Answering Moral Skepticism

Answering Moral Skepticism

SHELLY KAGAN

OXFORD
UNIVERSITY PRESS

Oxford University Press is a department of the University of Oxford. It furthers
the University's objective of excellence in research, scholarship, and education
by publishing worldwide. Oxford is a registered trade mark of Oxford University
Press in the UK and certain other countries.

Published in the United States of America by Oxford University Press
198 Madison Avenue, New York, NY 10016, United States of America.

© Oxford University Press 2023

All rights reserved. No part of this publication may be reproduced, stored in
a retrieval system, or transmitted, in any form or by any means, without the
prior permission in writing of Oxford University Press, or as expressly permitted
by law, by license, or under terms agreed with the appropriate reproduction
rights organization. Inquiries concerning reproduction outside the scope of the
above should be sent to the Rights Department, Oxford University Press, at the
address above.

You must not circulate this work in any other form
and you must impose this same condition on any acquirer.

Library of Congress Cataloging-in-Publication Data
Names: Kagan, Shelly, author.
Title: Answering moral skepticism / Shelly Kagan.
Description: New York, NY, United States of America : Oxford University Press, [2023] |
Includes bibliographical references and index. | Identifiers: LCCN 2023004632 (print) |
LCCN 2023004633 (ebook) | ISBN 9780197688984 (pb) | ISBN 9780197688977 (hbk) |
ISBN 9780197688991 (epub) | ISBN 9780197689011
Subjects: LCSH: Ethics. | Ethical relativism. | Skepticism.
Classification: LCC BJ1012 .K238 2024 (print) | LCC BJ1012 (ebook) |
DDC 171/.7—dc23/eng/20230512
LC record available at https://lccn.loc.gov/2023004632
LC ebook record available at https://lccn.loc.gov/2023004633

DOI: 10.1093/oso/9780197688977.001.0001

Paperback printed by Marquis Book Printing, Canada
Hardback printed by Bridgeport National Bindery, Inc., United States of America

For my fellow ELFS

Frances Kamm,
Jeff McMahan,
and Larry Temkin

Contents

Acknowledgments   xi
A Note to the Reader   xiii

Introduction   1

1. What Would Morality Need to Be?   8
   1.1 Job Descriptions   8
   1.2 Possible Elements   16
   1.3 Satisfying the Job Description   39

2. Basic Positions in Metaethics   42
   2.1 Cognitivism versus Noncognitivism   42
   2.2 Nihilism versus Moral Realism   46
   2.3 Varieties of Moral Realism   52
   2.4 Moral Skepticism   61

3. Nihilism   65
   3.1 The Nature of Nihilism   65
   3.2 The Case for Nihilism   68
   3.3 Disregarding the Arguments   71
   3.4 Normative Nihilism   77

4. Noncognitivism   79
   4.1 The Nature of Noncognitivism   79
   4.2 The Case for Noncognitivism   87
   4.3 Objections to Noncognitivism   96

5. Disagreement   104
   5.1 The Argument from Disagreement   104
   5.2 The Implications of Disagreement   108
   5.3 Explaining Moral Disagreement   114
   5.4 Nonconvergence   125

6. Relativism   129
   6.1 Moral Relativism   129
   6.2 Clarifying Relativism   133
   6.3 Arguing for Relativism   141
   6.4 Relativized Foundational Theories   151

7. Knowledge — 158
- 7.1 The Analogy to Observation — 158
- 7.2 Appearances — 162
- 7.3 Dismissing Moral Intuitions — 167
- 7.4 Reliability — 177
- 7.5 Intuitionism — 185

8. Evolution — 191
- 8.1 The Argument from Evolution — 191
- 8.2 A Second Try — 196
- 8.3 Truth and Advantage in Ethics — 202
- 8.4 Common Ground — 209
- 8.5 The Continuity Problem — 214
- 8.6 Path Dependence — 220

9. Explanation — 225
- 9.1 A Metaphysical Test — 225
- 9.2 Explaining Empirical Facts — 228
- 9.3 Reduction and Explanation — 232
- 9.4 The Normative Aspect of Moral Facts — 238
- 9.5 The Unrestricted Test — 242

10. Motivation — 248
- 10.1 Motive Internalism — 248
- 10.2 An Argument for Noncognitivism — 254
- 10.3 Rejecting Motive Internalism — 259
- 10.4 Rejecting the Humean Theory of Motivation — 265
- 10.5 The Direction of Fit — 271

11. Reasons — 277
- 11.1 Reasons Internalism — 277
- 11.2 Reasons — 280
- 11.3 Refining the Argument — 286
- 11.4 Hypothetical Reasons — 291
- 11.5 Rational Support — 296
- 11.6 Categorical Reasons and Motivation — 300

12. Reductionism — 308
- 12.1 The Appeal of Reductionism — 308
- 12.2 The Nature of Reduction — 313
- 12.3 The Open Question Argument — 317
- 12.4 Properties of the Wrong Kind — 325
- 12.5 The Significance of Reasons for Reduction — 329
- 12.6 Reducing Reasons — 335

13. Simple Realism — 342
    13.1 Simple Normative Realism — 342
    13.2 Objections to Irreducible Normativity — 347
    13.3 Nonnatural Properties — 353
    13.4 The Metaphysics of Morals — 361

14. Moral Realism — 364
    14.1 Answering the Moral Skeptic — 364
    14.2 Systematic Moral Theory — 369

Notes — 373
References — 387
Index — 389

Acknowledgments

I am a professor of moral philosophy. As such, I have often found myself in discussions with others where I am attempting to explore or defend a view concerning the rightness or wrongness of some act or policy. With surprising frequency, at some point in the discussion someone will shift gears and announce that it is silly to argue about what the right answer might be with regard to the particular moral question we were considering. After all (they may confidently assert), there is no such thing as objective moral truth, no right answers to be had, no moral facts to discover. So isn't the whole discussion really something of a waste of time, a pointless attempt to investigate the details of something that doesn't really exist? Others may be less adamant in their skepticism, but they may still confess to being *troubled* by these sorts of worries. How can *I* be so confident—they may ask—that there is such a thing as an objective morality, something whose contents we might strive to discover? Why believe in anything like objective moral facts or objective moral truths?

The questions are sincere and heartfelt. The people I am talking to—sometimes students, sometimes not—are thoughtful and intelligent. They wonder whether belief in morality can withstand careful, rational scrutiny. They worry (or they may even have concluded) that it cannot. There are things about the very idea of there being an objective morality that strike them as problematic and troubling, and they are genuinely curious to know what sorts of answers, if any, might be given on behalf of morality.

A few years ago I began to teach a class devoted exclusively to discussing and responding to the different skeptical worries that animate these misgivings, since the truth, of course, is that adequate answers take time, and so the quick replies which are ordinarily all I have time to offer outside of the classroom are never satisfying. A short answer—a few sentences, or even a few dozen sentences—can do little more than gesture in the right direction. But if morality is real, as I think it is, and if it is important, as I take it to be, then it is important as well to say enough so that one can really understand just how and why belief in morality is intellectually defensible. Teaching that class ("Moral Skepticism") has helped me better understand the concerns about morality that most commonly trouble nonphilosophers. And it has helped me to see as well when one has crossed the line from giving an acceptably full answer to a question to piling on technical philosophical details that are likely to be of interest only to professional specialists.

In this book I have tried to stay on the right side of that line—saying enough, but not too much (though I rather fear that there is more than one passage where I fall short of that ideal). This means, of course, that there is more to be said about each of the issues that will be discussed here. It is the nature of philosophical debate that answers to philosophical questions generate new questions in turn, and initial replies to objections prompt still further objections. I have deliberately stopped well short of pursuing all these dialectical twists and turns. But I hope I have said enough so that one can see why belief in the existence of objective morality is indeed an intellectually respectable position that someone might reasonably embrace.

I am grateful to Larry Temkin and Mark van Roojen for commenting on the book as it neared completion. Larry also read and commented on earlier versions of several of the individual chapters, as did Frances Kamm and Jeff McMahan. I am of course very grateful to the three of them—Larry, Frances, and Jeff—for doing that; but the simple truth is that I cannot possibly thank them enough for everything that they have taught me about moral philosophy over the years.

In the discussion that follows I draw upon countless ideas that have been developed and defended by other moral philosophers. Some of these debts are acknowledged in the Notes. But my deepest and most abiding debt is to all of the nonphilosophers who have taken the time to share with me their worries about morality. To the friends and students who have listened to my replies, asked further questions, and pressed me once again when what I had to say simply didn't satisfy them: thank you.

A Note to the Reader

This is a long book, and any given reader may not be equally interested in all of the topics that we will eventually discuss. So let me provide a quick overview of the chapters that follow.

As the Introduction explains, the goal of this book is to examine arguments that aim to show that there is something especially problematic about belief in morality or objective moral truths. It does not attempt to answer more general forms of skepticism.

But whether we believe in morality or not, we first need to be clear about the nature of the thing whose existence we are wondering about. Accordingly, chapter 1 discusses various features that one might conceivably require of something if it is to be thought worthy of the name "morality" or "objective morality." Chapter 2 then lays out some of the basic alternative positions—some skeptical, some not—that we will be returning to throughout the rest of the book.

Since many readers will not have thought much about the exact nature of moral skepticism, the next two chapters explore the two most important skeptical positions in greater detail. Chapter 3 examines moral nihilism; chapter 4, noncognitivism.

The survey of particular skeptical arguments begins in earnest with chapter 5, which asks whether the prevalence of interpersonal moral disagreement supports the conclusion that there are no moral facts at all. Chapter 6 asks whether the differences in the moral codes of different societies give us reason to believe, instead, in moral relativism.

Chapter 7 asks how we could possibly have knowledge of moral facts and argues that moral intuitions provide an essential part of the answer. Chapter 8 then examines the objection that since those intuitions have been shaped by evolution that should leave us skeptical about their reliability.

Chapter 9 looks at the claim that moral facts would never explain anything and so we should deny the existence of any such facts.

Chapter 10 asks whether moral beliefs could have the motivational force we normally take them to have, while chapter 11 asks whether moral requirements could really entail the sorts of reasons we normally take them to involve.

Chapter 12 examines the prospects for "reducing" moral facts to metaphysically less controversial ones. Chapter 13 then asks in turn whether it would indeed be problematic if we decided to posit irreducible moral or normative properties after all.

Chapter 14 explains why—given everything that has come before—belief in the existence of morality is intellectually defensible.

Finally, the Notes section offers suggestions for further reading. It also comments on some complications not discussed in the main text, and it identifies the places where I have directly borrowed from the work of others.

Introduction

Every reflective individual worries at some time or the other about the existence of objective moral truth. Or so I imagine. It isn't merely that one wonders whether this or that particular moral belief is correct. (Is it really true that harming others in self-defense is morally permissible? That white lies are morally acceptable? That there is intrinsic moral value in giving people what they deserve?) Rather, one worries about whether the very attempt to find answers to our specific moral questions is somehow misguided, whether the common belief in objective moral facts of any sort at all is nothing more than a widely shared illusion. Perhaps instead of debating which particular moral claims are correct we should realize that there are actually no right answers in ethics at all, precisely because there really are no facts about right and wrong to be arguing about in the first place.

Whether or not one is convinced of such skeptical conjectures, I imagine that everyone finds themselves at least periodically troubled by them—anxious or uncertain about whether and how they can best be answered.

Such worries have a variety of sources. Here is a brief sample. If there were ethical facts, how could we possibly know about them? (Empirical methods of inquiry certainly seem inadequate to the task.) Short of positing some "spooky" and unscientific faculty for gaining access to moral facts, how could we ever come to know anything about ethics at all? But in the absence of a method suitable for gaining moral knowledge, why even believe that there *are* any such moral facts to be discovered in the first place? Wouldn't it be more reasonable to reject the entire subject altogether? Furthermore, given how widespread moral disagreement is, with one person confident of moral claims that others in turn reject as morally abhorrent, and with different societies teaching widely divergent views about the purported moral "truths," isn't it more reasonable to conclude that there are no truths to be discovered here at all, that morality is in fact just a matter of opinion—or, more precisely, just a matter of one's personal tastes and preferences (or, perhaps, those of one's society)? Indeed, how could one reasonably think otherwise? Doesn't belief in moral facts fly in the face of what science has taught us about the fundamental nature of reality? How could one possibly find a place for anything like objective moral values in a scientific worldview? How could anything like right and wrong, for example, possibly emerge in a world simply composed of protons, neutrons, and electrons? Isn't it more reasonable to conclude that our moral beliefs, instead of somehow reflecting an obscure and scientifically dubious moral realm, are the result, rather, of nothing more than evolutionary shaping or cultural conditioning? Isn't it hopelessly naive to think otherwise?

Some people, convinced by thoughts like these, do indeed embrace a skeptical position with regard to morality. Perhaps our practice of making and debating moral claims should be abandoned altogether. At the very least, we should leave behind any thought of there being right and wrong *answers* in ethics, abandon any commitment to the existence of objective moral facts, or an objective moral code.

We probably all know people who have adopted this sort of unflinching skepticism about morality. Others adopt a less extreme position. They may continue to engage in moral deliberation and discussion, but they believe, nonetheless, that there is something shady or slightly embarrassing about belief in morality—something second-rate and not quite intellectually respectable. Belief in morality is questionable and intellectually precarious, they insist, especially in comparison to one's justified confidence in genuinely rational areas of inquiry, like math or the empirical sciences. So even if we cannot quite see our way to abandoning (or radically altering) our allegiance to moral discourse, we must recognize that morality is on a tremendously less secure foundation than we would like it to be.

Still others—perhaps the rest of us—are a bit less radical still. Even if we are not swayed by the various skeptical arguments (nor sufficiently moved by them to view morality as intellectually second-rate), we may still find ourselves at times worried by troubling thoughts of the kind I have described, wishing we had some notion of what adequate replies to them might look like. Even if we are not convinced that there is something questionable about the belief in objective moral truths, we might still wish we were better able to come to morality's defense, better able to see just why a belief in morality might be an intellectually respectable position to maintain.

My aim in this book is to say something in defense of the belief in morality—to say something in defense of the belief in objective moral facts and objective moral truths.

Admittedly, one of the first things we will discover is just how difficult it is to try to spell out precisely what it is that one means by this sort of talk—what it would take for there to be an objective morality, for morality to be "real" (in this sense). But this is an issue that skeptics must face as well, since if skeptics are going to deny the reality of anything genuinely worthy of the name morality, then it is important for them to be clear about just what it is, precisely, that they mean to deny.

Nonetheless, we won't actually try to settle on a single account of what it would take for morality to be objective (what it would take for there to actually be objective moral truth). There is simply too much disagreement, I think, for that to be a useful exercise. But I hope to say enough so that you will be able to see that it is indeed legitimate to accept a position that might reasonably be described using this sort of language. A bit more precisely, we will be exploring a variety of positions that might, I think, be plausibly described as embracing the existence of objective morality (or objective moral facts, or an objective moral code, and so on). And—even more to the point—I hope to show how and why these different positions have the resources to provide plausible, intellectually respectable answers to the skeptical challenges that might be raised against them.

While I hope that this is a sufficiently ambitious undertaking to hold the reader's interest, I want to acknowledge upfront that there are two other ways in which one might aspire to be even more ambitious. These are goals that I have not set for myself.

First, although this book is an attempt to respond to various arguments for moral skepticism, in no way is it an attempt to respond to the more *general* forms of skepticism that philosophers sometimes entertain. My goal is only to argue that ethics is in no worse a position than, say, other familiar subjects of systematic study (such as biology, or history). So if, at some point, I offer a reply to a particular skeptical argument aimed at morality by noting that—if it worked—that same argument would also undermine belief in physics, or biology, or geology, I will assume that for our purposes we are justified in concluding that the argument goes wrong *somewhere*. I won't go on to ask whether we really are justified in believing in any of these other subjects as well.

To be sure, as a philosopher I am of course genuinely interested in such general skeptical challenges. In principle, at least, it is perfectly legitimate to wonder whether any of our beliefs are justified at all, whether we really know anything about *anything*. Perhaps we should give up not only our belief in ethics, but all of our beliefs, covering all other areas of inquiry as well. Perhaps we cannot actually know anything at all about the external world—not even whether there is such a thing. Perhaps we cannot even know anything about the contents of our own minds (or whether there even are such things as minds). Perhaps we should be skeptics across the board.

I do not myself believe in such general forms of skepticism. But in any event, they are simply not our concern in this book. My goal is only to argue that ethics—the attempt to work out the basic truths of morality—is no worse off (in the relevant ways) than other subjects that we are not normally inclined to doubt or dismiss. If I can establish that much, then even though it certainly falls short of putting general skepticism to rest, I am content.

Second, in philosophy there is always more to say. I will do my best, in what follows, to present this or that skeptical argument fairly, and then consider what replies might be given to it. Typically, then, I will go on to consider some of the ways in which the skeptic might renew the attack, sharpening the original argument, or modifying it so as to deflect the suggested reply. And then I might note some of the ways that those who believe in morality might plausibly respond to that sharpened or modified argument. But at that point I might well end the discussion of the particular skeptical argument in question and move on to a different one.

So I want to confess—right here at the outset—that I am fully aware that from the philosophical point of view the matter hardly ever really ends there. There can be further sharpenings or modifications that might be suggested by the skeptic, with still further replies by the defender of morality, and so on and so forth, well beyond the point at which we will leave any given debate. In real life, philosophical debates rarely come to an end; they mostly just deepen. So I would not want anyone to think that the various arguments on behalf of morality that I offer here are the last words on the subject.

Still, as the dialectic—the point and counterpoint of argument, objection, replies, and so on—grows ever deeper, one is eventually entitled to insist that, at the very least, one's own position should not be simply dismissed out of hand as naive or simple minded. At any rate, I take that to be true for the defense of morality that I will present here. Perhaps the moral skeptic will eventually be able to come up with an argument or objection for which there is no compelling reply. I doubt it; but only time will tell. But in the meantime, or so it seems to me, one can reasonably insist that a belief in objective morality is among those positions that are indeed intellectually respectable.

So this represents a second way in which this book is less ambitious than some might hope. It is not my goal to present "knock down" replies to the various skeptical challenges—responses so brilliant and conclusive that intellectual honesty requires the skeptic to abandon their skepticism! Rather, my goal is only to show that there are reasonable replies that can be offered on behalf of morality, replies sufficiently plausible so that one need not be embarrassed to continue to engage in moral debate, to continue putting forward one's various first-order moral claims. I will not *prove* that morality is for real (whatever, exactly, that would look like). But I do hope to say enough to show why it is intellectually respectable to continue to believe that it is.

Suppose we were to agree that moral inquiry is legitimate, that there are such things as objective moral truths. It would then make sense for us to wonder about the particular moral questions that we normally find ourselves debating. (To revert to the examples from above, I mean questions like whether self-defense is permissible, whether telling white lies is wrong, whether giving people what they deserve is intrinsically valuable, and so on.) Obviously enough, deciding that there *are* answers to questions like these wouldn't yet *provide* us with those answers. We would still need to do the important philosophical work of discovering them.

The part of moral philosophy that attempts to answer first-order questions like these is called *normative ethics*. It attempts to articulate and defend the basic moral principles (as well as exploring what the ultimate basis or foundation of these principles might be). Unsurprisingly, there are rival theories that have been proposed within normative ethics, and there are ongoing debates about the relative strengths and weaknesses of these different views. But in this book I will not attempt to lay out these rival normative theories; nor will I attempt to adjudicate between them. (At best I will occasionally use a particular normative claim or theory as an example or illustration, so as to make our rather abstract discussions slightly more concrete.) Our concern here is solely with what we might think of as second-order questions, questions about the nature and reality of morality—whether there really are objective moral facts, what they might be like, and how we might know them.

This second part of moral philosophy, the part that investigates the second-order questions, is called *metaethics*. Metaethics isn't at all limited to exploring the skeptical worries that will be our focus, but such worries do indeed fall squarely within its domain. So in one sense the present book can be thought of as an introduction to metaethics. But it doesn't attempt to survey the entire subfield of metaethics, only those particular metaethical issues that arise while giving voice to, and responding to, those arguments that threaten to call into question the very existence of objective morality, or objective moral truths, altogether.

Let me close this introduction with a word of warning. At any number of places in the chapters that follow, the discussion becomes complicated. So please understand. This book presupposes no background in philosophy, and my aim, at least, is to carefully explain to the reader any philosophical concepts or theses that might not already be familiar. But there is no point in pretending that the discussion to come is always an easy one to follow. As I have already noted, it is in the nature of philosophical dialectic that initial arguments and replies get refined or replaced with more subtle, sophisticated, or complex ones; and the truth of the matter is that, as the discussion proceeds, it often becomes increasingly difficult to keep all the various moves and countermoves straight in one's head. Raising skeptical worries is easy. Answering them adequately is not. But this isn't because adequate answers aren't available; rather, it is because the adequate answers are not *simple*.

In more than one way, this is unfortunate and disappointing. Most of the skeptical worries that we will be examining occur to people naturally, often spontaneously, and at least in their initial formulations many of the skeptical questions we will be exploring are easy ones to pose. Since these questions occur naturally to reflective individuals, it would certainly be convenient—and reassuring—if the answers to these questions could also be laid out in similarly easy, simple terms. But that just doesn't seem to be the case—at least, not in many instances—and certainly not once we have moved to answers that occur at later stages in the relevant philosophical dialectic.

I don't think there is anything particularly unusual about our topic in this regard. It is often easy to understand a question whose answer is nonetheless surprisingly difficult to spell out. For example, any child can ask and understand the question, why do objects fall to the ground? But the *answer* to that question—involving as it does the concept of gravity as an invisible attractive force (whereby each physical object attracts every other physical object in proportion to each object's mass), the idea that an unimpeded object will accelerate when force is applied to it (but only to a degree that is inversely proportional to its mass), and the fact that everyday falling objects are tremendously smaller in mass compared to the earth—is one that is significantly more complicated to lay out, even if one avoids most of the technical details. So while the question can be asked and understood by just about anyone, the answer can be grasped only by someone with both a sufficiently advanced intellect and the patience to attend to at least the basic outlines of what is, after all, a relatively complicated answer.

For better or worse, the same thing is true, I think, with regard to the existence and nature of morality. The questions that might lead to skeptical misgivings are easy enough to get a feel for; but in many cases suitable answers—even though they are available—turn out to be relatively complicated, at least in comparison to the questions themselves. If I am right about the claims that I make in the rest of this book, then belief in objective moral truth is a reasonable philosophical position to hold. But seeing that this is the case—and why it is the case—turns out to be a complicated affair.

1
What Would Morality Need to Be?

1.1 Job Descriptions

Many of us believe in the existence of objective moral truths. We believe that certain acts are morally required, for example, while others are morally forbidden, and still others morally optional (permissible, but not required). We recognize, of course, that we may be mistaken, with regard to some particular act, or act type, as to whether it really does have the particular moral status we take it to have. But for all that, we believe that there is a *fact* of the matter as to whether or not the given act (or act type) really does have the particular status we take it to have.

Thus, for example, I believe that under ordinary circumstances it is morally permissible to harm another in the course of defending oneself against their unprovoked attack. That is to say, I believe that acts of self-defense are morally permissible. I take this to be an objective fact about the nature of self-defense. Of course, I also realize that there are others, pacifists, who disagree with me about this. Normally, they too believe there are objective facts about what morality does or does not permit; but they believe that, in point of fact, harming another person—even in self-defense—is morally forbidden. Such pacifists therefore disagree with me about the first-order normative question, whether defensive violence is permissible or not. But—and this is the crucial point—they agree with me about the second-order *metaethical* question, as to whether there is a correct *answer* to our debate, whether there really is a fact of the matter as to whether or not self-defense is permissible.

The pacifists and I could say that although we disagree about the *contents* of morality, or the details of the relevant moral facts, we nonetheless agree that there *is* such a thing as morality (whose contents we are attempting to determine), that there really is an objective fact of the matter as to whether self-defense is morally permissible or not; we agree that our debate has a correct answer. We could try to express this point of agreement by saying that although we disagree about what the moral facts are, we nonetheless agree that there *are* moral facts. Similarly, we could say that despite our disagreements about some of its contents, we nonetheless agree about the existence of something that deserves to be called "objective morality." To put the point more simply still, we could say that we are in agreement about the *existence* of morality.

Still others, of course, are more skeptical. Rather than engaging in first-order debates about whether or not self-defense is truly permissible, they reject the metaethical picture that is common ground between these pacifists and myself. Such skeptics insist that our debate actually has no right answer, because there are, in fact, no *moral* facts at all, no objective moral truths which could serve to make one side of this debate right while making the other side wrong. These skeptics deny the very existence of anything that deserves to be called objective moral truth. They thus deny the very existence of the sort of thing that the pacifists and I were trying to affirm. As we might put the point, they deny the very existence of morality (that is, they deny the existence of anything like the kind of objective morality that the pacifists and I mean to affirm).

It is this latter debate, this second-order, metaethical debate, which will be our exclusive concern in this book. I want to put aside the sundry first-order normative arguments about what the precise contents of morality might be (crucially important though these questions are). I want to ask, rather, whether the skeptic is right that we should reject the very existence of anything like moral facts, or an objective morality, in the first place. Should we indeed embrace some form of moral skepticism? Or can we instead plausibly affirm the existence of an objective morality of the sort that the skeptic means to deny?

It is, I think, easy enough to get at least a rough feel for this metaethical disagreement, with one side affirming what the other denies. But it is actually surprisingly difficult to pin down precisely what it is that the two sides are arguing about. One side posits the existence of something that might reasonably have a claim to being called "objective morality," while the other side denies the existence of anything like that. But what, exactly, does each side mean by this term? What is it, exactly, that people have in mind when the one side affirms, and the other side denies, the existence of objective moral truths (or an objective moral code, and so on)?

I suspect, in fact, that as people enter into this debate they often have at least somewhat different conceptions of what morality is (or what it would need to be, if it really were going to exist). Even people on the same side of the debate may disagree about what a genuine (objective) morality would need to be like, what features it would need to have. Thus, a particular conception of morality—an account of what something would need to be in order to actually *count* as morality—might satisfy one person (whether or not they believe that such a thing actually exists), while leaving another quite dissatisfied. One person might be fully prepared to proclaim the existence of morality, *provided* that we really could establish the existence of something that meets the requirements of a given, particular account, while a second might insist that even if something like *that* does indeed exist, it surely wouldn't suffice to establish the existence of anything that we should be prepared to call an *objective morality*. All of which is just to say that different people build somewhat different ingredients into their very concept of morality, and so they disagree, not only about whether such a thing exists, but what it would even *take* for such a thing to exist.

This fact will complicate our discussion in the following way. Suppose the skeptic argues that there is (and can be) no objective morality, because an objective morality would need to have feature F and nothing could possibly *have* such a feature. If you are persuaded by the argument that nothing could actually have F, *and* you agree that an objective morality must indeed have F, then such an argument will appropriately threaten your belief in the existence of an objective morality. But of course, if you never included feature F in your conception of what morality is (or would need to be) in the first place, then you might not be troubled at all by the skeptic's argument. You might happily concede that nothing could have F, but think the point simply irrelevant with regard to settling the existence (or nonexistence) of morality!

In such a situation I don't think there would be much point in one side insisting that we simply *must* include F in any account of morality that is going to warrant being called "objective," as though what we really care about is whether one is entitled to use that label or not. The simple fact of the matter is that people disagree about what exactly it is that they are looking for, what they are trying to establish or deny, when they argue about the existence of morality. So instead of trying to settle on a unique account of what an objective morality would need to be, we will do better if we acknowledge that there are a variety of different positions here that people actually take, and so people will differ, one to the next, with regard to which skeptical arguments they will find even initially troubling.

What we need, then, is a list of features that people frequently want to build into their very concept of morality, so that we can see the various points at which the skeptic might try to mount an attack. At the same time, we will want to recognize that not everyone will embrace each of these features, that not everyone will agree that anything lacking the given feature must fall short of constituting objective moral truth.

Furthermore, in producing this list there is no point in focusing exclusively on trying to work out the concept of *objectivity* per se. Presumably, anything that you would be willing to count as an objective morality would need to have a *variety* of features, several of which might not have anything much to do with morality's being *objective* per se, but each of which might be such that you would be troubled by a skeptical argument to the effect that nothing could actually have the feature in question.

So the issue that should centrally concern us isn't really one of wondering what features morality must have if it is to lay claim to being objective. Rather, what we need to ask, more broadly, is what are the various features that morality must have if it is indeed to count as constituting (a genuine) *morality* at all. In principle, at least, any of the features I will eventually list might represent a potential opening for a skeptical challenge. But whether you will find any given challenge troubling will depend on whether you agree that the feature in question is indeed one that you would prefer to build into the very concept of morality.

(Of course, despite my talk of people having different "concepts" or "conceptions" of morality, I don't mean to be claiming that people are simply talking past one another, intending altogether different things when they talk about morality's existing or not. It is hardly as though we don't understand one another, even if we disagree about whether some particular feature is indeed an essential ingredient in an adequate account of morality. You may be *surprised* if I claim that morality can exist perfectly well even if it lacks some particular feature. Perhaps you will want to insist that, on the contrary, *nothing* truly worthy of the name morality can lack the feature in question. But normally you will still *understand* my position well enough, for all that.)

You can think of it this way. If we are going to argue whether morality actually exists or not, we need something like a job description, an account of the various features that something should have if it is to lay serious claim to counting as (or constituting) an objective morality. But since people disagree about which features really belong in morality's job description, instead of creating a single such description and then looking to see whether anything could actually meet it, we will have to satisfy ourselves with listing some of the main ingredients that might go into producing something suitable.

You'll have to decide for yourself which of the possible elements are the truly essential ones.

Of course, once you decide just what it is that you do want to hold out for (before you would be prepared to declare that objective morality genuinely exists) you open yourself up to a relevant set of skeptical arguments. For each feature F that you include in the job description, there arises the possibility of a skeptical argument to the effect that there is and can be no objective morality, precisely because nothing could possibly have feature F. Similarly, the skeptic might argue that there is some *set* of features—F, G, and H—that you have included in the job description, where the various features are *jointly* incompatible, such that nothing could possibly possess all of the requisite features simultaneously. Either way, if the skeptic is right and nothing can really meet the job description, then you will have to conclude that objective morality doesn't actually exist after all.

That, at least, is the conclusion that the skeptic hopes you will reach. But it must be acknowledged that things aren't always that clear. Even if you become convinced that nothing can fully meet the job description that you were initially inclined to put forward, this need not force you to deny the existence of objective moral truths. Perhaps some of the features you included in the job description were never intended to be genuine *requirements* at all, but only things that it would be desirable to have if one could—preferable but not mandatory. (This is akin to listing certain work experiences in a job posting as "desirable" though not essential.) Or perhaps some of the features you initially took to be essential when you first developed the job description will turn out, on further reflection, to be ones that you are willing to do without after all. (Changing your sense of what it will take to fill a position isn't the same as deciding that it cannot actually be filled at all.) No doubt, certain features in the job description will indeed remain nonnegotiable. But in real life, at any rate, deciding exactly which features these are may turn out to be significantly less straightforward than one might have initially assumed.

Consider a few examples that have nothing to do with morality. I imagine we all agree that there are no witches (that is, witches like the ones found in fairy tales). Why not? Perhaps because our "job description" for being a witch looks something like this: a woman with the ability to perform magic, who communes with or worships the devil, who wears black clothes (and a pointy hat!) and lives alone, cursing and casting spells over others. Since we believe that no one actually can perform magic, we conclude that there are, in fact, no witches.

Contrast that with the case of whales. In the past, people would presumably have said that being a very big *fish* was part of the very concept of what it was to be a whale. But as it turns out, whales are not in fact fish at all (they are mammals, not fish). Yet we all agree—despite this—that there *are* whales! What we say is this: there *are* whales, it just turns out that whales aren't exactly what we took them to be. Rather than concluding that whales don't exist, we decide that part of our concept of whales needs to be revised. Apparently, then, something needn't meet *all* of our initial job description for us to conclude that the sort of thing we were looking for really does exist. It only needs to do this sufficiently well.

But then why don't we say something similar about witches? Why don't we say that there *are* witches, it just turns out that witches aren't exactly what we thought they were? After all, there presumably are (or have been) women who wear black clothes, live alone, worship the devil, and attempt to curse others. Admittedly, they cannot perform real magic, as there is no such thing; but why not conclude that this part of our concept of being a witch simply needs to be revised?

Perhaps some are indeed inclined to do just this, but what most of us will hold, instead, is that certain elements in the job description are too central to be abandoned or modified in this way. We might be willing to allow for the possibility of witches that wear colors other than black, or of witches who are good rather than evil, but the ability to do magic is simply too central to our concept of being a witch to give up. Since no one can perform magic, no one is a witch.

So some elements in any given job description are essential, and others are not. But it isn't always easy to tell which are which. I don't merely mean that we may disagree with one another about which are which, I mean that each of us may be uncertain about which answer we *want* to give. Consider a few more examples. Imagine that the world was ruled—but not created—by a tremendously powerful but decidedly non-omnipotent being, someone who was neither all-knowing nor especially just. Would it be appropriate to call such a limited being a *god*? Initially it might seem not—omnipotence, omniscience, and perfect goodness being among the features we might be inclined to build into the very job description. But on reflection the answer is less clear. We may not *believe* in the Greek gods, for example, but if, say, Zeus existed, wouldn't it be appropriate to say that Zeus was a god? Maybe. But maybe it would be better to say, instead, that strictly speaking, the Greek "gods" were merely extremely powerful beings, but not gods at all. Just what does it take to *count* as being a god, anyway? I don't think the answer is at all obvious.

Or take the idea of being *solid*. An initial account of the concept of being solid might include the feature of being something with no empty space inside. But as atomic theory has taught us, ordinary "solid" material objects—like a block of wood or marble—are in fact mostly empty space. So should we conclude that there are no genuinely solid objects after all (except, conceivably, certain subatomic particles)? Or should we say, instead, that the notion of having no empty space inside needs to be removed from our job description of solidity and replaced with something more suitable (perhaps something about being highly resistant to bending or deformation). Or perhaps that notion—lacking empty space within—was never part of the concept of solidity in the first place?

The answer, I think, isn't clear. It isn't always clear what one should say or do, in cases like this. Indeed, it isn't always clear what exactly one is doing even when one does it. Thus, on the one hand, it may not be obvious (even to yourself) whether you want to say that lacking empty space inside is indeed essential and nonnegotiable for solidity, so that—surprisingly enough—it turns out that nothing (or almost nothing) counts as being solid after all. And, on the other hand, even if you do decide that things like tables and desks and blocks of marble are genuinely solid, it may not be clear (even to yourself) whether what you are doing, in saying this, is a matter of *modifying* your initial account of solidity (but in a way that is close enough to the original to still count as an account of *solidity*), or, alternatively, more a matter of realizing that certain elements that you may have initially *taken* to be part of your account of solidity were never really there in the first place.

This sort of uncertainty will attend skeptical arguments aimed at dislodging one's belief in morality as well. Not only will we disagree with one another with regard to which features we want to build into the job description for morality (what it would take for there to be such a thing as morality, or an objective morality), each of us may be less than confident about at least some of the features that we do include, as to whether they are indeed essential to our conception (so that nothing that lacks the given feature could possibly count as constituting a genuine morality after all), or whether, alternatively, the features may be merely desirable or preferable without quite counting as essential (so that something that does well enough with regard to the *other* features in the job description might still count as being an objective morality, even if it fails to have the particular feature in question). And, of course, in still other cases we may be uncertain (even in our own minds) about whether we really do want to include a given feature in the job description at all.

All of this means that the targets of skeptical arguments will be less stably fixed, in real life, than it might seem in principle. Insofar as any given skeptical argument turns on this or that particular feature (or set of features) that one might include in one's job description for morality, not only can the argument be resisted by those who never included the given feature (or features) in the first place, it can also be answered by those who do include the feature but don't take it to be essential, and even by those who may have initially taken it to be essential, but who are now willing to reconsider this commitment after due reflection. And, of course, this is not yet to mention the most interesting possibility, that of responding to the given skeptical argument by showing—contrary to what the skeptic is claiming—that it is indeed possible to have something that has the feature (or features) in question, so that the job description of morality can indeed be filled, even *if* the relevant feature or features are taken to be essential.

Still, be that all as it may, if one is to maintain a belief in morality one must have at least *some* concept of morality at hand, some notion of the sort of thing it is, the existence of which one is asserting. That notion may be somewhat fluid (with regard to which elements are included, and which of those elements are essential), but if the belief in morality is to have content, we need to have at least some sort of job description initially in place. And similarly, of course, if the skeptic is going to attempt to undermine the belief in the existence of morality, they too need an account of just what it is the existence of which they mean to deny. Skeptics may insist that the job description of morality can never be adequately filled; but to do this they too need an account of what it is that something would need to be, if it really *were* to be worthy of the name morality.

One final point. It is worth noting explicitly that not all skeptical arguments turn on the claim that nothing could possibly meet one or more of the essential elements of morality's job description. That is, it isn't as though the skeptic is restricted to arguing that the existence of an objective morality is something that is necessarily *impossible*. On the contrary, the skeptic will often prefer to argue, more modestly, that belief in the existence of morality is simply less *plausible* than belief in moral skepticism. It isn't so much that the existence of morality is literally impossible (they may say), it's just that it is far more reasonable to conclude, instead, that there simply *is* no such thing.

Obviously, however, that's still a sufficiently strong conclusion to trouble anyone who is committed to the existence of morality.

Several of the skeptical arguments that we will eventually be discussing will be of this alternative, more "modest" form. But it is important to recognize the fact that, even here, the skeptic will be drawing on an understanding of just what it is that morality would need to be, if there were really going to be such a thing. Even in those cases where all that the skeptic hopes to do is to convince us that belief in morality is less plausible than skepticism, they still need at least a minimal account of the nature of the thing whose very existence they deny.

1.2 Possible Elements

I have been suggesting that people have different conceptions of morality (what morality is, or would need to be), and so differ over what they are looking for, what they are affirming or denying, when they argue about the existence of morality. Rather than try to settle upon a single such concept, I think we will do better if we acknowledge these differences and simply note some of the main elements that are commonly thought to be part of what I have been calling the "job description" of morality. I won't try to settle here which of these possible elements we should embrace; you can decide that for yourself.

Furthermore, I won't actually be saying all that much about any one of the particular proposals that follow. My goal here is the minimal one of saying just enough about each of them so that you can grasp the main idea underlying each and recognize the fact that each such feature is indeed something that many people will want to build into the very concept of an objective morality. You may decide against doing this yourself, for some of the features that follow; but even if you do, I hope you will find it easy to agree that each of these features is something that *many* of us, at the very least, will want to incorporate into morality's job description.

Many of the ideas that follow will come in for much more detailed examination later, once we turn to particular skeptical arguments. For the time being, I merely want to introduce them and to give a sense of at least some of the details that one would need to work out in a fuller discussion.

Function. One of the most common thoughts about morality is that its function or purpose is to guide action. So if there is such a thing as morality, many will argue, then at least part of what it does is to sort or classify actions as being, for example, better or worse, or perhaps permissible or forbidden. Morality must tell us what to *do*, or at least, what it is better to do.

Of course, accepting this general idea still leaves a tremendous amount unsettled. Must morality assign each type of action a specific moral status (required, forbidden, permissible)? Or would it suffice if it merely ranked any given act we might perform as being morally better or worse than some (or all) of the relevant alternatives? Similarly, if we imagine morality as consisting of a set of rules, must these rules govern all cases whatsoever, so that there is never a "gap"—an area where morality simply doesn't speak to the choice one might face? Or would that fail to count as being sufficiently action guiding? What about the possibility of moral dilemmas, cases where all of one's alternatives are classified as morally forbidden? Would a morality that allowed for this possibility still count as being action guiding (since it tells us that one must not do any of the alternatives, even though there are no further ones), or must a truly action guiding morality always mark out at least one available alternative as morally permissible?

For that matter, what exactly is required for it to be true that morality marks or classifies an act as being, say, permissible? Does it suffice if this is a logical implication of the relevant moral rule (or set of rules), when this is combined with the empirical facts of the given situation—even if it would be difficult or impossible for an ordinary person to realize that the given act is being so classified? Or does being genuinely action guiding require that it be possible, or even easy, for an average person to *figure out* what the given act's moral status is? Must morality be something that any given person can *use* to determine what it is that they are required to do? Or would it suffice if only experts in moral theory could manage to do that?

Finally, if morality is to count as being action guiding, must it do this directly, saying of any given act what its moral status is? Or would it suffice if morality guided our actions only indirectly, telling us, instead, what kind of *person* to be (and then suggesting that the thing to do in any given case is whatever a person like *that* would do)? A view that is content with the latter possibility might conceive of morality in terms of a set of ideal character traits or virtues; one satisfied only with the former possibility might demand, instead, a set of general rules or principles.

Clearly, even those drawn to the idea that morality must be action guiding in *some* sense of this term can differ among themselves—and be uncertain, at the individual level—regarding just what exactly it takes for something to count as being action guiding in the relevant sense. Nonetheless, in what follows I will always talk as though morality should be conceived of as being comprised of a set of general moral rules. Admittedly, not everyone believes this; but it will simplify the discussion if we help ourselves to this assumption. (Those who think morality can or should take other forms should be able to find suitable ways to modify the discussion that follows without affecting its main points.)

Content. As I have already remarked, in this book I hope to avoid detailed first-order debates concerning the contents of morality. Our question is whether we should believe in the existence of morality at all, not whether this or that particular first-order moral claim should be believed.

Of course, it is perfectly reasonable (as well as common) for people to assume that anything worthy of the name morality must require certain specific types of acts (such as telling the truth, or keeping one's promises) and forbid other specific types of acts (such as killing innocents for fun). So it will hardly come as a surprise to learn that people often build into the job description of morality a requirement that some particular set of first-order moral claims be part of the contents of morality. (They might hold, for example, that nothing that permits the killing of innocent children for the sheer sport of it can count as a *moral* code.) Nonetheless, since I want to avoid getting bogged down in first-order debates over specific normative claims, I won't here further examine views according to which the endorsement of some particular set of normative claims is said to be part of the very concept of morality.

There is, however, a more *general* view about the content of morality which may be worth noting. Some have suggested that above and beyond whatever particular normative claims are made (or implied) by a set of rules or principles, if those rules are indeed to count as *moral* rules, then they must speak to or otherwise address significant human interests (or, perhaps, more widely, the interests of all sentient beings). According to this idea, moral rules must be concerned, directly or indirectly, with promoting or protecting well-being, or perhaps with relevant ways of showing respect for other people and their interests. Morality cannot be about just anything at all.

Suppose, for example, that some society accepted a set of rules which required howling at the moon when it was full, and which prohibited stepping on the cracks in sidewalks at noon on sunny days. According to those who accept the restrictive view concerning the possible contents of a moral code, and who build the corresponding restriction into morality's job description, such rules simply cannot be properly thought of as being *moral* rules at all (not even mistaken moral rules). Or rather—a bit more cautiously—rules of this sort simply won't count as moral rules unless they are somehow thought of as being indirect means of promoting individual welfare, or of showing proper respect for others, and so on. In the absence of such a connection to human interests, rules like this would simply have the wrong sort of *content* to count as being even *candidate* components of a proper moral theory.

Others, however, will decline to build anything like this requirement with regard to content into the very concept of morality. They will insist, in contrast, that if rules like the ones just imagined were in fact widely taught in a society, and taken to have a suitably important and central role in deciding how one should act, then it would indeed be appropriate to describe these as being the moral rules accepted by that society—however unusual such moral rules might be, and however convinced we might be that any such rules must be mistaken. Conceivably, they might say, the true or best moral rules will be suitably concerned with protecting human interests. But that doesn't mean that we shouldn't even count a given set of rules as being *candidate* moral rules unless this is, in fact, what they are about.

Truth. Recall the debate between pacifists and those, like me, who believe in the permissibility of self-defense. Imagine that in the course of a discussion of this issue, I say that killing in self-defense is morally permissible. Perhaps I utter these very words: "Killing in self-defense is morally permissible." How are we to understand what I am doing in saying these words?

The most obvious suggestion here is that in saying this sentence I am making an assertion. I am making a claim about the permissibility of self-defense, and in doing so I am saying something that I take to be *true*. If I am right, then what I am saying really *is* true.

The pacifist, of course, disagrees with me about self-defense. She may say something along the lines of this: "Killing is never permissible, not even when defending oneself." But here too, the obvious suggestion is that in saying these words she too is making an assertion, putting forward a claim that she takes to be true.

On this natural proposal, then, each of us is asserting something that we take to be true, though we disagree about who is right. We disagree about whether it is really true that killing in self-defense is permissible. But we both agree that claims like this are the *sort* of thing for which it makes sense to assign a truth value. Claims about the permissibility of self-defense are either true or false.

Generalizing, it is natural to take a similar stance with regard to a wide range of first-order moral claims. If I say that slavery is wrong, or that telling white lies is permissible, or that one must never break a promise, you may agree with me or you may disagree with me, but you are likely to think that these claims are indeed assertions, things that are appropriately assigned a truth value: each of the things I have said is either true or false.

Philosophers use the term *truth apt* to refer to sentences that are capable of being true or false (though people may disagree, or be uncertain, about which are which). Truth apt sentences needn't actually be *true*; but they must be the sort of sentence for which it makes sense to assign a truth *value* (true or false).

Using this jargon, we can say that according to the natural proposal, claims about the moral permissibility of self-defense are truth *apt* (though the pacifists and I will disagree about which ones are true and which ones false). And more generally, according to the natural proposal, the various first-order normative claims that one might make about slavery, or telling lies, or breaking promises, and so on, are all truth apt as well (though here too we may disagree about which ones are true and which ones are false).

I say that this is the *natural* proposal about how to understand our various first-order normative utterances, for it is important to realize that this view can be rejected. For not all sentences *are* truth apt; many perfectly fine and useful sentences do not have truth values at all. For example, if I ask you, "What time is it?" I have uttered a perfectly grammatical sentence. But it would be silly and inappropriate to argue about whether my question was true or false; questions can't be either. Similarly, if I command you, "Tell me your name!" this too is a perfectly grammatical sentence, but it too is not truth apt, as imperatives can be neither true nor false.

Accordingly, it is important to ask whether first-order moral claims are genuine assertions or not. Are we right to take such utterances to be truth apt? Or might it be the case that something else is going on when we say things like "it is permissible to kill in self-defense"? Perhaps we are merely expressing our personal tastes about moral questions, rather than making assertions that can genuinely be true or false?

Many will insist that if there really is to be such a thing as an objective morality then first-order moral claims must indeed be truth apt. Unless one side of a moral debate can be saying something true, while the other side is saying something false, any notion of there being an objective morality or an objective moral code must be a mere illusion.

Others, however, might want to claim that even if it is not appropriate to regard first-order moral claims as being *truth apt*, there is, nonetheless, some other notion nearby that might do similar work. Even if we should not think of moral claims as being true or false, perhaps we can somehow distinguish between appropriate and inappropriate moral claims, or between justified and unjustified claims, or between valid and invalid ones. Conceivably, some such distinction might still allow us to make sense of the notion of there being right answers in ethics. And this, in turn, might leave room for belief in the existence of something worthy of the name morality.

Nonetheless, I suspect that many people will want to include truth aptness in the job description for morality. They may insist that an *objective* morality can only exist if at least some substantive first-order moral claims can be literally true, full stop.

Facts and Error. If we do embrace the idea that first-order moral claims must be truth apt, certain other closely related ideas can soon follow. To be sure, even if moral claims *are* truth apt, this doesn't yet entail that any of them are *true*. (The skeptic might insist, for example, that since there is no such thing as morality, all first-order moral claims are simply *false*.) But suppose one decides that at least some first-order moral claims are indeed true. Perhaps self-defense really is morally permissible, or slavery is wrong, or telling the truth is always morally required, and so on. If this is the case, then it seems appropriate to talk as well of the existence of moral *facts*. It will be a *fact* that self-defense is permissible, a fact that slavery is wrong, a fact that truth telling is obligatory, and so forth. Intuitively speaking, truths and facts go hand in hand in any given domain, and the same will presumably be the case when it comes to morality. So if there are first-order moral truths, there will be (first-order) moral facts as well.

(The precise connection between truths and facts is a matter of philosophical controversy; but for our purposes, I think, there is no need to enter into this debate. I will follow common practice in saying that a given statement attempts to describe the facts, that it asserts the existence of certain facts, and that if the facts are indeed as the statement claims, then the statement is true. For our purposes we needn't ask what metaphysical picture of truth and facts might make the best sense of such talk.)

Note, next, that if certain first-order moral claims are true, then it follows that anyone who denies those claims is *mistaken*. There will be right answers to (at least some) moral questions, and there will be wrong answers as well.

This possibility of making a mistake concerning such questions will strike many as getting close to the heart of what it would take for there to be anything like an objective morality. Typically, after all, when we are prepared to say that there is an objective fact of the matter about some question, an important part—perhaps the most important part—of what we mean to be asserting is the existence of a distinction between answers that are correct and answers that are mistaken. If there is an objective fact of the matter about some given domain, then certain claims about that domain will simply be false, full stop. Objectivity in a domain requires at least the logical possibility of making a *mistake* about that domain.

So another idea that we might want to build into the job description of morality is the idea that it is possible to say something *false* about morality, that not every view is as good as every other, so that in principle, at least, one could say or believe something mistaken about, for example, what acts are right or wrong, or about what one is obligated to do. If there is to be such a thing as objective morality, then there must be something to be mistaken about.

Though attractive, this idea must be expressed with care. For even if objectivity entails the existence of a distinction between right and wrong answers, it could still turn out that in certain areas, at least, each of us is infallible. For example, I take it that there is an objective fact of the matter as to whether you are in pain right now. If you are, then it would be a mistake for me to say otherwise; I would be getting the facts wrong, and asserting something false. And similarly, of course, if you really are in pain, then even if *you* were the one who said otherwise, you would be getting the facts wrong, and saying something false. But for all of that, most of us believe that you can't in fact be *mistaken* (have false beliefs) about this matter. If you are in pain, you will realize it, and so will never sincerely assert otherwise. If you *did* say otherwise, you would be "mistaken"; but that doesn't mean this is the kind of mistake you are actually capable of making.

Conceivably, then, some may be prepared to allow for a comparable infallibility with regard to certain moral questions. Perhaps we can make sense of a moral view according to which each person can never, in fact, be mistaken about what she herself is morally required to do. Any sincere judgment on this matter will inevitably be correct. Perhaps, for example, each of us has a conscience that is *infallible*, but only with regard to our own obligations, not the obligations of others. I don't think such a view is particularly plausible, but suppose it were true. If it were, I could only be mistaken about what *others* are obligated to do, not about what I myself am obligated to do, though I would still be speaking *falsely* if I (insincerely) stated a view about my own obligations that I didn't actually believe.

Would a view like this sufficiently capture the idea of objectivity in ethics, given the necessary connection between objectivity and the possibility of making mistakes? Or rather, more precisely, would the notion of objectivity that was captured here suffice to give a sufficiently *robust* account of objectivity in morality? Some may want to build a more demanding conception into the job description, one according to which any given individual can, in fact, be mistaken about any moral question at all, no matter *how* sincere their judgment. As usual, there is little value in arguing about what precisely is required for us to have an "objective" morality. But it remains important to ask whether we want to build into our concept of morality the possibility of error, and if so, of what kinds.

Knowledge. If there are moral facts, are they ones that we can come to know? I imagine that that's the view that most of us accept. But could it be, instead, that moral facts are somehow inaccessible to us? Would it be acceptable for someone to hold that although there *are* indeed objective moral facts, it is simply impossible for us to know them? Could morality exist, and yet be beyond our grasp?

For many people such a suggestion will seem absurd. It would be akin to saying that there are facts about etiquette, even though, for all that, no one can know them, or that there are facts about the meaning of this or that word, although no one can know what those meanings are. Words cannot do their job if we cannot know their meanings, and rules governing polite behavior cannot do theirs if we cannot figure them out. Similarly, then, many will insist, if we cannot know what the relevant moral facts are, then morality cannot perform *its* job either. For the job of morality—and here I revert back to an earlier suggestion about the very purpose of morality—is to guide our action. And morality cannot possibly do that if we cannot know its contents. So if there really are moral facts then it must be possible to come to *know* those facts.

Or so it might be argued. But as I have previously observed, even if we agree that in some sense morality must be action guiding, this still leaves considerable room about how exactly this notion is to be understood. Would it suffice if morality were simply a system of rules that assigned to each possible act a particular moral status (forbidden, required, or permissible)?

If so, then couldn't morality exist—couldn't there be an objective fact of the matter about which rules were the *valid* ones—even if, in fact, we could never come to know which particular rules these are? These rules would, after all, still be valid, still properly classify acts as forbidden or permissible, and so, in some sense of the term, still "guide" action, in that morality would still say, of any given act, whether it was permissible to do that act or not. Morality wouldn't be something we would *use*, but for all that, it would still classify acts as right or wrong.

Alternatively, if you feel that this wouldn't suffice to count as being "action guiding" in the relevant sense of the term, perhaps that merely shows that we shouldn't really include the idea of being action *guiding* in morality's job description after all. Perhaps we should be satisfied, instead, with morality's being action *classifying*. Conceivably, then, we shouldn't insist that moral facts (if such there be) must be ones that we can know.

Nonetheless, I assume that most of us will indeed want to insist that knowledge of moral facts must be possible (if only because we also insist on a robust notion of what it takes to be action guiding). But even if we do insist upon the possibility of moral knowledge, this still leaves room for debate about the *extent* of that knowledge.

Consider, as a possible analogy, our knowledge of the rules of our language. It does seem plausible to suggest that language simply couldn't do its job if those who spoke a given language had no understanding of the meaning of its words, had no knowledge whatsoever of how to form grammatical sentences, and knew nothing at all about how to understand and interpret those sentences. But for all that, of course, most of us would find it difficult or impossible to *state* the relevant rules of our language. (Doing this provides a challenge even to professional linguists.) Indeed, most of us would find it difficult or impossible to provide adequate definitions of countless words that we regularly use on a daily basis. So although it does seem right to suggest that in *some* sense language users must have knowledge of the rules of their language, it does not seem correct to insist that ordinary users of that language must be able to spell those rules out in an accurate and systematic fashion. Language use requires that we know how to *follow* the rules of our language, and no doubt it requires as well that we typically are able to say of this or that particular sentence *that* it is grammatical or not (and so on), but it certainly doesn't require that we know that the relevant rules are *such and such*; for we may not be able to articulate the rules at all.

Could something similar be true in the case of ethics? Arguably, if morality is to be action guiding in a sufficiently robust sense, then we must be able to use our knowledge of morality so as to classify at least some of our available actions as being permissible or not. But for all that, perhaps our knowledge is limited to these sorts of "local" judgments, and we have no ability to state, let alone know, the general rules of morality. Would it be acceptable if we could know, of this or that particular act, whether it was permissible or forbidden, and yet, for all that, we could not know anything about the underlying moral rules that grounded and explained these more particular moral facts?

Alternatively, would it be acceptable to hold, instead, that as far as moral knowledge is concerned, what we can know most readily and directly are, rather, the more general principles? Perhaps it is our knowledge of the morality of particular *acts* that sometimes gives out! On a view like this, we might indeed have knowledge of the fact that, say, lies tend to be immoral, that it is generally wrong to harm the innocent, and that we are generally required to aid those in need, and so on. If knowledge of such general moral principles were readily available, morality would still be (at least somewhat) capable of guiding our actions. We would, for example, know to try to avoid telling lies! In many cases—ones where the morally relevant factors all support the same course of action—we might know exactly what it is that we are required to do. But for all that, in more complicated cases—ones where different factors pull in different directions—we might be incapable of gaining the kind of certainty we normally associate with knowledge, never knowing for sure whether a given act is permissible or not. Would this limited capacity for moral knowledge be good enough?

If knowledge of general moral principles is indeed possible, how much about them must it be possible to know? Suppose we build the possibility of moral knowledge into morality's job description; what exactly is it that it must be possible to know? Working out the details of any given moral rule is often a difficult and complex undertaking. So would it suffice, for example, if all I knew was that self-defense is "often" morally permissible? Or must it be possible for me to state the precise circumstances in which defensive force is permissible and the precise circumstances in which it is not?

Going beyond knowledge of individual moral rules to questions about morality as a whole, must it also be possible for us to figure out how the various individual rules hang together in a systematic whole (supposing that this is indeed the case)? On some views, the familiar basic rules of morality have an underlying basis or foundation (whether God's will, or a social contract, or overall utility, or what have you). If this is so, if the rules of morality really do have an underlying foundation, must it be possible for us to know this as well? Must it be possible for us to figure out what that basis is?

In short, must the answer to *every* moral question be within our grasp? If not, which ones need to be? It is one thing to insist that certain types of moral knowledge must be available to us. But it is quite another thing to specify exactly which types of moral facts are the ones that we must be capable of knowing.

Variability. Let's continue to suppose that a genuine objective morality would take the form of a set of rules. What we need to ask next is whether the true or correct moral rules (if there is to be such a thing as an objective morality) must be the same for everyone, across all societies and cultures, valid at all times, past, present, and future.

Some people are what we might call *absolutists* about morality. They hold that if morality genuinely exists, if there are objective moral truths, then there must be a set of moral rules that hold for *everyone*—rules that are binding upon everyone equally, regardless of where they live or when they live or what they happen to believe. If, for example, killing innocent people is wrong, then it is wrong everywhere: the moral prohibition against killing the innocent must be *universally* valid—regardless of whether or not everyone in all societies has recognized that fact. Similarly for other basic moral rules. The true principles, if such there be, must hold everywhere and always.

In contrast, others are prepared to at least allow for the possibility of variability in the basic moral rules, such that a rule that is binding and correct in one society, or at one time, may still, for all that, not be binding and correct in other societies or at other times. For example, while we would all agree that slavery would be immoral and utterly unacceptable in our own society, those who allow for the possibility of moral *relativism* might allow for the possibility that slavery simply *was not wrong* in ancient Greece, that a different set of moral rules applied to that society than the one that applies to our own, with each set of rules being perfectly correct and valid when applied to the relevant society and time.

Of course, absolutists about morality will never allow anything like this sort of relativity. If slavery is indeed wrong (as we can suppose that it is), then it has always been wrong, whether or not the ancient Greeks realized it. Their society may have *allowed* slavery, and so it may have been permissible "socially," as it were; but morally speaking, it was *wrong*, period, regardless of whether anyone recognized that fact. So say the absolutists. But relativists are open to the possibility that the very same moral rules may not, in fact, be valid across all places and all times. What is truly and validly morally permissible in one place, or at one time, may come to be truly and validly morally forbidden at another place, or at another time.

This debate between absolutists and relativists serves as a nice illustration of a point I have repeatedly emphasized, that an account of morality that might satisfy one person may nonetheless leave another utterly dissatisfied. Suppose, if only for the sake of argument, that we could establish the existence of binding rules, rules that each person had compelling reason to obey, rules that spoke to how we were permitted to treat one another. But imagine as well that there was variation from society to society with regard to *which* rules were the valid ones for the members of the given society. Would that count as a defense of an "objective" morality?

Those who build absolutism into the very job description of morality might answer in the negative: if there is really going to be an *objective* moral code, they might say, then the rules themselves must be universally valid, valid across all places and times. But relativists need not agree: there could, they will point out, be a perfectly objective fact about which particular rules were binding upon any given society, and so there could be an objective fact about how the members of *that* society were permitted to treat others. That should suffice, the relativists might insist, for us to say that there are objective moral *truths* about what people are to do.

My own view, of course, is that while it is indeed important to decide whether we want to build absolutism into the job description of morality—or whether, instead, we want to allow for moral relativism of some sort or another—we should not get delayed over the question of who has a better understanding of what it takes (or would take) to have an objective morality. Debates about the label "objective" are unimportant. What is important, rather, is the disagreement between the absolutist and the relativist about whether variability in moral rules is acceptable or not.

Of course, in thinking about that disagreement, it is crucial to avoid certain potential misunderstandings. The debate between absolutists and relativists is about whether the valid moral rules vary from society to society (or across times). It is not a debate about whether moral *beliefs* have varied in this way. Almost all of us are prepared to recognize that different societies have held different moral *beliefs*: the ancient Greeks, to revert to our earlier example, believed that slavery was morally permissible; we do not. The absolutist certainly does not have to deny any of this. But the debate isn't about variability in beliefs; it is about whether there is variability in the moral facts. Could it really be that slavery was *in fact* morally permissible in ancient Greece, even though it is not morally permissible now? That is the kind of question that the absolutists and relativists are arguing about.

Unfortunately, the line between absolutism and relativism is somewhat harder to pin down than one might initially think. For even absolutists believe in moral relativity at *some* level. Suppose, for example, that you have promised your mother to call her this afternoon. Then you have a moral obligation to do just that, to call your mother. But *I* have no such obligation—no obligation to call *your* mother, or for that matter *my* mother—because I haven't made any such promise! So you have a moral obligation that I do not. Presumably no absolutist ever intended to deny this kind of relativity or variability. What they will claim, instead, is that there is an underlying basic moral rule (perhaps something like "keep your promises") and while this underlying rule can generate variable *derivative* moral obligations (depending on who has promised what), it is the underlying, more fundamental moral principle ("one should keep one's promises") that is universally valid. Absolutists happily allow relativity at a sufficiently derivative level. It is only the most basic moral principles that are said to be universally valid.

But once we say something like this, then it may turn out that even relativists believe in absolute principles, once we go *sufficiently* deep. After all, even the relativist believes in an absolute underlying principle, roughly along the lines of "one should obey the moral principles valid for one's own society." That is to say, the relativist takes the truth of relativism to be *universally* valid, valid across all places and times!

So just about everyone in this debate agrees that at a deep enough level, there may be some universal moral truths, and at a sufficiently superficial level, there may be some variability. This makes it difficult to articulate a precise line separating the absolutists and the relativists.

Nonetheless, despite this point, I imagine that there would be a fair amount of agreement about which particular positions to classify as absolutist and which relativist. The trick is to focus on familiar "basic" moral rules, like those requiring truth telling and promise keeping, or those forbidding harming the innocent or enslaving others, and the like. If you are prepared to believe that rules like this might be valid in certain societies or at certain times, but not in other societies or at other times, then you should think of yourself as a relativist. If not, an absolutist. At the very least, this rough and ready test should suffice for our purposes.

Unsurprisingly, there are more fine-grained distinctions that can be made within each of these two camps. If you are a relativist, for example, and want to allow for the possibility that valid moral rules might vary from society to society, might they vary even more radically than that? Could they, for example, vary from individual to individual? Just how much variability would you be prepared to allow? (Could valid moral principles even vary *within* a given individual's life, changing from one moment to the next?) Moving in the other direction, similar questions arise for the absolutist as well. Absolutists hold that the basic moral rules are valid for everyone, at all places and all times. But who, exactly, do we mean to include when we use the term "everyone"? If you are an absolutist, are you merely claiming that all *humans* are bound by the same set of basic rules? Or, more ambitiously still, do you mean to claim that all *rational beings whatsoever* must be bound by those very same rules? Imagine, say, the existence of intelligent Martians: would *they* be bound by the same moral rules?

Necessity. As I have just noted, some want to build absolutism into the job description for morality: if there really is to be such a thing as an objective morality, then the same basic moral rules must hold at all places and times. But some want to go further still, insisting that if there really are moral facts, then the same principles must be valid not only throughout the world as it actually is, but in any conceivable world whatsoever. According to this view, if there really are any moral truths at all then true claims about the basic moral principles must be *necessary* truths, truths that couldn't have been otherwise.

This belief in the necessity of morality is in fact a bolder claim than the one just put forward by the absolutist (though it is, of course, compatible with absolutism). The absolutist holds that one and the same moral principles are valid in all places and at all times—throughout the universe, as we might put it. But accepting this idea does not yet commit you to the further claim that moral truths are *necessary* truths, in the sense I have in mind here. For it could be, instead, that the basic moral principles, though valid throughout the world, are, nonetheless, *contingent*, in that the principles *could* have been different.

To see the contrast, consider what most of us believe about the laws of physics. These laws hold, we believe, without exception, at all times and at all places, throughout the universe. In this way they are "absolute" (in the sense of the term we have been using). But for all that, the laws of physics seem to be *contingent*, in the sense that they could have been different from what they actually are. Thus, for example, it is easy to imagine that the gravitational constant might have been higher or lower, or that gold might have had a different melting point from the one it actually has, or that objects in motion might have required continual application of force to remain in motion, and so on. The actual laws of physics hold throughout the universe, but it is easy to imagine alternative possible worlds where the relevant laws would be rather different from the ones that actually do hold in our own world.

In contrast, most of us believe that the laws of mathematics hold not just in the actual world, but in any conceivable world whatsoever. It isn't merely that it happens to be the case that in *our* universe $1 + 1 = 2$, while in other possible universes $1 + 1 = 3$ or $1 + 1 = -5$. No! What we believe about math is that the truths of mathematics are necessary ones, holding not just in the actual world, but in any possible world at all. It is a contingent truth (albeit one that holds throughout our world) that gravity works in keeping with an inverse square law. But it is a *necessary* truth that $2 \times 2 = 4$.

So we need to ask: if there is to be such a thing as morality, must the basic moral truths be necessary? Or might they be contingent? Even if the same moral rules are valid in all places and times in *our* world (our universe), might they nonetheless differ in *other* possible worlds? Could it be, for example, that although the killing of innocents is immoral in our world—the world as it actually is—nonetheless the world could have been sufficiently different so that within those alternative possibilities killing innocents would not have been forbidden at all, but rather permissible, or even obligatory? Or should we claim, instead, that when we are dealing with basic moral principles (if such there be), the relevant truths are necessary ones, so that the killing of innocents would be immoral in any possible world at all, just as one plus one would equal two in every possible world?

Relativists, at least, must hold that moral truths are contingent. Since relativists think that such truths needn't even hold across the entirety of our own world, they will certainly agree that they need not hold across all possible worlds. But even absolutists can embrace the idea that moral truths are contingent. If they want to, absolutists can claim that the laws of morality are like the laws of physics—exceptionless in our own world but different in other possible worlds. Nonetheless, many absolutists do indeed believe that basic moral truths are necessary ones. And some of them may want to build this idea into the job description of morality, insisting that if there is indeed to be such a thing as objective morality then it must be the case that the same basic moral principles would hold in any possible world whatsoever.

In thinking about whether to accept this sort of necessity for morality, it is important to bear in mind the fact that on any plausible moral view *some* moral facts will be contingent. After all, if it is true (as we can suppose it is) that it is morally wrong to feed your baby brother milk laced with cyanide, this is surely because cyanide is poisonous to humans and so cyanide will kill your brother! But the poisonous nature of cyanide is presumably a contingent fact; it is easy enough to imagine an alternative possible world where human biology evolved in a slightly different way, so as to be immune to cyanide's effects. In such a world, conceivably, there would be nothing morally objectionable at all about giving someone cyanide-laced milk. Accordingly, pretty much everyone can agree that at least some moral facts are contingent ones; they could have been otherwise.

But what those who believe in the necessity of morality have in mind, of course, is a claim about the *basic* moral principles or rules ("keep your promises," "don't harm the innocent," and so on). Even if it is true that had we evolved differently we would be immune to cyanide (and so there would be nothing wrong with serving it), there might still be other ways to harm or kill one another, and those ways would still be forbidden. That, at least, is the sort of claim that those who believe in the necessity of morality will want to put forward. They will readily admit that *derivative* moral truths can be contingent; but they will insist that the validity of the *basic* moral principles is fixed across all possible worlds. If objective morality is more than an illusion then in *no* world could it be morally permissible to kill the innocent, or to disregard one's promises, and so forth.

Grounds. Consider the claim that murder is wrong. If this really is a fact—as most of us take it to be—we can ask: by virtue of what does this fact obtain? What does it take for it to *be* a fact that murder is wrong?

In one way, of course, the answer to this question may seem obvious. If it is indeed a fact that murder is wrong, then this is so by virtue of the ("underlying") fact that a certain type of action, murder, has a particular property, the property of *wrongness* (that is, the property of being morally wrong or forbidden). This answer is similar to the one we might give if we were asked, instead, about what it would take for it to be a fact that murder is *difficult*: this too, we might say, would be a fact by virtue of the fact that a certain type of action, murder, has a particular property—the property of being difficult (that is, being difficult to perform).

But suppose we dig deeper. We might ask, for example, for more information about the nature of this first property, wrongness. What exactly does wrongness *consist* in? Can it be explained in terms of something more basic or fundamental? Similarly, we might ask about why it is that certain acts or act types have this property while others lack it. What, if anything, is the ultimate basis or grounding of this fact? Can moral facts—like the fact that murder is wrong—be reduced to, or explained in terms of, something more basic or fundamental?

In raising this question, I don't (merely) mean to be asking *which* acts are right or wrong, or what, if anything, all wrong acts (like murder) have in common. (There may well be general moral principles that allow us to appropriately sort acts into the permissible and the forbidden.) Rather, I mean to be focusing on the property of wrongness itself. What is the nature of that property, and what is the ultimate *basis* of the fact that certain types of acts are wrong? If there really are moral facts, what are they ultimately *grounded* in?

At this point a wide range of possible answers become available. I want to distinguish between two broad groups of replies.

On the one hand, some hold that moral facts ultimately reduce to, or "boil down to," more fundamental facts about the relevant attitudes or reactions of certain minds. Perhaps being wrong is a matter of being contrary to God's will. Or perhaps it is a matter of the members of a given society disapproving of such acts. Or maybe it is just a matter of my own personal likes and dislikes. Similarly, perhaps being morally required is ultimately a matter about what an ideal lawgiver would command, or what rational bargainers would demand of one another.

Although views like this obviously differ from one another in all sorts of important ways, what they have in common is the shared thought that moral facts are *mind dependent*—moral facts ultimately reduce (at least in part) to facts about the reactions or attitudes of the relevant sorts of minds. (On some of these views, what matters are facts about the *actual* reactions of the relevant minds; on others, what matters are facts about how those minds *would* react, or would react under suitably ideal conditions. Either way, morality boils down to facts about the relevant minds.)

Others, however, are uncomfortable with the idea that moral facts might be mind dependent in this way. They insist, instead, that moral facts cannot truly be objective if they (largely) reduce to facts about minds. Rather, basic moral facts must be *mind independent*, having nothing to do with what this or that mind might think or believe, like or dislike. Just as facts about physics have nothing essential to do with what we believe or think, or what anyone else believes or thinks, facts about morality (if there are to be such things) must have nothing essential to do with what we or anyone else would like or favor or command. Otherwise, the vision of morality being put forward cannot lay claim to being a truly objective one.

To be sure, it might be a basic moral fact that, say, pleasure is good, or that promoting virtue is morally obligatory; and obviously enough, facts about pleasure are facts about (the experiences of) minds, just as facts about virtue are facts about (the character traits of) minds. But what those who insist on the mind independence of basic moral facts are claiming, rather, is that the *goodness* of pleasure or the *obligatoriness* of promoting virtue do not reduce to facts about the reactions or attitudes of these or other minds.

On this second sort of view, it might turn out that basic moral properties—like the property of being morally required—simply cannot be reduced to anything further at all. But even if such properties can somehow be reduced to, or explained in terms of, more fundamental ones, those who hold this second view insist that moral properties *cannot* be reduced to facts about how certain *minds* happen to react. Any approach along these lines would threaten the objectivity of morality.

As usual, I don't think it a fruitful debate to argue about whose account can best lay claim to the label "objective." But it is important, nonetheless, to decide whether to build mind independence into the very job description of morality.

So the first thing to notice is that there do indeed seem to be facts that are mind *dependent*. If a joke is funny, for example, there certainly seems to be a fact here, the fact that the joke is funny. But for all that, this seems to be a mind dependent fact. Arguably, a joke's being funny ultimately boils down to the fact that members of the relevant group (the relevant audience) would *find* it funny—that they would react to it in a certain way. Similarly, if going over 70 miles per hour in a certain stretch of highway is illegal, then this certainly seems to be a fact as well. But here too, that fact ultimately seems mind dependent. The illegality turns on the fact that certain minds (the relevant legislators) voted for a law prohibiting going faster than this.

Or consider the fact that in English you are required to have agreement (in number) between noun and verb. This too is a fact, and it too seems to be a mind dependent one. Ultimately, this grammatical requirement boils down to complicated facts about what sorts of linguistic behavior English speakers are or are not prepared to accept. Indeed, if enough English speakers began to react and speak differently—routinely violating a rule they had previously accepted—what was once ungrammatical would cease to be ungrammatical. As a little reflection reveals, the rules of English grammar depend entirely on the relevant reactions of the relevant minds. (No one ever thinks to herself, "Thank God our Anglo-Saxon ancestors were able to discover the mind independent rules of English grammar. How lucky we are that they got it right!")

What is particularly interesting about this last example is that despite it being the case that facts about grammar are clearly mind dependent, it is nonetheless the case that any one of us—indeed all of us—can be quite mistaken in our beliefs about what is, or is not, grammatical. It certainly isn't true that the rules of English grammar are simply whatever it is that we *say* they are; on the contrary, the nature of the mind dependence is far more indirect than that. So common views about the rules of grammar, or even about particular sentences, can be thoroughly mistaken. In this way, an earlier feature that we connected to our ideas about objectivity—the possibility of getting things wrong—is in place here, despite the fact that facts about language are undeniably mind dependent.

Similarly, then, even if we allow for the possibility that *moral* facts might ultimately be mind dependent ones, nothing in this rules out the possibility that we might be frequently mistaken in our beliefs about those facts. There can still be right answers in ethics; there can still be a fact of the matter about which answers are *correct*.

Nonetheless, it remains the case that some demand more out of morality than this. They are dissatisfied with the idea that moral facts might depend in this way on the particular reactions of the relevant minds. They demand something more secure. If there are to be moral facts, they insist, these facts must not reduce to facts about minds. Like the laws of physics, the basic moral facts must be mind *independent*.

Reasons. Suppose I promise to meet you after work tomorrow. Most of us would accept the thought that I now have a *reason* to do what I have promised you I would do. There is at least some justification for my acting accordingly. Conceivably the reason is an extremely strong one, maybe even a decisive one. But certainly I now have at least *some* reason to meet you after work. After all, I promised.

A bit more cautiously, what I suppose most of us accept is the thought that *if* there really is such a thing as morality—if there really are moral facts, including facts about our various moral obligations—then I now have at least some reason to do what I promised to do. Moral requirements, if there really are such things, provide you with reasons to perform the acts in question. (Similarly, if there really are moral *virtues*, then one has a reason to have the character traits in question, and if certain outcomes are morally *good* ones, then one has a reason to promote and maintain such outcomes, and so on. But in what follows I will continue to focus on moral *requirements*.)

So here we have yet another feature that many will want to build into the job description: morality must provide reasons for action, justification for doing what it asks of us. According to this view, no purported moral obligation can be a real one unless we have at least some justification for meeting that purported obligation. Not everyone accepts this view, but many do: if there are to be genuine moral obligations, they must entail reasons.

A view like this posits a kind of inner necessary connection between the existence of moral requirements, on the one hand, and the existence of reasons to do what is morally required, on the other. Providing an appropriate reason is part of what it takes to *be* a moral requirement. Accordingly, the view that that there is indeed this sort of inner connection between moral obligations and the existence of reasons is sometimes called *reasons internalism*. In contrast, the alternative view, according to which obligations need not entail reasons at all, can be called *reasons externalism*.

That's not to say that reasons externalists think that there can be no connection whatsoever between moral obligations and reasons. In many circumstances, no doubt, we do have a reason to do what morality requires of us; and for some individuals, perhaps, there is typically or even always a reason. But this is indeed a further question, says the externalist. Merely knowing that there is a moral requirement to do such and such does not yet—in and of itself, without further ado—tell us anything at all about whether anyone has any kind of *reason* to do what the requirement demands. Moral requirements may often be accompanied by reasons. In fact, it is even conceivable that, as it happens, they are *always* so accompanied. But there is no *necessity* in any of this. There is no inner conceptual guarantee that a valid requirement will always be backed by a reason. In principle, at least, there could be obligations—perfectly genuine obligations—for which there is simply no reason to act upon the obligation at all.

So say the reasons externalists. But most people, I think, will find some version of reasons internalism more congenial instead. They will insist that there must be *some* kind of necessary connection between moral requirements and reasons. As usual, however, there is room for disagreement about what exactly this connection guarantees. Is it really the case that the mere *existence* of a requirement suffices to guarantee the existence of a reason to act? Or is it rather—more modestly—that the existence of such a reason is only guaranteed when the person who is under the obligation *recognizes* the existence of that obligation? Do moral requirements provide reasons even to those who don't recognize the existence of the requirement in question? Or are the reasons generated only when the requirement is acknowledged as such? (The latter view is more modest, but we can still count it as an internalist position since it holds that there is a necessary connection between the *recognition* of a requirement and the existence of a reason.)

There are other questions as well. If we suppose that obligations do entail reasons (though possibly only when the obligations are recognized), just how strong must those reasons be? Is it sufficient that there be *some* reason to meet one's obligations, no matter how weak that reason turns out to be? Or must the reason be stronger than that?

The most modest form of internalism holds that, indeed, all that is guaranteed is that there be *some* reason to perform any given required act. This minimal view is compatible with it being the case that the reason provided can nonetheless be outweighed by other reasons, reasons that oppose doing the act in question. So it could turn out that it will sometimes be *irrational* to do what morality demands of us. Because of this implication, many internalists will insist upon a bolder version of internalism, one where the reason is guaranteed to be stronger. Perhaps, for example, the internalist will demand that if there is indeed a genuine moral obligation to act, then this must guarantee *sufficient* reason to justify doing that act, so that it is always at least rationally *permissible* to meet one's moral obligations. Or perhaps the internalist will want to insist that the reasons generated by moral requirements must always *outweigh* any opposing reasons, so that the *balance* of reasons will always favor doing the required act. Finally, and more boldly still, some internalists will insist that whenever there is a genuine moral requirement to act in a given way, the corresponding reason must always be *so* strong that the act in question will be rationally *required*, as well as being morally required.

Why accept any form of reasons internalism at all? Perhaps because it offers a natural way to distinguish between those rules that are valid or binding and those rules that are not. Imagine that some madman on the corner makes up some rule and announces loudly that you are required to obey it. Intuitively, it seems plausible to think that the rule is not genuinely binding on you, no matter what the madman declares. But what exactly do we mean by that thought, the thought that the madman's rule is not a valid or binding one? Perhaps just this: that you have no real reason to conform to his rule. That's why the rule is not valid or binding *on you*. Accordingly, many people will want to insist that if there really is to be such a thing as objective morality, then the rules of that morality will have to be different from the madman's ravings in precisely this way. They must *apply* to you, not merely in the thin sense that they are telling you what to do, but in the more robust sense of there being some genuine reason for you to *do* what the rules say.

That, at least, is the view of the reasons internalists: if there really is to be such a thing as objective morality, then it must be the case that we always have some justification for doing what morality asks of us. There must always be at least some sort of reason for doing what morality demands.

Motivation. Imagine, once again, that I have promised to meet you after work tomorrow. Other things being equal, then, we would normally expect that I will now do what I have promised you to do.

It is important not to lose sight of the frequency with which we somehow manage to meet our moral obligations (assuming, for the moment, that there really are such things). We do what we are morally required to do. We keep our promises, we avoid telling lies, we go out of our way to help those in need. We are *moved* to act in keeping with our obligations. And of course it isn't as though this is just a coincidence—as though we just happen to be motivated to do the things we are obligated to do. The connection seems tighter than that: we are motivated, at least in part, precisely *because* of the fact that we are obligated. Moral obligations seem capable of motivating us, moving us to action.

Some want to go further. They insist that this is part of the very job description of morality: if there really are to be moral facts, then they must be capable of moving us.

Here then is yet another idea that many will want to build into the very concept of morality. Just as some—the reasons internalists—believe that there is (or would need to be) a necessary connection between moral requirements and the existence of reasons, so too there are those who assert a necessary connection between moral requirements and the existence of *motivation* (to do what those requirements demand). The view that there is this sort of inner conceptual connection between morality and motivation is sometimes called *motive internalism*. And the alternative view, according to which moral obligations need not entail anything about motivation at all, can be called *motive externalism*.

If one does accept motive internalism, there remain further questions, analogous to those that arise for those who accept *reasons* internalism. For example, if there is a necessary connection between obligation and motivation, is it the very existence of a moral obligation that guarantees the corresponding motivation? Or is motivation guaranteed, instead, only for those who *recognize* the existence of the obligation in question? (What about cases where the individual mistakenly *believes* in the existence of an obligation?) And if motivation must indeed be present, how strong does it need to be?

An extremely bold version of motive internalism would hold that when there is a genuine moral obligation (or, perhaps, when it is recognized as such) the motivation to act in keeping with that obligation must be so strong that it necessarily outweighs any competing motivation that one might feel. Which is just to say, where there is an (acknowledged) obligation, one will inevitably perform the obligatory act. Admittedly, this view may seem to fly in the face of the familiar fact that we sometimes fail to do what we take ourselves to be morally required to do. But perhaps such cases only show that what we took to be an obligation really wasn't one after all, or that we didn't truly believe in the obligation in the first place.

Be that as it may, I suspect that what most motive internalists accept is a more modest version of the view, one according to which although obligations do entail the existence of at least some motivation, it needn't be *sufficient* motivation to guarantee that we will perform the act in question. Although there must always be at least some motivational pull toward meeting the relevant moral requirement, it can be outweighed by competing motives—motives pulling us in other directions—so that we won't necessarily do what we are obligated to do.

Motive externalists, on the other hand, think that even this more modest version of internalism goes too far. There is no necessary connection at all, they say, between obligations and motivation. Of course, the motive externalist needn't deny that we are often or even typically motivated to meet our various moral obligations. Conceivably, in fact, there may be some individuals for whom such motivation is *always* present. But the presence of such motivation is always a further matter, not guaranteed by the mere existence of the obligation alone (nor by its recognition). In principle, at least, an obligation could exist (and be recognized as such) without the relevant individual having any motivation at all to try to meet it.

One might wonder whether there is really a need to distinguish between the views of the motive internalist and the reasons internalist. If obligations entail reasons, after all, won't there necessarily be at least some motivation to act accordingly as well? And if obligations *don't* entail reasons, why would someone be motivated to act on them? But in principle at least it is one thing to talk about what someone has reason to do, and quite another thing to talk about what they are motivated to do. Perhaps if we were perfectly rational what we would be motivated to do would always align completely with what we have reason to do. But in real life, at any rate, the two can come apart, so we need to ask about each in turn. Just as we need to ask whether there is (or would be) a necessary connection between the existence of moral obligations and the existence of reasons to act on those obligations, we also need to ask whether there is a necessary connection between the existence of such obligations and the presence of at least some motivation to meet them.

1.3 Satisfying the Job Description

We have now considered ten features that might be added to a possible job description for morality. There are, no doubt, still others that some might want to include. And there is certainly much more to be said about the details of any given feature (including more about the various ways of developing each underlying idea). But it does seem likely that anything that had all of the features we have already examined would be appropriately acknowledged as constituting an objective morality.

Imagine that there were a set of rules that exhaustively classified all possible actions as permissible or forbidden, rules which (when acted upon) helped to promote or protect a wide range of significant human interests. Imagine that the very same basic rules were valid and binding at all places and at all times, and indeed, in all possible worlds whatsoever. Imagine that the ultimate basis of these rules did not turn on facts about our own minds, nor the minds of anyone else; on the contrary, there were simply facts, waiting to be discovered, about which potential rules were the *valid* ones. Imagine that we could come to know the contents of those valid rules and could then use our knowledge of the rules to decide how to act. Finally, imagine that one was always rationally justified in conforming to these rules, so that there was decisive and overriding reason to do what they asked of us, and that once one had determined just what it was that the relevant rules demanded, one would always experience at least some motivational pull toward behaving accordingly.

If there really were rules with all these features, I imagine we would all agree that morality was not a mere illusion, but a reality. Presumably even those committed to moral skepticism agree that if there *were* anything like what I have just described then there really would be an objective morality. Rules like these would so clearly satisfy the job description of morality that it would be pointless to pretend that there was no such thing as objective moral truth. To be sure, moral skeptics may not believe that there *is* in fact anything that comes nearly this close to meeting morality's job description; but even they will readily acknowledge that if there *were* something like this, that would do the trick.

What is significantly more controversial is what it would be appropriate to say about cases that are less clear cut than this. Imagine that we discovered rules that had some, but not all, of the features I have just described. What if the rules were absolute, but not necessary? What if they were backed by decisive reasons, but one could nonetheless remain unmoved by the recognition of one's obligations? What if the ultimate basis of the rules turned on facts about how certain minds would react? Or what if we could have only limited knowledge of the contents of the rules?

Which of these cases, if any, would still count as ones in which there existed something worthy of the name objective morality? Here, I think, people will disagree. For people disagree with one another about what it takes to constitute an objective morality. We disagree over which features are necessary ones. We disagree about the forms those necessary features must take. We disagree about which features are negotiable. Sometimes we even disagree about whether a given feature is so much as preferable, let alone essential. Elements that one person might place at the center of morality's job description will be readily left out by others.

Because of this disagreement, people will sometimes disagree as well about whether a particular reply to a given skeptical argument would even constitute part of a genuine *defense* of morality. After all, the reply might involve denying or modifying a feature that some would want to insist upon, while others may never have included the relevant feature in the first place (or they may at least be open to reconsidering the matter). In such cases, a defense of morality that some will find perfectly satisfactory others may find utterly unacceptable.

There is, I think, no getting around this fact. Each of us will have to decide for ourselves just what it would take for there to be something worthy of the name objective morality. Accordingly, in the chapters to come, when I present possible answers to various skeptical arguments, I will leave it to the reader to decide for herself which (if any) of these answers should be avoided if one is to assert the existence of objective moral truth. Still, as I hope to show, there are indeed plausible answers to the skeptic's arguments. Belief in an objective morality remains an intellectually respectable position.

2
Basic Positions in Metaethics

2.1 Cognitivism versus Noncognitivism

Our main concern in this book is to explore and evaluate skeptical worries about morality. We want to better understand how, exactly, some of the most troubling skeptical arguments go, and we want to see what replies can be made to these arguments. But before turning to the arguments themselves it will be useful to distinguish between some basic positions that one might take in metaethics. This will make it easier, in those later discussions, to keep track of who is saying what, and who is *entitled* to say what, as we repeatedly move back and forth between possible arguments and possible replies. In effect, I want to introduce the basic philosophical positions that will be regularly appearing in the following chapters.

We can introduce the most important distinctions by means of the following flow chart.

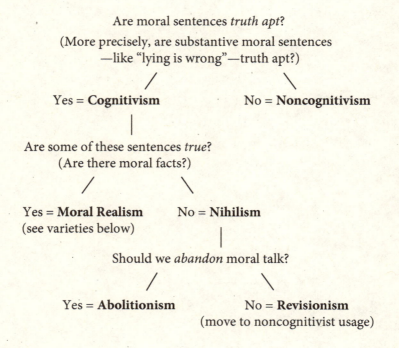

To understand this chart, we should begin by recalling the concept of being *truth apt* (introduced in 1.2). A sentence is truth apt if it is the kind of sentence that can take on a truth value, that is to say, be true or false.

Thus, for example, consider sentences like the following: "The Moon is made of cheese." "Snow is white." "Ducks are rectangles." "Laurette's computer was purchased last year in France." "Two times three equals six."

Each of these five sentences is truth apt. Some of them are true, some are false, but all of them are the kinds of sentences that can appropriately be assigned a truth value of one sort or the other. These sentences make claims. They are statements, whether true or not, that attempt to tell us how things are.

(Arguably, rather than saying of sentences like these that they make claims, or that they try to tell us how things are, or that they are assertions about how things stand, and so on, it might be more accurate to say instead that we *use* these kinds of sentences to make claims or assert things, and so forth. But in what follows I will help myself to both ways of talking. For our purposes, I think, there is no need to be fastidious about this point.)

Contrast these sentences with some others: "Go to your room!" "What is the name of that song?" "Mind your own business!" "Who is that?" "Blue cheese, yuck!"

These are, of course, perfectly grammatical and meaningful English sentences. But for all that, they are not truth apt. They are neither true *nor* false. They do not have truth values at all, one way or the other. They are not making claims about how things are; they are not making assertions.

To be sure—and this is an important point—the sentences in the second group have perfectly legitimate linguistic uses. There are other jobs that can be done by sentences in our language beyond that of making assertions. So these sentences are perfectly acceptable, and in the right contexts they might be quite useful. But they are not truth apt.

So that makes them different from, say, the sentence "the moon is made of cheese." That sentence is truth apt, even though it happens to be false. It is making, or can be used to make, a factual claim. As it happens, of course, the particular factual claim it is making isn't true (since the moon isn't made of cheese), but for all that, the linguistic job of a sentence like that is to *assert* something, to *make* a claim about how things are.

Of course, in saying that a sentence is truth apt, that it is the sort of thing for which it would be appropriate to assign a truth value, we are not saying that we necessarily *know* what that truth value is! Maybe we do, or maybe we don't. But even if we don't, the sentence can still be truth apt. Take, for example, the sentence "the number of atoms in the universe is even." I have no idea whether this is true or not, and for all I know no one will ever be in a position to know. But for all that, it remains truth apt, since it is making a claim about what the facts are, and that claim is either true or false.

Returning now to ethics, our first question is this: are moral sentences truth apt or not? More precisely, are substantive, first-order moral sentences—sentences like "it is permissible to kill in self-defense"—truth apt or not?

Now as I have previously remarked, most of us think that the sentence "it is permissible to kill in self-defense" is true. Trivially, then, we think it is truth *apt* as well. In contrast, of course, pacifists do not think that killing in self-defense is permissible. So a typical pacifist will want to insist that the sentence in question is *false*. But even a pacifist can agree that the sentence is truth *apt* since, as I have already noted, a sentence need not be true to be truth apt; it only needs to be the kind of sentence for which it is appropriate to assign a truth value—whether true *or* false. And the sentence "it is permissible to kill in self-defense" certainly seems to be a sentence of that sort. It certainly *seems* to be making a factual claim about morality—whether or not one accepts the particular claim it is making.

Our first question, then, is this: is it really doing that or not? More generally, are sentences of that *sort*—sentences that appear to be making first-order substantive claims about morality—genuinely truth apt? In raising this question about these sorts of sentences we are not asking of any particular moral remark whether it is true (or, alternatively, if it is false). We are asking a more fundamental question: Are these sorts of sentences actually *making* factual claims, as they appear to be doing? Or are they doing some *other* linguistic job?

Now it might seem that the answer to our question is obvious. After all, a sentence like "killing in self-defense is permissible" has the grammatical form of a statement. And aren't statements precisely the subset of sentences that are used to make claims about how things are? Admittedly, statements can turn out to be false. But even then, they are truth *apt*.

Compare the statement "killing in self-defense is difficult." Whether correctly or not, this statement ascribes a certain property (difficulty) to a certain type of action (killing in self-defense). It attempts to state a fact. That's what statements do. So this sentence is obviously truth apt.

Similarly, then, shouldn't we all agree that the sentence "killing in self-defense is permissible" is truth apt as well? It too seems to be ascribing a property (permissibility) to a certain type of action (killing in self-defense). So whether we think it is correct or incorrect to ascribe that property, shouldn't we at least agree that it is *attempting* to state a fact? "Killing in self-defense is permissible" has the grammatical form of a statement; so shouldn't we agree that it too is truth apt?

Conceivably, however, the surface grammar is misleading. Perhaps, despite appearances, moral sentences of the kind we have in mind are not actually in the fact-asserting business after all. Maybe they are doing something else, performing some other linguistic job—all the while being grammatically dressed as statements?

Consider the imperative "don't kill!" That sentence clearly isn't in the fact-stating business at all: it is a command, not an attempt to state how things are. But then compare that to the sentence "killing is wrong." It is difficult to see how this second sentence differs in content or meaning in any significant way from the first. So if the first isn't in the fact-stating business—and it isn't—then perhaps the second isn't either. In which case, the second wouldn't really be truth apt after all, despite its having the grammatical form of a statement. And more generally, perhaps something similar is true for all first-order substantive moral sentences. Although they look like they are in the fact-stating business, perhaps they actually have a different job altogether.

So what should we say? Are sentences of this sort truth apt or not?

Cognitivists about morality say that these kinds of moral sentences really *are* truth apt. They are doing just what they appear to be doing: asserting facts (rightly or wrongly) and making moral claims. Accordingly, sentences like this are the sort of thing that can be believed or denied. Conceivably, we can even come to know which are the true ones and which the false ones. If first-order moral sentences are indeed truth apt, then when we assert what the sentences claim we will either be right or wrong—depending, of course, on whether the facts really are what we are saying they are. (In contrast, one cannot possibly *believe* "shut the door!" One cannot *know* that "shut the door!" Imperatives lack truth values, so are not the sort of thing that one can believe or deny, let alone know. And so on.)

In contrast, *noncognitivists* about morality hold that moral sentences are *not* genuinely truth apt (despite appearances). So when we use them we are not actually making assertions at all, and in particular we are not making claims about purported moral facts. We are doing something different when we use these sentences, something other than attempting to state facts. And this means, of course, that we cannot be right or wrong in the same way that we can be under cognitivism. For if we are not making assertions, there are no assertions to *be* correct or mistaken. Indeed, if first-order substantive moral sentences are not truth apt, then strictly speaking they cannot be the sort of thing that can be believed at all (let alone known). For to believe a sentence is to believe it to be true, and according to the noncognitivists these sentences *lack* truth values. So just as one cannot (strictly speaking) *believe* the question "what time is it?" or the command "sit down!" one cannot believe first-order substantive moral sentences either. We don't use these sentences to make assertions about facts (which *could* be believed), but rather to do something else.

Just what is it, on the noncognitivist account, that we *do* use moral sentences to do? That is, of course, an important question for the noncognitivist to answer, and we will come back to it in a later chapter (see 4.1). But for the time being, the crucial point is simply that noncognitivists deny what cognitivists assert—that first-order substantive moral sentences are truth apt.

I should note, however, that in the discussion that follows I will often express this idea a bit carelessly. I will say things like "according to noncognitivism, moral claims are not truth apt," or "noncognitivists hold that moral assertions lack truth values." Strictly speaking, of course, this isn't what one should say at all. For if these sentences aren't truth apt, then they aren't really making claims after all, and they aren't really being used to make assertions. So if one were being scrupulously careful, one should instead say things like "according to noncognitivism, sentences that appear to be moral assertions or appear to be making moral claims are not, in fact, truth apt at all (and so are not, in fact, assertions or claims after all)." But being scrupulous in this way would quickly grow tedious, so I won't insist on being careful in this way. Having been warned, you won't be confused if (while speaking loosely, but intuitively) I sometimes say things like "noncognitivists think that moral claims lack truth values." You'll understand what I mean and be able to provide the more careful translations on your own.

2.2 Nihilism versus Moral Realism

The first question we needed to consider concerned the truth aptness of substantive first-order moral claims.

But why did I need to qualify the question in that way? Why ask about whether *substantive first-order* moral claims are truth apt (and attempt to state facts), rather than just asking, more simply, whether *moral* claims are truth apt?

Part of the answer is that even noncognitivists think that *some* remarks about morality are indeed truth apt. Consider, in particular, the central claim of the noncognitivist, the claim that moral assertions are not truth apt. *That* claim is (in some broad sense) a claim about morality—it is, after all, a claim about the nature of our moral discourse. And it is certainly a claim which the noncognitivist thinks is perfectly true! But it is a second-order claim, not a first-order one. It isn't a substantive claim on the ground level, as it were, about which acts are right and which wrong, or which states of affairs are good and which bad, but rather a second-order claim about the nature of those first-order claims. When the noncognitivist tells us that our various (first-order) moral assertions are not, in fact, genuine assertions at all, that second-order remark—that very assertion about the lack of truth aptness—is one that the noncognitivist takes to be true, full stop. And this, of course, means that it is one that the noncognitivist takes to be truth apt. Similarly, when the *cognitivist* insists, instead, that (first-order) moral assertions are indeed truth apt, the *non*cognitivist thinks that this second-order claim made by the cognitivist is *mistaken*. But again, that means that even the noncognitivist agrees that the cognitivist's claim is truth *apt*! So it isn't second-order (metaethical) claims that are said by the noncognitivist to lack truth aptness; it is, rather, the substantive, first-order claims—claims like "murder is wrong," or "one must keep one's promises," or "pleasure is intrinsically valuable."

There will be much more to say about noncognitivism later. But for the moment, let us suppose that it is the cognitivist who is right, and that (first-order) moral claims really are truth apt after all. Note that to say this is not yet to say whether any of these substantive moral claims are *true*! It is perfectly compatible with cognitivism to hold that although first-order moral claims are indeed attempting to accurately describe moral facts, nonetheless they are all mistaken. It is compatible with cognitivism to hold that each and every substantive moral claim is false.

So the second question we need to ask—though it is a question that only arises for cognitivists—is whether any substantive first-order moral claims are true.

If some of them *are* true, then there are substantive (first-order) moral facts. The true moral claims will be the ones that state or describe those facts accurately. But if, instead, none of them are true, if every single substantive moral claim is false, then there are no substantive moral facts at all. Given the truth of cognitivism, it will still be the case that substantive moral claims make *assertions* about (supposed) moral facts. They attempt to say how things are. But for all that, there will *be* no substantive moral facts to describe accurately; the claims will all be false.

It is natural to wonder whether this second possibility—according to which all substantive moral claims are false—is really coherent. After all, doesn't any given act have to be either permissible or not? Suppose, for example, that it is mistaken to claim that all white lies are morally wrong. Won't it follow, trivially, that at least some white lies are permissible? But if so, then "some white lies are permissible" will be true—and so there will be some true substantive moral claims after all. Alternatively, if "some white lies are permissible" is false, then doesn't it trivially follow that "all white lies are forbidden" is true? Won't one or the other of these two claims have to be true? But if so, then regardless of which it is, there will be some moral facts, some substantive moral truths.

Although tempting, I think this argument is mistaken. To see why, it may be helpful to consider some analogous questions as they arise in connection with theology. Imagine that a theist asserts that God is good, or that God is all powerful, and so on. These certainly look like substantive claims about God and his nature. They look like the sorts of things that can be either true or false. That is, they seem to be truth apt. Accordingly, almost all theists are cognitivists about substantive first-order theological claims.

Interestingly enough, though, even the *atheist* is likely to be a cognitivist about such claims. The atheist agrees that substantive theological claims are indeed genuine assertions; they attempt to accurately describe (supposed) theological facts. First-order theological claims are truth apt.

Nonetheless, the atheist insists that all of these claims are *false*! There is no God, so it is false to say that God is good. There is no God, so it is false to say that God is all powerful. However—and this is the crucial point—it would be a mistake to conclude that since it is false that God is good, it must be true that God is evil or imperfectly good, or that since it is false that God is all powerful, it must be true that God is limited in his powers. No, says the atheist, *all* of the substantive first-order theological claims are false. There are no first-order theological facts, so all claims about them are mistaken.

Admittedly, we might wonder what to say about the central claim of the atheist, namely, that there is no God. *That* claim is certainly one that the atheist thinks is true. So doesn't that show that there must be at least one first-order substantive theological fact after all—that God doesn't exist?

If we wanted to, I suppose, we could say that. Then we would need to describe the atheist's position as being, rather, that there are no substantive first-order theological facts *other* than this very fact. Beyond the fact of God's nonexistence, there are no other substantive facts about theology. (Equivalently: there are no substantive first-order theological *truths* beyond this very one, that God does not exist.)

Alternatively, it might be that instead of simply asking whether there are any first-order theological facts at all, we should ask whether there are any *positive* (first-order) theological facts. (Of course, some will have understood talk of "substantive" facts in this way already, from the start.) Presumably the nonexistence of God is at best a *negative* fact, not a positive one. So the atheist can then be construed as holding that the only first-order theological facts are negative ones. (Equivalently: that the only first-order theological *truths* are negative ones.)

Regardless of which of these two proposals we adopt on behalf of the atheist, analogous moves can be made by those who want to deny the existence of *moral* facts. Perhaps someone who holds this view will want to say that there are no first-order moral facts *other* than this very one. That is, beyond the fact that all other substantive moral claims are false, there are no further first-order moral facts. Or perhaps someone who holds this view will prefer to say instead that there are no *positive* moral facts, where the nonexistence of such positive moral facts is, at best, a negative fact, not a positive one.

Either way, the crucial point is that this kind of wholesale denial of (positive) first-order moral facts appears to be a coherent possibility (just as atheism is a coherent possibility). So it would be a mistake to conclude—as we were tempted to do, a moment ago—that if it isn't true that all white lies are morally wrong, then it must be true that at least some white lies are morally permissible. For both of these claims assert the existence of certain positive moral facts—either that all white lies are forbidden or that some white lies are permissible—and it could be, rather, that there are no such positive moral facts *at all*.

Moral nihilists hold that, indeed, there are no first-order moral facts of this sort. More carefully, of course, we can describe what nihilists believe by saying either that there are no positive first-order moral facts or that there are no first-order moral facts beyond this one. For simplicity, however, in the discussion that follows I will typically describe the nihilist as holding the view that there are no moral facts, *period*. Although this description is slightly inaccurate—for reasons we have now explored—adopting this convention will free us of the need to be constantly adding the relevant qualifications.

In contrast to the nihilists, *moral realists* hold that there *are* moral facts. Of course, this description is slightly misleading as well (since even nihilists believe in the *negative* fact that there are no positive, first-order moral facts); but here too it would be tiresome to constantly make the relevant qualifications explicit. So I will typically describe the difference between moral realists and nihilists in the intuitive, though slightly inaccurate, language that I have just adopted for the nihilist: I will say that moral realists believe that there are moral facts, while nihilists do not.

If there are moral facts, then some moral claims are *true*. Of course, that doesn't yet tell us *which* of these claims are true, and unsurprisingly, moral realists can and do still differ among themselves about this matter. But despite these disagreements, moral realists are united in their belief that *some* moral claims are true. There are, indeed, moral facts. That belief is what distinguishes the realists from the nihilists. (Moral realists also agree, of course, that many substantive moral claims are *false*—so it is important for us to try to figure out which are the true ones.)

In the next section I am going to note some of the most important distinctions among moral realists. First, however, let's distinguish between two different types of *nihilism*.

Suppose, then, that there are no moral facts. All (first-order) moral claims are false. At this point, it would seem, we have an important choice to make. Should we continue *using* moral language?

One obvious possibility is this. We could decide that in light of the fact that there are no moral facts, we should simply stop talking about morality. This is analogous to the typical atheist proposal, that in light of the fact that there is no God, we should stop *talking* about God! We should stop making claims about what God is like, or what God might want us to do. Since all theological claims are false (but for this very one), we should abandon theological talk altogether. Similarly, then, one might decide that if all moral claims are false, we should give up moral talk as well. We should stop making claims about whether self-defense is permissible or forbidden, stop arguing about whether giving someone what they deserve is intrinsically valuable or not. Since all such claims are false, we should simply stop making them. For obvious reasons, we can call this the *abolitionist* position.

Less obviously, however, we might decide, instead, that there is a *different* use to which we could helpfully put our moral language. Even if there are no moral facts, and so there is no need to use our moral language as we typically intend to be using it (as a way of making claims about those moral facts), there might still be other jobs that need doing, jobs for which moral language might still be well suited. So perhaps we should *reform* our use of moral discourse. We should stop using our moral language to make moral *claims*, since all such claims will inevitably be false. But we can continue *using* moral language anyway, provided we use it in a suitably revised way: not to make assertions, but to do some other job, a job that still needs to be performed. We can call this the *revisionist* position.

What might this revised approach to moral language look like? What would we use our moral discourse for, if not to make assertions? Perhaps it would be the very same use of moral language as the one (or ones) put forward by the *noncognitivists*!

Here's what I have in mind. The noncognitivist says that there are no moral facts, and that moral talk was never meant to be making assertions about such things in the first place. (The only reason we think there are such things as moral facts is because we mistakenly think moral claims are talking about them.) But for all that, moral discourse has an important and legitimate role to play nonetheless. Of course, I haven't yet tried to spell out any of the relevant details here (they'll come later), but the noncognitivist points to some of the other things we can do with language besides making assertions, and then claims that, in point of fact, all that moral language was ever actually doing was one or another of these other jobs.

The revisionist nihilist agrees that there are no moral facts. But, they say, it isn't that moral talk was never *meant* to be making assertions about such facts. It was. But since there are no such facts, we have no need to continue using it for this misguided purpose. Still, there is an important and legitimate role for moral discourse to play—the very role that noncognitivists were pointing to all along. If the noncognitivists are right that the job that they have in mind is one that needs filling, then we need some sort of vocabulary to fill that job. And if the noncognitivists are right as well that our already available moral vocabulary is suitable for doing that job, then we might as well *use* it for that purpose.

Thus, say the revisionists, the noncognitivists were wrong about what moral talk is intended to do. Contrary to what they say, it is indeed intended to be making assertions about purported moral facts. But for all that, they were right about what moral language can and should be used to do.

Seen from this perspective, there is very little difference between noncognitivists and revisionist nihilists. Although they disagree about the truth of cognitivism (since nihilists—including revisionist nihilists—are cognitivists), the two positions are in other ways very similar.

Imagine that we had begun by simply asking, are there moral facts? Nihilists and noncognitivists agree that the answer is no. (They just disagree about what moral language is trying to do.) That already shows that the two positions are fairly close to one another. And then imagine that we had asked next, what legitimate role can moral language be used for? Revisionist nihilists and noncognitivists can agree about that as well. (They just disagree about whether that is what moral language is *already* being used for.) That is very close indeed. So although revisionism and noncognitivism can look to be rather far apart—especially when viewed from the standpoint of the flow chart shown at the start of this chapter—there are, in fact, rather significant points of similarity between the two positions.

2.3 Varieties of Moral Realism

Unlike both the noncognitivists and the nihilists, moral realists think that there are moral facts. There are true moral claims. Of course, they disagree with one another about *which* moral claims are the true ones. Some think, for example, that self-defense is morally permissible; others think it forbidden. Some think that virtue is intrinsically valuable; others think that it only has instrumental value. Some think that telling a lie can never be morally justified; others disagree. In countless ways, moral realists differ among themselves concerning just what the facts really are.

But in addition to these various first-order disputes, there are important second-order disputes that separate realists from one another as well. I have in mind questions about the *nature* of moral facts—what exactly it *comes* to for a given act to be forbidden or permissible, or what exactly it is for something to be intrinsically good, or valuable, and so on. Even if we put aside the disagreements concerning the *contents* of the first-order facts, there remain questions about the *nature* of those facts, questions about what facts like that are *like*. That is to say, there are second-order questions as well as first-order ones; and while moral realists are united in their agreement that there *are* moral facts, they still disagree with each other with regard to many other second-order questions.

2.3 VARIETIES OF MORAL REALISM

For our purposes, we can introduce some of the most important distinctions here by means of three questions. The first question is this: are moral facts *natural* facts?

Unsurprisingly, there are two basic positions one can take on this issue. *Naturalists* say that moral facts are, indeed, natural facts. They are, metaphysically speaking, facts about the natural world. (Alternatively: moral facts are *part* of the natural world.) Of course, natural facts come in all shapes and sizes. It is a natural fact that water is H_2O. It is a natural fact that snow is white, and that the heart pumps blood. But it is also, in the relevant sense of the term, a natural fact that people live in houses, and that the American Civil War was fought in the nineteenth century. (The relevant contrast is not between natural facts and *social* facts, but rather between natural facts and facts that somehow lie "outside" the natural order.) According to this first view, then, along with biological facts, astronomical facts, psychological facts, linguistic facts, economic facts and more, moral facts are simply one more aspect of the natural world.

In contrast, nonnaturalists hold that moral facts are not, in this way, simply part of the natural world. There is more to reality than the natural world alone, say the nonnaturalists. There are other facts besides natural ones, and moral facts are among these. Of course, any examples I might offer of nonnatural facts will inevitably be controversial, but if only for the sake of illustrating the general idea, imagine that the theist is right, and there really is a God. Presumably God is not part of the natural order, so facts about God—what God is like, or what God commands us to do, or the very fact that God exists—are not natural facts at all. Such facts are, for all that, perfectly genuine facts (if theism is right), but they are not *natural* ones. Or consider the view held by many concerning mathematics and the nature of numbers. Arguably, although it is a fact that $7 \times 9 = 63$, this too is not a natural fact. (It isn't as though we think that numbers are natural objects, things that exist within the natural order.) So although there are facts about arithmetic, and facts about mathematics more generally, perhaps these are not natural facts either.

According to the nonnaturalist about morality, then, we need to say something similar about *moral* facts. Although there are such facts—they are perfectly real, and perfectly significant—we should not think of them as being part of the natural order.

We can sharpen the dispute between the naturalists and the nonnaturalists by means of the following observation. Presumably, if there really are moral facts (as the realists claim), then such facts consist in a given act or act type (or object, or state of affairs, and so on) having the relevant moral property (being right, or wrong, or good, or bad, or just, or valuable, or permissible, and so on). Thus, to take our stock example, if self-defense is permissible, then this fact consists in a certain type of action (self-defense) possessing a particular moral property (permissibility). And if my killing of an innocent bystander is unjust, then this fact consists in my particular act (killing the bystander) possessing a different moral property (being unjust). Similarly, if sadistic pleasures are vicious, then this fact consists in a particular type of entity (sadistic pleasure) having yet another moral property (viciousness—being an instance of vice).

But notice that, in these examples, the actions (or states of affairs, or individual entities, and so on) are all natural objects of one sort or another. Acts of self-defense are, in our sense of the term, natural events (they are completely part of the natural world). Similarly, the killing of a bystander is a natural event as well (in the relevant metaphysical sense). And although sadistic pleasures are not external events, they are, for all that, natural psychological states (again, metaphysically speaking). Obviously, the nonnaturalist doesn't mean to deny any of this.

So when the nonnaturalist insists that moral facts are not natural ones, she doesn't mean to be claiming that the *objects* which figure in these facts must be nonnatural; she only wants to claim that the various *moral properties* are nonnatural ones. The properties of being permissible, or forbidden, or just, or vicious, or intrinsically good, and so on, should not be taken to be natural ones, she says. And for that reason, even when a natural *object* has one of these properties, that fact—the fact that some act is forbidden, or that some state of affairs is desirable—cannot be taken to be a (wholly) natural fact. That is what nonnaturalists mean when they say that moral facts are nonnatural: they are nonnatural because they involve *properties* which are not, themselves, natural ones.

(As an analogy, consider the claim that God loves you. You are, presumably, a natural entity. But since God would not be part of the natural order, being loved by God would be a nonnatural property, not a natural one. So the fact that you are loved by God would not be a (wholly) natural fact; it would be a nonnatural one.)

We can thus understand the dispute between the naturalists and the nonnaturalists this way: naturalists believe that moral properties are natural properties; nonnaturalists deny this.

Of course, we might still find ourselves wondering, what exactly does it take to *be* a natural property? That turns out to be a difficult question to answer. Despite our rough intuitive feel for the distinction between the natural and the nonnatural, it is difficult to pin down just what it takes for something to fall within the one category rather than the other. But we can postpone further consideration of this issue until later (see 13.3).

As we have now seen, the first question we put to moral realists—whether moral facts are natural facts or not—ultimately concerns the nature of moral properties. The second question we should pose to realists concerns the nature of moral properties as well. Do these properties (whether natural or not) reduce to something more *basic*? That is, do moral properties "boil down" to even more fundamental ones?

Consider the property of being an uncle. This is, of course, a perfectly real property; some organisms have it, and others do not. But it is not a fundamental property, in that it can be reduced to other properties that are, intuitively, more basic. Thus, in particular, being an uncle consists in being a *male sibling* of someone who is a *parent*. The "complex" property of unclehood reduces, in this way, to more basic ones.

We can raise a similar question with regard to the various moral properties. Do they too reduce to something more basic?

In thinking about this question it is important to bear in mind the fact that pretty much everyone agrees that *some* properties reduce to others (after all, the property of unclehood reduces to other ones). But virtually no one thinks that *all* properties reduce to more basic ones. (For if this were the case, we would have an infinite regress, with properties being reduced to more basic properties, which would then be reduced in turn to even more basic properties, which would then be reduced to still more basic properties, and so on, without end.) In short, there is fairly widespread agreement that some, but not all, properties are basic and cannot be reduced further; some, but not all, properties are *irreducible*. So our question is this: are moral properties among the irreducible ones?

More precisely, the crucial question here is whether *any* moral properties are among the irreducible ones. For it might turn out that some moral properties can indeed be reduced, while others cannot. And in particular, it might turn out that certain moral properties can be reduced provided that we reduce them to other (more basic) *moral* properties. But given reductions of this sort—where complex moral properties are reduced (in part) to other moral properties—we would then want to know about these more basic moral properties as well. Can they too be reduced, to even more fundamental ones?

Ultimately, what we really need to know is this. When this process is taken to its logical conclusion, so that all that we are left with are properties that cannot be reduced further, will there be any *moral* properties among the set of irreducible ones? Or can all moral properties ultimately be reduced to *nonmoral* ones?

It may be helpful to have an example in front of us.

According to consequentialists, an act is morally permissible just in case the consequences of that act would be as good as the consequences of any alternative act available to the agent. Conceivably, then, a consequentialist might want to take the *further* step of claiming that the property of being permissible simply *is* the property of having good results overall. That is, perhaps this particular moral property—permissibility—is nothing more than a complex of more basic properties (roughly, the property of bringing about particular results, where those results in turn have the further property of being good overall).

(Most consequentialists don't actually take this further step. One can certainly be a consequentialist without claiming that the property of being permissible simply *is* the property of having the right combination of these more basic properties. The consequentialist might insist, instead, that although an act has the property of being permissible in all and only those cases where it also has the property of promoting the overall good as much as any available alternative, the former property is nonetheless a *distinct* property from the latter property, rather than being reducible to it. Still, some consequentialists *do* accept this reduction; so imagine one who does.)

Don't worry about whether you find this a plausible reduction or not. The important point to note for present purposes is that even if one *does* accept this particular reduction, one of the more basic properties to which our initial property—permissibility—has been reduced is itself a moral property (since the proposed reduction involves reference to the *goodness* of the act's results). So even if this view were accepted, we would still only be reducing moral properties to other, more basic *moral* properties. We would not yet have reduced moral properties to *nonmoral* ones alone.

Of course, one might try to push the reduction further. Can the property of being a *good* outcome be reduced in turn? If it cannot be, then at least some moral properties will be among the most fundamental ones, the irreducible ones. On the other hand, even if it should turn out that goodness can indeed be reduced to something even more basic, we would still need to know whether the properties to which it is reduced include any (even more fundamental) moral properties among them, and if so, whether *they* can be reduced as well.

As we move to ever more basic properties, do we eventually reach a stage where only nonmoral properties are left? Or are at least some moral properties among the most fundamental ones, incapable of being reduced further?

Reductionists hold that all moral properties can in fact be reduced to more basic ones. In particular, then, all moral properties can ultimately be reduced to nonmoral ones. (And this means, of course, that all moral facts can ultimately be reduced to nonmoral facts.) *Nonreductionists* deny this. They hold that at least some moral properties are irreducible, and so, in particular, are incapable of being reduced to nonmoral properties. (Which means, in turn, that at least some, and perhaps all, moral facts cannot be (wholly) reduced to nonmoral ones.)

In thinking about this choice, keep in mind that reductionists need not accept the particular candidate reduction we just considered, according to which permissibility reduces to bringing about good results. I offered that merely for the sake of illustration. You might well prefer some other reduction for permissibility instead. The point is simply that reductionists believe that there is *some* suitable reduction for permissibility, along with one for goodness, and one for justice, and one for obligation, and so on down the line for each moral property or relation. In point of fact, reductionists may not be at all confident about what the correct reductions *are*; they only need to believe that such reductions do in fact exist. What unifies reductionists is simply the shared thought that all moral facts ultimately boil down to a suitable set of *nonmoral* facts.

For those moral realists who are in fact reductionists, there is one final question to be posed: what *sort* of (nonmoral) facts do moral facts ultimately reduce to? Various answers are possible, of course, but it will be helpful to recall (from 1.2) the broad division between those views that hold that moral facts are (in large part) ultimately facts about the attitudes or reactions of relevant minds, and those views that hold that moral facts are, rather, mind independent.

In principle, even a reductionist can embrace a mind independent account. That is to say, one could hold the view that moral facts do indeed reduce to nonmoral facts, but that the relevant nonmoral facts have nothing in particular to do with the reactions or attitudes (or feelings or desires) of minds. Rather, moral facts reduce to nonmoral facts that are mind independent.

Nonetheless, what I take to be the most common reductionist approaches are, in fact, mind dependent ones, according to which moral facts ultimately reduce to relevant facts about the relevant minds. Perhaps morality is ultimately a matter of the commands given by God, or the rules favored by society, or the principles that would be endorsed by rational bargainers. Or maybe morality ultimately turns on the preferences or desires I have or would have, or the choices we all would make under suitably idealized conditions. For present purposes the details are unimportant. What matters, rather, is the shared thought that basic moral facts ultimately boil down (in large part) to facts *like* these, facts about how the relevant mind or minds do or would react.

I will call reductionist views that accept this sort of mind dependent approach *constructivist*, since they hold that moral facts can be "constructed" out of facts about the relevant minds. Admittedly, other forms of reductionism might have a claim to a similar label, since they too think that moral facts can be constructed out of more basic materials. But as I have already noted, the mind dependent versions of reductionism are by far the most common varieties of reductionism. Since it is useful to have a handy (short) label for views of this kind, I am going to reserve the term "constructivism" accordingly.

All constructivists are reductionists. That's true by definition. But it may be worth emphasizing the point that constructivists need not be *naturalists*. After all, as I have already noted, one prominent version of constructivism holds that moral facts are ultimately facts about God's will (God's commands), and presumably those who accept this particular view do not think of God as being part of the natural order. So although a divine command theory of morality is constructivist (since moral facts are ultimately facts about the reactions and attitudes of a particular mind), moral facts are not *natural* facts on such a view (since God is not part of the natural world). To be sure, many constructivist views *are* naturalist as well (they hold that the relevant minds are or would be part of the natural order); but constructivism per se is not committed to naturalism. The categories cut across one another.

Return now to the *non*reductionist position within moral realism. According to this view, whether or not certain moral properties can be reduced to more basic ones, this cannot be done across the board. There are at least some moral properties that are irreducible; they cannot be reduced further, to something simpler or more basic. In contrast to complex properties, then, which can be "broken down" or "decomposed" into more basic parts, these irreducible moral properties are *simple*, in the sense that they themselves cannot be built up out of even more basic materials. So unlike the reductionists, who think that all moral properties are complex ones, nonreductionists think that at least some moral properties are (metaphysically) simple. Since it will sometimes prove useful in the discussion that follows to have a reasonably short label for nonreductionist moral realists, we can also call their view *simple realism*.

Note that to say that certain moral properties are irreducible is not yet to say *which* moral properties are the irreducible ones. Perhaps there are only a few (like, say, being right, or being good), or perhaps the number of irreducible moral properties is considerably larger. Similarly, it is not yet to say whether the basic moral properties (however many there may be) are *natural* ones or not. Simple realists can still differ on this point as well. (That too is an issue to which we will need to return.)

Since the distinctions we have been drawing within moral realism cut across one another, it may be helpful to display them all in a single table.

Varieties of Moral Realism

	Reductionist		Nonreductionist
	Mind Dependent	Mind Independent	
Naturalist	Naturalist Constructivist Reductionism	Naturalist Nonconstructivist Reductionism	Naturalist Simple Realism
Nonnaturalist	Nonnaturalist Constructivist Reductionism	Nonnaturalist Nonconstructivist Reductionism	Nonnaturalist Simple Realism

There remains one more variety of moral realism that I want to mention. Imagine a view according to which all moral facts can indeed be reduced to more basic ones, provided that we reduce them to facts (of the right sort) about what there is *reason* to do. (Perhaps, for example, for an act to be forbidden simply *is* for there to be a reason of the right sort to avoid performing that action; and so on.) Arguably, a view like this should count as a reductionist one (where the moral has been reduced to the nonmoral), since the notion of there being a reason to do something is a broad one, encompassing far more than moral reasons. (For example, you have a reason not to put glue in the gas tank of your car, and you have a reason to believe that 2 × 2 = 4, but neither of these have anything in particular to do with morality.)

Suppose, however, that facts about reasons could not be reduced any further, so that the property of being supported by a reason (which some acts have, and others lack) is itself an irreducible property, incapable of being broken down to anything simpler or more fundamental. Many reductionists, I think, would be troubled by a theory like this. For there seems very little space between talk of what there is reason to do, and talk of what one *ought* to do (other things being equal); and part of the appeal of reductionism for many people is the hope of showing how all such normative talk (about what we should do, or ought to do, or must do, or are required to do, and so on) can be reduced to something less "suspicious" and more familiar. So if moral facts can only be boiled down to facts about reasons and no further, this will leave many reductionists dissatisfied. We will have reduced moral facts to more basic *normative* facts, but we won't have reduced them to something *nonnormative*.

In many ways, then, a view like this—where the property of being supported by a reason cannot be reduced further—has striking similarities to the nonreductionist view of the simple realist. Strictly speaking, perhaps, we should not think of it as a genuine version of simple realism (since, according to this view, moral facts *can* be reduced to facts about reasons, and facts about reasons need not be, in and of themselves, moral facts). But perhaps it makes sense to extend our use of the label "simple realism" to cover views like this as well. Instead of restricting the category of simple realism to those positions that hold that there are some irreducible *moral* properties, let us use it a bit more broadly, so that it covers as well any view according to which there are irreducible normative properties of any sort whatsoever. And let us hereafter *restrict* the class of reductionists in a corresponding way, so that we will call a position a reductionist one only if it holds that moral facts can all be reduced, not merely to nonmoral facts, but (more demandingly) to nonnormative ones more generally.

With these revisions of our labels in place, we can now say that even if moral facts can be reduced to facts about reasons, if such facts cannot themselves be reduced any further, then the resulting view is indeed a version of simple realism. And on those occasions when it is important to distinguish this particular version of simple realism—according to which moral facts reduce to facts about reasons, but facts about reasons are themselves irreducible—I will refer to it as simple *normative* realism.

It should be noted, finally, that even simple normative realists can differ among themselves about the metaphysical nature of these irreducible facts about reasons. Some will hold that facts about reasons are natural ones; others, that they are nonnatural.

2.4 Moral Skepticism

We have now distinguished a number of different positions within metaethics. But I haven't introduced any position that's actually called *moral skepticism*. Why not?

The short answer is, because "moral skepticism" is the name for any view at all that denies the existence of morality as you conceive of it. And people conceive of morality in rather different ways.

Here's a slightly longer version of the same thought. Many theorists put forward and defend something that they are prepared to call "morality." But unless the thing being posited comes sufficiently close to meeting what *you* take to be morality's job description, you won't think that what you are being offered is the genuine article. That is to say, regardless of whether the position *describes* itself as a skeptical one, you will inevitably take it to *be* a skeptical view if what it puts forward falls too far short in terms of your own favored version of the job description—your own account of what morality would need to be, if there really is to be such a thing.

To be sure, as I have suggested, there may be some wiggle room here. Some elements of your initial job description may be ones that, on reflection, you are prepared to do without. Perhaps they are negotiable, or modifiable. Perhaps certain elements in the job description are merely preferable, rather than essential. Or perhaps you will decide that you actually shouldn't have included some particular element in the first place. But at some point you will need to decide what the minimal conditions are that must be met if something is to truly count as morality at all (or as an objective moral code, and so on). If a given view fails to support belief in something like *that*, you will inevitably think of it as actually constituting a *skeptical* view, no matter how it is described. And since different people disagree about what, exactly, should go into the job description, they will differ as well over which positions should be thought of as skeptical ones.

Admittedly, there is one position we've described which pretty much everyone is going to think of as a version of moral skepticism: abolitionist nihilism. After all, according to this view moral claims are all *false*, since they are attempting to describe a sort of fact that simply doesn't exist. What's more, there is no *other* useful job for our moral vocabulary to take on, so abolitionists think that we would do well to rid ourselves of such talk and stop engaging in moral discourse altogether. That's clearly a skeptical view, by anyone's accounting.

But things immediately grow less clear once we move from abolitionist to revisionist versions of nihilism. For on such a view, although it remains true that there are no moral *facts*, and we are mistaken in trying to describe them, there is still, for all that, a significant and worthwhile job that we can perform using moral discourse; there is still a legitimate and important purpose that can be served by making moral claims and discussing them with one another. Something meaningful will still be happening if, for example, I say that killing in self-defense is morally permissible, and you then deny it. So although there is no doubt that many people will want to classify revisionism as a form of moral skepticism, I imagine that there will be at least some who think that it is actually a *defense* of morality, albeit one that requires modifying some of the beliefs we might initially have had about morality's nature.

Things grow murkier still when we ask whether noncognitivism is a skeptical view or not. Many people will certainly think so, since, like the nihilists, noncognitivists deny the existence of moral facts; indeed, in one way they go even further than the nihilists, insisting that moral "assertions" are not genuine assertions at all, not the sort of thing that could be so much as true or false. But at the same time, other people (including many noncognitivists) may not think of noncognitivism as a skeptical position at all. After all, according to noncognitivism there is nothing flawed or misguided about our use of moral vocabulary, no reason for us to stop uttering moral sentences and arguing about which to accept. Once we realize that moral discourse was never intended to be in the fact-stating business in the first place, we can free ourselves of worries about its legitimacy, and appropriately continue to engage in moral debate, just as we have always done. Seen from this perspective, then, noncognitivists may not seem to be offering a rejection of morality at all, but only a more sophisticated understanding of it. Nonetheless, despite this, many people—perhaps most—will insist that merely providing a legitimate use for moral utterances isn't sufficient for noncognitivism to escape the charge of skepticism. They will insist that no view that denies the existence of moral facts and moral truths can really count as an adequate defense of *morality*.

Coming at things from the other direction, can we at least agree that moral *realism* should *not* be classified as a version of moral skepticism? That may seem obvious, but in point of fact the issue remains complicated, even here. For some versions of moral realism may still strike you as quite unacceptable. Suppose, for example, that you think that if there really is to be such a thing as objective morality, then basic moral facts must be mind independent (just as the laws of physics are mind independent). It follows, then, that you will think that any *constructivist* account of morality is a nonstarter, not merely wrong in details but utterly misguided as to what it would take for there to *be* such a thing as morality. If the best we can do on morality's behalf is to try to show how it might reduce to facts about relevant minds, then that may seem tantamount to admitting that there really is no such thing as morality after all.

Of course, realists who do *not* build mind independence into their job description may decide that in principle, at least, a constructivist view might be acceptable. Such accounts might or might not succeed, but at the very least, constructivist accounts of morality would be defending something worthy of the name. But if mind independence seems to you to be an essential element in the very idea of objective morality, then constructivist theories will turn out to be just another version of skepticism.

Thus, depending on just what it is that you insist on building into the job description for morality (in an essential, nonnegotiable way), you may find that even certain versions of moral realism strike you as abandoning belief in a genuinely objective morality. Versions of moral realism that fall too far short—in terms of your own conception of what morality would need to be—may strike you as equivalent to, or no better than, skepticism.

The bottom line is that since people disagree about morality's job description, they disagree as well about which views should count as skeptical ones. Nonetheless, in what follows I will assume that if we are to avoid moral skepticism, at the very least we must fend off both nihilism and noncognitivism. That is, a suitable defense of morality must involve a version of moral *realism*. When I refer to the "moral skeptic," then, without further specification, I have in mind someone who rejects moral realism, and who thus accepts either noncognitivism or nihilism (in either its abolitionist or revisionist modes). I will never refer to a moral realist as a moral *skeptic*.

But for all that, you should not lose sight of the point that depending on the details of your own favored conception of what morality needs to be, you may not find all versions of moral realism acceptable. When evaluating skeptical arguments, I will point out different replies that might be offered by the realist. But you will need to take careful note of the assumptions that lie behind any given reply, since some of these replies may be ones that you cannot avail yourself of, given your own favored account of what morality would have to be. In such cases you will have to turn to one of the alternative replies instead.

3
Nihilism

3.1 The Nature of Nihilism

Skeptical worries about morality are common enough. But precise articulations of skeptical positions are not (except, perhaps, among philosophers). Though thoughtful individuals at least occasionally find themselves worrying that skepticism might be right, they rarely try to work out what, precisely, such a skeptical position would look like.

But we have now distinguished two different approaches to moral skepticism—nihilism and noncognitivism—and it may be helpful to examine each of them a bit more fully. In part, this is worth doing because the differences between the two may initially be a bit difficult to keep straight for those who have only just started thinking about moral skepticism. Exploring each in turn should make it easier, going forward, to remember how the two positions differ from one another. But beyond this first point, it is important to treat each in turn as well, precisely because nihilists and noncognitivists really do differ from one another in important ways, and so the details of the skeptical arguments that each puts forward will sometimes differ as well. Although it remains true that both nihilism and noncognitivism are skeptical positions, different arguments for skepticism (or different versions of those arguments) are available to each.

We can start with moral nihilism.

Nihilists deny the existence of moral facts. Of course, noncognitivists do this as well, but nihilists don't do it for the same reason that noncognitivists do. Noncognitivists, as we know, claim that, despite appearances, moral sentences don't actually assert the existence of moral facts at all; such sentences are, rather, doing something else entirely. But nihilists are *cognitivists*, and as such they believe that moral sentences really are making assertions, just as they appear to be doing. It is just that nihilists are cognitivists who believe that, in point of fact, there simply *are* no facts of the sort that these assertions aim to describe. Thus, moral claims really do attempt to state truths, but there simply are no substantive truths in this area.

As I noted in the previous chapter, this means that the nihilist is a bit like the atheist. The atheist says that theological sentences (like "God loves the poor") are indeed to be understood as making genuine assertions about purported theological facts. However, for all that, there simply *are* no such substantive facts, since there is no God.

In effect, the atheist points out that there is a *presupposition* of all substantive theological claims, namely, the assumption that God exists. But the atheist believes that this presupposition isn't true. So all such theological claims are *false*.

Similarly, then, the nihilist holds that moral sentences are indeed to be understood as making assertions about purported *moral* facts, but these sentences are all false, since there simply are no substantive moral facts to be described. In effect, there is a presupposition of all substantive moral claims, namely, the assumption that *morality* exists. But the nihilist believes that this presupposition isn't true; so all such moral claims are false.

For this reason it is important not to confuse nihilism with the quite distinct view that everything is morally *permissible*. Admittedly, it is certainly tempting to conflate these two positions. (If nihilism is true, then nothing is actually morally forbidden; and if nothing is forbidden, doesn't it follow that everything is permissible?) But what the nihilist actually believes is that there are no moral facts *at all*, including facts about moral permissibility. In contrast, a view that holds that everything is permissible seems to be asserting that there are indeed moral facts, it just turns out that the facts are significantly different from what we ordinarily take them to be. Morality is simply far more permissive than we might have thought.

A view like that isn't nihilism at all. What nihilists believe, rather, is that *all* substantive talk of what morality does or does not require of us is mistaken, including talk of what morality permits. There are *no* substantive facts about morality, and this means, in particular, that it is a mistake to say of anything at all that it is morally permissible. Nothing is morally permissible, nothing required, nothing forbidden, nothing morally good, nothing morally bad, nothing morally neutral, and so on. Nothing. Any claim of this sort, any claim at all, is false.

Of course, the nihilist knows full well that most of us do not agree that every single substantive (positive, first-order) moral claim is false. We naively think that some of them are true, though we disagree about which they are. That's why nihilists sometimes talk about accepting an "error theory" concerning morality. They think that the rest of us—or, at least, the moral realists among us—are in error, in thinking that at least some moral claims are true.

We might well wonder why this mistake (as the nihilist sees it) is so common. If there simply are no moral facts at all, why is the belief that there are such facts so widespread?

Nihilism per se isn't committed to any particular account of the origin of the error, though individual nihilists may have their own favored explanations. (For example, perhaps we unwittingly "project" our internal preferences and desires "onto" the world, and then misread these as features *of* the world, thus mistaking our personal preferences for objective values.) I won't take the time to explore and evaluate such possible explanations. For our purposes the more pressing question is this: why should we agree that we are indeed making a mistake in the first place? The nihilist *tells* us that all moral claims are false, that there are no moral facts. But why should we believe her?

In one way, at least, the *noncognitivist* has an easier time of it as compared to the nihilist. It would, after all, be easier to see why we should be skeptical about the existence of moral facts, if we have never actually been making claims about such things in the first place. Why believe in the existence of a sort of fact that no one was so much as asserting the existence of?

(Admittedly, even if noncognitivism is true, it is probably an exaggeration to say that *no one* has been using moral sentences to make assertions about purported moral facts. But if the *rest* of us aren't using moral sentences that way then it shouldn't be all that hard for us to believe that there are no such facts. Why believe in the existence of something we never asserted the existence of?)

But precisely because the nihilist is a cognitivist, this line of argument isn't available to her. According to the nihilist, when we use moral language we really are trying to describe moral facts. We are mistaken in thinking there *are* any such facts; but there is little point, they say, in denying that what we are *trying* to do is to describe these supposed facts.

And in this regard, I think, it is actually the *nihilist*, as a cognitivist, who has the better of it, as compared to the noncognitivist. For on the face of it, at least, it does seem as though moral sentences are in the fact-stating business. Whether or not there really are any such facts, it certainly does seem as though moral sentences are attempting to describe them. We go around arguing with one another about which moral claims are true. We say that we believe some of these claims, and disbelieve others. We certainly talk as though moral claims are making genuine assertions. At the very least this makes a fairly strong presumptive case for the cognitivist claim that what we are doing when we make moral utterances is indeed making *assertions* about a putative domain, the domain of moral facts. Whether we are misguided or not in thinking that there *is* any such domain, it certainly looks as though moral sentences are making claims about it.

All of which is just to say, cognitivism seems to be the more natural position to take with regard to moral sentences. So while we need to remain open to the possibility that the appearances here are deceptive, for the time being at least it does seem reasonable to tentatively grant to the nihilist the claim that moral sentences are indeed genuine assertions, just as they seem to be. (We'll consider arguments for the noncognitivist's alternative view in the next chapter.)

But of course, if we really are inclined to grant (even if tentatively) the truth of cognitivism, this just sharpens the question, why think that all of these assertions are, indeed, *false*? If moral sentences really are making claims about purported moral facts, why believe the nihilist when she asserts that every one of them fails—that the entire enterprise is misguided?

To be sure, if nihilism really is correct—if all substantive moral claims are false—we will have to face the question of whether to stop using moral sentences altogether (as the abolitionist proposes), or continue using them (as the revisionist suggests) for some alternative purpose, distinct from the misguided attempt to make claims about (nonexistent) moral facts. If we become convinced of the truth of nihilism, this is a decision we will eventually need to make.

But the nihilist first has to convince us that it really is true that there aren't any moral truths at all. Why believe that?

3.2 The Case for Nihilism

Nihilists typically defend their view by going on the offensive. If we continue to (tentatively) assume the truth of cognitivism, the question is simply whether moral *realists* are right when they assert that at least some of our substantive moral claims are true. So nihilists offer a variety of objections to moral realism, attempting to point out one or another difficulty with the realist's position. If these objections are compelling, then realism has to be abandoned. And so—given cognitivism—nihilism follows.

For example, we might find the very notion of a moral fact metaphysically troubling. Such facts seem to involve properties hopelessly unlike everyday, familiar ones; they seem to involve properties that are unacceptably "weird" or "queer." Or we might find the notion of a moral fact epistemologically troubling. Shy of positing some spooky faculty of "moral insight" how could we ever learn anything about these supposed moral facts at all, or even come to know that they so much as exist? Or we might find it implausible to believe in moral facts given the ubiquity of disagreements concerning their contents. If there really are such facts, why can't we agree about what they are? And there are, of course, still other worries about realism that the nihilist can raise as well.

Thus, the nihilist offers a series of arguments *against* moral realism. These are, unsurprisingly, the very arguments we will go on to examine in detail in later chapters. If they are sound, then they give us reason to reject moral realism, and they thus offer support for the nihilist's skeptical alternative.

But if they are *not* sound, then we are left with no particular reason to embrace nihilism. Nihilism emerges as the more plausible position only given the assumption that one or another of the attacks on realism is found compelling. Indeed, in the absence of a successful attack on realism, we are likely to judge the realist position the more plausible of the two.

And this means, I think, that it is premature to render a verdict on nihilism until we have had a chance to survey those skeptical arguments with care. The mere fact that one can list a series of potential concerns about realism in the breezy way we just did hardly shows that there are no convincing answers to those concerns. An adequate defense of nihilism takes more than merely raising a few questions; it requires showing that realist replies to these questions are inadequate. Unless that can be shown, the argument for nihilism falters.

One might wonder, however, whether in spelling out what the nihilist needs to do I have been unfair to the nihilist. Suppose the nihilist's arguments against realism fail. What then? I have just suggested that in that situation it will be more plausible to accept realism. But why should that be the case? Why should the burden of proof fall on the shoulders of the nihilists rather than the realists? Instead of demanding that nihilists find some *flaw* with realism, why not insist, rather, that it is *realists* who must do the work, that it is realists, rather, who must provide compelling arguments in *favor* of moral realism, and that in the absence of such arguments it is nihilism, rather than realism, that is the more plausible position to adopt?

Indeed, it might be urged that placing the burden of proof on the nihilist rather than the realist runs afoul of the practice we would normally adopt when considering disputes of this kind. Don't we place the burden of proof upon those who *posit* some domain (or set of facts, or entities, or properties) rather than on those who *deny* the existence of that domain? For example, if someone asserts the existence of demons, or angels, or Martians, we normally place the burden of proof on them, demanding that they give us evidence, reason to believe in the extra entities they posit. If someone asserts the existence of astrological facts, or supernatural facts, or facts about the paranormal, we rightly place the burden on them, too, to show us why we should indeed believe in the existence of these supposed facts.

So shouldn't the nihilist insist that it is the *realist* who has the burden of proof, rather than the nihilist? It is the realist, after all, who posits the extra set of facts—moral facts. So isn't it the realist who faces the argumentative burden, the realist who must somehow establish that we have reason to prefer their view? In the absence of any compelling argument one way or the other—no compelling arguments for or against realism, no compelling arguments for or against nihilism—doesn't parsimony favor nihilism over realism?

As it happens, I think that determining where the burden of proof falls in any given debate is often a tricky matter. But whatever the relevant rule here is, it certainly isn't anything as simple as holding that the burden always falls on those who posit something that others deny. After all, imagine that someone denies the very existence of the external world. That is, they insist that there are no material objects at all, nothing external to the mind. Surely the burden of proof is on anyone who puts forward such a remarkable claim. Despite the fact that the rest of us are positing a kind of fact that this skeptic denies (to wit, facts about external, mind independent material objects), it seems clear that the burden of proof lies upon the skeptic here, rather than on those who believe in a domain that the skeptic rejects. In this case, at least, it is indeed the skeptic who owes us good reason to deny what we ordinarily believe in. If they cannot provide such reason, we are entitled to retain our belief in the existence of an external world.

So when does the burden of proof fall on one party rather than the other? Just who is it that is obligated to offer robust arguments on behalf of their favored position, when one side affirms the existence of something that the other side denies? Unfortunately, I think the answer isn't always clear. And so—returning now to the dispute that particularly concerns us—if we ask whether it is the moral realist or the moral nihilist who must offer some initial argument on behalf of their own view (or against their opponent), I think it would be difficult to definitively settle the point.

Happily, however, I believe we can sidestep this particular debate. In a later chapter (chapter 7) we will see how the moral realist can argue that moral *intuition* provides at least some evidence for the truth of various moral claims. So even if realists do have the initial burden of proof, perhaps that will suffice for having met it, in that this will at least constitute a *presumptive* case for realism.

To be sure, it will only be a presumptive one. Perhaps the appeal to moral intuition can be successfully undermined. But at the very least, once a prima facie case for using moral intuition is in place, the ball will be in the moral skeptic's court. The nihilist will need to give us some *reason* to reject this presumptive case, some reason to believe that moral intuition is unreliable. That is, the nihilist will need to give us reason to be skeptical about the pronouncements of our moral intuition.

Such reasons for skepticism can take various forms, of course. In principle any convincing argument to the effect that there are no moral facts should do the trick. For if there are no moral facts, then our intuitions cannot possibly be accurately reporting them.

In short, what the nihilist will need to do is to offer any of the various skeptical arguments that we would have considered sooner or later in any event. Which is just to say, regardless of who has the initial burden of proof, the case for nihilism will ultimately turn on our deciding whether the various arguments for moral skepticism are convincing or not.

3.3 Disregarding the Arguments

It would be natural to think that the only legitimate way to decide whether particular skeptical arguments are compelling involves examining them in detail. As it happens, however, there is an argument that can be offered on behalf of the realist that suggests that it may not actually be necessary to do this. If successful, this argument would free us of the need to examine the various skeptical arguments at all, for we would be confident that ultimately we would not find any of them convincing.

In essence, this antinihilist argument says that nihilism is so utterly *implausible*, that we would never be justified in accepting any particular skeptical arguments that appear to support it. So we are justified in simply disregarding those arguments.

Admittedly, this way of putting the idea may make it seem like it is doing nothing more than begging the question against the nihilist. But the idea actually has a certain amount of plausibility. Let me try to spell it out more carefully.

Imagine that someone gives you a philosophical argument for a surprising conclusion. Suppose there is something you are strongly inclined to believe—let's call it Q. But the argument aims to show that, surprisingly enough, Q is false, and so we should instead believe Not Q. That's the conclusion of the argument, Not Q. (That is, the conclusion states that Q is *not* the case.) For the moment, the details of the argument itself don't matter, so let's just call the premises of the argument A, B, and C. What matters is that the premises of the argument seem plausible. (That's why you are inclined to accept them as premises of an argument!) But we are supposing that when one combines these assumptions together they logically entail the surprising conclusion, Not Q. So you now have an argument for Not Q. Should you accept it?

Not necessarily. For the whole point in saying that Not Q is a *surprising* conclusion is that you don't find Not Q at all plausible, considered in its own right. Indeed, you are inclined to think that Not Q is *false*. What you find intuitively plausible, after all, is the opposite of Not Q, which is to say, what you find plausible is the claim that Q! You find Q very plausible indeed. That's why the argument's conclusion is so surprising: it's an argument for something you are very strongly inclined to deny.

When you find yourself in a situation like this, what is it reasonable for you to do? Are you required to accept the surprising conclusion? After all, it followed from A, B, and C, and those all strike you as plausible. So don't you need to embrace the conclusion, Not Q?

No, this isn't always the right thing to do. For it could be that on reflection you will realize that what you should do instead is abandon one of the premises of the initial argument! Now that you see what it leads to—Not Q—it might be that you should decide that one or more of the initial premises (A, B, or C) turns out to be false. It is often perfectly respectable to revise your initial judgment about some claim, once you see what it leads to. Indeed, sometimes this is the *best* thing to do.

Suppose you are utterly convinced of, say, B and C. You are inclined to believe A as well, but of course once combined with B and C, these three assumptions together yield Not Q, and you are very strongly inclined to believe that Not Q is *false*. This very fact might then give you reason to believe that A isn't really true after all, despite your *initial* inclination to accept it. After all, if you are utterly convinced of B and C, then what it all boils down to is that you must choose between continuing to accept A (and thus giving up Q, despite how plausible it seems), or continuing to accept Q (and thus giving up A, despite how plausible it seems). You can't continue to believe *both* A and Q. One of them will have to go.

Which is the more reasonable choice? Often it will simply be a question of which of the two—A or Q—is the one that strikes you as more plausible, which of the two is the one you are more confident of. If you are more confident of the truth of A than you are of the truth of Q, then you should retain your belief in A, and abandon your belief in Q. This is, of course, what the creator of the argument hopes you will conclude. But it could just as easily be the case that you are, rather, more confident, perhaps even far more confident, of the truth of Q than you are of the truth of A. And in that case you won't be moved by the argument at all. You will retain your belief in Q and decide, instead, to abandon your belief in A.

Either way, you will have to give up something that you found initially plausible. But the point is that it needn't be the belief in Q that has to go. If you are more confident of Q than you are of A, then despite A's initial plausibility, it could still be the case that the right thing to do is to give up the belief in A. The presence of an argument for Not Q does not force you to *agree* that Not Q is true; indeed, it might well be that this would be an unreasonable conclusion for you to reach.

Suppose, next, that you are not "utterly convinced" of the truth of B and C. Each of the initial premises (A, B, and C) seems plausible, perhaps none significantly more so than the others. Even so, it needn't be the case that you should accept the surprising conclusion Not Q. If Not Q strikes you as *sufficiently* implausible it might be that all you should conclude, instead, is that one or more of the premises of the original argument must be false. Perhaps you don't know which it is. That's disappointing, but it doesn't change the fact that it might be most reasonable to conclude that at least one of the premises *must* be false. Here too, it is really a matter of your confidence in Q, as compared to your confidence in the various premises, A, B, and C. You might just find yourself saying that although you don't know where the argument goes wrong (whether it is A, B, or C that is actually false, despite their initial plausibility), nonetheless you are confident that the argument goes wrong somewhere—precisely because you are more confident of the truth of Q than you are that each and every one of the individual premises that together make up the original argument is true instead.

After all, all that the argument can really demonstrate is that it is logically inconsistent to accept A and B and C *and* Q. So one of these things has to go. To be sure, it may have been the intent of the creator of the argument to get you to give up Q. But that is neither here nor there. If your confidence in Q is greater than your confidence that all of the premises of the argument are true, then it may be more reasonable to conclude that your belief in at least one of these premises must be mistaken, rather than your belief in Q. (You could even turn this very same fact about the logical incompatibility of A, B, C, and Q, into an argument to this effect: since Q is true, it must be the case that at least one of A, B, or C is false!)

Thus, when faced with an argument for a highly implausible conclusion, the reasonable thing to do may not be to accept that conclusion, but to decide, instead, that one or more of the premises of the argument must be mistaken. Whether this is the right thing to do largely depends on what you are more confident of—the truth of all the premises, or the falsity of the argument's conclusion. If it is the latter, then you may be reasonable in refusing to accept the conclusion of the argument—even if you are uncertain which premises are to be rejected.

Armed with this point, we can now see why one might well hold that we don't actually need to examine the details of the various skeptical arguments after all. For you might already know that you are far more confident of the falsity of the nihilist's conclusions than you could ever be of the sundry contestable premises of their arguments.

To make this thought concrete, suppose we take some moral claim of which you are utterly confident—for example, that it is wrong to torture human infants for the passing pleasure of hearing them scream. Almost everyone believes that this is true, indeed I imagine that there are few things of which you are *more* confident. But if nihilism is correct, then it isn't really true at all that it is wrong to torture infants for this reason. For if nihilism is true, nothing is wrong, period, including the torturing of infants. This means, of course, that you should find nihilism highly implausible. So imagine, next, that you have been presented with some argument for nihilism. Inevitably, at least some of the premises of that argument will be abstract philosophical claims of a kind that have been endlessly debated. You may find them plausible, but you are unlikely to be *certain* that they are all true. Still, let us suppose that taken together they do yield the surprising conclusion that nihilism is true.

So something has to go; one of your initial beliefs has to be revised. It could be that you should abandon your rejection of nihilism. But that would also require giving up your belief that it is wrong to torture infants! So what we really need to ask is this: what are you more confident of? The premises of the nihilist's argument, or the wrongness of torturing infants? If, as seems almost certain, you are far more confident of the wrongness of torture than you are of any particular philosophical premise that might figure in the nihilist's argument (let alone of the likelihood that *all* of these philosophical premises are true), then perhaps you are already in a position to know that you should *reject* the argument, as being based on a mistaken premise of some sort.

Of course, I haven't actually presented you with any particular skeptical argument. Perhaps, if you had one spelled out for you, you would be able to put your finger on the particular premise you would now take to be false (despite whatever plausibility it might initially have had). Or perhaps you couldn't actually do that. But even if you couldn't, you might still be entitled to assert that since you are *more* confident of the wrongness of torture than you are of the various philosophical premises themselves, one or more of the premises *must* be mistaken; and given that that's the case, you certainly needn't accept the argument's nihilistic conclusion.

But doesn't this mean that we don't really need to examine the arguments for moral skepticism at all? Can't we just say, even before we've heard the details, that they must go wrong somewhere? That we are far more confident of the wrongness of torture than we could ever be of the various philosophical premises that would inevitably have to figure in these skeptical arguments? Even if we are initially inclined to find the premises plausible, surely we find the wrongness of torture far more plausible, and so, forced to choose, we will inevitably and justifiably decide that one or more of the premises must be mistaken after all. Accordingly, we don't really need to consider the specific arguments at all. We are justified in believing that they must go wrong.

(The worry may linger that all of this must just be begging the question against the skeptic. But it is hard to see what would make that a fair criticism. Suppose the skeptic has actually presented you with one of their arguments. They say that since A, B, and C are each plausible, one must agree that Not Q is true, despite its initial implausibility. Is it really question begging for you to reply that since Not Q is *implausible*, one must agree instead that either A, B, or C is *false*, despite their initial plausibility? Isn't it question begging for the skeptic to reply to your argument by repeating their own? How can it possibly matter who stated their argument *first*?)

Although I think there is a great deal of truth in the line of thought I've just been describing, I am less confident about its ultimate conclusion—that we can be excused from the need to examine the skeptical arguments altogether. For surely in at least some cases we really can be provided with compelling reasons to accept surprising conclusions, even ones that we might initially have found extremely implausible. And sometimes the cumulative force of a series of arguments suffices—and justifiably so—to *reduce* our confidence in some claim, a claim that we might initially have thought quite unassailable. Yet precisely as we become increasingly less confident of the claim in question, we become correspondingly less justified in simply dismissing the arguments that seek to convince us that our initial confidence is misplaced. To be sure, it might still turn out that this or that surprising conclusion can be justifiably dismissed; but often enough that decision really will turn on the details of the arguments in question. The more plausible the premises of the arguments, the less justified we are in dismissing those arguments out of hand. Ultimately, of course, everything does still depend on comparative judgments of plausibility. But where the balance of plausibility lies may well be something we cannot be genuinely certain of, until we actually look at the arguments themselves.

Furthermore, even if we do remain confident that the nihilist's skeptical arguments must go wrong someplace, it may still be worth our while to do our best to identify exactly where and how they do that. Our understanding of morality may be deepened by seeing how and why skeptical arguments fail. If nothing else, our confidence in the existence of an objective morality may be made even more secure, once we see exactly how the various skeptical challenges can be answered.

Accordingly, I think it remains important for us to examine the arguments for moral skepticism after all. We may be confident that they go must go wrong someplace; but even if so, we can profit by seeing in detail exactly how moral realists can respond to them.

3.4 Normative Nihilism

Moral nihilism declares that there are no moral facts. This is a bold position to stake out, since, as we have seen, it means not only that there are no moral requirements and no moral prohibitions, but also that nothing is morally permissible. Nor is anything morally good or morally bad. Indeed if there are no moral facts, then there are no moral *reasons* either. For if there is no such thing as morality, then there is no morality to so much as provide us with a *morally good reason* to do one thing rather than another. Moral nihilism is, as I say, a bold position.

But there is another version of nihilism which is even bolder than moral nihilism, more sweeping still in terms of what it denies. It will be of interest to us, now and again, in later chapters. So it may be useful to introduce it here, precisely so as to distinguish it from its somewhat more modest cousin. According to this even bolder view, there are no reasons *at all*, no reasons of *any* sort whatsoever. Indeed, there are no normative facts of *any* kind. Unlike moral nihilism, then, which restricts itself to the claim that there are no *moral* facts, this bolder view rejects all of normativity *across the board*. For obvious reasons, then, we can call this view *normative nihilism*.

Normative nihilism entails moral nihilism, for if there are no normative facts of any sort, then, in particular, there are no moral facts either. But it goes beyond moral nihilism in that it denies not only the existence of moral facts, but of any normative fact at all. Thus all talk of what one ought to do (whether morally or otherwise) is mistaken, all claims about what one has reason to do, simply false. (We can construe the normative nihilist as a cognitivist about normative utterances, taking them to be genuine attempts to describe supposed normative facts, but holding that, as there *are* no such facts, all such claims are false.)

Should we accept normative nihilism? I hope it is clear that any view remotely like this is very hard to believe. Very hard indeed. It would mean, for example, that there is no reason to get out of the way of a car headed toward you on the road. No reason to move your hand from a hot stove. No reason to believe that trees have leaves, or that $7-5 = 2$. No reason to do or believe anything at all. Speaking personally, I find it very hard to take seriously the suggestion that anything like that could possibly be right. Indeed, I find the idea sufficiently incredible that I really am prepared to insist that it simply must be false. I imagine that you are prepared to say that too.

So why do I bring up such an implausible view? Because it seems to me that at least some of the arguments that get used to support *moral* nihilism would, if they worked at all, actually push us all the way to *normative* nihilism. And given how utterly implausible normative nihilism is, I think perhaps we really would be justified in concluding that these arguments simply must be mistaken, whether or not we are able to identify where, exactly, they go wrong.

Of course, we still haven't considered any particular skeptical arguments, so at best we should think of this as a cautionary note, warning us to keep our eyes open for arguments that would "prove too much" if only they worked at all. Still, even if only in a preliminary way, it isn't hard to see how attacks on moral reasons (which, of course, the moral nihilist must mount) run the risk of becoming attacks on all reasons whatsoever. If moral reasons are *metaphysically* troubling, why wouldn't the same be true for *all* reasons? If they are *epistemologically* troubling, wouldn't that be true for reasons of any sort at all? If we should be bothered by the fact that there is disagreement about moral reasons, shouldn't disagreement about other sorts of reasons bother us as well?

Questions like this prove little, of course, because everything depends on the details. But they should put us on guard. And if we do find ourselves thinking that a given skeptical argument would lead not merely to moral nihilism but all the way to full-blown normative nihilism, that may serve to reinforce our sense that the argument *must* go wrong somewhere, even if we disagree about where precisely it does.

One final point. Normative nihilism will not figure in our discussion with anything like the regularity that moral nihilism will. Accordingly, in what follows when I mention "nihilism" (or "the nihilist") without qualification, it will always be *moral* nihilism (or the *moral* nihilist) that I have in mind. On those few occasions when I do want to be talking about the bolder view, I will be sure to use the fuller expression, "*normative* nihilism."

4
Noncognitivism

4.1 The Nature of Noncognitivism

Cognitivists take substantive, first-order moral claims (like "lying is never permissible") at face value—as genuine assertions attempting to say something true about the moral facts. To be sure, *nihilists* think that such claims are, in fact, always false (since there are no moral facts to be accurately described); but for all that, as cognitivists even they take such claims to be genuine (if mistaken) assertions.

But *noncognitivists* think it is a mistake to interpret moral claims in this way. Strictly speaking (the noncognitivists say), they are not genuine *claims* at all, since they are not so much as even attempting to describe some putative domain of moral facts. According to noncognitivists, when we utter sentences like this, we are not actually using them to make assertions; we are doing something quite different.

(Accordingly, the noncognitivist thinks that if we were being careful it would be more accurate to use scare quotes in discussing these matters. Instead of talking about moral claims and assertions, we should instead talk about moral "claims" and moral "assertions"—that is, sentences that *look* like claims or assertions but are not actually either. Nonetheless, since a profusion of quotation marks quickly grows tiring, I will continue to refer to the relevant sentences in the intuitive, familiar way.)

If noncognitivism is right, of course, then moral realism is mistaken, since realists hold that such claims are indeed genuine assertions (and what's more, some of them are true). Thus, noncognitivism will strike most of us as a form of moral skepticism.

Admittedly, a noncognitivist need not take this view of their own position. They might claim that they are not skeptics about morality at all; rather, they only want to free us from some common but mistaken beliefs about what we are up to when we engage in moral discourse. Nonetheless, precisely because noncognitivists deny that there are moral facts (why believe in something that we never so much as assert the existence of?) and deny that there are moral truths (how can there be any, if our moral utterances don't really assert anything at all, and so aren't even truth apt?), most of us will indeed view this position as a skeptical one. So noncognitivism is a view that we'll want to examine with some care.

At first glance, if nothing more, noncognitivism seems like a difficult position to maintain. After all, our substantive moral claims certainly *look* like they are making assertions; they certainly *appear* to be statements to the effect that the moral facts are one way rather than another. Obviously, any particular such claim might well be mistaken. But why believe that such claims are not really making assertions at all? They *look* like assertions. Why think otherwise?

Presumably, the noncognitivist is not going to deny that the appearances are as I have just described them. Substantive moral utterances do indeed look like genuine claims. But they will insist that the appearances are deceptive. We are misled by the surface grammar. Such sentences *look* like ordinary assertions. They have the grammatical *form* of ordinary assertions. But if we dig below the surface, the noncognitivist assures us, we will discover reason to believe that surface appearances are here leading us astray.

We should, I think, be prepared to concede that at least in principle something like this could be the case. For sometimes it really does seem plausible to suggest that a sentence that looks like it is making an assertion (it has the grammatical form of a statement) is actually—below the surface—doing something rather different.

Consider, for example, the sentence "I order you to shut the door." At first glance, this seems to be making a factual claim, to wit, that I am engaged in a certain activity, the activity of ordering you. But it would be silly to suggest this is what the sentence is really up to. A sentence like this isn't really in the fact-stating business at all. On the contrary, it seems plausible to suggest that it is actually an imperative. We use sentences like this to give orders, not to state facts. So despite having the grammatical form of a statement (a form that is normally used to make assertions), in this particular instance what is really going on is that this sentence and sentences like it are used to give commands.

Here's another example. Suppose you point to someone attractive across the room and say to me, "I need to know what his name is." Here too, at first glance this looks like a factual claim; you are telling me that you need something—information about someone's name. But once again, it seems somewhat strained to suggest that this sentence is being used to state facts.

4.1 THE NATURE OF NONCOGNITIVISM

Rather, it is plausible to suggest that below the surface this sentence is actually being used to ask a question ("what's his name?") or perhaps to give a command ("find out what his name is!"). We needn't quibble about which of these it is (questions may themselves simply be disguised imperatives). The important point is simply that although this sentence also has the grammatical form of a statement, it is actually being used to do something other than to state facts.

So we shouldn't dismiss out of hand the noncognitivist's claim that something similar is going on when it comes to substantive moral utterances. Perhaps here too we should ultimately conclude that although these sentences look like they are being used to state facts, that appearance is simply an illusion brought about by the surface grammar. Perhaps if we dig below the surface we will find that such sentences are actually being used to do something else altogether. That, at any rate, is the central claim of the noncognitivist.

Note, however, that so far all we have from the noncognitivist is a *negative* thesis—that substantive, first-order moral sentences are *not* used to state facts. We don't yet have a *positive* proposal concerning just what it is (according to the noncognitivist) that these sentences *are* being used to do. If sentences that look like they are stating facts are actually doing something else, what is the something else that they are doing?

In principle, I suppose, a noncognitivist could make any alternative positive proposal that they feel like. But as it happens, there is an answer that is extremely common among noncognitivists: the sentences in question are really being used to *express and reveal certain attitudes*. Thus, for example, according to this view my saying that lying is wrong is (roughly speaking) a way of expressing (revealing, showing, displaying) my attitude of disapproval toward acts of lying; my saying that one is required to keep one's promises is a way of expressing my approval of acts of promise keeping (and disapproval of acts of promise breaking); saying that equality is intrinsically good is a way of expressing my favorable attitude toward states of affairs with less inequality; and saying that honesty is a virtue is a way of expressing my approval of people who are honest. And so on.

(A view like this is sometimes called *expressivism*, to capture the thought that the relevant moral sentences are used to express attitudes, rather than to state facts. Sometimes the view is called *emotivism*, to capture the thought that what is expressed is a kind of emotional attitude, a strong liking or disliking of the acts (or states of affairs, or character traits) in question.)

As it happens, working out the details of this general proposal consumes a fair bit of time among contemporary noncognitivists. But for our purposes the details mostly won't matter. What is important is that if something like this is right, then we now have a positive thesis in place concerning just what it is that substantive moral claims *are* being used for when we utter them. It supplements the negative thesis that such claims are *not* being used to make assertions.

I hope it is clear that in terms of posing a threat to the moral realist, what is crucial is the noncognitivist's *negative* thesis. For on the face of it, at least, there is no obvious reason why a moral realist couldn't agree with the noncognitivist's positive thesis, that substantive moral claims are used to express attitudes. It does seem plausible, after all, to suggest that expressing attitudes is at least *one* of the things that we are doing when we make such claims. That is to say, even the realist might and perhaps should agree that if, for example, I say that stealing is wrong, part of what I am doing in saying this is revealing my disapproval of stealing! It is hard to see why the realist should resist acknowledging such a plausible thought. The realist only wants to insist that this is not the only thing we are doing when we say things like this—that part of what we are doing, and indeed the central part of what we are doing, is asserting something that we take to be a *fact*, namely, that stealing is *wrong*. As the realist might put it, it is precisely because I believe it to be *true* that stealing is wrong—precisely because I take this to be a moral fact—that I disapprove of it. So while it is certainly true that when I say that stealing is wrong, I am indeed expressing my disapproval of it, acknowledging this fact (accepting the noncognitivist's positive thesis) doesn't give us any reason to accept the noncognitivist's *negative* thesis, that I am not actually making any kind of *assertion* about the moral domain.

For the realist, then, what is most centrally going on when I make a substantive moral claim is that I am attempting to accurately describe a set of moral facts. To be sure, I may also be revealing or expressing my emotional attitudes when I do this, but it is the describing that is primary. But for the noncognitivist there is no such describing going on at all. There is *only* the expression of approval and disapproval. There is no attempt to state facts.

For this reason it is important not to confuse noncognitivism with a view that holds that when I say to you, for example, that stealing is wrong, what is really going on is that I am *telling* you that I disapprove of stealing—that I am stating a fact about my attitudes, and saying, in particular, that I have a disapproving attitude toward theft. On this alternative view, when I make a moral claim I am indeed making a factual claim after all: I am making a claim about my attitudes. I am telling you what I approve and disapprove of.

We can call a view like this *subjectivism*. But subjectivism isn't a form of noncognitivism at all. On the contrary, it is actually a form of cognitivism! For according to the subjectivist, when I make a moral claim I am indeed making assertions about facts (facts about my attitudes, to be sure, but facts nonetheless). And so, if I have described my attitudes accurately (if, say, I really do disapprove of theft), then what I have said is true! And if I have misdescribed my attitudes, then what I have said is false. Far from being a form of noncognitivism, subjectivism is actually a *realist* view, albeit one that most realists would never find acceptable. (It is, in particular, a constructivist view, since according to the subjectivist, moral facts boil down to facts about the reactions or attitudes of the relevant minds—in this instance, the mind of the speaker.)

In contrast, the noncognitivist insists that when I make a moral claim I am not *describing* my attitudes at all. I am not telling you what I approve or disapprove of. I am, rather, *showing* you. I am *revealing* my preferences, not describing them.

To help make this distinction clear, suppose that I sit down in front of you and eat a gallon of chocolate ice cream. In doing this, I obviously am not saying that I like ice cream. Indeed, I am not saying anything at all. I am however *showing* you that I like ice cream. I am revealing this fact to you through my behavior. I am not *reporting* anything about my tastes, but I am nonetheless showing you what they are.

Turning next to a slightly more complicated example, suppose that I say to you, "It is raining outside." Here I am indeed asserting something: I am asserting something about the weather. Note however that something further is going on here as well. When I (sincerely) tell you that it is raining outside, I am revealing something about my *beliefs*. I am revealing to you that I believe it is raining! But of course, for all that, I am not *saying* that I believe it is raining. I am not *describing* anything about my psychology. I am not talking about my psychology at all, I am talking about the weather! And yet, for all that, I am revealing to you something about my beliefs. Although I am not reporting anything about my beliefs, I am showing you what they are.

Similarly, then, according to the noncognitivist, when I say that stealing is wrong, I am displaying or revealing my disapproval of theft. But I am not *saying* anything about my disapproval; I am only showing it to you. My utterance is an *expression* of my disapproval, but it is not a *statement* to the effect that I disapprove of theft. I am not reporting anything about my attitudes; I am only showing them to you.

So far, the three examples are similar. But according to the noncognitivist this last case—the moral case—differs in an important way from the first two examples. In the case of eating ice cream or the case of telling you about the weather, the fact that I am revealing something about my tastes or beliefs may be largely incidental to what I am doing. My primary aim is to eat ice cream or report on the weather. But when I tell you that stealing is wrong, the fact that I am revealing my attitudes by expressing them in this way isn't at all incidental to my fundamental aim. On the contrary, says the noncognitivist, this is my *very purpose* in using this language. I say these things (stealing is wrong, inequality is bad, and so on) precisely so as to show you what my attitudes are. I am deliberately revealing them to you. That's the whole *point* of using moral language.

There certainly do seem to be places where language functions in just this way, precisely to reveal (rather than report) one's attitudes. Suppose you offer me some strawberry ice cream, and I reply, "Strawberry ice cream, yuck!" Here I express my dislike of strawberry ice cream, and I do it verbally. (I could of course do it nonverbally instead, by throwing it out!) What's more, the act of expressing my attitude isn't incidental to some other purpose, it is my very goal in using this language in the first place. I reveal my attitudes without reporting them; and the very point of having language like this ("yuck") is to make this sort of expression possible.

Similarly then, says the noncognitivist, when I say, "Lying is wrong," the entire point of having and using sentences like this is simply to express my disapproval of lying. Moral language exists precisely to *show* you my attitudes by expressing them in this way.

So as a very rough first approximation, we can translate "lying is wrong" as something like "boo, lying!" or "lying, yuck!" And (again, roughly) we can translate "you are required to keep your promises" as something like "promise keeping, hooray!" or "yay, promise keeping!"

Of course, putting the idea this way runs the risk of making it seem as though the noncognitivist thinks that making a moral claim is doing something silly and unimportant. But that's not at all the case. The *kind* of approval and disapproval involved in moral cases is far from silly or trivial. For when we use our moral vocabulary, we are talking about matters incomparably more important to us than whether someone eats strawberry ice cream or not. We are revealing our attitudes toward acts of murder, or theft, or promise keeping; we are responding to the possibility of a society's being just or fair, or of people being honest, or compassionate, as opposed to being cruel or disloyal; we are contemplating the thought of widespread inequality, or of people being happy rather than suffering. We care incredibly *deeply* about whether people perform these sorts of acts, whether outcomes have these sorts of features, whether people have these character traits and so on. For these matters are utterly central to how we live with one another and to what sorts of people we are going to be.

Unsurprisingly, then (say the noncognitivists), we have a special vocabulary that we use only in cases that involve this deep form of approval and disapproval. It is the vocabulary of right and wrong, good and bad, forbidden, permitted, and required. It is our moral vocabulary.

So that is one main thing that noncognitivists typically think we are doing when we make moral claims: we are using a special vocabulary to express the deeply felt attitudes of approval and disapproval that come into play when we are concerned with these central questions about how we are to live.

There is, in fact, a second thing, closely related, that noncognitivists typically think we are doing as well—beyond expressing our attitudes of approval and disapproval—when we make moral claims. We are uttering imperatives, giving commands. We are telling people to behave in certain ways, to bring about certain kinds of outcomes, to be a certain type of person.

Thus, for example, part of what I am doing when I say that stealing is wrong is issuing an imperative: "don't steal!" When I say that promise keeping is obligatory, I am saying "keep your promises!" When I say that inequality is bad, I am ordering people to "minimize inequality!" I am giving commands—and not just to others, but to myself as well. I am telling everyone (myself included) to avoid theft, keep promises, and reduce inequality.

Here too, we can think of our moral vocabulary as something we reserve for commands that concern these central questions about how we want all of us to behave, and what we want all of us to bring about. If it is cold outside, I may utter the everyday imperative "shut the door!" But I won't say anything "stronger" than this, because normally this isn't a matter of life and death. Yet if we imagine that somehow it were—if, say, someone's life depended on it—then I might well appropriately insist that it is *wrong* to leave the door open. I would still be issuing a command, but I would be doing it using the specialized vocabulary that we save for imperatives that have this more pressing significance.

So what is the function of substantive moral claims? According to the noncognitivist it is a combination of these two things: expressing (in this special way) my attitudes of approval and disapproval, and issuing commands (to myself and to others) to act accordingly. This is the positive account of our moral utterances that is put forward by the noncognitivist.

There are, of course, in-house debates among noncognitivists. Some emphasize the expressive aspect of moral discourse; others, the imperatival aspect. For our purposes, I think, there is no need to choose between them. And there are any number of technical details that need to be worked out as well, once you try to take either of these basic ideas and refine them so as to make them precise. This is very much a live research program among contemporary metaethicists. But here too, I think these details won't much matter for our purposes.

(For the curious, though, here's a quick example. How does the noncognitivist propose to translate the claim that killing in self-defense is morally permissible but not morally *required*? This certainly isn't the giving of a *command* to kill in self-defense (since I just said that doing this isn't required); nor is it a matter of expressing an attitude roughly equivalent to "yay, killing in self-defense!" (for we used that locution to explicate moral *requirements*). So what's going on here? It would seem that the noncognitivist will need to introduce the idea of an expression whose function is to mark the explicit *absence* of a command or the absence of certain attitudes. But as I say, we needn't worry about these sorts of details.)

What is important for our purposes is acknowledging that the two basic roles for moral vocabulary that we have identified on behalf of the noncognitivist—revealing attitudes and issuing commands—are important ones to fill. We care deeply about how people act, and so it is crucially important to have a way to communicate our attitudes of approval and disapproval and to command one another (and ourselves) to act accordingly. So the noncognitivist certainly thinks that moral utterances play a significant, indeed central, role in our lives. The jobs they perform are important ones. But they do not include the attempt to state or describe any purported moral *facts*.

4.2 The Case for Noncognitivism

I have suggested that it is helpful to think of noncognitivism as putting forward two theses. The negative thesis says that substantive moral claims are not, in fact, genuine assertions at all; they are not used to describe purported moral facts. The positive thesis says that such claims *are*, however, used to express attitudes of approval and disapproval and to issue commands.

Now as I have also already suggested, on the face of it there is no obvious reason why a moral realist should need to reject the positive thesis, if we understand that thesis as indeed restricted to making positive claims about the use of moral utterances. For there is no obvious reason why a realist should resist the suggestion that *among* the things moral language is used for are expressing attitudes and giving commands. All that the realist needs to insist upon is that these are not the *only* things that moral language is used to do. In particular, one further use—indeed the central use—of moral claims is to make assertions, to attempt to say what the moral facts *are*. So on the face of it, at any rate, it certainly looks like there is no reason for the realist to resist accepting the noncognitivist's *positive* thesis. It is only the noncognitivist's negative thesis which must be rejected.

Indeed, it seems a virtue of realism that it can take this sort of pluralist attitude, that it can acknowledge that we use moral language not just for describing, but also for expressing and commanding. For just as it seems natural to take moral claims at face value as attempts to make genuine assertions, it also seems obviously correct to say that we also use them to reveal our attitudes of approval and disapproval and to give commands. On the one hand, when I (sincerely) say, for example, that murder is wrong, surely part of what I am doing is revealing to you my disapproval of murder. So it does seem undeniable that part of what moral claims are used for is to express attitudes. And, on the other hand, when we think of how easily we move between moral claims ("it is wrong to lie") and moral rules ("don't lie!"), it also seems undeniable that part of what moral claims are used for is to issue commands. So the positive thesis seems highly attractive in its own right, and it is an advantage of realism that it can so readily embrace it.

Accordingly, it looks like we can focus our attention on the negative thesis, the claim that substantive moral claims are *not* used to *describe*. And here, I think, it really does seem as though the burden of proof will fall squarely on the noncognitivist. After all, as I have several times suggested, the sort of moral sentences we have in mind ("inequality is bad," "white lies are wrong," and so on) certainly *look* like they are attempts to make claims about purported moral facts. If the noncognitivist thinks that this isn't really the case—if they hold that the claims aren't merely false (which is what the nihilist believes), but not genuine claims at all—then surely it falls upon the noncognitivist to explain to us why we should believe that this appearance is indeed a mere illusion. Moral claims look like claims. Why think otherwise?

It might seem as though the noncognitivist should here avail herself of the same skeptical arguments that are routinely used to challenge moral realism. We haven't yet examined them, but can't the noncognitivist simply insist that if one or another of these arguments works, realism is defeated and we should, accordingly, embrace noncognitivism?

But any suggestion like this would be too quick. For even if some argument convinced us that there are no moral facts and so realism must be rejected (perhaps because, say, any such facts would be metaphysically dubious), that would apparently still leave untouched the cognitivist claim that moral claims really do *attempt* to describe such facts. Even if they inevitably fail to say anything true (precisely because there are no such facts), that wouldn't yet give us reason to think that moral claims aren't really claims at all. An argument to the effect that moral claims are all false isn't at all the same thing as an argument to the effect that they aren't really assertions.

In short, even if there are no moral facts, it seems as though ordinary skeptical arguments are actually going to support *nihilism*, rather than noncognitivism. To be sure, if we do become nihilists, we will then face the question of whether to *abandon* moral language. And at that point we might well decide that even if there are no moral facts there is still value in using moral language to express our attitudes of approval and disapproval and to tell people how to live. So we might well become *revisionist* nihilists, suggesting that we *stop* using moral utterances to make claims and use them instead only to express attitudes and issue commands. That would certainly be an intriguing proposal, but still, for all that, it would be an articulation of a cognitivist position (since even revisionist nihilism is a form of cognitivism), not at all a defense of noncognitivism.

So we need to ask again, just how does the noncognitivist propose to argue that despite the surface grammar, despite the fact that moral claims *look* like genuine claims, in point of fact these sentences are not genuine claims at all?

Interestingly enough, the most promising line of argument appeals to the thought that despite appearances, the various proposed uses of language are not in fact all compatible, that if it really is the case (as surely it is) that moral claims are used to express attitudes and issue commands, then it just can't be the case that they are also used to describe (purported) facts. In effect, the noncognitivist argues that the positive thesis *entails* the negative one, that the positive thesis suffices, all by itself, to rule out the cognitivist's claim that moral claims are used to make assertions as well.

Let's look at this strategy at work. (Warning: the arguments that we'll be considering until the end of this section may be a bit hard to follow the first time through.)

One version of the argument focuses on the fact that we use moral claims to express our approval and disapproval. The noncognitivist then asks how we are to reconcile this with the cognitivist's insistence that such utterances also assert the existence of various moral facts. For suppose that substantive moral claims really were assertions. It would seem, then, that I could in principle *believe* the given assertion (agree that the facts are just as described) and share this thought with you, without yet telling you anything at all about what I approve or disapprove of. After all, if I really thought there were moral facts, how could my merely *acknowledging* them tell you anything about what I favor?

Suppose, for example, that the sentence "murder is wrong" really does assert something, namely, that acts of murder have the property of being wrong. It would seem, then, that I might sincerely believe that the facts are just as described. Accordingly, I might communicate that belief to you by uttering the sentence "murder is wrong." Surely I could do that—state my belief about those facts—without indicating in any way whether I *disapprove* of murder.

So imagine someone giving the following speech: "Murder is wrong. That is a simple fact. Murder really does have the property in question, wrongness. But what of it? I just don't *care* about the fact that murder has that particular property! Indeed, I *favor* murder under certain circumstances. It is wrong, but I don't disapprove of it at all!"

It seems that if cognitivism were right, this would be a coherent speech to give. Sincerely asserting murder's wrongness would not necessarily commit you to any form of disapproval at all.

But—the noncognitivist continues—that gets things completely backwards. It really does seem obvious that (sincerely) saying that murder is wrong necessarily expresses *disapproval* of murder. So cognitivism must be mistaken. For if cognitivism were correct, one could think something wrong without disapproving of it. Since one can't, cognitivism has to be rejected.

(The same basic argument could have been presented in terms of approval rather than disapproval: if cognitivism were correct one could think something obligatory without *approving* of it; but one can't, so cognitivism has to be rejected.)

This argument against cognitivism is certainly suggestive. But we might still wonder: what is it about disapproval (or approval, for that matter) that necessarily takes us beyond merely acknowledging a given set of facts? What *more* does moral disapproval involve?

A natural suggestion for the noncognitivist to make at this point is that there is a necessary connection between disapproving (in the morally relevant sense) and being motivated to *act*. To disapprove in this sense requires at least some minimal motivation to *avoid* the relevant acts or act type. (Thus, for example, if I truly disapprove of lying then I am at least somewhat motivated to avoid lies.) So perhaps the noncognitivist's argument is really this: There is a necessary connection between thinking something wrong and disapproving of it, and another necessary connection between disapproving of something and being at least somewhat motivated to avoid doing it. But the cognitivist cannot acknowledge these connections, since mere beliefs cannot motivate. So cognitivism is false.

If something like this captures what the noncognitivist has in mind, we can simplify the argument a bit by dropping the references to disapproval and appealing instead directly to the implied connection between moral utterances and motivation. The resulting argument would then look like this: There is a necessary connection between thinking something wrong and being at least somewhat motivated to avoid doing it. But the cognitivist cannot explain that connection. So cognitivism is false.

This revised argument involves an appeal to *motive internalism* (introduced in 1.2), one version of which holds that moral beliefs necessarily motivate, at least somewhat. The noncognitivist is thus claiming that motive internalism is incompatible with cognitivism. Therefore, given the plausibility of motive internalism, cognitivism should be rejected.

Here's the argument spelled out a bit more fully. If an agent sincerely believes that an act is wrong, this entails at least some motivation to avoid doing the act. But if cognitivism is correct, then the belief that an act is wrong is indeed a genuine *belief*, namely, the belief that a certain fact holds (to wit, that the given act has the property of wrongness). But a belief cannot, all by itself, guarantee any motivation to do anything. So cognitivism is mistaken.

(Moral "beliefs" are not genuine beliefs at all, and moral "claims" are not genuine assertions.)

In effect, the noncognitivist is arguing that cognitivism cannot accommodate the truth of motive internalism. (How could a mere *belief* guarantee motivation?) In contrast, it might be added, noncognitivism easily accommodates motive internalism. For if moral claims are not genuine assertions at all, one cannot literally *believe* them and so we needn't worry that one might have the relevant belief and nothing more, and thus not have the corresponding motivation at all. On the contrary, if noncognitivism is correct then when I sincerely say that murder is wrong, *all* I am doing is expressing my attitude of disapproval (and, perhaps, issuing a corresponding command). So if an agent sincerely "believes" that murder is wrong, they will necessarily be motivated (at least somewhat) to avoid killing others, since they really do *disapprove* of it.

How might the cognitivist reply to this line of thought? The issues turn out to be quite complicated, and so I am going to postpone detailed examination of them until a later chapter (chapter 10). But let me quickly note two basic possibilities.

One possible response, of course, would be to reject motive internalism. After all, if moral beliefs needn't entail anything about motivation, then it won't be any sort of problem for the cognitivist to concede that on their view one might sincerely believe that murder is wrong and yet not be motivated to avoid killing.

Is the denial of motive internalism plausible? Some—the motive externalists—certainly think so. They claim that we can easily imagine someone who is completely unmoved by his moral beliefs. For example, a hit man for the Mob might say, "Of course murder is *wrong*, but so what? I just don't care about morality!" If that is indeed a genuine possibility, then it seems as though motive internalism is mistaken, and so the noncognitivist's argument (which presupposes it) fails.

In effect, a position like this defends cognitivism by rejecting part of the noncognitivist's positive thesis (or, alternatively, by modifying our understanding of it). Instead of agreeing that substantive moral claims are *always* used to express approval and disapproval, the cognitivist would claim, rather, that they are only *usually* used to do this. So it won't threaten cognitivism to note that mere beliefs per se won't entail anything about motivation; it can still be the case that moral claims are indeed genuine assertions. (The cognitivist might say: moral beliefs are *typically* accompanied by the relevant motivation; but not always.)

But not everyone believes that a thoroughgoing amoralist (like our imaginary hit man) is a genuine possibility. (Does the hit man *really* think it wrong to kill?) And in any event, not all cognitivists are willing to embrace motive externalism. Some will think that anything genuinely worthy of the name morality must inevitably move us, at least a little. So it is worth noting as well a second possible defense of cognitivism, one that embraces motive internalism.

According to this second possible reply, it isn't really true that a mere belief can *never* motivate. No doubt, most beliefs are motivationally "inert." (The mere belief that snow is white surely doesn't move me to do anything at all.) But perhaps some beliefs really are such that they do guarantee the presence of at least some motivation. What sort of beliefs might be like that? Unsurprisingly, the cognitivist's answer might be: *moral* beliefs!

Here the cognitivist would be agreeing that if someone genuinely thinks that murder is wrong, then they must be moved by this thought (at least a *little*) to avoid killing. Thus the cognitivist would be accepting the unqualified version of the positive thesis, where that thesis is construed to mean that moral claims are *always* used to express approval and disapproval. And the cognitivist would be agreeing as well that the relevant notion of approval and disapproval necessarily involves motivation. But they would simply be insisting that moral claims *can* be genuine assertions for all of that, since it is the nature of moral beliefs that they do necessarily motivate (at least somewhat), unlike more ordinary beliefs. Here too, then, if this is indeed a genuine possibility—if certain beliefs (and in particular, moral beliefs) can motivate all by themselves—then the noncognitivist's argument (which presupposes that this is impossible) fails.

In principle, then, there are two different ways that the cognitivist might try to respond to the noncognitivist's argument. So if the noncognitivist is to shore up her attack on cognitivism she must rule out both of them. She must argue both that *genuine* beliefs alone cannot motivate (so as to rebuff the second cognitivist reply), and that moral "beliefs" necessarily *can* (so as to rebuff the first).

At this point, I suspect that most of us will agree that it isn't obvious who has the better of this dispute. Adjudicating it will require a much more thorough examination of the various connections between motivation, on the

4.2 THE CASE FOR NONCOGNITIVISM

one hand, and morality and belief, on the other, than we have yet undertaken. Indeed, the topic is sufficiently complicated that we will later devote an entire chapter to it. For the time being, then, I only hope to have made it clear just how much turns on the outcome of that discussion.

Instead of considering this argument further now, I want to note a second argument that is similar to it—except that instead of focusing on our use of moral claims to express attitudes, it focuses on our use of moral claims to issue commands. Since we certainly do use moral claims in this way, it concludes that these claims cannot be genuine assertions.

Despite the shift in focus, the general strategy of this new argument is similar to that of the first one. It starts by pointing out that if cognitivism is true, substantive moral claims make genuine assertions about purported moral facts. But if that were the case, then it seems that one could *believe* that the facts are, indeed, just as the claim described. And if so, one could then appropriately communicate that belief by uttering the claim in question. But—the argument continues—surely one could assert the *existence* of such facts without thereby offering any commands at all about how to behave. The mere act of acknowledging facts cannot commit one to issuing imperatives. So cognitivism has to allow for the possibility of making moral claims without issuing commands. Since that possibility is absurd, cognitivism must be rejected.

After all, suppose for the moment that the sentence "murder is wrong" really did assert that acts of murder have a certain property: wrongness. It seems as though I could then use that sentence to make that very assertion, and do so without yet issuing any kind of command at all. For saying or thinking that the world is a certain way (that the facts are a certain way) does not, in and of itself, commit me one way or the other to telling people how to behave. In particular then, I could believe murder is wrong without commanding anyone (myself or others) to avoid killing.

But this, the noncognitivist argues, is unacceptable. Surely if I believe that murder is wrong this is equivalent to accepting some principle along the lines of "murder is morally forbidden." And there is no real difference between accepting such a principle and accepting the corresponding moral rule "don't kill!" But rules just *are* imperatives; so it is obvious that believing that murder is wrong necessarily involves the acceptance of certain commands, and saying it necessarily involves the *issuance* of such commands. Since cognitivism has to allow for the possibility of making moral claims without issuing commands, it has to be rejected.

Just as the strategy of this second argument is very similar to that of the first, the replies open to the cognitivist are similar as well. Once again, there are two of them, and here too I am only going to note them quickly.

First, then, the cognitivist might try to reject the assumption—crucial to the argument—that accepting a moral claim necessarily involves the giving (or accepting) of a command. Perhaps this is only *usually* the case, not always. Perhaps one really can think an act wrong without issuing the corresponding imperative. Consider our hit man once again. Imagine that he says to his assistant, "I want you to kill Frank! Admittedly, killing is *wrong*, but what of it? I just don't care about morality." If that's a coherent possibility, then moral claims can indeed be genuine assertions after all, affirming the existence of relevant facts. It won't be a problem for the cognitivist to admit that the mere recognition of such facts need not result in the issuing of imperatives. (Taking this position would of course require rejecting or at least somewhat modifying the positive thesis, if that thesis is construed as asserting that moral claims are *always* used to issue imperatives.)

Once again, not everyone will accept the idea that this kind of amoralist (the hit man) is a genuine possibility. And in any event, many cognitivists will agree with the noncognitivist that there is an extremely tight connection between making moral claims and issuing commands. So a second possible cognitivist response would be to insist that it isn't really true that mere assertions never bring commands in their wake. No doubt most assertions are "imperatively inert" (if I tell you that snow is white, no particular commands follow, one way or the other). But there may be particular assertions which nonetheless have a uniquely close connection to commands. What sorts of assertions might be like that? Unsurprisingly, the cognitivist's answer might be: moral beliefs!

Here's the idea. We all have an intuitive distinction between valid and invalid commands. If a random stranger standing next to you turns and says, "Give me $100!" this is going to strike you as a command in name only, nothing you need pay attention to. Why? Because there is no good reason to do what he said. In contrast, most of us think that the imperative "don't tell gratuitous lies!" is a *valid* command, one backed by compelling reasons. (Recall the related discussion in 1.2.)

Perhaps then the cognitivist should insist that there is a necessary connection between the truth of a given moral claim (what it would take for the claim to be true) and the existence of compelling reasons. This is a version of *reasons internalism* (introduced in 1.2.) Suppose then that I sincerely claim that murder is wrong. Given reasons internalism, I have in effect committed myself to the existence of compelling reasons not to kill. This would not in any way undermine the thought that I have made a genuine claim. Indeed, part of what I would have been saying or implying was that such reasons exist. So in saying that murder is wrong, I would have committed myself to a further claim, namely, that the imperative "don't kill!" is a *valid* one, a command backed by good reasons. Thus, although the claim that murder is wrong would still be a genuine assertion, in sincerely making that claim I would be committing myself to the validity of the corresponding imperative. Perhaps, strictly speaking, making a moral claim would not automatically involve *issuing* a command, but it would come very close to doing that, since I would be implying that there were good grounds for issuing such a command. And under ordinary circumstances, at least, saying that there were such grounds might constitute one familiar way of (implicitly) issuing that very command.

Thus there are at least two ways the cognitivist might try to resist the second version of the noncognitivist's argument. She might deny that there is any necessary connection between making a moral claim and issuing commands, or she might insist that—thanks to the truth of reasons internalism—whenever you sincerely make a moral claim, you implicitly commit yourself to the validity of the corresponding imperative.

(Note, in passing, that the second response also offers a possible reply to a different argument that the noncognitivist might propose, *the argument from synonymy*. This argument starts with the idea that uttering a moral principle like "it is wrong to tell lies" is basically the same thing as uttering the command "don't lie!" But the latter of these two sentences is undeniably an imperative, while it is at least a possibility that the former only *appears* to be a genuine assertion. So if they are truly synonymous, it is more plausible to conclude that a claim that killing is wrong is actually an imperative as well, not a genuine assertion. Against this argument the cognitivist can now reply that although the two sentences (principle and imperative) are closely related, they are not truly synonymous. Rather, the principle implies the existence of good reasons for obeying the imperative, and the imperative presupposes the existence of such reasons. Thus anyone who affirms the principle is likely to be ready to issue the command; and anyone who issues the command is likely to be ready to affirm the principle. But for all that, the two are not synonymous: one is an imperative, while the other is indeed an assertion.)

To be clear, I don't take these quick responses to the noncognitivist's arguments to be decisive. We still need to take a closer look at the possibility of amoralists like the hit man, and we need to think further about the plausibility of both reasons internalism and motive internalism. These are issues to which we will eventually return. But I do think these quick replies suffice to show that providing a successful defense of noncognitivism (if such can be given) won't be a trivial undertaking. So for the time being, at least, it seems reasonable to tentatively retain our natural inclination to take moral claims at face value—as genuine assertions about purported moral facts.

4.3 Objections to Noncognitivism

So far, we have imagined the cognitivist on the defensive, trying to respond in one way or another to the noncognitivist's attack. But it is worth pointing out that the cognitivist can also go on the *offensive*, noting various difficulties with *non*cognitivism. Beyond the most obvious objection—the simple fact that moral claims certainly *look* like they are attempts to describe a moral reality—there are additional problems that may further reduce noncognitivism's plausibility. To the extent that noncognitivism has a difficult time responding to these objections, this will reinforce our sense that it is indeed cognitivism that is the more plausible of the two views.

However, given that our main interest lies in evaluating skeptical challenges to moral realism, a survey of noncognitivism's difficulties is less important to us than the attack against cognitivism that I sketched in the previous section. Accordingly, I won't dwell on any of the objections that I am about to describe. Still, it is worth saying enough to show that noncognitivism really does face some significant problems of its own.

First, then, consider the noncognitivist's claim (part of their positive thesis) that when I make a moral assertion I am (often, or maybe even always) expressing an attitude of approval or disapproval. That does seem a plausible enough thing to suggest. But it is important to bear in mind that not all approval or disapproval is *moral* approval or disapproval. If, for example, I tell you, "That's an ugly blouse!" then although I am clearly indicating my disapproval of your choice of clothing, this isn't an instance of moral disapproval. Similarly, if I say, "What a delicious cookie!" then although I may be indicating my approval of your culinary skills, it isn't moral approval that is being displayed.

So what is the particular sort of approval or disapproval that is involved when I make a moral claim? What differentiates *moral* approval or disapproval from *other* forms of approval and disapproval?

One natural suggestion is that the relevant forms of approval and disapproval are those that are based on judgments about the act's being right or wrong. I *morally* disapprove of an act if my disapproval is due to my thinking that the act is morally forbidden. I morally *approve* of an act if my approval is due to thinking the act permissible or required. (Similarly, my disapproval of an *outcome* is moral disapproval if it is due to my thinking that the outcome is morally inferior. And so on.)

Unfortunately for the noncognitivist, however, any proposal along these lines presupposes that I have a logically prior belief about the moral status of the act (or outcome) in question. My approval or disapproval can be based on my moral judgments only if I *have* moral judgments—only if I take the relevant moral claims to be *true*. And while a cognitivist can certainly allow for this possibility (since cognitivists take moral claims to be truth apt, and thus the sort of thing that can be believed or rejected, providing the basis for one's moral attitudes), the noncognitivist cannot. According to the noncognitivist, moral claims are not genuine claims at all, so there is nothing to believe; there are no moral beliefs to provide the basis for one's approval or disapproval.

Thus, the noncognitivist needs some alternative way to pick out what it is that distinguishes moral approval and disapproval from *other* forms of approval and disapproval, a way that doesn't covertly smuggle in an appeal to genuine moral assertions. The noncognitivist needs a way to characterize moral attitudes without presupposing the truth of cognitivism! And while there are various proposals that might be made, it is far from clear which, if any, are satisfactory.

A second challenge facing noncognitivism grows out of a criticism which is, I think, fairly easily answered. The criticism is this. It certainly seems as though people disagree about moral matters. One person thinks white lies permissible, while another thinks them forbidden. Some people think all pleasures have intrinsic value, others do not. Disagreement is a familiar fact of our moral discourse. But how is the noncognitivist to explain what is going on when people disagree?

The cognitivist has a straightforward account of the nature of moral disagreement. One side of a given debate is asserting—genuinely asserting—that the moral facts are such and such, and the other side is denying this. Each side is making a truth apt claim, but they are disagreeing about which of the two claims is the true one, which claim describes the facts correctly. That's the nature of moral disagreement: one side asserts what the other denies.

But this natural account isn't available to the noncognitivist, since the noncognitivist denies that moral claims are genuine assertions. Instead, according to the noncognitivist, all that is happening here is that each side is revealing their preferences. But if neither side is actually asserting anything, what could it possibly mean to say that they are *disagreeing*? If I reveal that *I* like chocolate ice cream, while you reveal that *you* prefer strawberry, there is no incompatibility here between what you are doing and what I am doing! So where's the disagreement?

As I say, this initial criticism is readily answered. Unlike the case of ice cream, where it is fine with me if you prefer strawberry and it is fine with you if I prefer chocolate, in the kinds of cases where moral attitudes are involved it is not in fact a matter of indifference to any of us how other people choose. We may not have differences of opinion with regard to the facts (says the noncognitivist) but we can still have disagreements concerning how we want ourselves and others to behave.

This sort of *practical* disagreement occurs even in nonmoral contexts. If you and I are deciding what to do tonight, and you prefer the movies, while I prefer to go to a concert, there is no disagreement in our beliefs—neither of us is making an *assertion* that the other denies—but for all that we have a genuine disagreement, a disagreement about what to do! All the more so, then (says the noncognitivist), when we are disputing a moral question. If you think abortion is morally wrong, for example, while I think it is permissible, we will both care deeply about whether abortions are available. This won't be a disagreement of belief, but it will be a disagreement about what sorts of behavior we are going to disapprove of. This is a perfectly genuine— and important—form of disagreement.

So far, so good. The noncognitivist can meet the initial criticism. But now a new challenge arises in its wake. For what we might want to know, next, is this: given our moral disagreement, what is it, on the noncognitivist's account, for us to engage in moral *argument*? Here too it seems as though the cognitivist has an easier time of it. For normally when we engage in a rational dispute with one another we try to sway those on the other side by offering reasons to believe that our own view is *true*. And if cognitivism is correct, then this is what we are trying to do in moral disputes as well: we are trying to persuade the other side by providing compelling reasons to believe that the particular claims *we* are putting forward are the true ones.

4.3 OBJECTIONS TO NONCOGNITIVISM

But what kind of account of moral argument can the noncognitivist provide? If moral claims are not genuine assertions, then I am not trying to get you to change your beliefs but only your attitudes; I am simply trying to get you to change your *preferences*. Can this be anything other than an attempt on my part to influence your tastes by "pushing" your psychic buttons? I may succeed in tugging at your heartstrings. But is that argument, or just manipulation?

In some cases, no doubt, it may be possible to provide reasons for changing one's preferences. Perhaps you deeply want something, X, and don't realize that Y will help bring X about. So you don't currently want Y; you may even be opposed to Y. But in the course of arguing with you, I may be able to persuade you that Y really is an effective means of getting X. I have given you a reason to want Y, and in light of it, you may change your attitude toward Y. In cases like this, cases involving "derivative" preferences, even the noncognitivist can point to something that we will recognize as an instance of offering a rational argument for changing your attitudes.

But even if the noncognitivist can do this for derivative preferences, it seems difficult to see how a similar account could possibly work when it comes to more basic or "ultimate" preferences. Here, it seems, noncognitivists have to dig in their heels and insist that no further reasons can be given for having one (fundamental) attitude rather than another. Anything that looks like rational argument can be nothing more than manipulating your psychology in such a way as to cause you to *change* your preferences without actually providing you with *reasons* to do so.

(Why must the noncognitivists concede that on their view there cannot be good reasons to embrace one ultimate preference rather than another? Because if even ultimate preferences were subject to rational evaluation, then a moral realist could simply insist that right and wrong is ultimately a matter of which preferences are justified all the way down; and then there would be moral facts after all! For example, they might hold that a claim to the effect that a given act is wrong is true if and only if there is good reason (all the way down) to disapprove of it. And that's a form of cognitivism, not noncognitivism.)

So if we accept noncognitivism, won't we need to hold that at a certain point in any moral "argument," what passes for the giving of good reasons will inevitably be nothing more than verbal posturing and psychological manipulation? That rational argument about *fundamental* moral questions must actually be impossible? That seems a rather disappointing conclusion to reach. (In contrast, the cognitivist can insist that even for basic moral issues the question is always whether a given moral claim is *true*, and there is no reason to *assume* that such questions are beyond our rational grasp.)

Perhaps there is a way for the noncognitivist to avoid this unhappy conclusion. At the very least, perhaps noncognitivists can find a satisfying way to distinguish between acceptable ways to influence another's basic preferences and sheer propaganda and brainwashing. That might at least somewhat reduce the unattractiveness of the view. Or perhaps some noncognitivists are prepared to bite the bullet here and concede the point. Once again, I won't consider the matter further. My goal remains the more modest one of pointing out some of the different ways in which noncognitivism faces its own challenges.

Here's a third objection. According to noncognitivism's positive thesis we use moral claims to express attitudes and issue commands. So if I say, "White lies are wrong," I am expressing my disapproval of white lies and issuing a command (to myself and others) not to tell them. That noncognitivist interpretation of what I am doing when I use moral language is a tolerably clear proposal when we limit our attention to simple ("atomic") sentences like the one I just mentioned. But we often use moral language in more complex sentences than these, and it is not yet at all clear what the noncognitivist thinks we are up to when we do. Suppose, for example, that I say, "If white lies are wrong, then it is wrong to tell one to your roommate." What am I doing if I say something like *that*?

As usual, the cognitivist has a relatively straightforward answer. I am asserting that if one set of facts holds (that is, if it is indeed a fact that white lies are wrong), then a second set of facts holds as well (that is, then it is a fact that telling such a lie to your roommate is wrong). In effect, I am asserting that there is a relationship between the truth of the first clause of the sentence and the truth of the second clause, such that if the former is true then the second is true as well. Note, however, that in saying this, I am not actually committing myself to the truth of the antecedent. I am not taking a stand on whether it really *is* true that telling white lies is wrong. I am merely claiming that *if* such lies are indeed wrong, then something follows from that. Details aside, all of this is more or less straightforward if we are cognitivists.

But what should we say if we are *non*cognitivists? It won't be acceptable for the noncognitivist to say that I use this more complex sentence to express my disapproval of white lies—for as we just noted, in saying this sentence I am not yet committing myself to the claim that telling white lies *is* wrong.

4.3 OBJECTIONS TO NONCOGNITIVISM 101

Nor am I commanding others not to tell them. What I am doing, of course, is saying that *if* white lies are wrong, so is telling one to your roommate. But how is the noncognitivist to capture this idea armed only with the notions of expressing attitudes and issuing commands?

(Even if we agree that in uttering the sentence I am expressing my disapproval of your telling a white lie to your roommate *if* such lies are wrong, or I am ordering you not to tell such a lie *if* they are wrong—how is the noncognitivist to make sense of the conditional nature of such commands and attitudes? The most natural way to interpret them might be to say that if a certain moral claim is true—if telling white lies is wrong—then I do disapprove and command accordingly. But of course, the noncognitivist cannot help herself to such talk of moral truths. Alternatively, is there some logically complex attitude or command at play? Am I somehow trying to express my disapproval of your telling your roommate a white lie in those circumstances where I (first?) disapprove of white lies more generally? But that doesn't seem to adequately capture the content either. It would be more accurate to say that I disapprove of your telling the lie to your roommate if white lies are *worthy* of disapproval. But how is the noncognitivist to capture that last bit?)

Closely related problems show up everywhere, once we start looking for them. Sometimes in moral deliberation we work our way from premises to conclusions about right and wrong. I might, for example, argue as follows: (1) if white lies are wrong, then telling one to my roommate is wrong; but (2) white lies *are* wrong; so (3) telling a white lie to my roommate is wrong. That certainly seems to be a logically valid argument: the conclusion, (3), really does seem to follow logically from the premises. That is to say, if the premises are true, the conclusion is true as well.

That, at least, is how we would ordinarily describe the logical force of an argument like this. We may be uncertain about one or more of the premises of this argument (in particular, we might be uncertain about the second, which says, of course, that white lies really *are* wrong). But we ordinarily wouldn't hesitate to say that the truth of the conclusion really would follow if the premises were true.

Yet none of this talk—about how the truth of the conclusion would follow from the truth of the premises—can be taken literally if we are noncognitivists, since noncognitivists don't think that sentences like (2) and (3) are so much as truth apt! What could it possibly mean to talk about how the truth of the conclusion would follow from the truth of the premises, if the conclusion and at least one of the premises are not the sort of thing which can even have a truth value? (And of course, as we have already noted, it remains obscure what the noncognitivist wants to say about (1) in the first place.)

Abstractly stated, the problem is this. When we evaluate arguments we ask whether the conclusion follows from the premises. But this very notion of "following" seems to be one that we most naturally understand by means of the notion of truth. Yet if noncognitivism is right and simple moral claims are not truth apt, what can this notion of one thing *following* from another even mean?

(How is this second version of the problem, which concerns the idea of logically valid arguments, related to the first, which concerns complex moral utterances? Both involve contexts in which something more complicated than simple assertion is going on, and it is difficult to see how to make sense of the phenomena without appealing to the idea that moral claims can be truth apt.)

As usual, none of this is problematic for the cognitivist. For the cognitivist thinks that all of the relevant claims in the argument are indeed truth apt, so it makes perfect sense to ask whether the truth of the premises really would guarantee the truth of the conclusion. But the noncognitivist needs some alternative account of what it means for the conclusion of a moral argument to "follow" from its premises, and it certainly isn't clear what this alternative account would look like.

Let me close with one more example of what is probably the same underlying problem at work. Imagine that I am trying to decide whether or not it is permissible to tell a white lie. Perhaps I am planning a surprise party for my wife, and she has asked me what our plans are for the evening. Imagine that I ask myself, "Are white lies permissible?" What is going on when I raise this question? (Note that this is yet another area where I am using moral language, but not making a simple assertion.)

Here too, the cognitivist has an easy time of it. According to the cognitivist, the claim that white lies are permissible is truth apt—it is either true or false. In asking my question, I am wondering which it is. (Even the nihilist, who thinks there are no moral facts, can recognize that I am here assuming there are such things, and wondering what the relevant facts are.) But once again, the noncognitivist's account of what I am up to in asking my question is difficult to make out. Obviously enough, it can't be that I am expressing approval or disapproval of white lies, since in my current state of uncertainty I don't yet approve *or* disapprove. I am trying to figure out which to do! But if we rephrase my question as "what should I do with regard to white lies,

4.3 OBJECTIONS TO NONCOGNITIVISM

approve or disapprove of them?" no real progress has been made. For the obvious thought here is that I should disapprove of them just in case they are indeed wrong—if it really is true that white lies are wrong. And this is a thought that the noncognitivist cannot appeal to. (Similarly, I clearly am not issuing a command not to tell white lies. At best, I am trying to decide what commands are *appropriate* here. But how is the noncognitivist to make sense of that notion?) So here we have yet another case—an everyday, familiar case—of moral language being used in a way that the noncognitivist cannot easily explain.

In short, noncognitivism runs into trouble whenever we move away from the simplest cases of moral assertion. The account of moral language that views it simply in terms of offering commands and expressing attitudes may seem adequate when we restrict our attention to simple assertions like "murder is wrong" or "inequality is bad." But extending that account to more complex linguistic contexts (including ones where we aren't straightforwardly making moral assertions at all) remains a challenge.

None of this is meant to suggest that no proposals can be offered by the noncognitivist to explain what is going on in these more complex cases. There are, in fact, any number of proposals that have been made, though the details rapidly become extremely technical and complicated. Here again, then, the point is not at all to claim confidently that the noncognitivist's difficulties are insuperable, but only to note that they are indeed difficulties. In comparison, at least, the cognitivist seems to have the upper hand.

Of course, we must bear in mind that we have yet to give the noncognitivist's attack on *cognitivism* a full hearing. It may be that when we examine it more carefully we will ultimately decide that cognitivism must indeed be rejected after all—and moral realism with it. I don't believe that this will, in fact, be the most reasonable conclusion to reach; but for the time being this is merely a promissory note on my part. Still, until such time (if ever) as we find a compelling reason to prefer the noncognitivist's account of moral discourse, I think it is more reasonable to take moral claims at face value: as genuine assertions about purported moral facts.

5
Disagreement

5.1 The Argument from Disagreement

People regularly disagree about first-order moral questions. Is capital punishment morally justifiable? Is it permissible to tell a lie to save someone from embarrassment? Is it wrong to kill in self-defense? Are abortions ever morally permissible? Are promises made under false pretenses binding? Is it ever permissible to deliberately harm an innocent person? These questions, and countless others like them, are a source of endless debate.

What should we make of this fact, the fact of there being so much disagreement? One possible reply, I suppose, is this: Ethics is hard, and the answers to these questions just aren't obvious. We find ourselves disagreeing because it is difficult to figure out the truth. There is nothing more to it than that, no deeper moral to draw. It is easy to imagine a moral realist suggesting something along these lines.

But there is a more troubling response which may suggest itself instead: The ubiquity of disagreement gives us reason to believe that there actually are no right answers to be had. We disagree precisely because there are no substantive first-order moral facts to figure out, no moral facts "out there" to push us in the direction of accepting one set of answers rather than another. From this more troubling perspective the fact of moral disagreement gives us reason to be *skeptical* about morality, to deny the existence of moral facts altogether.

We can call this second line of thought—the skeptical one—the *argument from disagreement*. Our goal in this chapter is to evaluate it.

Here's the argument again, spelled out more fully. There is a lot of disagreement about substantive moral questions. That's a simple fact, but it needs explaining. Why does this disagreement exist? Of course, since we could doubtless make up any number of potential explanations, what we really want to know is, what is the *best* explanation of this widespread disagreement? The skeptic's proposal is this: the best explanation is that moral realism is false, that there aren't really any moral facts at all. That's why we can endlessly argue about the supposed moral facts without ever getting anywhere.

Contrast the situation in ethics with domains where a realist approach is clearly appropriate, chemistry, for example, or astronomy. Here we tend to have consensus. People agree about the chemical composition of water, for example; they agree that the earth rotates around the sun; and so on. Here, then, we find agreement, rather than disagreement. This too needs to be explained, and the most plausible explanation is a realist one: there are facts (about chemistry, astronomy, physics, biology, and so on), and these facts constrain and influence our beliefs about these domains in various ways, such that we tend to *converge* on the correct beliefs about the underlying facts.

Thus, agreement within a given domain is a sign that a realist approach toward that domain is appropriate. Admittedly, it doesn't guarantee that realism is correct. But it is a relevant and compelling piece of evidence. And, in contrast, disagreement within a given domain is a sign that a realist approach is *inappropriate*. (Here too, it may not decisively settle the question, but it is a highly relevant piece of evidence.) And what we find, when we think about moral questions (in contrast to questions about physics and biology and the like) is that there is so much disagreement, it is reasonable to conclude that there are no moral facts at all. Therefore, we should embrace moral skepticism.

Although suggestive, these brief remarks don't make it transparent how, exactly, the argument from disagreement is supposed to go. For I presume that anyone putting forward the argument will want to concede the (undeniable) point that we find disagreement in the sciences too. It is hardly as though astronomers, for example, agree about everything! So the idea had better not be that the presence of any disagreement whatsoever is sufficient to support a skeptical position with regard to a given domain. Rather, the complaint about morality will have to turn on some view about the *amount* of disagreement (or perhaps the *kinds* of disagreement) that we find there (but presumably not in astronomy or chemistry, and so on).

So perhaps the skeptic's thought is this: when there is *widespread* disagreement with regard to a given subject matter, the best explanation of this disagreement is (likely to be) the skeptical one, according to which there are no (substantive) facts concerning the given domain.

(Admittedly, what it takes for disagreement to be "widespread," rather than narrow or limited, isn't something we can pin down with precision; it doesn't have sharp boundaries. But for all that, this principle could still be true. Having terms with imprecise boundaries needn't render a given claim unacceptable.)

If this is the right way to understand what the skeptic has in mind, then the argument from disagreement boils down to two claims: first, that there is widespread disagreement in ethics; and second, that where there is widespread disagreement, the best explanation of this is likely to be that there are no facts concerning the domain in question. Accordingly, what we need to do is ask whether these claims are actually true.

Most of us, I imagine, will be prepared to grant the skeptic the first premise of the argument—the claim that moral disagreement is widespread. I began this chapter with half a dozen examples of controversial moral questions, and I take it to be obvious that the examples could easily be multiplied, many times over. So perhaps we should concede that the first premise of the skeptic's argument is true and focus our attention solely on the second.

Nonetheless, I do want to register a note of uncertainty concerning this point, for speaking personally it isn't actually obvious to me that it is correct to say that our moral disagreements are widespread. It is of course obvious that there are many, many points of moral disagreement. But we should not lose sight of the fact that there are also many, many points where people tend to agree, rather than disagree, about what morality asks of us (or which outcomes are better, and so on). Indeed, I rather suspect that there is far more that people agree about, morally, than what they disagree about.

Unsurprisingly, when we engage in first-order normative ethics in a systematic way, trying to state general moral principles and combining them into a systematic whole, it is often useful to focus on the points at which our rival theories disagree with one another. For these are the places where we are best able to see what is at stake in accepting one theory rather than another. That's certainly what I do, at any rate, in my own classroom: I focus on the points where people disagree. But this practice, understandable and appropriate as it may be, may create the illusion that moral disagreements are far more common than they actually are. If, instead, discussions of moral theory emphasized the fact—and I do take it to be a fact—that people tend to agree that it is wrong to kill infants for the pleasure of hurting them, that it is wrong to enslave someone on the basis of the color of their skin, that special circumstances aside it is wrong to make a promise that you have no intention of keeping, that it is unjust to deliberately frame an innocent man for a crime he did not commit, and so on, then perhaps our confidence that moral disagreement is widespread, rather than being relatively limited and narrow, would be reduced or even eliminated. To be honest, I really don't know how widespread our moral disagreements are (as compared to the countless points where we largely agree), and I bet you don't either. So at the very least, I am not at all sure that the moral realist should simply concede the first premise of the skeptic's argument.

Well, can we at least agree about this? That disagreement is *more* widespread when it comes to moral questions than in other areas (like the sciences) where we find realist positions obvious and compelling? The skeptic had certainly better hope that this comparative claim is true, for if it isn't, then almost no one will be prepared to accept the skeptic's argument. After all, we find plenty of disagreement in the sciences as well; it isn't as though scientists speak with one voice on all scientific questions. Yet no one is tempted to suggest that there are no scientific facts—no facts about astronomy, or biology, or chemistry, or physics. So if moral disagreements are no more common than scientific ones, we will presumably conclude either that (1) moral disagreements are not widespread after all, and so the *first* premise of the skeptic's argument is mistaken, or else (2) *scientific* disagreements are widespread too, so the mere presence of widespread disagreement does not give us reason to accept skepticism, and so the *second* premise of the argument is false. Either way, the argument from disagreement would be in trouble.

Accordingly, the skeptic has to insist that while it is true that we find disagreement in the sciences too, it isn't at anything like the scale that we find when we are discussing moral issues. So while it remains reasonable to maintain a realistic attitude toward the sciences (there are facts about chemistry, and physics, and evolution), nonetheless, given the tremendously greater amount of disagreement we find in ethics, the best explanation of this disagreement is that in this domain (in contrast to the various scientific domains) there are actually no facts at all.

But is it really true that there is more disagreement in ethics than there is in other areas (such as the sciences) where we are inclined to take a realist stance? Is disagreement in ethics genuinely *more* widespread?

Speaking personally, I actually have no idea at all whether this comparative claim is correct. Has a careful empirical study (comparing the extent and type of disagreements to be found in ethics with that found in, say, physics) ever actually been done? I rather doubt it. Admittedly, like you, I am under the impression that something like this *might* be true—that there might be more disagreement about ethics than there is with regard to scientific disciplines. But for all I know, this might be little more than an artifact of the fact that people tend to discuss moral questions more frequently than they do questions about cosmology or quantum mechanics! Or consider the fact that newspaper articles routinely describe debates over what are, ultimately, moral questions (for example, disagreements about politics, criminal justice, and public policy, and so on), while *scientific* debates are only rarely covered. Perhaps all of this merely creates the illusion that disagreements are more widespread in ethics than elsewhere. As I say, I really don't know, and I doubt anyone does.

But suppose we *grant* the thought that disagreements in ethics are more widespread than they are in areas (like physics, or biology—or psychology, or history!) where a realist stance is relatively uncontroversial. While I am far from confident that anything like this is true, I imagine that most of us will agree that it might well be. It certainly does *seem* to be true; so let us suppose that it is. Where does that leave the skeptic's argument? Once we grant this point, the skeptic no longer has to worry that the presence of disagreement in the sciences poses a threat to their argument against ethics. They are free to insist that disagreement is indeed widespread in ethics (but *not* in, say, physics or biology), and that this gives us reason to be skeptical about morality. They can offer the argument from disagreement without worrying that it might undermine belief in the sciences as well (or, a more likely outcome, that our confidence in the existence of scientific facts might lead us to reject the skeptic's argument instead). If moral disagreements are widespread in a way that scientific disagreements are not, then the argument from disagreement can still be put forward.

Of course, I have given some reason to be uncertain whether it really is true that moral disagreements are *sufficiently* common to count as widespread for the purposes of the skeptic's argument. But here too I imagine that most will be prepared to grant the skeptic this claim. So let us suppose that the skeptic is right about this point as well, and that disagreements really are widespread in ethics (though not in the sciences). Does this give us reason to reject moral realism? Everything will turn on whether it is indeed plausible to believe that *widespread* disagreement in a given domain makes it likely that there are no substantive facts with regard to that domain. So let's consider that claim next.

5.2 The Implications of Disagreement

The argument from disagreement, as we are currently interpreting it, has only two premises: first, that disagreements are widespread in ethics, and second, that when there is *widespread* disagreement about a subject it is likely that there are no substantive facts about that subject. If we grant the first of these premises to the skeptic, the moral realist can only avoid the skeptical conclusion—that it is likely that there are no moral facts—by rejecting the second. Happily, however, this is a very plausible thing to do. Indeed, if we stop to think about it, we will see just how dubious the principle stated in the second premise really is.

The basic thought underlying this objection was already at work (behind the scenes) when we raised the question of whether scientific disagreements might be widespread as well. For if such disagreements are indeed widespread, we would surely take this as compelling reason to reject the second premise. Almost all of us are committed to realism with regard to the sciences, and so if the principle had supported the claim that there are no *scientific* facts, we would have taken this instead as a decisive argument against the principle in question. We would have concluded, sensibly, that the mere presence of widespread disagreement does *not*, in fact, give us good reason to be skeptical about a given domain.

Of course, we are currently assuming (if only for the sake of argument) that disagreements in the sciences are *not* sufficiently widespread to fall under the scope of the skeptic's principle. So that particular attempt to challenge the principle is one that we are here putting aside. But that hardly shows the principle to be a plausible one, since it is easy to find other cases where it certainly has unacceptable implications.

As readers familiar with some of the many debates in areas of philosophy other than ethics will already know, there are countless subjects where there is widespread disagreement as to what the facts might be: people argue endlessly about the metaphysical nature of properties, or the nature of substance, or numbers, or space, or time, or causation. Surely, if it is appropriate to say there is widespread disagreement in ethics, then it is also appropriate to say that there is widespread disagreement about all of these topics (and more) in metaphysics. But if we were to accept the skeptic's claim that where there is widespread disagreement it is likely that this is because there are no facts in that domain, we would then have to conclude, accordingly, that (it is likely that) there are no facts about the nature of space, time, causation, substance, and numbers.

Yet any such skeptical claim strikes me as being not merely false, but close to unintelligible. Skepticism about metaphysics is a view that deserves no more than a moment's consideration. That's true regardless of whether we try to imagine the metaphysical skeptic as a nihilist or as a noncognitivist.

Suppose, for example, that we try to imagine a *nihilist* about metaphysics. That would be someone who concludes that the various metaphysical claims people make are indeed truth *apt*—they are trying to describe purported facts about metaphysics—but that all such claims are simply false (because there are no such facts). But what could a view like this possibly mean? How could there be no facts about the nature of space, no facts about the nature of time, no facts about the nature of causation? (No facts at all about when events take place, or whether lighting the fuse caused the bomb to explode, and so on.) Any given metaphysical view might be false, of course, but how could they *all* be false? One would have to deny the very *existence* of space and time and substance and causation, and similarly for other metaphysical categories, pretty much across all of metaphysics. Who could possibly think that such a sweeping skepticism is preferable to deciding, instead, that the skeptic's principle is simply false—that widespread disagreement doesn't actually give us reason to deny the existence of facts in a given domain.

And if anything, an attempt to be a *noncognitivist* about metaphysics (instead of a nihilist) seems even less credible. On such a view, we aren't actually making genuine *assertions* when we put forward our various philosophical theses about the nature of space and time and causation and so on, we are merely expressing our attitudes of approval or disapproval about—well, about *what*? What is it we are supposedly so worked up about? Is it how people *talk* when they are discussing metaphysics? Are we supposed to believe that although there are no right *answers* in metaphysics, we care deeply about what people *say* about these subjects? That seems ludicrous. But if not that, then what? (It is one thing to care deeply about how others act. So noncognitivism about ethics is a view worth taking seriously. But why care deeply about how others speak about time, for example, if there are no facts they are getting wrong?) And if the noncognitivist tells us that when we make metaphysical claims we are doing some *other* job with our metaphysical discourse (not making assertions, and not expressing our preferences), what job could that possibly be?

When we think about the widespread disagreements we find in metaphysics, it is certainly reasonable to conclude that figuring out what the relevant facts *are* is a difficult undertaking. But it seems absurd to conclude, instead, that there simply are no facts at all (about space, time, and so on) to figure out! Accordingly, we have good reason to reject the skeptic's claim that widespread disagreement means it is likely that there are no facts in the given area to be discovered. But, of course, to give up on this general claim is to give

5.2 THE IMPLICATIONS OF DISAGREEMENT

up on the second premise of the skeptic's argument, and so to give up on the argument from disagreement.

This objection could just as easily have been supported by thinking about other areas of philosophy instead of metaphysics. We could have noted widespread disagreements about epistemology, or philosophy of mind, or philosophy of language, and more. If the skeptic were right we would have to conclude that there probably are no facts about the nature of knowledge, no facts about the relationship between the body and the mind, no facts about how words refer, and so on, through a virtually endless list of philosophical subjects. But it is simply not credible to suggest that there are no substantive facts at all about any of these topics. So we have compelling reason to reject the skeptic's principle instead.

There is, as it happens, one particular area of philosophy where the objection I am raising against the skeptic's principle takes a particularly interesting form. The subfield I have in mind is *metaethics*, the part of moral philosophy that attempts to answer second-order questions about the basic nature of morality (including, of course, the possibility that there is no such thing as morality). As we have begun to see—and as we will continue to see in later chapters—metaethics is certainly an area where there is widespread disagreement. Among other issues, realists disagree with skeptics about whether there *are* any substantive first-order moral facts, cognitivists disagree with noncognitivists about whether moral claims are even *attempting* to describe such facts, realists disagree with one another about the *nature* of those facts, and even skeptics disagree with one another about what moral facts would need to be (if there *were* to be such things). Presumably, then, if widespread disagreement in a given domain gave us reason to believe there were no facts for that domain, we would have to conclude as well that there simply are no facts about metaethics!

But what could such a claim conceivably mean? How could there be no facts about whether moral claims are assertions or not, no facts about whether there *are* moral facts or not? Skepticism about metaethics (as distinct from skepticism about normative ethics) seems virtually unintelligible. Yet that seems to be the implication of applying the general principle (that widespread disagreement gives us reason to deny the existence of facts) to the particular case of metaethics. So here too we have a compelling reason to reject the skeptic's principle.

Worse still, think about what it means for the skeptic to appeal to this principle, given its implications for metaethics. If the principle is right, and the best explanation of disagreement in metaethics is that there are no facts about metaethics, then, in particular, there are no facts to the effect that moral skepticism is true! But this is not a view that the skeptic can coherently maintain.

Suppose, for example, that the skeptic is a nihilist. Then they believe that nihilism is the *truth* about ethics. To be sure, the nihilist believes that there are no substantive first-order moral truths. But that doesn't mean that the nihilist thinks there are no *second*-order moral truths, truths about the nature of morality and moral discourse. On the contrary, the nihilist is a cognitivist: she believes that moral claims are *truth apt*, genuine attempts to describe purported moral facts. The nihilist takes that to be the *truth* about moral discourse. But that means that the nihilist is committed to the existence of *metaethical* facts—including, in particular, the fact that (first-order) moral claims are truth apt. So the nihilist cannot coherently embrace a principle that implies that there are no metaethical facts, given that the nihilist takes the very truth of nihilism to *be* a metaethical fact. Accordingly, the nihilist cannot actually embrace the principle in question after all: they must concede that widespread disagreement need not give us good reason to deny the existence of facts concerning a given domain. On pain of undermining their own view, the nihilist must reject the principle we have been examining. And that means, of course, that the nihilist cannot put forward the argument from disagreement (or at least, not in its current form).

The noncognitivist does no better. For noncognitivism is also a substantive view within metaethics—it is the substantive claim that moral discourse is not, in fact, used to make genuine assertions. The noncognitivist takes this to be a fact about first-order moral discourse. Thus the noncognitivist too is committed to the claim that there are metaethical facts, since she takes the very truth of noncognitivism to be such a metaethical fact. So the noncognitivist cannot embrace the principle in question either! On pain of undermining her own view, the noncognitivist must reject the principle, and thus she cannot use it to put forward an argument from disagreement.

To belabor the point a moment longer, the nihilist and the noncognitivist are both attempting to say something *true* about first-order moral claims (although they disagree about what the truth is). So if either position is correct, then there are second-order *metaethical* facts (about the nature of first-order claims). Thus neither can coherently embrace a principle that implies that most likely there are no metaethical facts at all. So neither can coherently put forward an argument that appeals to such a principle.

In short, not only will the realist want to reject the skeptic's principle, not only will all of us who think there are facts about metaphysics and other branches of philosophy want to reject the principle, even the *skeptic* has compelling reason to reject it.

It is conceivable that the attack on the skeptic's principle can be taken even further. I imagine that the sorts of considerations I have been raising as challenges to that principle will be convincing to many. But it also seems likely that there will be still others who will remain attracted to it. Perhaps then we should acknowledge that the issue remains controversial; there is disagreement about whether the principle is true.

Would it be fair to say that there is *widespread* disagreement about the principle? Surely even those who accept the principle must acknowledge that it wouldn't be close to the truth to insist that *most* of us accept it. At most, then, those who accept the principle can only assert that although the principle is true, there is widespread disagreement about it.

But if that's right, then shouldn't we apply the principle to itself? Suppose for the moment that the principle is true and so where there is widespread disagreement we have reason to believe that there are no facts about the relevant subject matter. If there is indeed widespread disagreement about whether the principle is true, it would then follow—given the truth of the principle—that we have reason to believe that there is no fact about whether the principle is true! But if there is no *fact* of the matter about whether the principle is true, then it cannot be true! So if the principle is true we have reason to believe that isn't actually true at all. Thus the principle might undermine itself. Anyone who puts it forward is likely to find themselves in a situation where, at best, they have to admit the principle probably isn't true. But if it probably isn't true, why are they appealing to it?

(Could a fan of the principle try to wiggle out of this objection by insisting that the principle doesn't apply to itself, since almost everyone *rejects* it? Perhaps. But they would then be in the uncomfortable position of having to claim that where there is widespread *disagreement*, there is probably no fact of the matter, yet where almost everyone *rejects* a view, it might yet be true! Obviously, there is nothing to commend such a position.)

Thus, it may turn out to be paradoxically incoherent to put forward the skeptic's principle. Arguably, if it *were* true, we would have reason to believe it probably isn't. In contrast, there is nothing incoherent at all about simply rejecting it: after all, if it is false that disagreement indicates the absence of facts, then even if there is disagreement about the principle, that won't give us any reason to deny that it is a *fact* that the principle is false. So while affirming the principle may be incoherent, rejecting it is not.

Whether or not this last charge—that the skeptic's principle refutes itself—is correct, we have already seen other reasons to reject it. So it looks as though the moral realist has a compelling answer to the argument from disagreement, namely, that even if we grant the first premise of the argument (the claim that there is widespread disagreement about first-order moral questions), we still have good reason to reject the *second* premise of that argument. The bottom line, I suppose, is this: in and of itself, disagreement simply doesn't tell us much of anything at all about whether to look for corresponding facts.

5.3 Explaining Moral Disagreement

The argument from disagreement as we have been interpreting it fails because one of its premises is implausibly broad. It simply isn't plausible to insist that the best explanation of widespread disagreement is usually or even typically that there simply are no facts with regard to the given domain. Although there may be some cases where that is indeed the best explanation, it certainly isn't true across the board, and for all we know (given all the counterexamples) it may not even be the best explanation in *most* cases.

But this diagnosis points the way to a different form the argument might take, one that might fare better. Instead of offering broad generalizations about what normally explains, or is most likely to explain, widespread disagreement, the skeptic might try focusing more narrowly on the particular case that concerns her—moral disagreement. The skeptic doesn't actually need a principle to the effect that widespread disagreement is probably best explained *wherever it occurs* by the nonexistence of relevant facts; it will suffice if she argues that in the particular case of *moral* disagreement the best explanation is the skeptical one.

An argument of this more focused kind requires a comparison of a sort that wasn't necessary before. If it really were the case that skeptical explanations of widespread disagreement were usually correct (or were likely to be correct) that would suffice to give us at least a presumptive reason to believe that this was the correct explanation for moral disagreement as well. But once we restrict the skeptic's claim to one about *moral* disagreement, so that the skeptic is only claiming that skepticism is the best explanation here, rather than more generally, it becomes necessary to compare the skeptic's explanation of moral disagreement to any alternative explanations that might be offered by the moral realist instead. We can no longer think, "Skepticism is *usually* the best explanation of widespread disagreement, so it is probably the best explanation for disagreement in morality as well." Instead, we have to actually look and see how the skeptic's explanation measures up when compared to the alternatives put forward by the realist. Of course, despite these differences, the underlying thought remains the same as before: moral disagreement needs to be explained, and the best explanation of that disagreement is the skeptical hypothesis that there simply are no moral facts to guide or push us toward one set of moral assertions rather than another.

(Note that whether we accept moral skepticism or not, it does at least seem *coherent* to deny the existence of moral facts, so that at the very least, skepticism about morality is not a complete nonstarter. In contrast, as we noted, it is almost unintelligible to deny the existence of metaphysical facts, or metaethical facts, so that skepticism there was never really a serious possibility. That's why the current version of the argument might succeed even if the original does not.)

So what we need to do is to compare skeptical and realist explanations of moral disagreement. If we decide that the best explanation involves the denial of moral facts, that gives us a reason to accept that explanation and thus embrace moral skepticism. But everything will turn on our considered judgments of how the proposed explanation compares to any alternative explanations which might actually be compatible with realism. The argument's success ultimately depends on our agreeing that the relevant skeptical hypotheses are better explanations than any realist alternatives. Accordingly, we can start by asking what, exactly, the skeptic's explanation comes to.

The basic idea is clear enough: we disagree about moral matters because there are no moral facts to constrain or shape our beliefs about these questions. Our moral beliefs "spin freely" without coming into contact with a moral reality that might push them in one direction rather than another. But the details of this explanation will vary, depending on whether the skeptic is a nihilist or a noncognitivist.

If the skeptic is a nihilist, they will say something like this: Our moral disagreements are genuine theoretical disagreements. We correctly take ourselves to be attempting to describe the moral landscape. But we disagree because there is no landscape to be described!

Note, however, that any such explanation is seriously incomplete as it stands. We will want to ask the nihilist why we take there to *be* a moral landscape, given that there isn't one, why we think there *are* moral facts when there actually aren't any. Furthermore, even granting that we do labor under such an illusion, we will want to know, what are the processes that lead us to form the particular moral beliefs that we do? More particularly, why do these processes lead us to form *different* moral beliefs? To insist that our moral beliefs are not constrained by a moral reality is not yet to explain why we end up with beliefs that vary from person to person.

At this point the nihilist will need to help herself to one or another psychological explanation, an explanation that will offer an account not only of why we would take there to be moral facts if there are none, but of why we would end up with differing views about those nonexistent facts. (Why don't the relevant psychological processes lead us, instead, to a *shared*, though mistaken, moral perspective?) I won't here try to examine the psychological hypotheses that the nihilist might offer. I will only pause to note that until some such account is on offer it may be premature for the nihilist to triumphantly announce that they have the superior explanation of moral disagreement.

Suppose, next, that the argument from disagreement is put forward by a noncognitivist, rather than a nihilist. Their explanation of moral disagreement will inevitably differ in at least some of the details. According to noncognitivism, after all, our moral disagreements are not theoretical disagreements at all, only practical ones. If we take ourselves to be attempting to describe a moral landscape then we are confused about what it is that we are actually up to, since moral "claims" are not genuine claims, but only expressions of attitudes or disguised imperatives. Keeping this point in mind, if we now ask why people disagree morally, the answer is simply that people differ in terms of how they want others (and themselves) to behave. In the absence of moral facts putting pressure on our preferences, people just end up endorsing or condemning different types of behavior.

But this explanation is incomplete as it stands as well. Here, too, we want to hear more. There is, of course, the obvious question, of why so many of us take ourselves to be attempting to describe a moral landscape if this isn't actually what we are doing at all. (And if the noncognitivist replies that we are misled by the surface grammar—the fact that moral claims take the form of statements—we can then ask, why have we adopted such a misleading linguistic form?) Beyond this, however, there is the further question: even if all we are doing in making moral claims is expressing attitudes and issuing

5.3 EXPLAINING MORAL DISAGREEMENT

imperatives, why do our preferences on these matters differ so much? To insist that our attitudes and preferences are not constrained by any sort of moral reality is not yet to explain why we end up with *different* attitudes and preferences.

So the noncognitivist too will need to avail herself of some further psychological hypotheses, if she is to genuinely provide us with an account of moral disagreement. We will want to know not only what psychological (or linguistic) processes lead us to express our attitudes in such a potentially misleading way, but also why people vary so much, from one to the next, in terms of the underlying attitudes to which we are giving voice. Here too, I won't try to examine the different hypotheses the noncognitivist might propose. I merely repeat the point that until some such account is actually given it is premature for the noncognitivist to assume that their own explanation (once it is provided) will be superior to the realist alternatives.

So both the nihilist and the noncognitivist versions of the argument from disagreement are incomplete. Details still need to be filled in. Of course, in making this observation I do not mean to imply that the requisite psychological accounts cannot be provided. Indeed, various potential hypotheses have no doubt already begun to suggest themselves to you. But if nothing else, recognizing the gaps in the skeptical explanations should put us on guard against rushing to embrace the argument's conclusion. We can hardly confidently affirm that moral skepticism provides the best account of moral disagreement if we haven't really been told how the skeptic proposes to explain that disagreement in the first place.

Still, let us suppose, as seems likely, that plausible-sounding hypotheses can be provided, so that one or the other or both of the two skeptical explanations can be made more complete.

(It is important not to be confused about what these explanations would need to do. Just as the skeptic need not claim that moral realism is somehow *incompatible* with the existence of disagreement, she need not claim that if moral skepticism is true this somehow *guarantees* (or even makes it likely) that we will have widespread moral disagreement. She only needs to claim that given the *existence* of disagreement, skeptical explanations of it are better than the realist alternatives.)

Before turning to particular realist explanations of moral disagreement, it is worth reminding ourselves that there must indeed be *some* explanations of disagreement that are compatible with realism. As we have already noted, there are disagreements even within physics—and chemistry, and biology, and psychology—yet despite these disagreements we continue to embrace a realist stance toward these subjects. So there must be processes or "mechanisms" capable of generating disagreements which are nonetheless compatible with realism. Presumably, then, even the skeptic will concede that there are realism-compatible explanations of disagreement.

But if there are explanations of disagreement compatible with realism, why shouldn't we appeal to them even when it comes to ethics? Even if we suppose that disagreement is *more* widespread in ethics than in physics, why can't we appeal to realism-compatible explanations for *both* subjects?

The skeptic's answer, of course, is that when it comes to ethics (whatever might be the case elsewhere), the skeptical explanations are *superior* to the realist ones. For even if it is true, as I claimed above, that the skeptical explanations are a bit thin on details, even a "thin" explanation is preferable to having none at all—or to the bare assertion that there must be realist-compatible explanations of moral disagreement of *some* sort, since there are realism-compatible mechanisms that explain disagreement elsewhere. If the best the realist can do is to hold out the vague hope that some sort of explanation compatible with moral realism *must* exist, then perhaps we really should agree that the skeptic has the better of the argument.

The truth, however, is that the realist isn't at all limited to offering vague promises about possible realist explanations.

Let's start with a possibility that is easy to overlook. As I have already explained, if the skeptic is to offer anything like an adequate account of moral disagreement, they will inevitably need to supplement their initial account with an appeal to one or more psychological processes that (they will claim) play a central role in generating our different moral beliefs. These processes, whatever exactly they are, need to be capable of leading us to *diverging* moral beliefs.

But if there really are psychological processes that can have this effect, then why can't the moral realist simply appeal to them as well? That is, if the psychological mechanisms in question are capable of explaining differences of opinion on moral issues, why shouldn't the moral realist simply help herself to an explanation based on those very same mechanisms? Why can't the realist say that although there really are moral facts, these psychological mechanisms—the same ones appealed to by the skeptic—get in the way of our reaching *agreement* about these facts?

The problem for the skeptic is this. It looks like the *skeptical* portion of the skeptic's explanation isn't doing any real work toward explaining moral *disagreement*. Rather, it is the appeal to the relevant psychological mechanisms, whatever they might be, that explains our differences of opinion. But if that's right, then the realist can, it seems, appeal to these very same processes, thus offering an explanation of moral disagreement that is nonetheless fully compatible with realism.

If this is correct, then it won't be possible for the skeptic to claim that skepticism offers a better explanation of disagreement than realism can offer. For the realist will be able to offer the very same explanation as the skeptic does, once the skeptic's explanation is stripped of its inessential elements. All the skeptic will have done is offer an explanation fully compatible with realism, but an explanation that is wrapped up in eliminable skeptical garb. If it really is true that the skeptical elements of that explanation are doing no explanatory work, the skeptic will have inadvertently provided the realist with a suitable realism-compatible explanation.

So we need to ask: is it indeed *true* that the skeptical addition to the promised psychological account adds nothing essential to the adequacy of that explanation? Conceivably the skeptic might claim that the relevant psychological processes are only capable of generating disagreement in the *absence* of moral facts—that if there *were* moral facts the processes in question would be incapable of leading us to differing moral beliefs (or at least, would be incapable of leading to disagreement on the scale that we actually find). If that's right, then perhaps the moral realist cannot avail herself of the very same explanations after all. However, until the skeptic actually tells us what the relevant psychological processes *are*, and then shows us why they would generate disagreement only in the *absence* of moral facts, it is difficult to see why we should grant the skeptic this further claim.

Speaking personally, I find this initial realist reply intriguing, though I wouldn't want to put a great deal of weight on it. Happily, however, the realist can do even better. Instead of waiting for the skeptic to fill in the missing details of their own account, and then trying to show why these same processes—whatever they turn out to be—are compatible with realism, the realist might simply proceed ahead on their own terms, taking the initiative and pointing to explanations of moral disagreement that do seem clearly compatible with moral realism.

As it happens, there are at least two plausible realist proposals that deserve our attention. The first starts with the observation that many of our moral beliefs depend on relevant *nonmoral* beliefs. Thus, to take an easy example, my belief that it would be wrong to serve you this cup of tea may depend on my empirical belief that it contains poison! In effect, the particular belief in question is a "derivative" one: I have an underlying belief that it is wrong to harm others, and when this combines with the relevant nonmoral beliefs (that this tea contains poison, and that drinking poison will harm you), together they yield the (derivative) moral conclusion that I shouldn't give you the tea. If I didn't believe the tea was poisoned, I wouldn't believe it wrong to serve it to you.

Imagine, next, that Abigail believes that this is an ordinary cup of tea. She might then think it permissible (or conceivably even obligatory) for me to serve you the tea, since she knows how thirsty you are, and believes that drinking tea will help quench your thirst. Here too, the particular belief in question—that it is permissible to serve the tea—is a derivative one, depending as it does on Abigail's empirical belief that the tea will be good for you.

So here we have a case of moral disagreement. Abigail thinks it permissible to serve you the tea, while I think it forbidden. But this disagreement is completely explicable in terms of our varying nonmoral beliefs, and it is easy to see why disagreements of this sort pose no threat to moral realism. For even if there are moral facts—including, in this instance, whether it is wrong to serve the tea—those moral facts often depend on nonmoral facts. So when we disagree about those nonmoral facts, as we do here, we will disagree about the derivative moral facts as well. In cases like this the explanation of our moral disagreement is perfectly compatible with the truth of moral realism; our moral disagreement is simply due to whatever it is that explains our disagreement about the relevant nonmoral facts.

Admittedly, if there were no fact of the matter concerning the relevant *empirical* question this might in turn entail that there would be no fact of the matter concerning the derivative moral question either. But no one is tempted to infer skepticism about empirical facts from this sort of familiar empirical disagreement. So to the extent that *moral* disagreements can be explained in terms of underlying disagreements concerning *nonmoral* matters, the explanation of those moral disagreements will be one that is compatible with moral realism.

(Of course, if it really is true that disagreements are more widespread when it comes to ethics than it is when it comes to, say, empirical questions, then the moral realist will also have to claim that the nonmoral assertions that play a role in generating our derivative moral beliefs are more controversial, on the whole, than such assertions generally are. Otherwise, we still won't know why we disagree more frequently when it comes to moral questions. Happily, I think it might well be *true* that ethically relevant nonmoral assertions are more controversial overall than their ethically irrelevant siblings—in part for reasons to be given below.)

Suppose we grant that disagreements about derivative moral claims pose no particular threat to moral realism, because the sources of these disagreements can be traced to disputes about nonmoral matters rather than to disputes about the underlying moral principles. That prompts the obvious question, just how much moral disagreement remains, once we focus on the underlying moral principles themselves? While the moral realist hardly has to claim that *all* moral disagreements arise at the derivative level (there are, after all, disagreements about fundamental issues in physics, too, yet we don't normally take that to be a compelling consideration against realism there), still, the more widespread the remaining disagreements, the more troubling the argument from disagreement is likely to seem.

So how widespread are our disagreements concerning basic moral questions? I think the answer is far from obvious. If nothing else, I think we should recognize that once we dig below the surface, countless moral disputes do indeed depend, at least in part, on nonmoral issues, and so are really derivative disagreements after all. To take just a few very quick examples, debates about the legitimacy of capital punishment turn, at least in part, on empirical questions about whether such punishments have a significant deterrence effect, historical justifications for slavery often turned on nonmoral questions about the character and intelligence of Blacks, and religiously based arguments against homosexuality often appeal to nonmoral claims about God's will. (Of course, whether God condemns homosexuality may not be an *empirical* question, but for present purposes it still counts as a *nonmoral* premise.) I suspect—though I cannot prove—that the vast majority of our moral disagreements are indeed about derivative moral claims, thus posing no threat to moral realism at all.

Of course, nothing that I have said is meant to deny that people *do* often disagree even about underlying moral principles. Anyone who has been in a class on moral philosophy (or read any significant amount of the philosophical literature on ethics) knows that. Although, as I have suggested, our sense of the *extent* of that disagreement may be at least in part an artifact of the standard practice of focusing on issues where we disagree rather than agree, I take it to be a plain fact that there are numerous places where people disagree about underlying (rather than derivative) moral issues. Here too, a few examples seem sufficient to establish the point. Thus, people disagree about whether it is always permissible to perform the act with the best results (as consequentialists claim) or whether certain types of acts might be impermissible despite their good results (as deontologists claim); people disagree about whether basic moral rights (like the right not to be harmed) are inviolable, or whether, instead, they can be permissibly overridden when enough is at stake, and if so, how *much* must be at stake before the right is outweighed; and people disagree about how much we are morally required to sacrifice for the sake of helping others or bringing about a morally preferable outcome.

Actually, even here it isn't always clear that all of these disagreements are indeed at the underlying level, in the sense of not depending on still further nonmoral assumptions. For some theories about the ultimate foundations of ethics have the basic normative rules turn on questions about what rules might have good results (rule consequentialism), or what rules rational bargainers might settle upon (contractarianism), or what rules God commands us to obey (divine command theories), and so on. All of these questions seem to involve nonmoral matters as well—whether about the results of alternative rules, the choices of rational bargainers, or the contents of God's will. If so, then even moral principles that would ordinarily be considered relatively "basic" may turn out to be *derivative* in our sense.

Still, I do take it to be the case that there really are moral disagreements that *cannot* be traced to further nonmoral disagreements. So what we would like to know is this: is the amount of disagreement that can be found at this fundamental, nonderivative level sufficiently great that it should trouble us? Just how much disagreement at this level is there, anyway? I imagine that no one really knows for sure.

But be that all as it may, there is a second explanation of moral disagreement available to the moral realist, one that seems available even when we are discussing disagreements at the fully underlying (nonderivative) level. This second explanation starts with the observation that we seem to get *more* disagreement (even in fields where a realist stance seems uncontroversial) when the particular questions being debated speak to our self-conceptions or are relevant to nontrivial human interests. Thus, to take just a few familiar examples, questions about IQ and race, the impact of potential tax cuts on the economy, the causes of climate change, the long-term effects of social welfare programs, and whether one's sex makes a genetic difference to one's psychology, are all subjects of deep and emotional debates. In all of these cases, getting straight on the facts here may ultimately make a difference to how we think of ourselves, how people will be treated, how we will need to behave, and who gets what. With so much at stake, perhaps it shouldn't surprise us that disagreements emerge here—despite these being factual questions—at a greater rate than they do elsewhere.

Intuitively, what we suspect about cases like this is that many of the beliefs in question are held, at least in part, precisely because to hold other beliefs on the given subject might affect some of our significant interests in ways that would be costly or upsetting. It isn't so much that we deliberately *decide* to hold one set of beliefs rather than another because of the advantages (in terms of our interests) in doing so; rather we are unconsciously led to accept (or retain) those beliefs partly because of that advantage. We are unwittingly motivated to find certain beliefs more attractive precisely because of their connection to serving our interests.

This isn't yet to spell out the precise underlying psychological mechanisms that are at work in such cases; but I think we needn't pursue the details here. I presume that we all recognize that there *are* psychological mechanisms capable of producing what we can call *motivated beliefs*. (The thought behind the label, of course, is that in such cases we are at least partially motivated by something other than the desire for truth, and this distorts our ability to *recognize* the truth.)

There are two main ideas worth emphasizing in connection with this concept. First, we would expect to find more disagreement when motivated beliefs are involved, and second, we would expect to find more motivated beliefs in areas where the contested questions more closely touch on nontrivial human interests. Accordingly, in an area where many (let alone all) of the relevant claims have a bearing on significant human interests we shouldn't be surprised to find a lot of disagreement—even if, as we might suppose, realism is true with regard to that domain.

But surely ethics is just such a field! Every aspect of morality touches on significant human interests in countless and varied ways. The facts about morality—supposing for the moment that there really are such facts—will have a direct bearing on how we are to resolve conflicts of interest, how we are to treat one another, what is involved in showing respect for ourselves and others, what we must do for others, what we must avoid doing to others, what we must aim for, what sorts of sacrifices we must make, what sorts of sacrifices we may impose, what sorts of people we must be, and more. In innumerable ways, the facts about morality will make a tremendous difference to whether we can regard the way we live our lives as *acceptable* or not. So if ever there were a field where we might anticipate the existence of significant disagreements as a result of motivated beliefs, surely it is ethics.

Note, furthermore, that motivated beliefs are capable of generating disagreements at all levels of morality, fundamental as well as derivative. Indeed, we might even anticipate that an appeal to motivated beliefs will also explain many of our disagreements about the various *nonmoral* beliefs that figure in our moral deliberations. Precisely because these nonmoral beliefs play a role in supporting corresponding derivative beliefs, our beliefs about these nonmoral facts will connect (indirectly) to significant human interests as well. Accordingly, perhaps we shouldn't be surprised if we find that nonmoral beliefs that figure in moral deliberation are themselves more frequently the subject of disagreement than is ordinarily the case (with nonmoral beliefs more generally).

So an appeal to motivated belief can go a long way toward explaining moral disagreement. Yet as should be clear, there is nothing in such an appeal that is in any way incompatible with the existence of moral facts. An appeal to the mechanisms underlying motivated beliefs can explain why we would find moral disagreement even if moral realism were true.

Of course, none of this shows that moral realism *is* true. Even if these explanations are correct, they don't *require* the truth of moral realism; they are only compatible with it. But establishing the truth of moral realism was not our goal here. Our goal was the more limited one of responding to the (revised) argument from disagreement. And I think it reasonable to hold that our current discussion does suffice to do that. For the skeptic's claim was that the skeptical hypothesis that there are no moral facts is a *better* explanation of moral disagreement than any the realist might propose, and we have now seen at least two highly plausible explanations of moral disagreement that are nonetheless perfectly compatible with the truth of moral realism.

Are these realism-compatible explanations *better* than the skeptic's? I am inclined to think so (especially if it turns out to be true that, once the details of the skeptic's explanations are filled in, the *skeptical* aspects of those explanations play no significant role). But the realist need not insist on this comparative claim. If the skeptic is to provide us with compelling reason to reject the belief in moral realism, they must show that *their* explanations—the skeptical ones—are *better* ones than any the realist might provide. The burden is on them. If they cannot do this—and it seems to me that they cannot—then the existence of moral disagreement need not trouble the moral realist.

5.4 Nonconvergence

There is one more version of the argument from disagreement that merits our attention. Sometimes it is suggested that what is truly problematic for moral realism is not the fact that we *do* disagree, but the fact that such disagreement is inevitable and cannot be eliminated. No matter how long we debate morality—the thought goes—no matter how ideal the conditions under which we discuss it, we will *never* come to (complete) agreement about morality's contents.

We can call this the *nonconvergence claim for ethics*. Spelled out a bit, we can think of it as saying something like this: even if perfectly rational individuals were given full knowledge of all relevant nonmoral facts (including all relevant empirical—and theological!—facts) and were given the ability to recognize various forms of bias and motivated thinking as well as the ability to correct for the influence of these things, even if they were given unlimited time to think about moral questions and to discuss them with one another in a calm and rational manner, carefully weighing and evaluating all the relevant arguments, it would *still* be the case that they would disagree about at least some moral issues.

There is, I think, no need to quibble about whether I've actually listed all the conditions required for ideal moral deliberation. If you happen to think that I have overlooked something that deserves to be added to the list, feel free to add it. We should construe the nonconvergence claim as holding that *whatever* the ideal conditions might be, even under *those* conditions moral disagreements would not altogether disappear. Though we might reach agreement about derivative moral matters in those cases where we shared the same underlying moral commitments (given the stipulation of perfect knowledge of relevant nonmoral facts), moral disagreement would never disappear completely. Even under ideal conditions, moral beliefs would never totally converge.

The skeptic might then suggest that this is quite different from what would be the case with regard to scientific fields, like physics or psychology. Here, although it is certainly the case that there *are* disagreements about various questions, nonetheless under *ideal* conditions—given enough time and resources to run all the relevant experiments and evaluate all the evidence, given the ability to identify and correct for biases and motivated thinking, and so on—perfectly rational individuals would eventually agree about all empirical questions. That is to say, unlike the case for ethics, with the empirical sciences we *would* have convergence under ideal conditions.

Suppose, for the moment, that these two claims are correct—convergence for the sciences, nonconvergence for ethics—what would that show? The skeptic might then claim that they provide us with reason to reject moral realism. The argument would go like this: In domains where there *are* substantive, first-order facts (like physics or psychology), under ideal conditions we would get convergence of beliefs. But we would *not* have convergence in ethics, even under ideal conditions. So there are no substantive (first-order) moral facts and moral realism must be rejected.

To evaluate this argument let's start by asking what work is done by the claim that we *would* get convergence in the sciences. Why didn't the skeptic simply argue as follows: we would get convergence in domains where there are genuine facts, but we wouldn't get it in ethics, so realism in ethics is mistaken. Why mention the empirical sciences at all?

The answer, of course, is that if we didn't agree that we would get convergence in the sciences, we would never be prepared to grant the first premise of the skeptic's argument—that where there are facts, there would be convergence. For I take it that we are far more confident that realism is the appropriate view when it comes to the sciences than we are about the skeptic's sweeping claim to the effect where there are facts it must be the case that under ideal conditions there would be convergence. Accordingly, if we were to conclude that even in the sciences there might *not* be convergence (even under ideal conditions), we would never grant the skeptic the first premise of their argument.

So perhaps we should ask, is it really true that under ideal conditions we would get convergence of belief with regard to all scientific questions? I don't think the answer is at all obvious. No doubt, given unlimited time and resources to undertake scientific investigations we would reach agreement about many, perhaps even most, scientific questions. But would we necessarily reach agreement about *all* of them? (To take just a few examples, *must* we get convergence about whether there was anything before the Big Bang (and if so, what it was like)? About whether the hidden variable interpretation of quantum mechanics is true? About whether there is a unified field theory for all of physics?) Couldn't it be the case that for at least some scientific questions (in physics and elsewhere), disagreements would remain, even under ideal conditions for inquiry?

If you are prepared to allow for the possibility that disagreements might remain in science even under ideal conditions, then you will want to reject the skeptic's assumption that where there are facts it must be the case that there would be convergence. But the truth of the matter is, no matter what your prediction about convergence in science, it is difficult to see why we should agree that any such claim must hold true across the board, in *all* areas of inquiry, no matter what. Why couldn't there be truths in some domain that are simply too hard to figure out, no matter what the conditions under which we investigate? Why in the world should we agree that the mere existence of facts in a given domain somehow *guarantees* that under suitable conditions there would be convergence of belief about that domain? Speaking personally, I don't think it is remotely clear that we should grant the skeptic the first premise of their argument.

But suppose, nonetheless, that we do decide to grant this premise. There remains the further question: why believe the *second* premise of the skeptic's argument? Why should we accept the nonconvergence claim for ethics? Is it indeed true that even if we were perfectly rational and were reflecting on moral questions under ideal conditions we would, nonetheless, continue to have moral disagreements?

As far as I can see, we haven't the slightest idea whether this is so or not. Certainly we don't have any particularly compelling evidence on the question, one way or the other. At the very least, it seems obvious to me that our *current* conditions are so extremely far from any set of ideal conditions for moral inquiry that it would be foolish to try to extrapolate from our *actual* disagreements to any conclusion to the effect that such disagreements are inevitable.

Indeed, if it really is *true* that where there are facts there would be convergence of belief under suitable conditions of inquiry, then why shouldn't the moral realist simply insist that the nonconvergence claim for ethics is false? After all, if there really are moral facts—as the moral realist believes—then once we grant the skeptic's claim that facts guarantee convergence (under ideal conditions), it will follow that we *would* have convergence after all. In the absence of independent reason to think otherwise, there is no particular reason for the realist to agree that we would never get convergence in ethics.

I suspect that for those who offer the argument from disagreement (in its current form) it simply seems *obvious* that the nonconvergence claim for ethics is true. It isn't so much that there is any compelling evidence (or for that matter, any evidence at all) that we could never get convergence in ethics; rather this is simply a thought that seems obvious to those who are independently drawn to moral skepticism.

But if I am right about this, then this isn't so much an argument *for* skepticism as it is an expression *of* skepticism. Ultimately it does nothing more than beg the question against the moral realist. It seems obvious to the skeptic that there *are* scientific facts, and so they posit (without real argument) that there would be convergence in science; it seems obvious to the skeptic that there aren't any *moral* facts, and so they posit (without real argument) that there *wouldn't* be convergence in ethics. The skeptic has no real argument for either of these claims; it is simply that they seem overwhelmingly plausible to her. But the reason that they seem so plausible to the skeptic is precisely because she is already convinced that although there are scientific facts there are no moral ones. And while we understand her position, that isn't the same thing as her having given us reason to share it.

I conclude, accordingly, that the facts about moral disagreement do not provide the basis for a convincing argument against moral realism. While it may be distressing that we continue to disagree about moral questions—given the central importance morality should play in our lives—the existence of such disagreement does not give us reason to embrace skepticism. For all that we have seen so far, the realist can simply retain the view they put forward at the start of the chapter, that although there are moral facts they can be difficult to figure out, and so we sometimes disagree about them. There is nothing more to moral disagreement than that.

6

Relativism

6.1 Moral Relativism

According to *moral relativism*, morality is not absolute, but rather varies from society to society. Indeed, it may vary from one group to the next, even within a given society, or from one period to the next. Since there is no such thing as a single, unique moral code—valid across all places and all times—what a person ought to do in any given case depends on the particular moral code that happens to hold in their society (or group) at that time. Roughly speaking, one ought to conform to the code of one's society.

Is a view like this a form of moral skepticism? Certainly many people think of relativism in this way, including many of those who accept the view. The relativist denies the existence of a universally valid moral code. They reject the existence of an objective morality (in at least one natural reading of that term). What more could it take to be a skeptic about morality?

In fact, however, the issue is somewhat more complicated than it might initially appear. For on what I take to be the most common form of relativism, moral relativism actually seems to be a form of moral realism! After all, according to the relativist there is a *fact* about what the given person should do in any given situation: they should conform to the code of their society. And this seems to mean that there are indeed substantive first-order moral facts. If, for example, killing in self-defense is permitted by the moral code of your society, then according to relativism it is a *fact* that it is permissible for you to kill in such a case. And if, in contrast, killing in self-defense is forbidden by the code of your society, then according to relativism it is a fact that it is forbidden for you to kill. What the facts *are* will depend on the contents of your particular society's code, but for all that, there will indeed be moral facts about what you are permitted to do. Similarly, of course, for other moral issues. So whatever else is true of the relativist, she seems to be a realist.

Of course, sometimes people who embrace something they *call* "moral relativism" use this as the name for a view whose bottom line is that there really are no facts about what people ought to do at all (since different societies endorse different moralities). But this is not how we will be using the term. We will use it for the view just described, according to which there are indeed facts about what one ought to do, but the facts *vary*, depending on your society. And as I just noted, this makes the relativist a realist.

But still, we might ask, is the relativist really a *moral* realist? Do the obligations she posits genuinely count as moral obligations? More broadly, are the various first-order, substantive claims she puts forward really *moral* claims? The relativist clearly believes in facts of some sort, and she may well use moral language to describe them—talking, for example, about what is or is not morally permissible for a given person to do—but is it truly appropriate to describe these facts as facts about morality?

Your answer, unsurprisingly, will depend on what all you build into your concept of morality. If you built into the very job description of morality a requirement that basic moral principles must be universal (if there really is to be such a thing as morality at all), valid at all places and at all times, then the facts posited by the relativist will not count as moral facts, precisely because the relativist is open to the possibility that the basic principles vary (at least to some extent) from society to society. A bit more precisely, if you consider it an *essential* element of the job description that the basic principles be absolute, then you will consider it unacceptable for the relativist to hold that these principles may vary from one society to the next.

The situation is even worse if you consider it an essential element of the job description that basic moral truths must be *necessary* truths, holding across all possible worlds. (Recall the distinction—explained in 1.2—between requiring that moral truths be universal or absolute, and requiring that they be necessary.) For even if it should accidentally turn out to be the case that all actual societies accept the very same moral code, presumably it *could* have been otherwise. For the relativist, then, moral principles are not necessary, but contingent. Accordingly, if you think that anything worthy of the name morality must involve some basic truths that hold at all places and at all times—and especially if you think that these basic truths must be *necessary* ones—then you will conclude that if anything like relativism is true, there really is no such thing as morality after all.

Thus, anyone who includes necessity or absolutism as nonnegotiable elements of the concept of morality will want to say that what the relativist offers us isn't truly morality at all. Seen from this perspective relativism is indeed a form of *skepticism* about morality, and the relativist is indeed a kind of moral skeptic.

I imagine that most—not all, but most—of those who reject moral relativism do in fact think of it in these terms, that is, as a skeptical view. And, I suspect that the same thing is true even for those who *accept* moral relativism. That is to say, I suspect that even most moral relativists—not all, but most—think that if relativism is true (as they take it to be) then there isn't really such a thing as objective morality after all.

As I explained in an earlier chapter (in 2.4), I don't think it worth our time to try to settle whether a view like this is "really" a skeptical view or not. How you want to classify it will depend on which elements of morality's job description you consider nonnegotiable.

For similar reasons, I think that there is also little point in trying to settle the question of whether the facts posited by the relativist count as *objective* or not (again, see 1.2.) Certainly in one ordinary use of the term, they do count as objective, for there will be right and wrong answers about what, for example, a given person is permitted to do. If the code of the relevant society permits a given act it is permissible for the person to perform that act, full stop, and anyone who says otherwise is simply mistaken. Admittedly, *whether* the act is permissible will depend on facts about the agent in question (since it depends on whether the act is permitted by the code of *their* society), and so may vary from person to person (as we move from one society to the next), but all of this is compatible with there being an objective fact about what any given individual is permitted to do.

That this kind of relativity is compatible with objectivity (in one ordinary use of the term) is a familiar point in other contexts. Consider, for example, facts about diet and nutrition. These are often relative, depending on the particular individual in question. It might be, for example, that one person has a calcium shortage, and so should eat a diet that is rich in dairy products, while a second person is lactose intolerant, and so should avoid dairy products as much as possible. In cases like this, facts about what it would be good for a person to eat will vary, depending on the person in question. And yet, for all that, we would ordinarily say that there are *objective* facts, in any given case, about what the person should eat. The facts may be relative, but there are right and wrong answers for any given case, and in that sense of the term the relevant facts are objective ones. Similarly, then, even if moral relativism is true—so that the facts about what one should do can vary, depending on one's society—there will still be right answers in any given case about what someone is permitted to do (and so forth), and in that sense, at least, the relevant facts will be objective ones, not mere matters of opinion.

On the other hand, sometimes when people talk about something being an objective matter, they have in mind the idea that the relevant facts should not depend in any way on the beliefs, reactions, or attitudes of any particular minds. To be objective, in this second sense of the term, the facts in question must be mind *independent*. In *this* sense of the term, facts about chemistry, say, are objective ones, whereas facts about what's fashionable are not. To be sure, there may well be right answers about what is in fashion in any given place and time, but since such facts clearly depend on the tastes and attitudes of the relevant members of society, in this second sense of the term facts about fashion are not objective.

Given this second sense of the term, some people will find themselves inclined to say that if relativism is true then even though there may be facts about what a given person should or should not do (and so on), these are not objective facts at all. For as we will see, the most prominent versions of moral relativism are *constructivist* ones, where moral facts boil down to facts about the attitudes and reactions of the relevant minds. So if you think of mind independence as a requirement for genuine (or complete) objectivity, you aren't likely to think that a defense of moral relativism would constitute a defense of an *objective* morality.

Unsurprisingly, my own view is that just as there is little point in belaboring the question of whether under relativism the so-called moral facts are truly *moral* facts or not, there is also little point in trying to settle whether these facts truly count as objective or not. What does seem clear, I think, is that many people will find themselves inclined to *view* relativism as a form of skepticism, so I think it worth our time to ask whether there is good reason to *accept* relativism or not.

Furthermore, even those with a sufficiently encompassing conception of morality (and objectivity) as to allow for the possibility of moral principles that are relative rather than absolute may well be troubled or unhappy at the thought that this might turn out to actually be the case. It is one thing to say that relative moral rules would indeed still count as objective moral rules (provided that they are action guiding, reason giving, and so on); it is quite another thing to be indifferent as to whether or not moral principles really are socially relative in this way. So even if you don't think of relativism as a form of skepticism about objective morality, you may still wonder whether we have any good reason to believe in it.

One last point. If moral relativism is to be an interesting position, the kinds of moral differences it posits must be at a fairly deep level. After all (to return to a point noted already in 1.2), even those who believe in universal moral principles agree that differing circumstances will generate differences in terms of derivative moral obligations. If I have made a promise, and you have not, I have an obligation that you lack. That kind of relativity doesn't trouble those who believe in absolute moral principles. Similarly, then, if the moral code of your society requires something that the moral code of my society does not, but this is simply due to different circumstances in our two societies—so that the very same underlying principle can yield these distinct but derivative obligations—that too will not constitute the kind of relativity that the absolutist will find troubling. What the moral relativist believes, but the defender of absolute morality denies, is that there is relativity even at the level of the underlying, *fundamental* moral principles.

It is important not to lose sight of this point, since it is easy to be misled by surface differences. Different societies might have different ways of showing respect, for example, or they may adopt different conventions with regard to the division of moral labor, thus generating different role-based obligations. But as long as these are expressions of the same underlying principles (for example, a requirement to show respect, or a requirement to do one's part in achieving important social goals), cases like this needn't trouble the absolutist. If moral relativism is to be an interesting position—a challenge to the absolutist—it must posit differences in even the *basic* moral principles. That, at any rate, is how I shall understand it.

6.2 Clarifying Relativism

According to moral relativism, what a given person should do depends on the moral code of their society. Relativity comes in once we acknowledge the possibility that the moral code for one society may be different (in significant ways) from the code for a different society.

That's the basic idea, at any rate, and for many purposes that's probably enough. But there are a few further issues about the nature of relativism that it may be worth our noting before we turn to considering arguments for the view itself. First, and perhaps most importantly, we need to get more precise about who, exactly, is bound by a given society's code. Is it the *members* of the society? Or, alternatively, is it those who are located within its *boundaries*?

In ordinary cases these two views converge. If I am a member of a particular society, and I am currently at home, living within its borders, then both the membership and the location versions of moral relativism agree that I am bound by my society's code. But imagine, instead, that I am not at home, but rather temporarily traveling abroad in a society with a rather different moral code. Which code is it, then, that I am to follow? The membership approach says that so long as I remain a member of my original society, it is *that* code that I should obey. But the location approach says that so long as I am visiting the new society it is this *foreign* moral code that applies to me. The same question arises, of course, with regard to foreigners visiting *my* society: should they obey the code of *their* home society, or the code of *my* society? The membership view says the former; the location view, the latter.

Consider the saying "When in Rome, do as the Romans do," which is sometimes used as a quick expression of relativism. When used in this way it seems to be an expression of *location* relativism. Nonetheless, I suspect that if it is genuinely *moral* relativism that we are thinking about—where the issue is which fundamental *moral* principles one should obey, and not simply a question of diet or dress or etiquette—I suspect that most people have something more like member relativism in mind. So that is the version I will focus on, and that is why I have talked about relativism as holding that an individual ought to obey the code of *their* society. (Perhaps, then, the view should be expressed as "When you are a Roman, do as the Romans do.")

We might still want to ask, however, what is a person to do if they are a member of more than one group or society (with diverging codes)? Someone might be an American *and* a Hindu *and* a member of the Mob. If, as we might readily imagine, the moral codes of these three groups differ from one another, which code is the relevant one for the person to obey?

Should we go for the code of the largest group? The smallest? The group with which the person most identifies? Should we somehow try to identify the places where the relevant codes agree, and then just disregard the rest? Or might it be that some of these groups are of the wrong *sort* (from the perspective of moral relativism) and so don't even *count* as "societies" in the first place?

I don't think it is at all obvious what the relativist's answer to this question should be. So I propose to leave the issue unresolved. Let's just bracket worries about membership in multiple groups and simplify our discussion by supposing that someone can be a member of only *one* relevant group or society at any given time. (Similar questions would of course have arisen if we had adopted *location* relativism instead, as one might be located within a nested series of larger and larger groups or societies.)

6.2 CLARIFYING RELATIVISM

With this simplifying assumption in place, we can return to our earlier formulations and continue to say that according to moral relativism (as we are understanding it), any given individual should obey the moral code of their society. But this brings us to a different question. Just what is it for a given code to *be* the code "of" a given society? What makes it the case that one code, rather than another, is the code that is valid or relevant? By virtue of what, exactly, is one particular code the code that "morally governs" a society (as we might put it)?

In principle, I suppose, relativism per se is compatible with a variety of different answers to this question. It could be, for example, that there are facts about the climate or the environment (or the location, or the history, and so on) of particular societies that somehow make one code valid or binding for one society, while another code is valid or binding for a different one. But the most common answers, I take it, are *constructivist* ones, where a given code applies to a given society by virtue of facts about the attitudes or reactions of the relevant minds.

And whose minds are the relevant ones? Here too different answers are possible. A relativist could, for example, accept a "divine command" version of constructivism, where the relevant mind is God's. Perhaps God assigns one code to one society, while assigning a different code to another. But I imagine that the most common form of relativism is a *social* version of constructivism, where the relevant minds are those of the members of the given society. More particularly, the most common form of relativism holds that a given code is the relevant one by virtue of the fact that the members of that society *accept* or embrace (or strive to conform to) the code in question. (Which attitudes, precisely, are the crucial ones? Is it a matter of *believing* the principles of the code, or *approving* of acts that conform to the code, or what? For present purposes we need not try to settle this question, though a related issue will be relevant below.)

That's fairly straightforward, as long as we imagine that the various members of a given society agree about fundamental moral questions. If they all accept the same moral code, then that is the code that is valid for their society. But things are less straightforward if we imagine that the members of the society are not, in fact, in complete agreement about the basic moral principles. If some accept one code, while others accept a somewhat different code, is there nonetheless a fact of the matter concerning which code is the code that is valid for that society? Must there be complete agreement (including agreement about all the details), or else no valid code at all?

Presumably not. Presumably the relativist thinks it is possible for a given code to be sufficiently dominant in a given society for that code to be the relevant one, even though some members of the society don't accept it (or disagree about some of the details). The situation here might be similar to what holds with regard to the rules of a society's primary language. I take it, after all, that the rules of Spanish grammar that hold in Mexico, say, are valid by virtue of the fact that Mexican speakers of Spanish largely agree about their content (even if they might have trouble describing the underlying rules explicitly). Presumably it needn't be the case that every single Spanish speaker in Mexico accepts every single rule, or would agree with the majority concerning every single detail of Spanish grammar. Somehow, if there is sufficient agreement among a sufficiently large majority of the relevant population, this suffices to fix the rules of Spanish grammar, even in the absence of unanimity. Something similar might then be proposed by the moral relativist: a code can be the valid one in a given society, even if not all members of that society accept it, and even if some members disagree about some of the relevant details.

(But what if, for some question, the society lacks *sufficient* consensus to fix the content of the code with regard to that question? Perhaps the relativist will say that morality doesn't speak to that question in that particular society. Alternatively, perhaps the relativist will say that those acts not otherwise forbidden by the code are all morally permissible.)

So far, so good. We are taking moral relativism to be a constructivist view where facts about morality depend on details of the code embraced (in the right way) by a sufficient number of the members of the given society. But that raises, in turn, a further question: what will the contents of a given code *look* like? Normally, no doubt, much of the content will be only implicit, embodied in shared understandings (or, perhaps, dispositions) that may never reach the level of fully explicit expression. But suppose that we successfully stated the content of some code, explicitly and precisely. What would that look like?

It is natural to suppose that we might have a set of principles, like "lying is forbidden," or "killing is wrong, except in cases of self-defense," and so on. Perhaps some of the principles will speak to the value of outcomes ("equality is intrinsically valuable") or will stipulate what the most attractive character traits are ("honesty is a virtue"). For our purposes we don't need to worry about the details. What is important, rather, is recognizing that principles like this do not seem to be relativized in terms of who they apply to; they seem to be laying down moral edicts for *everyone*. The first principle, for example, does not say that lying is forbidden *if* you are a member of this society. Rather, this principle is most naturally understood as saying that lying is forbidden, *period*—regardless of whether you are a member of this or any other society. Similarly, the second principle seems to be saying that self-defense is permissible regardless of what society you belong to; it doesn't restrict the permissibility of self-defense to those individuals who happen to belong to the society whose code we are describing. In short, the principles seem to be making universal or absolute claims: such and such acts are permissible for everyone; such and such character traits are virtuous for anyone at all; such and such outcomes are intrinsically good ones regardless of what society you belong to.

But if that's right, then the relativist is in the rather odd position of having to insist that each and every moral code—regardless of its details—is mistaken. For if moral codes ever disagree with one another (and presumably that's what the relativist thinks is often the case), then oddly enough they will all be *wrong*!

Suppose, for example, that one society's code says that some white lies are permissible, while another says that all lies, including white lies, are forbidden. According to the relativist, then, a member of the first society is permitted to tell a white lie (under suitable conditions), while a member of the second society is not. But this means that the first moral code is *mistaken*, insofar as it implicitly claims—incorrectly—that *everyone* is permitted to tell a white lie in appropriate circumstances; and the second code is mistaken as well, insofar as *it* implicitly claims—also incorrectly—that *no one* is ever permitted to tell a white lie. Thus, if relativism is true, and yet moral codes are stated (as they seem to be) in terms of absolute or universal principles, then all of those codes are false! (Of course, not every single principle of every single code would have to be false. If there are principles *shared* across all societies, there is no problem. But wherever principles from two or more codes contradict one another, both principles will turn out to be mistaken.)

Perhaps there are some relativists who are comfortable with this result. (This would certainly reinforce the thought that relativism is indeed a form of moral skepticism.) But most relativists, I imagine, would rather say something like this: each society's code is actually *correct*, not mistaken at all, precisely because it applies only to the members of the corresponding *society*. If a code says, for example, that white lies are permissible, then appearances to the contrary notwithstanding, this doesn't actually mean that white lies are permissible for absolutely *everyone*; what it actually means, rather, is only that white lies are permissible for everyone who is a *member* of this society (that is, the society whose code this is).

On this alternative approach to thinking about the contents of moral codes, there is what we might think of as a hidden relativization parameter. When we say that a given code says that something is permissible, or valuable, or virtuous, and so on, the relevant principles are implicitly *restricted* to being claims about what is permissible (and so on) for those who are members of society S—where "S" stands for the particular society whose code we are describing. The claims do not extend to everyone, but only cover those who are members of the relevant society.

Of course, this implicit relativization may not be obvious at a quick glance. Indeed, when we first try to describe the contents of a given code we may not even recognize that this kind of relativization is taking place. That's the point of describing the relativization parameter as being "hidden." We may not realize it's there. Indeed, even the members of the given society—including people who might otherwise be quite adept at spelling out the contents of their society's code—may not at first recognize that this kind of relativization is taking place.

The situation here (according to this second approach) is similar to what we find when we try to make sense of talk about something being to the left or to the right of something else. Such language *looks* like it is absolute—as though something could be to the left or right of something absolutely, or unqualifiedly, rather than only being to the left or right *relative* to some frame of reference. But in fact, of course, there is no such thing as being to the left of something *full stop*; there is only being to the left of something relative to a frame of reference. That frame of reference might be mine, or it might be yours (if I am speaking to you); it might be the frame of reference you have now, or it might be the one you will have later (once you reach a certain location); and so on. Typically, of course, we don't bother to make the relevant frame of reference explicit—and so at first glance we might *seem* to be making claims about absolute directions. Indeed, very young children sometimes fall prey to this illusion. But whether or not we are fully aware of this fact, our spatial directions always involve a (typically unstated) reference to an implied frame of reference. Left and right is always a relative affair.

Similarly, then, the relativist may say, whether or not we are fully aware of this fact, our moral claims always involve a (typically unstated) reference to a particular society. Morality is always a relative affair. And once we remember to make the relativization parameter explicit, moral relativism no longer has the unsettling implication that all moral codes are false. If a given society's moral code says that telling white lies is permissible, then since it is (implicitly) only making a claim about what is permissible for members of the society whose code this is, then it is making no claims at all about what is permissible for people who are not, in fact, members of that society. And since, according to relativism, each person is bound by the code of their own society, the code will turn out to be correct—rather than mistaken—when it says that people (that is, the *relevant* people) are permitted to tell white lies. And if a different society's code says that lies are *never* permissible, this will be correct as well, since this code too will only be making a claim about a relevant group of people—in this instance, the quite different group of people who are members of that *second* society.

But if we do adopt this second approach to moral relativism, new worries arise. For now, it seems, it turns out that a society can never have a *mistaken* moral code! After all, if we do relativize the claims of moral codes in this way then each code is only making claims about the members of a certain society; and given relativism's insistence that each person should *obey* the code of their society, it follows that the code is *correct* when it makes its various claims.

Indeed, it cannot be otherwise. Whatever the given code says that people are to do, it will necessarily follow—given the truth of moral relativism—that people (that is, the relevant people) are indeed to do just what the code *says* they are to do. No matter what a given society's moral code says, it turns out to be impossible for the code to be mistaken.

Admittedly, in any given instance this or that individual may be mistaken about what the code of their society implies with regard to their particular situation. (And for that matter, those of us who are not members of the society in question may misunderstand what the code implies for those who *are* members.) A code can certainly be misapplied. But with regard to the most basic, underlying principles of the given code, it seems that there is no possibility of the code *itself* being mistaken at all. A society cannot have the wrong moral code.

Is that an unacceptable implication? Many relativists, in any event, will be comfortable with it. Perhaps they will say that the situation is like the one we find with regard to the rules of a given language. Roughly speaking, if enough people in a society consider a given type of sentence grammatical, doesn't it necessarily follow that it *is* grammatical? If everyone in a given society speaks a certain way (and accepts sentences of that sort, and so on), won't it be true, by virtue of that very fact, that this way of speaking is—in that society, at that time—correct? When it comes to the grammar of a given language (or dialect), it seems that there is no possibility of society as a whole being wrong. Individuals may misapply the rules of the grammar, but the rules themselves cannot be mistaken. Perhaps, then, something similar is true with regard to morality.

For closely related reasons, it seems that on this second approach it will also turn out that societies cannot actually *disagree* with one another about fundamental moral matters. For if the claims of a moral code are relativized and restricted to the members of the society whose code it is, then the codes of different societies are talking about different groups of individuals. Even if, for example, one society says that slavery is permissible, while another condemns it, all that is really going on is that the first code is saying that slavery is permissible for members of *that* society, while the second code is saying that slavery is wrong for members of the *second* society. Thus there is no real disagreement. Although it may *look* like the two societies are disagreeing with one another, given the implicit relativization of the codes such disagreement is actually impossible.

To be sure, precisely because the relativization is typically *hidden*, members of one society may not even *realize* that they are not actually making moral claims about members of other societies at all. So people from differing societies may *think* that they are disagreeing with each other about fundamental moral issues; but in fact, they're not.

Of course, people can still disagree with one another about what a given society's code *says*, or what it *implies* about a given situation. But as we have just seen, the code *itself* cannot be mistaken.

Given all of this, however, we might find ourselves wondering: if relativism is true, is anything like moral *reform* truly possible? If someone proclaims that the moral code accepted by their society is misguided in some way—allowing slavery, perhaps, though slavery is actually morally wrong—won't it follow that it is the would-be reformer who is actually mistaken on this point, and not the code itself?

As far as I can see, there are two possible replies the relativist might make. First, although the code itself cannot be mistaken, in at least some cases it does seem possible for there to be common misunderstandings about what the code actually permits. Even if we accept the constructivist account of relativism, where the relevant minds are the members of the given society, there can still be shared misunderstandings about the *contents* of the shared code. (Analogously, the rules of grammar depend on relevant facts about the reactions and attitudes of those who speak the language. But for all that, language speakers can be mistaken about what those rules permit, and these misunderstandings can be widespread.) Perhaps, then, the moral reformer is only attempting to correct some common misunderstandings concerning the contents of the code, rather than criticizing the code itself.

But suppose the reformer does indeed mean to criticize the code itself. Can they coherently do so? Here a second possible reply suggests itself. Suppose that the code of the society in question really does permit slavery. If the reformer gets up and announces that slavery is nonetheless actually morally forbidden, then—given the truth of relativism—what they say is simply *false*. But for all that, the reformer may be able to change hearts and minds. Appealing to some of the other values or sentiments shared by her compatriots, the reformer may succeed in changing underlying attitudes toward slavery. And if the reform movement becomes sufficiently successful, eventually it might be the case that enough minds are opposed to slavery (in the relevant ways) so that it is *no longer* the case that the moral code that obtains in the society permits slavery. In effect, although the reformer will have been speaking incorrectly at the start, if she is successful then what she is saying may end up being the truth. *At first* the code permitted slavery, but now it forbids it. (The analogy to language may be helpful here as well. Initially, when one violates some rule of grammar, one is simply mistaken. But if the ungrammatical way of speaking catches on sufficiently, the linguistic norms may change, and then the formerly ungrammatical form of speech may *become* grammatical.)

6.3 Arguing for Relativism

So far, all we have been doing is *describing* the moral relativist's position. We haven't yet asked whether there is any good reason to believe that relativism is correct. My own view is that despite the perennial appeal of the view (especially among those who have learned something about the moral practices of other societies), there is actually surprisingly little to be said in its favor.

In thinking about the plausibility of relativism it is important to distinguish the *normative* view that interests us—the claim that what a given individual ought to do is to conform to the moral code of their society—from the mere *descriptive* claim that, in point of fact, different societies accept (and have accepted) different moral codes.

Even if the latter is true—a point we will return to in a moment—that wouldn't immediately imply the truth of the former. After all, it seems as though it could be that societies *accept* different codes and yet, for all that, there is nonetheless a uniquely *correct* moral code. It could be, that is to say, that there are basic moral principles that apply to everyone at all places and at all times, and if some society accepts a moral code with principles incompatible with these, then to that extent the code in question is simply mistaken, nothing more.

If that's right, the situation would be analogous to what we think about subjects like, say, astronomy. Some societies have accepted the belief that the earth is flat and that the sun revolves around this flat earth, while other societies have accepted the belief that the earth is round and that this round earth revolves around the sun (rather than the other way around). But no one is tempted to conclude from these differences in astronomical beliefs that somehow the astronomical facts themselves vary from society to society. On the contrary, what we believe is that there is a single, correct theory of astronomy, and if a given society accepts beliefs incompatible with it, then to that extent the beliefs of the society are simply mistaken, nothing more. Similarly, then, even if the moral codes of societies differ in various ways from one another, we don't yet have reason to believe that the *validity* of a given principle somehow depends on which society one happens to be a member of.

For that matter, even if different societies have different moral codes, why not take them, for all that, at face value, as making incompatible but nonetheless absolute claims about how everyone should behave (and what things are good, and what character traits are virtuous, and so on). Instead of positing a hidden relativization (so that each code is speaking only to its own members), why not take these codes to be doing what they certainly *appear to* be doing—making absolute moral claims about everyone—and then conclude, more simply, that in light of these disagreements, at most one of these codes is correct? (Conceivably, of course, *no* society has yet articulated a completely correct moral code.)

Nonetheless, in what I take to be the most common line of thought in favor of moral relativism we do indeed begin with the descriptive claim that different societies have different moral codes. Somehow the fact of such intersocial disagreement is supposed to lend support to the normative claim that interests us, that people should *obey* the code of their own society. Accordingly, let us start by asking—if only briefly—whether it really is true that we find the kind of differences in moral codes that the relativist claims we find.

Given my discussion of disagreement in the previous chapter, it won't surprise you to learn that I am myself skeptical about the confident assertions that are frequently made in this connection. What we are wondering about, after all, is whether different societies accept different views concerning the most fundamental moral principles. Given this focus, it is irrelevant if it turns out that societies often have distinct *derivative* moral beliefs, since these may not indicate any differences concerning the basic principles themselves.

To revert to an earlier example, if one society believes that the death penalty helps deter crime, while another rejects this empirical claim, then this difference in the specified nonmoral *belief* may generate a difference in the social attitude toward the death penalty, even if it turns out that the two societies share the same fundamental views about the justification of punishment. Similarly (a closely related, though not quite identical point), if it turns out the *effects* of different policies would differ in one society as compared to another, then here too the first society might embrace a different value from the second without this indicating any genuine divergence at the level of the most *basic* principles or values. What we need to know, I have been suggesting, is how much difference we would find at the level of *fundamental* moral principles, and this, I suspect, is something concerning which we have far less empirical evidence than is normally assumed.

To be sure, I have previously acknowledged (in 5.3) that people do sometimes disagree about fundamental moral questions. But even this doesn't suffice to establish the point now at issue, since individual differences are irrelevant unless these differences are reflected at the *social* level. For the purpose of defending the claim that different *societies* have different moral codes, it doesn't help at all if, say, one Italian has different moral beliefs from those had by another Italian, or if one American has different beliefs from those had by another American. Rather, it has to be that Italians, on the whole, share the very *same* basic moral outlook, while that outlook differs from a second moral outlook, which is nonetheless shared by most *Americans*. Is anything like that claim true? My own view is that we really just don't know. Many superficial differences will disappear at the fundamental level, so even if there are some broad differences in the ethics of Italians and Americans (or the Japanese, or the ancient Romans, and so on) it is far from clear whether differences remain at the level of fundamental moral principles as well. (For example, comparative anthropologists sometimes argue for the existence of diverse moral codes by pointing to differences in sexual mores and mating practices, or by noting differing beliefs about appropriate ways to show honor and respect. But these are relatively superficial differences and may not reveal anything much about differences at the level of underlying moral principles. Similarly for when anthropologists point to differing conventions concerning the division of moral labor.)

In light of these points, I don't think that it is obvious whether social moral codes really do differ in the fundamental ways that relativists claim they do. But let us suppose that the descriptive claim is indeed true and there are deep differences in the codes of different societies. We still need to ask, why should that lend support to the *normative* claim, that what one ought to do is to obey the code of one's own society?

One initially tempting idea is this. Suppose that the *noncognitivist* is right, and moral claims are actually disguised imperatives, used to issue commands. We have, of course, yet to see convincing reason to *accept* noncognitivism; but for the moment put such concerns aside and simply consider the implications of noncognitivism in the current debate. If moral claims are simply disguised imperatives, then when my society's moral code tells me that, say, killing in self-defense is forbidden, I am being commanded to refrain from killing even in self-defense. But if, in contrast, your society's code says that killing in self-defense is permissible, then you are not being given that same command. Thus, you are being given a different set of commands than I am, precisely because of the fact that you belong to one society while I belong to a different one. So if noncognitivism is correct, and there is nothing more to making a moral claim than the issuing of imperatives (and the expression of the corresponding attitudes of approval and disapproval), doesn't the truth of moral relativism fall out more or less immediately—once we accept the descriptive claim that different societies have different moral codes? Principles are just (disguised) imperatives, and you are bound by one set, while I am bound by another.

Of course, if this defense of relativism is correct, then it was a mistake for me to characterize moral relativism (as I did at the start of the chapter) as a form of moral *realism*, since realism is a form of cognitivism and the argument we are considering presupposes the truth of *non*cognitivism. But we need not linger over this point. If the best defense of moral relativism is noncognitivist, so be it. (This would further vindicate those who view relativism as a form of moral skepticism.)

6.3 ARGUING FOR RELATIVISM

In fact, however, the breezy argument I just sketched is unsuccessful. For the moral relativist is not content to observe that members of different societies are being *given* different commands (*by* their respective societies); they also want to insist, essentially, that what any given individual ought to do is to *obey* the commands of their society.

We must not lose sight of the fact that the relativist is *herself* making a normative claim—that each person *ought* to obey the moral code of their society. And according to noncognitivism this normative claim is itself simply one more imperative, used to issue one more command. In particular, then, according to noncognitivism, the relativist is simply ordering each of us to obey the more specific imperatives contained within the moral codes of our respective societies. And in asking you to embrace relativism, the relativist is asking you to issue a similar imperative (and approve and disapprove of specific acts accordingly).

But why in the world would anyone want to issue such an imperative? Why would I want to tell each person to obey the terms of their society's moral code, regardless of the potentially abhorrent and objectionable things their code might enjoin? Suppose I live in a society whose code condemns slavery, but you live in one whose code permits or even requires it. And suppose as well that I fully embrace my society's condemnation of slavery. Why then would I ever want to command you nonetheless to go along with your society's practice of enslaving others? Far from wanting to command you to obey your society's code, I would presumably want to command you to reject it! And a similar point holds, of course, for any number of other ways in which your moral code might differ importantly from my own. As far as I can see, except in utterly extraordinary circumstances it is almost inconceivable that a reasonable person would ever want to issue a blanket imperative to everyone to obey the codes of their respective societies, *regardless* of what those codes might say. So it is almost inconceivable that a reasonable person would ever be willing to endorse the relativist's position—if this is construed as the noncognitivist would have us construe it.

(Sometimes people advocate moral relativism on the supposed ground that it is a highly tolerant view: let each person obey the code of their own society! Isn't that a reason for issuing the relativist's imperative? Unfortunately, however, there is no requirement within relativism that any given moral code *be* particularly tolerant. The relevant code might require killing others, for example, or forcing them to live lives they despise. Accordingly, no friend of tolerance should be prepared to issue a blanket imperative that tells each person to obey the code of their individual society.)

Suppose we put this attempted noncognitivist defense of relativism aside, and revert to the realist understanding of relativism that we had previously adopted. Relativism might then still turn out to be the truth. For even if we are *unhappy* at the prospect of each person obeying the code of their society (given how objectionable some codes might be), it could still be the simple truth of the matter that this is what each person is required to do. But now our earlier question returns. Supposing that different societies really do have different moral codes, why would that support the normative claim that one *ought* to obey the code of one's society?

The relativist might suggest that the answer to this question was already implicit in our earlier discussion: the truth of moral relativism follows from the descriptive claim (that different societies have different moral codes) once we recognize the truth of *constructivism*. Suppose, after all, that the constructivist is right, and moral facts really do boil down to the attitudes and reactions of the relevant minds. If it really is the case that the accepted moral codes *vary* from society to society, doesn't this show that the relevant *attitudes* of the relevant minds vary in corresponding ways, as we move from one society to the next? (What else could the fact that societies have different codes *consist* in other than the underlying fact that the relevant minds—the minds of their respective members—have different attitudes?) So given the truth of constructivism, won't it follow that basic moral facts really do vary as well, as we move from society to society?

Clearly, one way to resist this argument would be to reject the constructivist viewpoint that it appeals to. Some will insist that if constructivism supports relativism, perhaps that simply gives us a reason to reject constructivism as well. But the truth is, even a constructivist need not find this line of thought especially compelling. Admittedly, if constructivism is true then moral facts do ultimately boil down to the attitudes and reactions of the *relevant* minds. And it certainly does seem plausible to suggest, as well, that a given society's acceptance of a particular moral code ultimately boils down to the attitudes and reactions of its members. But why should we assume, without argument, that since the members of a society are the relevant minds when the question is what code is *accepted* by that society, they must also be the relevant minds when the question is instead what code is *valid* for the members of that society?

6.3 ARGUING FOR RELATIVISM

For example, couldn't a constructivist hold that it is *God's* will that settles the question of our obligations, even though it is presumably our *own* attitudes and reactions that settle the question of what code our society accepts? Alternatively, couldn't a constructivist hold that although the members of a given society are the relevant minds when the question is which obligations are *accepted* by a society, nonetheless, when the question is what obligations are morally *binding* on those members, the relevant minds include *all* of us—not just the members of the given society alone, but all humans (or perhaps, more boldly still, all rational beings)? It simply isn't the case that constructivism per se insists that the only relevant minds for fixing the obligations of a given group are the minds of that group's *members*.

Furthermore, even if we were given a convincing reason to believe that under the best version of constructivism it is indeed true that the only relevant minds for fixing the obligations of a given group are the minds of its members, there would still be no reason to assume that the *particular* attitudes and reactions (of those members) that are relevant are the same when it is a matter of fixing the group's *obligations* as when it is a matter of fixing the group's *beliefs*. Presumably, if we are asking what code is *accepted* by a given society, the answer will boil down to the *actual* attitudes and reactions of its members. But if, instead, we are asking what code is valid for or *binding* upon those members, the constructivist might well prefer to ask, rather, about the attitudes and reactions that people *would* have under suitably ideal conditions (for example, if they were fully informed and perfectly rational, and so on). Since there is no reason to assume that the attitudes people would have under ideal conditions are the very same as the ones that they do have, there is no reason for the constructivist to assume that the obligations that are binding upon people correspond to the ones that are actually accepted in any given society. Indeed, for all we know, under sufficiently ideal conditions people might have attitudes supporting a single, unique moral code.

Thus, even if constructivism is true, there is no particular reason to think that the diversity of moral codes among different societies somehow shows that valid moral obligations vary as well, as we move from one society to the next.

A rather different argument for relativism might begin with the thought that a genuine moral obligation must be something that someone who is under that obligation can be moved by. That is, if I have an obligation to do an act, then it must be the case that I can be moved by that very thought. The relativist might then argue that I can only be moved by the *thought* that

I have a given obligation if I do indeed *believe* that I have that obligation. But this seems to imply that something can be a genuine obligation of mine only if I accept that it is. Consequently if, as we are assuming, different societies accept different moral codes, the members of those societies will take themselves to be under different obligations, and this will mean, in turn, that they actually *are* under different obligations. For if some purported duty is not part of my society's moral code, I won't accept it, and so can't be moved by it, and so it cannot be a genuine duty after all. Thus, the relativist may conclude, your genuine moral obligations will depend on the principles contained within the code of your society. Given that moral codes vary from one society to the next, moral obligations will do so as well.

Although I suspect that some people are indeed attracted to relativism as a result of thoughts along these lines, I imagine it is clear to most that this argument faces a number of telling objections. Let me note two. First, and most obviously, any given individual need not actually accept the moral code of the society of which they are a member. So even if the rest of the argument went through, we couldn't actually conclude that you must obey the code of your *society*. (We might, instead, need to conclude—even more implausibly—that the only obligations you have are the ones that you yourself happen to recognize!) But second, and more importantly, even if we grant that a genuine obligation must be one that in some sense you "can" be moved by, it is quite implausible to conclude that this means that genuine obligations must be ones that you *already* accept. Presumably, the requisite connection between obligation and motivation (assuming that there is one) will be in place provided that you can *come* to accept the obligation in question (perhaps only after suitable reflection) and can *then* be moved by it. So your obligations needn't be limited to those that are *already* recognized in your moral code (whether your own personal code *or* the one embraced by your society). And this means that until we learn more about what moral principles one might reasonably come to accept, we won't yet have reason to think that basic obligations are relative rather than being absolute.

We have been examining different attempts to show that moral relativism somehow follows from the existence of diverging moral codes. Relativism is true, these arguments claim, *because* societies have different codes. I have argued, of course, that these various arguments are unsuccessful. Conceivably, however, it might be suggested that we have been looking at things backwards. Instead of suggesting that relativism is true because of the differences we find in moral codes, might the relativist do better if she argued, on the contrary, that these differences exist because of the *truth of relativism*? In particular, then, might the relativist argue that we should accept moral relativism because it offers the best *explanation* of the fact that societies have different moral codes?

After all, *something* must lie behind the fact (we are supposing it to be a fact) that different societies accept different principles. What better explanation than the hypothesis that societies put forward different principles for their members precisely because different principles are valid or binding, depending on *which* society you are a member of?

Of course, this is not the first time we have asked ourselves how best to explain moral disagreement. We previously considered the quite different suggestion that our disagreements about moral matters can best be explained by embracing the hypothesis that there are actually *no* moral facts at all! (That was the thought behind the argument from disagreement, examined in the last chapter.) Obviously, had that idea been accepted, that would have given us compelling reason to *reject* moral relativism (along with other forms of moral realism), since the relativist believes, on the contrary, that there are indeed facts about what each person should do.

I argued, however, that disagreement in a given domain should not normally be taken to be an indication that there are no facts concerning that domain, and further, that there is no good reason to think that *moral* disagreements are an exception in this regard. So it does remain open to the moral relativist to argue, instead, that if we find moral codes differing from one another, the best explanation is not that there are no moral facts at all, but rather that the facts are relative, differing from society to society. Would a defense of relativism along these new lines do better than the arguments we have already considered?

(Of course, for reasons already explained, if moral codes do involve a hidden relativization parameter, then strictly speaking they don't really disagree, and so, strictly speaking, there is no *disagreement* here in need of explanation. Still, we are supposing that different societies put forward different principles for their respective members, and the relativist can be taken as offering an explanation of why *these* differences exist.)

Unfortunately, even if it is open to the relativist to *propose* moral relativism as the best explanation of the differences we find in the codes of different societies, that doesn't mean that this is a particularly complete or compelling explanation. Consider what the relativist would now be suggesting. It wouldn't be that people are under different obligations because the codes of their societies vary, but rather the reverse: the codes are different—the claim would be—because they reflect the differences in obligation that exist *independently* of their being recognized by these codes. People in different societies are under different obligations (for reasons yet to be explained), and the codes simply reflect that fact.

I should note, in passing, that if an account like this is accepted, the resulting view is no longer committed to constructivism about morality. It isn't that people have the obligations that they do because the relevant minds have the attitudes that they do (as made manifest in their given society's code). Rather, people have the attitudes that they do (as made manifest in their code) because they "already" have the *obligations* that they do. The relativist will thus need some further account of why people *have* the obligations that they do, and there is no particular reason to assume that this further account will turn out to be a constructivist one (though it could be).

But this particular point need not detain us. If, despite initial appearances, the best account of moral relativism is not constructivist after all, that may be surprising, but it isn't problematic.

A more pressing point is this. It doesn't suffice for the relativist to put forward any old "further" account of why people have the particular obligations that they do. Rather, that account needs to generate *different* obligations for different people, depending on what *society* they happen to belong to. And it certainly isn't obvious how that further account should go in order to do that. Just why *is* it that the members of different societies have fundamentally different obligations?

No doubt we can dream up partial stories on behalf of the relativist. Perhaps the relativist should accept a divine command theory of moral obligation and then posit that God simply chooses to give different principles to different groups. But why would God do that? The answer isn't obvious. Or perhaps the relativist should insist that the fundamental conditions in different societies are so radically different that only distinct moral codes could adequately promote and protect human interests in such varying circumstances. But just what are the specific environmental conditions that make differing codes necessary? The answer isn't obvious here either.

I certainly don't mean to suggest that one cannot construct theories of the foundations or bases of our moral obligations that are capable (in principle, at least) of generating different obligations for different societies. Indeed, we'll return to that possibility in the very next section. But in the absence of details, the relativist's "explanation" of the differences in moral codes seems nothing more than a promissory note, the mere suggestion that *something* or the other generates distinct moral obligations, varying by society.

And this brings us to the most significant point. If our goal is simply to explain the differences in moral codes that we may find, do we really need to bring in the relativist's conjecture at all? Can't we readily explain these differences without supposing that the underlying, valid principles really do vary from society to society? (As an analogy, can't we explain the fact that different societies have had different astronomical beliefs without supposing that the underlying astronomical facts somehow vary from society to society?)

It certainly seems as though there are numerous possible explanations of why different societies might come to have different moral codes, explanations that take no particular stance as to whether the *valid* moral principles are absolute or relative. Given the variety of historical factors that may influence a society's culture—including accidents of which religion came to dominance when, which ethical teachers and literatures became culturally prominent, which moral outlooks best served the political and economic interests of those in power in the given society, and so on—it should hardly surprise us if different societies end up with moral codes that differ in at least some ways. Even if—as absolutists believe—there really is a single, uniquely correct moral code, valid at all places and at all times, given the sheer difficulty of working out its content and the constant danger of motivated beliefs (see 5.3), there is no particular reason to assume that all societies would agree about its details. We can explain differences without embracing relativism.

Of course, none of this establishes that the absolutist is right. Even if differences in moral codes can be adequately explained without positing the truth of moral relativism, that doesn't *prove* that the valid principles are absolute. But it does still leave the relativist searching for a compelling reason for us to *prefer* relativism.

6.4 Relativized Foundational Theories

Let me mention one final way the relativist might try to defend their position. All of the arguments for relativism that we have examined to date make essential use of the descriptive claim that different societies have different moral codes. Although these arguments differ in their details, they share the thought that this descriptive claim somehow lends support to the *normative* claim that particularly interests us, the claim that people have different moral *obligations* (depending on their society). Unfortunately for the relativist, however, the various attempts to establish the reality of this support have proven unsuccessful.

Perhaps then the relativist should abandon the attempt to defend the normative claim by means of the *descriptive* one, and simply look for some other, more direct, way of arguing for moral relativism.

In what I take to be the most interesting approach to doing this, the relativist would claim that the best account of the foundations of normative ethics already has relativity *built into it*. Let's consider this idea more carefully.

When we think about morality we normally have in mind basic principles like the claim that killing is wrong (except, perhaps, in self-defense), or that one is required to keep one's promises, as well as lists of basic moral rights (for example, the right to life, or the right not to be enslaved) and of various virtues (such as honesty, loyalty, or compassion), and so on. Much of moral philosophy is devoted to debating and articulating these items and working out their details.

But beyond that, moral philosophy also includes rival theories concerning the ultimate foundation or basis of all these basic principles, rights, virtues, and the like. These theories attempt to explain what it is *by virtue of which* certain principles are valid, while others that we might imagine are not. (Similarly for the basic rights and virtues, and so forth.)

For example, *contractarians* hold that the valid principles (and so on) are those that we would agree upon during a suitable bargaining session. *Rule consequentialists* hold, instead, that the valid principles are those that would have the best results if everyone were to accept them and act upon them. *Ideal observer* theories hold that the valid principles are those that would be endorsed by a suitably ideal lawgiver (perhaps God), while *universalizability* theories hold that the valid principles are those that can be rationally willed to be universally valid. Obviously enough, there are different ways of filling in the details of these various theories, so that each approach subdivides further, and there are, of course, still other theories I haven't mentioned. But what all of these foundational theories have in common is the thought that the various valid principles (and the like) are valid by virtue of the fact that the correct foundational "machinery" would select, or endorse, or produce them. (In contrast, *nonfoundationalists* believe that once we have listed the basic principles, and so on, there is nothing deeper that can be said about why the valid principles are valid, while others are not. These are simply brute facts about the ethical domain.)

It would be far beyond the scope of the present book to try to spell out the underlying ideas behind these rival foundational theories or to explore the different ways in which they can be developed. But it is worth noting that these theories are almost always put forward in (what we might think of as) a *universal* mode. We ask what *single* set of rules would be agreed upon if we were *all* to engage in the bargaining sessions. We ask what single set of rules would have the best results if we were *all* to conform to those rules. We ask what single set of rules would be given to *all* of us by the ideal observer. We ask what single set of rules are the ones we can all rationally will, and so on. (Even nonfoundationalists typically assume that there is a single set of rules—valid for all of us—even if nothing deeper can be said about why these rules are valid.)

But in principle, at least, it seems as though most or all of these foundational theories could be offered in *relativized* versions instead. Rather than looking for a single set of rules, valid for all, we could ask instead what rules would be agreed upon by the *members* of a given society (to be binding upon their society alone), what rules would have the best results if the members of a *particular society* were to conform to them, what rules would be given to a particular society by the ideal observer, what rules could be rationally willed as valid *within* a given society, and so on.

Perhaps, then, the moral relativist should simply insist that the *correct* foundational theory (whatever exactly that turns out to be) will actually take a *relativized* form rather than a universal one. What we will have then, unsurprisingly, will be moral codes tailored to individual societies, rather than a single moral code valid across all places and times. A bit more precisely, what we will have is a foundational theory that is *open* to the possibility of generating different moral codes for different societies, rather than building into the theory itself an assumption to the effect that one size fits (or had better fit) all.

The first thing to notice about an approach like this is that there is no longer any particular reason to think that the specific code that gets "assigned" to a given society will be the same as the code that is in fact *accepted* within that society. While it would still be the case that what you are required to do would depend on what society you are a member of, and so, in one sense of the term, you would still be required to conform to the code "of" your society, there is no particular reason to assume that this code—the code that is *valid* for your society—will have much in common with the code that is *accepted* by (or acted upon by) the members of that society.

So this approach to relativism yields a rather different version of relativism than the one we have considered so far. It isn't so much a matter of "When you are a Roman, do as the Romans do," nor even "When you are a Roman, do as the Romans *believe* the Romans should do," but rather something more like "When you are a Roman, do as the Romans *should* do (regardless of what they *think* they should do)." Unlike the version of moral relativism that we have been examining up to this point, with this new version there is no particular reason to think you can learn how to behave properly by learning the moral code that happens to be accepted within your society.

So this new approach to moral relativism differs in some essential ways from the more standard version of relativism that we have been discussing. But there is a further point worth emphasizing as well, namely, that it isn't yet clear whether relativized foundational theories really will *assign* different moral codes to different societies. Having a relativized foundational theory certainly opens the door, as we might put it, to the possibility of having different codes for different societies. But is there good reason to think this possibility will be realized? Even if the correct foundational theory *could*, in principle, assign different moral rules to different societies, why think that it *will*?

As far as I can see, it is impossible to settle this question decisively without taking a stand on what the correct foundational theory actually is, since the details of the relevant arguments would vary, depending on the foundational theory in question. But there is at least some general reason to be skeptical. For the crucial issue is whether the relevant facts about societies and their members vary *sufficiently* to have the foundational machinery generate different codes. It isn't clear why we should think that they do, especially when we bear in mind that we are asking not whether the codes might have different derivative implications (given local circumstances), but rather whether the codes will differ in terms of the fundamental moral principles themselves. Given the basic facts of the human condition I find it easy to imagine that the fundamental moral principles appropriate for any given society (from the perspective of the foundational theory) may turn out to be the same from one society to the next.

(If we do conclude that each society will in fact be assigned the very same basic moral principles, does this still count as a version of moral *relativism*? In a minimal sense, perhaps, since the theory *might* have given different obligations to different people depending on their society. But in a more robust sense, probably not, for everyone will turn out to be bound by the very same moral code.)

Still, as I have already remarked, I don't think we can settle whether a relativized foundational theory will truly assign different moral principles without first determining the correct foundational theory. And that is beyond the scope of the present book. So let us suppose—if only for the sake of argument—that if the correct foundational theory is put forward in a relativized form then it will indeed generate different moral codes. That still leaves the question whether we should *prefer* foundational theories in their relativized versions rather than the more common universal ones. It is hard to see why we should.

Conceivably, the relativist might try to offer some general considerations—points independent of any particular foundational theory—for preferring relativization. That is, she might argue that no matter *what* the best foundational theory turns out to be, we have reason to think that the best *version* of that foundational theory will be a relativized one.

But what might such general considerations look like? Presumably the relativist would want to appeal to independently plausible ideas about the very function and purpose of morality. Still, it remains difficult to see how, exactly, the argument would go. Suppose we grant, for example, the idea that one essential function of morality is to guide action (see 1.2). If the relativist could somehow make out the thought that morality can only *be* action guiding (or can only do an adequate job of being action guiding) if moral principles vary from society to society rather than being universal, that might give us reason to think that the correct foundational theory (whatever it is) will be relativized. But it seems obvious (to me, at least) that even absolute moral principles can do a perfectly good job of guiding action. Or suppose we grant the idea that moral principles must serve to protect, respect, and promote people's significant interests (again, see 1.2). If the relativist could somehow make out the claim that morality can only do this (or can do it better) if basic moral principles vary with the given society, that too might give us reason to expect that the correct foundational theory will be relativized. But here too, it is difficult to see why absolute moral principles should do less well in this regard.

Speaking personally, I cannot think of any compelling arguments along these lines, that is, arguments that start with independently plausible general remarks about the nature and purpose of morality and then move from these to the relativist's desired conclusion, that the correct foundational theory should be cast in a relativized mode.

Of course, that doesn't show that there is compelling reason to prefer foundational theories presented in a *universal* mode either. *Are* there general considerations that give us reason to prefer universal over relativized foundational theories? Perhaps. To the extent that part of the purpose of morality is to guide our interactions with others, protecting and respecting the interests of everyone, we might think that a foundational theory will serve that purpose most effectively if it generates a single set of rules, so that even when we interact (directly or indirectly) with people from *other* societies, all concerned parties will approach those interactions from the same shared moral perspective. If that's right, then perhaps we do indeed have reason to prefer universal rather than relativized foundational theories.

But there is no need for those who believe in absolute moral theories to insist upon this point. Our goal is not to establish the unique superiority of the view that valid moral principles are absolute, but only to deflect and disarm arguments that seek to establish the opposite. So in the absence of a compelling reason to think that foundational theories should be relativized, those who believe in absolute moral rules can reasonably maintain that their own favored position remains an acceptable one.

It is, of course, still a possibility that once we have settled on the correct account of the foundations of morality we will find something *specific* to that account that leads us to conclude that this *particular* foundational theory—the correct one—should indeed be cast in a relative rather than a universal mode. For example, perhaps there is something about *contractarianism* in particular that makes it appropriate to embrace it in a relativized form, even if the same wouldn't have been true for other foundational theories. Or maybe there is something special in this regard about rule consequentialism, or the ideal observer theory, and so on. Even if there is no reason in the abstract to prefer relativized theories to universal ones, it could still turn out that for the *particular* foundational theory that we ultimately endorse we will discover such reasons. I doubt that this is the case; but that does still remain a possibility.

To explore this question properly would require detailed consideration of each of the leading foundational theories (or, at the very least, detailed consideration of whatever foundational theory you already happen to prefer). It will not surprise you to learn that we won't undertake that sort of investigation here. To engage in it would be to turn our attention fully to normative ethics, and that would constitute a significant detour from our main concerns.

Perhaps then the conclusion that we should reach is this. While it remains possible that a full-blown systematic discussion of normative ethics and its foundations would lead us, eventually, to some form of moral relativism, there is currently no particularly compelling reason to think that it will. That should be good enough, I think, for our purposes. No doubt, those who believe in absolute moral truths—valid for all people and all times—should remain open minded. But they have not yet been given reason to think that they are mistaken.

7
Knowledge

7.1 The Analogy to Observation

One familiar source of skepticism about the existence of morality turns on the thought that even if there were moral facts, there would be no way we could know anything about them. After all, what could the basis of such knowledge possibly be? It isn't as though we can use our five senses to gain knowledge of basic moral principles. (What kind of empirical experiment could possibly establish fundamental moral principles?) Yet, if we can't actually know anything about moral facts, why believe that there *are* any? Indeed, given the plausible thought that part of the very point of there being such a thing as morality would be to guide action, how could anything possibly meet the job description of morality if there were no way for us to gain *knowledge* of the purported moral facts? How could we possibly be guided by morality if we can't know what morality asks of us? Accordingly, if there is no way to gain knowledge of morality, *skepticism* about morality may well turn out to be the most plausible position for us to adopt.

To be sure, given the knowledge of *some* moral principles it might be possible to gain further, *derivative* moral knowledge as well. To revert to an earlier example (from 5.3), if I know that it is wrong to harm others, my empirical knowledge that this glass of tea contains poison might allow me to come to know the derivative moral truth that it is wrong to serve you the tea. But how could I have ever come to know that it is wrong to harm others? While derivative moral knowledge might be explicable if we assume knowledge of underlying moral principles and relevant nonmoral facts, that just pushes off the moment of reckoning. How could we possibly have come to have knowledge of the underlying moral principles?

Admittedly, we might be able to push off the epistemic moment of truth for a while longer. Perhaps, for example, it is wrong to harm others because, say, a moral rule that permits harming innocents would have worse results than one that forbids it. That's the thought behind rule consequentialism, at any rate, and it certainly looks as though familiar empirical methods might

7.1 THE ANALOGY TO OBSERVATION

allow us know what the results of different rules might be. But how did we come to know just what it is that constitutes one result's being morally *worse* than another? And how did we come to know the truth of rule consequentialism itself, in the first place? Sooner or later, don't we have to reach moral claims that cannot themselves be justified in terms of our nonmoral beliefs? Won't we eventually find ourselves making "purely moral" claims of some sort or the other? Very well, then, the skeptic asks, how could we possibly have knowledge of moral claims like *that*?

In the absence of a compelling story about the possibility of basic (nonderivative) moral knowledge, the whole fabric threatens to unravel, and we are left with the skeptical thought that moral knowledge may be impossible after all. And with that comes the even more general skeptical conclusion, that we shouldn't believe in moral facts at all.

An adequate response to this skeptical worry needs to tell us how knowledge of moral facts is possible. When we argue for moral claims (and let us hereafter focus on the more purely moral elements of those arguments) what is it that we appeal to? What counts as evidence in a moral argument? As we try to work our way toward systematic moral theories, what justifies preferring one theory over another?

The full answer, of course, is complicated, too complicated for us to try to spell out here. But ultimately, I believe, the best answer will say this (among other things): we gain moral knowledge by making careful use of moral *intuitions*.

To unpack this answer, I think it is helpful to explore an analogy between theory building in ethics and empirical theory building (whether it's the grand theories of the natural and social sciences, or the less ambitious sets of beliefs we constantly form about our own personal surroundings). I want to suggest that moral intuitions function as *inputs* into our moral theories in something very much like the way that observations function as inputs into our empirical theories.

I take it to be a familiar point that we use our observations to generate, evaluate, and justify our empirical beliefs. Some of this happens directly. For example, I might see a tree, and thus come to know that there is a tree here. In cases like this, observation functions as a direct route to knowing specific things. In other cases the route to knowledge is less direct. My observations (say, of samples of white snow) may support some more general or comprehensive claim (perhaps, that all snow is white), which in turn might then give me reason to believe things I haven't observed (say, that the next sample of snow will be white as well). Similarly, I might test an empirical claim by extracting predictions from it, which I then compare to the observations I actually make in the relevant circumstances. And so on. The full story of how observations are used as evidence for empirical claims is a complicated one, and I won't try to sketch it further here. But I presume we are all in agreement that observations play this double role in our empirical knowledge—providing both direct and indirect evidence for our sundry empirical claims. This is what I mean by saying that observations serve as the *input* to our empirical theories.

Similarly, then, I think, for moral intuitions and ethics. Whether it is a matter of building a grand, systematic normative theory, or simply forming some moral beliefs about a particular situation, moral intuitions serve as the input to our moral theories. Some of this is direct, with particular moral intuitions giving me direct reason to believe specific moral claims; and some of it is indirect, with moral intuitions supporting relevant generalizations, and so on. Here too, unsurprisingly, the full story of how moral intuitions can provide evidence for moral claims is a complicated one, and I won't try to sketch the details much further. (I'll say a bit more below.) But the crucial suggestion I want to make is that just as observations play a central role in justifying our empirical beliefs, moral intuitions play the corresponding central role in justifying our moral beliefs. Moral intuitions are the inputs for our moral theories.

(Strictly, perhaps, on some views of the matter we should not talk of observations and moral intuitions as themselves literally constituting the inputs to our theories. Perhaps it would be more accurate to say that observations justify certain beliefs—for example, the belief that the contents of the test tube are blue—and that it is those *beliefs* that act as inputs into our broader empirical theories. Similarly, perhaps it would be more accurate to say that moral intuitions justify certain beliefs—for example, the belief that murdering innocents is unjust—and that it is those beliefs that act as inputs into our moral theories. But there is no need for us to be overly scrupulous about this point.)

Of course, as my remarks about the various ways in which observations can provide indirect evidence for our empirical claims suggest, there is much more to empirical theory building than just compiling an ever expanding list of observations. We want theories that are coherent, elegant, simple, and powerful. The creation of theories with such theoretical virtues is rarely a simple or straightforward matter. But be that all as it may, simplicity and

7.1 THE ANALOGY TO OBSERVATION

power (and so on) alone do not suffice; we ultimately need to build our theories with an eye toward accommodating (as best we can) the touchstones provided by observation.

The analogous situation holds for morality as well. There is far more to moral theory building than merely compiling a list of moral intuitions. Here too we want theories that are coherent, elegant, simple, and powerful. But the mere possession of these theoretical virtues will not suffice to render a moral theory adequate either. An acceptable theory must also go some significant distance toward accommodating our moral intuitions.

In both cases, then, an acceptable theory must significantly accommodate the relevant sort of input. In the empirical case, that input is observation. In ethics, it is intuition.

It is, however, important not to misconstrue this talk of "accommodating" the inputs—whether observation or intuition. While theory building needs to be *guided* by the appropriate evidence, doing this properly certainly doesn't require that the relevant inputs be considered *infallible*. Sometimes we ultimately decide that certain observations are best treated as erroneous. We reject them as somehow mistaken—illusions or hallucinations. (You may see pink elephants flying around the room after you've had too much to drink. But that doesn't mean that an adequate empirical theory must posit the existence of such creatures.)

I emphasize this point because even if it is true, as I am suggesting, that an adequate moral epistemology—a theory of how we come to know anything about morality—will ultimately be grounded in an appeal to our moral intuitions, there is no need to treat those intuitions as though *they* are infallible either. Sometimes critics of intuitions assume that those who give intuitions epistemic weight must indeed view them as infallible, as though the only alternatives are to think either that intuitions have no legitimate role in our moral epistemology at all or else that they are utterly incapable of being mistaken. Since the latter position—infallibility—is implausible, it is then concluded that the only reasonable alternative is the former one, where we disregard our moral intuitions altogether. But as the example of empirical observation makes plain, these are hardly the only two choices. We can think it appropriate to give weight to our intuitions while remaining fully open to the realization that they sometimes go wrong, just as we appropriately give weight to the reports of our five senses, all the while recognizing that they too are sometimes mistaken.

7.2 Appearances

Up to this point, I have been emphasizing a certain analogy, according to which moral intuitions function as inputs for our moral theory building in much the same way as observations function as inputs for our empirical theory building. But to talk of there being an "analogy" in this way is, in an important respect, misleading, for it suggests that there might turn out to be two rather different lines of justification required for relying on these inputs, one for observation and one for intuition. And this, in turn, would allow the skeptic to argue that although it may be true that we tend to *use* moral intuitions as inputs for our moral theories in the same way that we use observations as inputs for empirical ones, that doesn't give us any reason at all to think that we are *justified* in doing so.

Put slightly differently, the skeptic could concede the *descriptive* point—that we use both observations and intuitions as inputs in theory building—while still insisting on the *epistemological* claim that while there is indeed a justification for relying on *observations* in this way, there is no justification for relying on intuition. At best, I may have successfully sketched a rough account of what we are doing when we try to attain moral knowledge; but none of it gives us reason to think that moral intuition is indeed a legitimate *source* of knowledge in the first place, so none of it gives us reason to think that we actually *have* any moral knowledge at all.

Consequently, it is important to note that it is plausible to think, on the contrary, that the basic reason it is legitimate to rely on intuition is actually at bottom the same as our justification for relying on observation. In both cases what is going on is this: we are appropriately relying on how things *appear* to us. In both cases we start by tentatively *trusting* the appearances, and we continue to do so—and we are justified in doing so—until such time (if ever) as we discover that we should instead be skeptical about this or that appearance (or this or that broader class of appearances). It isn't that there is one sort of justification for relying on observation and another sort for relying on intuition. Rather, there is just a single underlying justification—the fact that we are justified in taking things to be the way that they *appear* to be, until we find compelling reason to think otherwise.

Thus if I seem to see a tree in front of me, things *appear* to me to be a certain way, and this very fact—that things appear to be a certain way—gives me some initial or tentative reason to believe that things are indeed as they appear to be. Similarly, of course, for other observations—that it appears that the needle is pointing to 5 on the meter (a different visual appearance), that it appears that my mother is calling me (an auditory rather than a visual appearance), that it appears that the bread is ready to come out of the oven (an olfactory appearance), that it appears that the water is frozen (tactile), or that the wine has spoiled (gustatory), and so on and so forth. In each case, things appear to be a certain way and unless I find myself with reason to dismiss the appearance as illusory, I am justified in believing that things are just as they appear to be.

But moral intuitions are appearances as well. If I have the intuition that killing in self-defense is morally permissible then something *seems* to me to be the case: it appears to me to be the case that self-defense is permissible! And similarly, of course, for countless other moral intuitions as well. In each such case, to intuit that something is right or wrong, or good or bad, or just or unjust, and so on, is for things to appear to me to be a certain way. And this very fact gives me some initial or tentative reason to believe that things are indeed as they appear to be—that self-defense really is permissible, that killing innocents really is unjust, that equality really is intrinsically good, and so on and so forth, for each of these ways that things seem to be.

For present purposes, of course, the crucial point to recognize is that both observation and intuition involve appearances; they are ways that things can *seem* to me to be the case. And in both cases it is this very fact—that things appear to be one way rather than another—which provides the tentative justification for holding the corresponding belief, for believing that things are indeed as they appear to be.

The epistemological idea at work here has been called *the principle of phenomenal conservatism*—"phenomenal" because it is concerned with appearances, and "conservatism" because it tells us that we are justified in accepting these appearances and preserving them in our beliefs (albeit in a presumptive or tentative way). Of course, strictly speaking it isn't the seeming or the appearance itself which is preserved, but what we might call the *content* of the appearance. If it seems to us that such and such is the case, then what we are tentatively justified in believing is that very proposition—that such and such is the case.

Note, in any event, that the view in question doesn't implausibly maintain that appearances are never mistaken. We know that is far from the case. Despite the name, then, the principle certainly doesn't say that we are to accept that things are as they appear, *no matter what*! Upon reflection we may well find that we have good reason to abandon certain appearances as illusory.

Nonetheless, appearances do give us a *defeasible* justification for belief: we are justified in thinking that things are as they appear to be until we find ourselves with compelling reason to think the appearances are misleading.

It is for this reason that the skeptic's attempt to drive a wedge between our reliance on observation and our reliance on intuitions is misguided. The very same principle warrants our use of both. Indeed, it is arguable that ultimately there is no other source of justification at all, that *all* justification ultimately traces back to our defeasible belief in how things appear. (For another example, consider the case of memories: ultimately, I think, we are defeasibly justified in believing that such and such happened, when we remember it, because it *seems* to us that it happened.)

None of this is to deny that there are different types of appearances. Intuitions may be like observations in that both involve things appearing to us to be some way, and both may have justificatory weight by virtue of being such appearances, but that is not to deny that there are distinctions between different types of appearances.

I have been talking freely about our intuitions as a potential source of knowledge, and I presume that we are all familiar with the experience of having an intuition that something is the case (for example, having the intuition that telling a particular lie would be wrong). Still, I can easily imagine someone wanting a fuller account of what exactly an intuition is. I find that a difficult thing to provide. At the same time, I must admit, I also find it difficult to say what exactly an *observation* is.

As I have been at pains to emphasize, both intuitions and observations involve things seeming to us to be a certain way. Much of the difficulty of explicating what an intuition is, or what an observation is, can be traced, I think, to the difficulty of explicating what this common aspect comes to, what it is for it to *seem* to someone that P (for a given proposition, P). I won't try to characterize this shared aspect further (which isn't to say the attempt wouldn't be worth undertaking). Instead, I will take this notion as given, and simply suggest that, roughly speaking, when the appearance is a sensory one (produced, or at least apparently produced, by the senses) it is an observation, and when the appearance is a rational one (produced, or at least apparently produced, by reason) it is an intuition.

Although our particular interest in this book lies with moral intuitions, the truth is that we have intuitions about many different subject matters. We have, for example, intuitions about math (for example, that one plus one equals two), or about logic (for example, that a claim and its negation cannot both be true). We have intuitions about epistemology and metaphysics and much more, including ethics. We use—justifiably use!—our mathematical intuitions to develop our mathematical theories, our logical intuitions to develop our theories of logic, our metaphysical and epistemological intuitions to develop our theories in metaphysics and in epistemology. And what I have been arguing, of course, is that we use—justifiably use!—our moral intuitions to develop our moral theories.

Even restricting our attention to moral intuitions, the scope of such intuitions is quite broad. That is to say, we have intuitions about a wide range of moral matters. We can, of course, have intuitions about specific cases (intuiting, say, that it is wrong for Frances to hurt that particular child). But we can also have intuitions about more general principles (intuiting, for example, that it is wrong to tell a lie to avoid minor embarrassment). We can have intuitions about specific moral concepts (say, that framing an innocent person is unjust) and more abstract ones (for example, that if some act is morally *required* then we have some sort of reason to do it). We can have intuitions about comparisons (that this act would be worse than that, or that this factor is weightier than that), about outcomes (that an outcome with less inequality is better than one with more), about character traits (that compassion is a virtue), and about relevance (that it makes a difference whether the patient consented to the surgery). And there is more still. As far as I can see, we can have intuitions about pretty much any aspect of morality. Accordingly, there are many different points at which we have relevant inputs to use in building (and critically evaluating) rival moral theories.

A further important point, already implicit in what I have said, is that having an intuition that something is the case is not the same thing as having a *belief* that this is the case. Intuitions may involve a *tendency* toward having the corresponding belief—a sort of disposition or inclination to have the corresponding belief—but they don't actually require *having* the corresponding belief. One needn't *accept* one's intuitions (which is to say, one needn't believe the contents of one's intuitions). The mere fact that it seems to you that something is the case is perfectly compatible with believing, nonetheless, that things are not in fact as they appear. That's part of what it means to recognize that intuitions are not infallible.

Unsurprisingly, the situation here is similar to what we find with observation. Think of what it is to look at an optical illusion. One line may look longer than the other: it *seems* to be longer than the other. Yet, precisely because you know that it is an optical illusion, you don't *believe* that the first line is longer than the second. Similarly, the earth can *look* flat to me—it appears flat—but for all that, of course, I know that it isn't. It is one thing for things to appear to you to be a given way; it is another matter for you to have the corresponding belief.

Normally, of course, if I "observe" something, this results in my believing it. Visual hallucinations and optical illusions are a familiar phenomenon, but they aren't a constant occurrence, and so typically when it looks to me like something is the case, I immediately (and justifiably) believe that it is indeed the case. It *seems* to me that there is a tree in front of me, and so I (appropriately) *believe* that there is a tree in front of me. But for all that, it is one thing to have the appearance and something distinct to have the corresponding belief. I might after all, realize that I am in a hall of mirrors, and so reject the appearance of a tree as a mere illusion.

Note, however, that even when I do reject the appearance as mistaken, that needn't mean that the appearance itself disappears. Even when I know I am looking at an optical illusion, the one line still *looks* longer than the other. The appearance can remain, even when I disavow it. And if the appearance does remain it may continue to "tempt" or "attract" me toward the corresponding belief. But whether or not this happens, it is one thing to have something look to me to be the case and something distinct to actually believe it.

Similarly, then, for moral intuition. If I intuit something, I will normally find myself believing it, until and unless I find myself with good reason to think the intuition is mistaken. Sometimes I do indeed discover such reasons, and in such cases I can reject the corresponding belief. Of course, even when this happens, the intuition itself needn't disappear, so I might have a residual inclination or disposition to believe. Still, I needn't have the belief itself. I can reject the intuition as mistaken.

Suppose, however, that I do not find myself with any particularly compelling reason to reject a given intuition as illusory. Normally, in such circumstances, I will simply accept the corresponding belief. If I have the intuition that P, then I will *believe* that P is the case. What's more, my belief that P will be justified—or, a bit more accurately, it will be *defeasibly* justified. It will be justified until such time (a time which may never come) as I find reason to reject it.

All of which is just to say that moral intuitions can function as a source of moral knowledge. We are presumptively *justified* in believing what they say, though various particular intuitions may get rejected in the course of synthesizing the contents of our intuitions into an overall theory that is simple, powerful, and coherent.

There are, obviously, countless details to be worked out here. Among other things, a complete moral epistemology would need to tell us how to combine our moral intuitions into larger theories, under what circumstances particular intuitions should be rejected, and whether some intuitions should be given more weight than others. These are all important issues, but they are not our concern here. My goal has only been the modest one of showing why the skeptic is too quick to claim that moral knowledge is impossible. On the contrary, just as we use observation to gain knowledge of the empirical facts, we can use our moral intuitions to gain knowledge of the moral facts.

7.3 Dismissing Moral Intuitions

When I have an intuition it seems to me that something is the case, and so I am defeasibly justified in believing that things are as they appear to me to be. That fact, I have been suggesting, opens the door to the possibility of moral knowledge. It is part of the defense of moral realism that can be offered by the realist against the skeptic's claim that moral knowledge would be impossible.

I realize, of course, that many people will find themselves incredulous at the suggestion that mere intuition can be a source of knowledge. Appealing to intuitions seems spooky and unscientific, too weird a proposal to take seriously. How can the mere fact that something *seems* to me to be the case provide me with a reason—even a defeasible reason—to think that it is so?

But this reaction, understandable and familiar as it may be, fails to keep in mind the point that observations are *also* appearances—appearances generated by our senses—and we are perfectly comfortable appealing to such appearances as a potential source of knowledge. So if we are going to find reasonable ground to dismiss our moral intuitions, it cannot be the mere fact that intuitions are "only" appearances.

Admittedly, there are philosophical skeptics who insist that in point of fact we lack knowledge of the external world as well. But as I explained in the introduction, our goal in this book is not to rebut such global skepticism but only to respond to the more limited skepticism that thinks there is something especially problematic about *morality*. Accordingly, in our discussion I am simply taking it as a given that empirical knowledge of the external world is possible. And since such knowledge does seem to be ultimately based on how things *seem* to us, it cannot be legitimate to dismiss moral intuitions on the ground that they (too) only tell us how things appear.

Presumably, then, *our* skeptic—the *moral* skeptic—will want to distinguish somehow between observation and intuition. She will want to give us reason to be skeptical about intuition, without raising analogous concerns about observation. More precisely, then, the skeptic might concede that appearances provide justification in the absence of compelling reason to reject those appearances, but insist, nonetheless, that although there is nothing troubling or problematic about observations as a class, the situation is rather different when it comes to moral intuitions, where, she might claim, we *always* have reason to be skeptical. That is to say, the skeptic may argue that we have compelling reason to reject moral intuitions *across the board*. And if that's right, of course, then we can't justifiably appeal to those intuitions as a way of grounding moral knowledge.

Let me be clear that in principle, at least, there is nothing illegitimate about the skeptic's trying to find something problematic about intuitions as a class. As I have repeatedly remarked, appearances provide only *defeasible* justification. That justification can be defeated or undercut in the right circumstances. And there is nothing in the principle of phenomenal conservatism that limits us to criticizing appearances *individually*; sometimes we have good reason to distrust entire *classes* of appearances. Conceivably, then, the skeptic could reinstate their objection to moral knowledge by insisting that we have reason to be skeptical of moral intuitions as a whole. If the skeptic can point to something troubling or problematic about the entire class of moral intuitions, something that gives us reason to dismiss the entire lot of them (without similarly challenging the class of observations), then the account of moral knowledge that I have sketched will be undercut.

The most radical suggestion along these lines would actually be one that rejected not just moral intuitions but all intuitions altogether, regardless of their subject matter. Instead of thinking that there is something uniquely problematic about our intuitions about right and wrong (or good and bad, and so on), perhaps it is the very appeal to *intuition* (as opposed to observation) that is problematic. We shouldn't just be skeptical about intuitions about *morality*; intuitions about other subjects (such as metaphysics) should be disregarded as well. If that's right, we should indeed disavow appeals to moral intuition, but the reason will be because we should not appeal to intuitions of any sort at all.

7.3 DISMISSING MORAL INTUITIONS

Though tempting, I think that any such wholesale rejection of intuitions must be resisted, since it will make not just moral knowledge impossible (as well as, say, knowledge of metaphysics), but *any* systematic knowledge whatsoever. For no matter what our area of inquiry, sooner or later—and most often, sooner rather than later—we rely on intuition to justify our beliefs.

In making this claim part of what I have in mind is the fact that much systematic inquiry relies on mathematics. (Think about the central use of mathematics in the empirical sciences.) Yet what is it that ultimately justifies our substantive claims about math other than an appeal to intuition? Ultimately, much of our knowledge of mathematics turns on what can be shown to follow logically from more basic mathematical assumptions; but it is intuition that guides us in the choice of the relevant axioms. Why are we confident that $1 + 1 = 2$? Because we have the intuition that this is the case.

Furthermore, think about those judgments about what does or does not follow from the given axioms. Here we rely on our knowledge of deductive logic. But what is it that justifies our beliefs about *logic*? I can't see any possible answer other than that we appeal to our logical intuitions to guide our judgments about what follows from what. (Why are we confident that if it is true that p, and true that if p then q, then it must also be true that q? Because we have the intuition that this conclusion necessarily follows from the premises.) So our use of mathematics relies on intuitions from start to finish.

But the truth, of course, is that *all* inquiry relies on logic, on our sense of what follows from what. More broadly still, all inquiry relies on our ability to tell good arguments from bad ones, arguments that offer compelling considerations for their conclusions from those that fail to do so. So if we construe the notion of "logic" broadly enough to encompass not just deductive logic but all our considered judgments about what makes an argument good or bad, then it seems impossible to argue for anything at all—on any subject whatsoever—without appealing (directly or indirectly) to underlying intuitions about logic.

In short, if we were to dismiss all appeals to intuition it wouldn't just be knowledge of morality (and other philosophical topics, like metaphysics) that would be threatened. On the contrary, all—or almost all—knowledge of any subject whatsoever would be impossible. And this means, of course, that if we are to avoid falling into a global skepticism which rejects the possibility of virtually any knowledge at all, we must reject the suggestion that intuitions per se are suspect and cannot be used to justify beliefs.

Accordingly, if the moral skeptic is going to dismiss moral intuitions as a potential source of knowledge it cannot be on the grounds that they are mere *intuitions*. The skeptic is going to have to point to something especially problematic about *moral* intuitions, as distinct from others. And it is far from clear what that might be.

Suppose we put this particular problem aside (that is, put aside the problem of finding objections to moral intuitions that don't apply equally to other intuitions, like our logical or mathematical ones), and simply ask, what is it that people find so troubling about appeal to intuitions anyway, moral or otherwise? Why is it that people find intuitions problematic in a way that observations are not?

One common suggestion here is that observations can be *confirmed*, while intuitions cannot be. But although this too is a tempting thought, I suspect it is mistaken as well. For it seems to me that individual intuitions actually can be confirmed in something like the way that we confirm individual observations.

What do we do when we confirm a given observation? Simplifying a bit, I suppose we do something like this. First, we tentatively accept the content of the observation in question. Then we derive some implications from the given belief (though of course it may only have these implications when combined with other, relevant, background beliefs), and then we check whether those implications obtain or not. If they do, we have at least some confirmation for our original observation. If they don't, we have at least some reason (perhaps defeasible) for rejecting it. (Alternatively, of course, sometimes what happens is that we retain belief in the original observation, but reject some of the background beliefs, or revise our views about what the relevant implications might be, or reject one or more of our later observations.)

So, for example, if I seem to see that one object is taller than another, I tentatively accept that it is indeed taller. I infer from this belief—along with background beliefs about how yardsticks work—that if I hold a yardstick next to the first object the number closest to the top of the object will be greater than that seen if I hold the yardstick next to the second object. Suppose, then, that I put the yardstick next to each object in turn, and compare the relevant numbers. If the number for the first is greater than the number for the second I have confirmed my initial observation (that the first object is taller than the second). If, however, the second number is greater than the first, I have disconfirmed my initial observation, and I now have (defeasible) reason to reject it as an illusion. (Alternatively, though less likely, I might revise my beliefs about how yardsticks work, or ask whether I accidentally switched which end of the yardstick was down, or wonder whether I read the numbers on the yardstick accurately, and so on.)

Essentially, then, what is going on here is this. Based on my initial observation I draw some predictions about what future observations will occur if I conduct the relevant "experiments." Thus I confirm or disconfirm my original observation by means of attending to still other observations. That's what it is to confirm an observation: I check it against other observations and see if they harmonize in the appropriate ways.

Now there are some who think that all of this constitutes an unacceptable vicious circle—confirming observations by means of still other observations. They conclude, accordingly, that observations cannot actually be confirmed after all, and we should reject observation as a source of knowledge. But as always, it is not our concern here to reply to those who accept such sweeping versions of skepticism. For our purposes it suffices to point out that if observations really can be legitimately confirmed—as we normally think—then the process is at least roughly like the one I have suggested: we confirm observations by means of seeing if they harmonize in the appropriate ways with still other observations.

But something analogous can be done with moral intuitions as well. Thus, I might have some particular intuition, and based on this intuition I might tentatively adopt the corresponding belief. I then derive some implications from this belief (typically, in conjunction with other background beliefs), and I look to see whether these implications obtain or not. Of course, as we are here dealing with moral issues rather than empirical ones, the relevant implications will be *moral* implications, and so I will be checking to see if the relevant *moral* facts hold or not. How do I do this? By generating moral intuitions about the relevant cases!

Thus, for example, if I have the intuition that it is always wrong to tell a lie, I might confirm this intuition by examining some of its implications, for example by thinking about cases that involve white lies (say, lying to my wife about her surprise party) or cases that involve lies that protect innocents (say, lying to a would-be murderer about the whereabouts of their intended victim). If it does seem to me that lies are wrong even in cases like this, then I have gone some distance toward confirming my initial intuition. And if it seems to me that in one or another such case the relevant lie is actually permissible, then I have gone some distance toward disconfirming the original intuition. (Alternatively, of course, I might find myself revising some of my background beliefs, or asking whether I have correctly deduced the implications of the original belief, or wondering whether to trust my intuitions about the relevant test cases, and so on.)

In short, I confirm or disconfirm my initial intuition by means of attending to still other intuitions. That's what it is to confirm an intuition: checking it against other intuitions to see if they harmonize in the appropriate ways.

No doubt some will be inclined to reject this idea out of hand. How can it be legitimate to check moral intuitions against other moral intuitions, if we are worried about whether there is such a thing as morality at all? But note that the corresponding objection about observation appropriately leaves us unmoved (at least, insofar as we are not contemplating adopting global skepticism). What we believe about observation is that individual observations *can* be legitimately confirmed, and that the way to do it (though this may not have been obvious at the outset) is by checking them against still other observations. If a process like this is indeed legitimate when it comes to observation—and we are, of course, here assuming that this is indeed the case—then there is no obvious reason why the corresponding process should be any less legitimate when it comes to intuitions (including moral intuitions). We confirm observations by testing them against still other observations. Similarly, then, we can confirm intuitions by testing them against still other intuitions.

The skeptic might press the point further and suggest that, despite what I have just said, there is an important difference between the possibilities for confirmation available with regard to observation and those available for confirming intuition. When it comes to "confirming" moral intuitions, *all* that we can do is to check them against other moral intuitions. But when it comes to empirical observation, we are not similarly limited to a single modality. We can "cross check" our senses, testing our visual observations against our tactile ones, our auditory ones against our olfactory ones, and so on. If I seem to see a rock, I can confirm this appearance by trying to touch it, and asking whether I seem to feel one as well. If I seem to hear a truck, I can confirm this appearance by asking whether I seem to smell its exhaust as well. But nothing like this is possible with regard to moral intuition. There is no other modality of appearances to check our moral intuitions against. Doesn't this inability to *cross check* our moral intuitions give us reason to be skeptical about them?

In thinking about this objection, I find myself uncertain as to whether it is truly the case that we have only a single mode of experiencing moral appearances. Phenomenologically speaking, the experience that I have when I coolly and calmly intuit that it is permissible to lie to my wife about a surprise party seems completely different from the experience I have when I emotionally recoil at the very thought of someone being tortured. In both cases, it seems to me that the moral facts are one way rather than another, but is there indeed only a *single* form of moral appearance at work here? Or are there two (intuition and emotion)? To be honest, it isn't transparent to me how best to *count* modes of moral appearances. Conceivably, then, this first premise of the skeptic's argument may be incorrect. (Don't say: but they are all just forms of *intuition*. Would we similarly say that vision and touch, for example, are all just forms of observation?)

But at any rate, I think the more interesting question is whether it is really true that we have reason to be skeptical about moral appearances in the absence of the ability to cross check across distinct modalities (however these are best distinguished). While I will concede that it is reassuring to have the possibility of cross checking, is it truly necessary before we are entitled to appeal to moral intuition?

Imagine that we had only a single empirical sense. Suppose that we had vision, say, but no sense of smell, touch, hearing, or taste. Obviously, our ability to attain knowledge of the empirical world would be more limited than it currently is, but would it really be illegitimate to *use* our vision to gain knowledge of the world? Would anyone actually conclude that since there was no way to cross check our vision against other sensory modalities, it was inappropriate to appeal to it? That seems highly unlikely to me.

(And for that matter, do we have more than one mode of *logical* intuition? It certainly isn't clear to me that we do; yet would anyone argue that we should therefore *disregard* our intuitions about what follows from what?)

So while it would perhaps be convenient if we had more than one modality for moral appearances, it is hard to see why it should undermine our claims to moral knowledge if it turns out that we don't.

Perhaps the worry about confirming our moral intuitions isn't so much about whether any given intuition can be checked against another (whether of the same or a different modality), but rather discomfort at the fact that people's intuitions differ so widely, from one person to the next. How can we justifiably appeal to intuitions as a source of knowledge when people so regularly disagree with one another in their intuitive responses? Indeed, even my own intuitions aren't always consistent, as I sometimes find that my intuitions change at a later point from what they were earlier.

We have, of course, already discussed at some length (in chapter 5) the supposed skeptical implications of moral disagreement. But that discussion focused on the (metaphysical) suggestion that disagreement might somehow give us direct reason to conclude that there are no moral facts. Here, instead, the suggestion is the epistemological one that the presence of disagreement somehow undermines the justificatory force that intuitions might otherwise be thought to have.

Of course, here too we might wonder why disagreement should be thought to have the skeptical implication in question. On the face of it, after all, all that intuitive disagreement shows, in and of itself, is that someone's intuition must be *mistaken*. If I have the intuition that self-defense is sometimes permissible, and you have the opposite intuition, at least one of us must be wrong. But as I have already noted, giving genuine weight to intuitions certainly doesn't require viewing them as infallible. Indeed, the entire point of saying that intuitions provide *defeasible* justification is to acknowledge the fact that sometimes they do go wrong (and that we may even have good reason to say of particular intuitions that they *have* gone wrong). Conceivably, then, all that disagreement does is provide us with cases where we can be confident that at least *someone's* intuition has indeed misfired.

It is worth reminding ourselves of the familiar fact that we also sometimes get disagreement when it comes to empirical observations as well. You see the two patches as having the same color; I do not. So at least one of us is mistaken. It looked to you like this runner crossed the finish line before that one; it looked to me like the opposite was the case. So at least one of us is mistaken. No one concludes from the existence of such disagreements that we are not justified in appealing to observation. At best, what disagreements involving observation show is that we need a fallibilist attitude toward observation: *sometimes* observations are mistaken. But then why shouldn't the same conclusion suffice when the disagreements involve intuition?

Ideally, of course, we would like to eventually identify the mechanisms as a result of which vision (for example) sometimes misfires. If we could offer a plausible account of how and why our visual apparatus sometimes generates illusory appearances, we might then be able to use that account to help settle who is right in some of the cases where different individuals have conflicting observations. But I hope it is obvious that we hardly need to wait until we *have* that story in place before we start using observations in building our empirical theories! Indeed, if we did have to wait, it is likely that we would never be able to work out the details of the error theory in the first place, never be able to discover the mechanisms that lead to mistaken observations. On the contrary, what we appropriately do is *use* our observations—fallible though they may be—to build up relevant empirical theories, the very theories that will eventually help us *identify* the error-generating mechanisms.

Similarly, then, for moral intuition. To the extent that people have incompatible intuitions, we will certainly need to conclude that intuition is fallible (a position we should hold in any event). And here too, ultimately we would like to identify the mechanisms which can lead to mistaken intuitions, since that might sometimes help us to confirm which intuitions are erroneous. But here as well, I see no reason to think that we need to wait until such an account is in place before we are justified in using our moral intuitions in theory building. Indeed, it is not at all likely we could ever arrive at an account of the error-generating mechanisms behind mistaken intuitions if we first had to figure out what those mechanism were before resorting to intuitions at all. Happily, however, since we do not impose a requirement to identify the relevant error-generating mechanisms before we appeal to *observation*, there is no reason to impose such a requirement when it comes to intuition either.

(A related point: if the skeptic suggests that we shouldn't rely on intuition since we have no adequate account of how moral intuition *works*—what mechanisms underlie it, even when it is supposedly functioning properly—we would do well to remember that for almost all of human history until quite recently we lacked anything like an adequate account of how vision, say, worked as well. Presumably, however, we would never have *discovered* that account—and we are, after all, still working out the details—if we had been unwilling to make use of our vision until that account was in place!)

At this point, the skeptic might insist that the problem is not the sheer fact of intuitive disagreement, but rather its *scale*. There is so *much* intuitive disagreement (she might insist) that we are justified in dismissing appeals to moral intuition altogether. In contrast (she might continue) disagreements in observation, though real, are sufficiently limited that a similarly skeptical stance is unwarranted.

Of course, this raises the question of just how widespread disagreements among moral intuitions actually are. It will not surprise you to learn that I think the answer is far from obvious.

In our earlier discussion about moral disagreement I suggested that diverging moral beliefs—especially about fundamental moral matters—may be less prevalent than we often think. But even if I am wrong about that, it won't settle the question currently under consideration. For as I have already explained, intuitions are not the same thing as beliefs, and one need not accept all of one's intuitions. (I certainly have various moral intuitions that I have come to regard as mistaken; I bet the same is true of you too.) Accordingly, even if it should turn out to be the case that people differ a fair amount in terms of their moral judgments, that won't yet tell us whether they differ in terms of their moral intuitions as well. To be sure, it isn't that I believe that we all actually do have the same moral intuitions; I'm reasonably confident that this isn't the case. But if the question is whether our moral intuitions vary *widely*, my suspicion is that no one really knows whether—or, to what extent—this is the case.

Suppose, however, that it really is true that in a wide range of cases there is a significant amount of intuitive disagreement. That is, suppose that for a wide range of cases a significant portion of the population have intuitions incompatible with the ones had by others (a significant number of others). Why shouldn't we simply take this to be good reason to reject the particular contested intuitions in question? Instead of dismissing all moral intuitions altogether, why not simply disregard (or, conceivably, give less weight to) those intuitions where there is substantial disagreement, and focus instead on intuitions that are indeed widely shared? That's more or less what we do in the empirical case, after all, where we give greater weight to observations that are widely shared, stable, and replicable, discounting observations that are controversial because people disagree about what they are seeing. Similarly, then, we could discount or altogether disregard moral intuitions that are not widely shared (or are unstable, and so on), all the while continuing to rely on intuitions that most or all of us possess.

(There are more refined versions of this same strategy: perhaps we should only discount intuitions that conflict where all the relevant parties are equally informed and reflective, and so on. For present purposes there is no need to explore the specifics.)

Note that such an approach is perfectly compatible with phenomenal conservatism which, remember, only says that appearances provide *defeasible* justification. Arguably, then, one of the things that can appropriately undermine or weaken that justification is when the relevant appearances are not widely shared and we have no independent ability to identify which of the competing appearances are illusory. But the mere fact that such disagreement undermines justificatory force in those cases where it exists, does not give us reason to think that *shared* appearances lack justificatory force as well. We rightly refrain from building empirical theories on the basis of observations that aren't widely shared; but this doesn't stop us from appealing to observations that are indeed shared (or replicable, and so on). Similarly, then, we can discount moral intuitions in the face of widespread disagreement, while still appealing to ones that most of us have—or that we would have, were we asked to think about the relevant questions.

(Of course, even if some intuition is widely shared, we may still discover a good reason to reject it. Optical illusions are still illusions, after all, even though we are all subject to them. Similarly, then, there may well be some universally shared "moral illusions" as well. That's certainly my own view, at any rate: even a universally shared intuition can be mistaken.)

Suppose, then, that it really does turn out to be true that disagreements involving moral intuitions are more common—perhaps even far more common—than disagreements involving observations. That may mean that we have a smaller stock of inputs for our moral theory building than we have for our empirical theory building. To that extent, at least, gaining moral knowledge may be more difficult than gaining empirical knowledge. But for all that, we don't yet have a reason to think it impossible.

7.4 Reliability

A rather different worry about appealing to intuitions as a source of moral knowledge focuses on what we might call the "contingency" of our moral intuitions. It seems obvious that if any number of things had gone differently—if history had gone differently, or the course of human evolution, or if my own upbringing had been different in various ways—then I wouldn't have the particular intuitions that I do have. Not only might I lack some of my current intuitions, I might have different ones instead, intuitions incompatible with the ones I actually have. So my intuitions could easily have been different. But it doesn't seem likely that the moral facts themselves would have been different. So doesn't this sort of contingency undermine the plausibility of thinking that we can appeal to intuitions as a way of gaining insight into moral truth?

Actually, though, I don't think it does. It isn't that I doubt that our intuitions are (at least to some extent) contingent. It does seem likely that at least some of our intuitions would have been different if certain external circumstances—we needn't quibble about which—had been different from what they were. But what of it? Why should we think that this undermines the legitimacy of appealing to our intuitions? Why think that this calls their reliability into question?

It is, after all, also true that the accuracy of our *observations* is a contingent fact as well. Presumably, if certain things had gone differently—whether in my personal history, or over the course of human evolution, or what have you—my visual system would not accurately represent the external world. But what of it? Why would the mere fact that my vision *could* have been inaccurate give me reason to think that it *is*, in fact, inaccurate?

Similarly, I take it to be obviously true that if I hadn't had the proper zoological education, I wouldn't be in a position to simply have it seem to me (visually) that there is a zebra in front of me. But what of it? I *did* have the relevant education, and I *am* in a position to have things appear to me in the relevant way. Why would the mere fact of contingency—if my personal history had been different I would lack some of the appearances I now actually have—give me reason to think that those appearances are not to be trusted?

Thus even if we suppose it to be true—as I imagine to some degree it is—that my moral intuitions are at least somewhat contingent, what of it? If I had lacked a proper moral education, I wouldn't be in a position to have some of the moral intuitions that I have. If human history or evolution had gone differently, perhaps I would have lacked moral intuitions altogether, or had radically different ones. But what of it? Why would the mere fact that intuition could have been inaccurate (or lacking altogether) give me reason to think that it *is*, in fact, inaccurate?

The question is not whether my intuition (or human intuition more generally) was influenced by various factors that might conceivably have gone otherwise. Of course it was. But that mere fact doesn't suffice to call into question the accuracy or reliability of intuition (just as the contingency of observation doesn't in and of itself call the reliability of observation into question).

What we really want to know, of course, is this: do I or don't I have reason to think that my moral intuition is *reliable*? As I've just argued, contingency per se doesn't call the reliability of intuition into question. But perhaps something else does. So let's consider the issue more directly.

Something like the following seems plausible. If I am justified in using individual moral intuitions as input (even if merely as defeasible input), it must be the case that moral intuition on the whole is reasonably reliable; it must largely get things right. To be sure, it need not be perfect, or infallible. (Vision, after all, is hardly infallible; but we justifiably rely on *it*.) But at the same time, intuition can't simply be random. Roughly speaking, moral intuition must be

7.4 RELIABILITY

correlated with the truth, typically getting it right, or at least, getting it right "often enough." (How often is often enough? I won't try to settle this here, though I do want to point out that there is a similar question about the reliability of observation.)

If we are to rely on intuition, then intuition must be sufficiently reliable. As a rough approximation, something like the following must be the case: if I have the intuition that P, then it must—usually, or often enough—be the case that P; were it not the case that P, I would not have the intuition that P.

Note that there is no similar requirement that if P is the case then I must (usually, or often enough) *have* the intuition that P. It could turn out that intuition is *silent* on many moral issues, leaving us without any initial, tentative impression of what the relevant moral facts might be. That might be disappointing, but it wouldn't in any way threaten our justification for relying on intuitions when and where we do have them. So the relevant requirement is only this: when I do have an intuition, it had better usually (or often enough) be right. (A similar requirement is in place with regard to observation. Though there are many empirical facts I cannot just "see," still, if I do seem to see something, it had better be the case—usually, or often enough—that the facts are as they seem to be. Otherwise, observation isn't reliable.)

Now if the rough correlation I've just described holds, then there is presumably some explanation of why this is so. There must be something that accounts for the connection (imperfect though it may be) between intuition and the moral facts. To be sure, it needn't be the case that we *know* what explains the connection—exactly how it works and why—but we must at least believe that there *is* some such explanation. And it would certainly be reassuring if we had at least a rough idea of how it might go.

But at this point we may grow concerned. For it can seem baffling how the supposed connection between intuition and moral truth could possibly exist. Without such a connection, intuition won't be reliable; yet what could possibly explain it? How *could* the two be connected?

On the face of it, it seems that there are two basic ways that a potential explanation—connecting intuition and moral truth—could go: (1) perhaps we have the intuitions that we do *because* of the moral facts (we intuit that P because it is true that P); or (2) perhaps the moral facts are as they are because we have the *intuitions* that we do (it is true that P because we intuit that P).

The first type of explanation—which runs from truth to appearances—is the obvious one to think of initially, for that is how the analogous connection is created when it comes to empirical observations and facts about the external world. In the case of vision, for example, ordinarily it seems to me that there is a tree in front of me because there *is* a tree in front of me: the particular fact in question (the presence of the tree) helps explain why it is that things look to me the way that they do. But in principle, at least, it is conceivable that a suitable explanation of the connection between moral facts and moral intuition might run in the other direction, from intuition to truth. That's what we would have, in any event, if somehow the moral facts could be what they are *by virtue of* my having the moral intuitions that I do (or by virtue of *our* having the intuitions that *we* do).

Explanations of this second type may seem unpromising. How could it be the case that the moral facts are what they are by virtue of their *seeming* to be a certain way? Nonetheless, there are domains where explanations of this second sort do seem to be more or less correct, so we shouldn't dismiss out of hand the possibility that an explanation of this second kind may be appropriate when it comes to ethics as well. Consider, for example, the nature of the connection between the facts about grammar—of English, say—and our intuitive reactions concerning what is grammatical ("this sentence is grammatical, that one isn't"). Presumably it isn't that there are mind independent facts about grammar (waiting to be discovered "out there") and somehow those facts explain why we all ended up having the reactions that we do. Rather, what makes a given sentence grammatical are a lot of facts about which sentences we are prepared to make and accept, that is, facts about our intuitive linguistic reactions. Very roughly speaking, a given sentence is grammatical because we have the intuitive reactions that we do. And if—as sometimes happens—our intuitive reactions change, and we start accepting sentences that we now reject, those sentences would in fact *become* grammatical. The full story is, of course, more complicated than what I have just said, but the basic thought here seems right: our linguistic intuitions are reliable (not infallibly, but largely so) because the facts about grammar are grounded in them. Loosely but intuitively speaking, the facts of grammar are ultimately grounded in our intuitions about grammar.

Could something similar hold true for ethics? Might our moral intuitions ground the moral facts?

Some constructivists can be seen as taking this second route. If it is the case, as constructivists hold, that the truth of a given moral claim boils down to the relevant reactions or attitudes of the relevant minds, then it could turn out that the moral facts are what they are to a significant degree because of our moral intuitions. After all, my seeing a given act as wrong is typically the same as (or closely related to) my disapproving of it, or opposing it; my seeing a given outcome as intrinsically good is the same as (or closely related to) my favoring it. If my reactions are among the relevant reactions (and are similar to those of the other relevant minds) and if constructivism is correct, then we can say that, roughly speaking, my intuitions (along with those of the relevant others) explain why the moral facts are as they are. A given moral claim may be true because we intuit that it is.

Of course, depending on what exactly the constructivist takes the relevant reaction or attitude to be, it might not be that the intuition in and of itself forms the ground of the corresponding moral fact. But as long as there is a tight enough connection between having the intuition and having the reaction in question, it won't be far from the mark to say that moral facts are what they are because we have the intuitions that we do.

One version of constructivism that might be understood along these lines is a simple subjectivist view that holds that the truth of a given moral claim boils down to my actually having the relevant intuition (or attitude). On such a view, "this act is wrong" would be true just in case I disapprove of the given act. So moral facts will be what they are because I have the intuitions that I do.

Admittedly, this sort of subjectivism is a very implausible account of morality. But there are cousins of the view that may do better. Imagine a view that says that the truth of a moral claim boils down not to the attitudes that I actually do have, but rather to the ones I *would* have under suitably ideal conditions—for example, were I fully informed, perfectly rational, and so on. I am not, of course, perfectly rational nor fully informed, but still, it might be the case that I am sufficiently informed and rational so that the intuitions I do have are at least roughly correlated with the ones I would have under ideal conditions. Here too, then, it might turn out that my intuitions, though far from infallible, are nonetheless reliable; the moral facts would be what they are because of the intuitions I do (and would) have. (On the other hand, if I am *too* very far from the idealized version of myself, my intuitions would not be reliable after all.)

Similarly, if one accepts an ideal observer account of morality—where right and wrong boil down to the attitudes of a suitably idealized lawgiver—if my current state, though falling short in various ways of the relevant ideal conditions, nonetheless *approximates* it sufficiently well, then my intuitions may be an imperfect but reliable guide to moral truth.

Or consider a contractarian theory, according to which the truth of a given moral claim boils down to facts about the moral rules that would be agreed upon by suitably specified bargainers. Here, too, provided that our actual intuitions are sufficiently close to the preferences we would have were we to meet the relevant specifications and engage in such bargaining, we can see how intuition could be sufficiently correlated with the output of such a bargain that it would be a reliable (though imperfect) guide to the moral facts.

So there may be constructivist views according to which we can say—at least, as a rough approximation of the truth—that the moral facts are what they are because our intuitions are what they are. Accordingly, if any of these views is acceptable, then moral intuition may be a sufficiently reliable guide to moral truth. For some people, in fact, this may be part of the appeal of constructivism.

At the same time, it must be admitted that not all versions of constructivism can avail themselves of an argument along these lines. If our minds are not among the *relevant* minds, then it won't be even approximately correct to say that the moral facts depend on our intuitions. Thus, for example, a constructivist view according to which moral facts ultimately depend on *God's* will won't be one where it is right to suggest that the moral facts are what they are by virtue of our having the moral intuitions that we do. And even on constructivist views where our minds *are* among the relevant minds, if the theory appeals to *highly* transformed versions of ourselves, it won't be plausible to suggest that the moral facts depend in any interesting way on our *current* intuitions. So if our (current) intuition is going to be thought reliable, a different explanation will be needed.

Furthermore, it is clear that *simple realists*—who, by definition, reject the idea that moral facts boil down to facts about the attitudes of relevant minds (see 2.3)—cannot avail themselves of this type of explanation at all. It cannot be that moral facts are what they are by virtue of our intuitions being what they are, if moral facts are, in the relevant sense, mind *independent*. Here too, then, if intuition is going to be reliable, the explanation can't be of this second sort, where moral truth is grounded in (or somehow constituted by) facts about our intuitions.

So simple realists, and at least some constructivists (as well as nonconstructivist reductionists), will want to consider the possibility of an explanation that runs in the *first* of the two directions mentioned above. Instead of suggesting that the moral facts are to be explained in terms of our intuitions, they will want to argue that our intuitions are explained by the facts. This is, as I have already noted, the relevant direction for explaining the reliability of observation: we believe that the external world appears to us as it does because of what the facts about the external world *are*. (It seems to me that there is a tree in front of me because there *is* a tree in front of me.) Is a similar sort of explanation available to the moral realist?

In the case of empirical observation, the explanation is, more particularly, a causal one: roughly speaking, and details aside, my observations are *caused* by the facts. (The presence of the tree causes me to have the sensory experiences that I do.) Could anything like that be true in the case of morality? Could the fact that torture is wrong, say, cause me to have the *intuition* that it is wrong?

At first glance this may seem an unpromising approach, since we don't normally think of moral facts as having causal powers. But if one is a *naturalist*, at least, so that moral properties are themselves *natural* properties (see 2.3), perhaps this possibility shouldn't be dismissed. If moral properties are (simple or complex) natural properties, there is no obvious reason why they shouldn't be part of the causal nexus, and as such it is at least conceivable that I have the particular moral intuitions that I do because of what the moral facts *are*. Just as the five senses are, roughly speaking, empirical fact "detectors," perhaps reason (or one's conscience) is, in turn, a *moral* fact detector.

It is less clear whether an approach along these lines is available to the nonnaturalist, though even here I think we can make sense of the idea of a faculty capable of generating largely accurate representations of independent moral facts. Suppose, for example, to take a familiar religious idea, that God has implanted within each of us a moral conscience, capable of representing moral facts accurately (though perhaps not infallibly). Presumably, the idea would be that God knows the moral facts, and consequently gives us the particular type of conscience that he does, precisely so that our moral intuitions will be largely correct and moral knowledge will be available to us. If anything like this were true, it would still be correct to say that we have the moral intuitions that we do because the moral facts are what they are, and intuition would be reliable. (On the other hand, we might wonder how *God* comes to know the moral facts. Would an appeal to "divine omniscience" answer the question, or merely point to a further puzzle?)

Suppose, however, that we would rather avoid theological hypotheses and so don't want to appeal to a divinely implanted conscience. We can, of course, still talk of conscience or reason—or intuition itself—as a faculty capable of reliably generating appropriate moral intuitions. But what other explanation might there be (divine intervention aside) for how we come to *have* a reliable intuition generator? If—as we are here assuming—moral facts are themselves mind independent (or, at least, independent of *our* minds, or of our *actual* minds), how does it come to be the case that we have a faculty that represents moral facts accurately?

We should, I think, resist the temptation to appeal to culture here, and the passing down of moral knowledge from one generation to the next. While it certainly does seem likely that some of our moral intuitions (and the mechanisms that generate them) are shaped by cultural influences, any such broad-brush appeal to culture will simply postpone, rather than answer, the inevitable question: how did our cultural ancestors come by *their* moral knowledge? Inevitably, we will find ourselves appealing to moral intuitions once again—though this time, the intuitions of our predecessors—and we will still need to know how it came to pass that our *predecessors* had a faculty capable of accurately representing moral facts.

As far as I can see, the only plausible alternative to the theological story will be one that appeals to *evolution*. If we have a faculty capable of generating accurate representations of moral facts, it must be that evolutionary forces shaped us to have such a faculty. Roughly speaking, there must be some evolutionary advantage in having a faculty that to a significant extent gets the moral facts right. Or rather, a bit more precisely, there must be some evolutionary advantage in having a faculty that gets at least some basic moral truths right. (Even if there is no evolutionary advantage in accurately representing more *advanced* or complex moral truths, we might simply get these "for free"—with intuitions generated by the same faculty that generates the more elementary insights.)

Compare the account we might give of how we came to have an intuitive faculty capable of accurately representing mathematical truths. Presumably there is an evolutionary advantage in having accurate intuitions about elementary arithmetic (such as addition and subtraction), and so evolution shaped us to have a faculty capable of generating largely accurate intuitions about basic math. And while there may have been no particular evolutionary advantage in also having accurate intuitions about *higher* forms of mathematics, like multivariable calculus or algebraic topology (that is, no advantage that would have been manifest among our primal ancestors, when our basic faculties were being formed), it might well be the case that a faculty capable of getting elementary math right is also capable (under suitable tutelage) of getting more advanced math largely right as well.

Perhaps a similar story can be told about moral intuitions. Arguably, there is an evolutionary advantage in having accurate intuitions about what there is reason to do in certain basic cases (including, perhaps, some basic moral situations), and so evolution shaped us to have a faculty (which we call *reason*) capable of generating largely accurate intuitions about such cases. And once in place, that very same faculty might also be capable (under suitable tutelage) of generating largely accurate representations about more advanced cases (including more subtle moral situations) as well.

Obviously, working out the details of such an evolutionary account would not be an easy undertaking. But we have no obligation to try to do that here. Our question was simply whether we could so much as sketch the outlines of a possible explanation of the reliability of moral intuition, and at first glance, at any rate, it does seem as though a suitable appeal to evolution might do the trick.

Interestingly enough, however, some people are attracted to the opposite conclusion. They argue that recognizing the extent to which our moral intuitions have been shaped by evolutionary forces should *undermine* our faith in the reliability of those intuitions rather than supporting it! Indeed, many contemporary moral skeptics think that evolution-based challenges to morality are among the most persuasive.

The relevant arguments are complex; sufficiently so, in fact, that rather than try to spell them out here we are going to devote an entire chapter to examining them. So perhaps it is best to end this part of our discussion with a conditional claim. If evolutionary challenges to morality can be successfully answered—as I believe they can be—then perhaps the moral realist should actually *appeal* to evolution (rather than worry about it), as evolution may provide a way of explaining the reliability of moral intuition. And with the reliability of intuition defended, the realist will have in place a plausible account of the basis of moral knowledge.

(As it happens, I believe that when all is said and done, an evolutionary account of the connection between moral intuition and moral facts may actually be best understood in terms of a *third* possible "direction" of explanation, one distinct from the two we have explored here. But this point can wait until later.)

7.5 Intuitionism

I have been arguing that the realist can account for the possibility of moral knowledge by appealing to our moral intuitions, using them as (defeasible) inputs for our moral theories. If we call theories that appeal to moral intuitions in this way *intuitionist*, then intuitionism offers, I believe, a plausible account of moral knowledge. Intuitionism tells us that we can appeal to our intuitions to argue for or against specific moral claims.

More than that, intuitionism gives us a reason—a defeasible reason, to be sure, but a reason for all that—to believe that there is indeed such a thing as morality, that there really are moral facts. For whatever the specific contents of this or that particular intuition, when I *have* a moral intuition it seems to me to be the case that some such specific moral fact obtains. That is to say, not only does it appear to me as though this particular fact obtains, it appears to me, more generally, that there are, indeed, moral facts of *some* sort. It seems to me that there are moral facts! So if intuitions provide defeasible reason to believe their contents, then I have defeasible reason to believe in moral facts.

This point is worth noting in light of our earlier discussion (in 3.2) about whether the moral realist has the burden of proof, such that it is the realist who must first give us some reason to believe in the sort of facts—moral facts—that are rejected by skeptics. Without conceding that it is indeed the realist who has the burden of proof, let me simply note that if intuitionism is right, then this burden is now met. In the absence of a compelling argument to the contrary, we should tentatively believe that things are as they appear to us to be. Since it appears to us that there are moral facts, then unless we are provided with compelling reasons to reject those appearances, we should believe that there are indeed moral facts after all.

To be sure, the skeptic might yet *provide* us with convincing reasons to reject those appearances. Suppose, for example, that we were to decide that moral facts are impossible because they would be metaphysically dubious in one way or another; then, of course, we would have good reason to dismiss our moral intuitions as illusory. Still, for all that, until these skeptical arguments are put in place and successfully defended we will have a presumptive justification for taking our intuitions at face value, as evidence for the very existence of moral facts. In short, an appeal to intuitionism should suffice to meet any initial burden of proof that the moral realist might face, and so now the burden will squarely move to the skeptic, who must try to provide compelling reason to deny the existence of such facts after all.

I should note, however, that despite these important virtues there are indeed moral realists who nonetheless reject intuitionism. As realists, they do believe in the existence of moral facts, but they reject the use of moral intuitions as a path to moral knowledge. (Perhaps they worry that there is no acceptable way to argue for the reliability of those intuitions.) Such realists, of course, will need to offer an alternative proposal concerning how moral knowledge can be acquired and how moral claims are to be justified. Typically such proposals start with claims about one or another metaphysical concept, such as the nature of rationality, or the nature of agency, or the function or "telos" of different types of beings, or perhaps they begin with claims about divine purposes, or what have you. They then attempt to derive particular moral conclusions from these various starting points.

Inevitably, however, or so it seems to me, any such attempt will sooner or later appeal to intuitions of one sort or another. For how is it that we can come to know anything at all about the nature of rationality, or agency, or the telos of a given type of being, and so on, except by means of our intuitions about these various topics? Indeed, even appeals to divine revelation will have to make use of our intuitions about the reliability of various potential sources of knowledge. Furthermore, once we turn to deriving particular moral conclusions from the relevant starting points, we will also need to draw on our logical intuitions, using such intuitions to guide us as we try to determine what follows from what.

Since realists cannot avoid appealing to intuitions of some sort, the question then becomes why they should resist the appeal to *moral* intuitions in particular. It certainly isn't obvious why intuitions about rationality, or agency, or the divinity, and so on, should be thought reliable, while intuitions about morality are not. As far as I can see, then, there is no compelling reason for the moral realist to avoid an intuitionist view, one which gives weight to our moral intuitions *along* with intuitions of these other sorts as well (should these other subjects indeed prove to be morally relevant). As I have repeatedly suggested, moral intuitions are not infallible. But that is not a reason to disregard them altogether.

It may seem obvious that even if moral realists should be intuitionists, moral *skeptics*, in contrast, must reject intuitionism. After all, such skeptics deny the existence of moral facts and moral knowledge, so don't they need to deny the epistemic force of our moral intuitions? Actually, however, I don't think that this is the case. Like everyone else, moral skeptics make use of their intuitions about logic, if nothing more, when putting forward their arguments. And of course, depending on the particular argument in question, skeptics also make use of intuitions about metaphysics, epistemology, philosophy of language, metaethics, and more. So I think that moral skeptics would be well advised to avoid a sweeping dismissal of all appeals to intuition whatsoever. On the contrary, it seems to me that the skeptic should acknowledge that appearances are the source of defeasible reasons for belief, and thus that intuitions—as a kind of appearance—are, quite generally, *also* a source of defeasible reasons. And this means, of course, that the skeptic should concede that even *moral* intuitions provide defeasible reasons for belief, and in particular that they provide defeasible reasons for believing that there really are moral facts (and that the facts are as they appear to be).

What the skeptic should insist upon, rather, is that we not lose sight of the fact that since these are *defeasible* reasons, they are indeed capable of being completely undercut. So we may yet find compelling reason to dismiss our moral intuitions—each and every one of them—as illusory. That is to say, the skeptic should concede that moral intuitions provide defeasible justification, but then go on to argue that moral intuitions are indeed all *defeated*, given the compelling skeptical arguments against the existence of moral *facts*.

In short, even the moral skeptic might embrace intuitionism, provided that we define that view broadly enough so that it is committed only to the *presumptive* possibility of moral knowledge through moral intuitions. Moral *realists* will then be intuitionists who believe that the presumption remains in place even after reflection, that skeptical attacks can be successfully rebutted. Skeptics, in contrast, will be intuitionists who believe that the presumption can be *overcome*, so that moral knowledge turns out to be impossible after all. Of course, making good on this skeptical version of intuitionism still requires the skeptic to offer a compelling argument *for* skepticism, since the arguments we have considered so far are unsuccessful.

Let me close with a few comments about noncognitivism and intuition. Like other moral skeptics, noncognitivists deny the existence of moral facts. But they insist that there are, nonetheless, important uses for our moral language; moral pronouncements express attitudes of approval and disapproval and are used to give commands. Similarly, then, although noncognitivists hold that moral intuitions are illusory (since when I have such an intuition it appears to me to be the case that some moral fact obtains, but—they claim—there are no moral facts), they typically hold that there is, for all that, an important use for those intuitions. Moral intuitions can influence us in deciding which moral principles to embrace.

The thought here is this. Since there are no moral facts, when I have a moral intuition all that is really going on is that my underlying dispositions to approve or disapprove of certain types of things (actions, states of affairs, character traits, and so on) are making themselves manifest. The intuition is simply an expression of my underlying preferences. Accordingly, it makes sense to take them to heart while I work my way toward moral principles that I am prepared to order myself and others to conform to. In effect, I can use my moral intuitions to guide myself toward discovering principles that, on the whole, I will be prepared to embrace. In practice, then, the noncognitivist may use moral intuitions in a way that will look very similar to the way that realists use them—as touchstones for shaping and selecting moral principles. It's just that, unlike the realist, the noncognitivist won't take this process to be one that aims to arrive at accurate representations of moral facts.

Nonetheless, moral intuitions do pose an interesting problem for the noncognitivist. For moral intuitions, like intuitions quite generally, are mental states in which something appears to be the case. When I have an intuition that lying is wrong, for example, it *seems* to me to be a *fact* that lying is wrong. As such, we would expect moral intuitions to at least *dispose* us to accept the corresponding beliefs—for example, the belief that lying *is* wrong. No doubt, we need not accept all, or perhaps even most, of these beliefs; but it would be strange if moral intuitions never led to any corresponding beliefs at all. To stick to our example, surely at least sometimes they might lead to the belief that lying is wrong, a belief I might then reasonably express with the claim that "lying is wrong." Yet according to noncognitivists, this doesn't actually happen! According to noncognitivists, when I say that lying is wrong I am not actually trying to express a genuine belief at all; I am not attempting to state a fact. Indeed, according to the noncognitivist I *have* no such belief; what looks like a moral belief is actually nothing more than an expression of my attitudes of approval and disapproval.

I must say, this all seems rather peculiar and implausible. In other cases, intuitions do at least sometimes lead to corresponding *beliefs* (about logic, or metaphysics, or epistemology, or metaethics, and so on). Why doesn't something similar happen in the case of moral intuitions? I suspect that the noncognitivist cannot provide a plausible answer.

In this regard, at least, the nihilist does better than the noncognitivist. The nihilist will agree that moral intuitions, like other intuitions, frequently lead to corresponding beliefs, so that moral beliefs are genuine beliefs, and moral claims, genuine assertions. It is simply that they are all false. I see no compelling reason to *accept* nihilism, but at least this view seems intelligible. In contrast, by denying the truth aptness of moral claims, the noncognitivist shuts the door to a similarly straightforward account of the influence of moral intuitions on our beliefs. And I cannot readily see what alternative account the noncognitivist might offer in its place.

Perhaps, then, those otherwise drawn to noncognitivism should accept, instead, *revisionist* nihilism (see 2.2). As a cognitivist, the revisionist can acknowledge that moral intuitions routinely lead us to accept corresponding moral beliefs. The revisionist thinks these beliefs are all false, but they are genuine beliefs for all that. Still, despite the illusory nature of our intuitions (since they represent moral facts as obtaining, even though there *are* no moral facts), and despite the fact that our moral beliefs are all false, the revisionist agrees with the noncognitivist that there are important jobs that still need to be done, and so moral language should not be abandoned. Rather, says the revisionist, it should be reconceived. Although moral claims are all false, we can still use these claims to express attitudes and issue commands.

Obviously, it is not my intent here to argue for revisionist nihilism. Along with other forms of moral skepticism, I think it is mistaken. Still, this does seem one important way in which the revisionist's view is more plausible than the noncognitivist's. But having noted this point, I will put this particular problem for the noncognitivist aside. *Our* question remains the more general one, whether there is any good reason to accept some form of moral skepticism in the first place.

8
Evolution

8.1 The Argument from Evolution

There is a familiar, nagging worry that recognizing the role of evolution in shaping our moral beliefs somehow threatens, or should threaten, our belief in moral realism—our belief in objective moral facts. It is, I suppose, easier to feel the force of this worry than it is to pin down how, precisely, the threat is supposed to work. But the basic thought, I imagine, goes something like this: It seems likely that evolutionary forces explain why we have many of our most central moral emotions, intuitions, attitudes, and beliefs. Yet once we recognize this fact—or perhaps, more precisely, once we recognize just what it is that evolutionary shaping actually responds to—we can see that there is no good reason to think that those beliefs, emotions, intuitions, and the like are to be trusted. That is to say, given the role of evolution in generating our moral beliefs, there is no reason to think that they accurately represent an objective moral reality.

So construed, the worry is most directly and primarily an epistemological one: we are led to worry about whether we have any adequate evidence for the various purported moral facts we find ourselves inclined to believe in. We normally take our moral intuitions and emotions to be evidence for the corresponding moral beliefs; but the relevant evolutionary considerations leave us wondering whether we are justified in trusting our emotions and intuitions on this score at all.

To be sure, if this epistemological worry can't be turned aside it might lead us—as we have previously noted—to a metaphysical one as well: if we have no *evidence* concerning these purported moral facts, why should we so much as believe in their existence? But since this particular metaphysical worry presupposes the epistemological one, we can focus on the latter.

In terms of our previous discussion of the possibility of moral knowledge, the worry might be stated like this. Even if I was right to argue in the last chapter that intuitions provide defeasible justification for holding the corresponding beliefs, recognition of the role that evolution played in shaping those moral intuitions might leave us worried that this presumptive justification has indeed been *defeated*—not just for this or that particular intuition, but across the board. Evolutionary explanations for our moral intuitions seem to give us reason to be skeptical about the reliability of those intuitions quite generally. If that's right, then the particular path to moral knowledge that I've argued for will be closed, and (or so it seems to me) the prospects of having any justified first-order beliefs about morality at all will be rather dim.

Now as skeptical worries about morality go, concerns about evolution are of relatively recent vintage. One could hardly think of evolution as posing a threat to moral realism before the introduction of the theory of evolution in the nineteenth century; and even then, I imagine, few people worried much about evolution's potential threat to the justification of belief in morality until the emergence of modern evolutionary psychology in the twentieth. But be that as it may, I suspect that a concern about morality and evolution is nowadays a fairly common one, and it is certainly worthy of our attention.

Here, then, is a first stab at expressing a skeptical argument based on an appeal to evolutionary theory. Many or most of our moral beliefs are the direct or indirect result of evolution. Evolution has simply "designed" or "shaped" us to have the moral beliefs we do. Accordingly, we have no reason to accept those beliefs as *accurate*. Even if there *are* moral facts, we have no reason to think that our evolutionarily generated moral beliefs are *reliable*.

Let's call this *the argument from evolution*. No doubt, stated in this crude way the argument is inadequate. Much of what follows in this chapter is an attempt to see whether a more successful version of the argument can be mounted. But first, let me offer some general, clarificatory remarks.

First of all, then, talk of evolution as "designing" or "shaping" us (or "building" us, and so on) is potentially misleading, suggesting as it might some deliberate intentional process. But I very much doubt that anyone reading this book will be misled by such talk. It is, of course, common to use anthropomorphic locutions like this as shorthand for the fuller, nonanthropomorphic accounts provided by evolutionary theory. Happily, since nothing that follows turns on this issue, there is no need to avoid these familiar bits of shorthand.

Second, while there are various accounts that have been suggested by evolutionary biologists and evolutionary psychologists about how to explain different parts of our commonsense moral outlook in evolutionary terms, the details of those accounts will not concern us here. Indeed, it isn't even my intention to sketch a few likely stories. I will simply assume that you are familiar with these sorts of explanations, at least in broad outlines—or, at the very least, that you believe that such explanations can be provided. Perhaps you've heard, or read, accounts of why reciprocal altruism would be evolutionarily advantageous, or you can see the possible evolutionary advantages of caring for one's children, punishing cheaters, keeping one's promises, having a sense of fairness, and so on. Be that as it may, I will not rehearse those possible accounts here. Nor will I ask whether those accounts are correct or if, failing that, other, superior evolutionary accounts might do the trick. For our purposes, I am simply going to assume that something along these lines is correct. I know that there are those who doubt whether evolution can provide an adequate account of much (let alone all) of our commonsense moral outlook. Our goal is to ask what would follow if it could.

I will however say this much. It seems very unlikely that evolution would have straightaway implanted many, if any, moral beliefs. More likely the process was slow and indirect. Over the long sweep of our evolutionary history, evolution may have initially favored certain behaviors, and only then later favored certain emotional attitudes toward those behaviors (in ourselves and in others), and then later still favored our having certain moral intuitions (having things appear to us as being "called for" or "to be done" or "supported by the situation"). It is, no doubt, only quite recently in our evolutionary history that anything like explicit moral judgments or beliefs would have emerged.

And even today, where we undeniably have such judgments, it is unlikely that many of those moral beliefs are innate, directly "hard wired" into us. Evolution's influence on our moral beliefs remains somewhat indirect. Evolution may have bequeathed upon us something like our various moral emotions and intuitions (or so we are assuming), or more precisely, faculties capable of generating such emotions and intuitions. But it is only as a result of reflection—both individual and cultural—that these evolutionarily provided materials get turned into full-blown moral beliefs. So evolution's impact on our moral beliefs is largely an indirect one. But it is (we are assuming) pervasive for all that.

It might, of course, turn out that for *some* of our moral beliefs, the influence of evolution is *highly* indirect. Perhaps for some of our moral beliefs an adequate explanation of why we have come to have those views will give pride of place to instances of reflection, abstract thought, and culture. But presumably, even here, the more basic moral beliefs (those more directly shaped by evolution) will have had a very significant influence, for we use them as touchstones—albeit defeasible ones—for our moral reflections. So even if it turns out that we have come to accept certain moral beliefs only as a result of highly reasoned and abstract arguments, insofar as much of the "raw material" for this reasoning—our initial emotions and intuitions—was provided by evolution, we may have reason for concern. If the moral beliefs more directly influenced by evolution are largely suspect, then even those conclusions *less* directly influenced by evolution will be suspect as well.

With these clarifications in place, let's return to the skeptic's argument. As a first pass, it seems that the skeptic's thought might be something like this: Evolution built us to have the moral beliefs that we do. It did this by means of giving us a faculty capable of generating relevant intuitions and emotions. But recognizing this fact—that our moral beliefs are the result of evolutionary shaping—gives us reason to doubt the reliability of these beliefs. Since the faculty that *creates* the intuitions (and emotions) was the result of evolutionary selection, we can't justifiably trust it. We can't trust the intuitions that it generates, nor the beliefs that we arrive at as a result of having these intuitions.

(Going forward I will talk only about evolution's role in shaping our moral *intuitions*, dropping further reference to our moral emotions. Parallel remarks apply, of course, with regard to our emotions as well, but it would add nothing substantive to the discussion that follows to continue mentioning them explicitly. For simplicity, then, in what follows I will limit myself to talking about intuitions, leaving the corresponding claims about emotion implicit.)

It should be obvious, however, that if what I just said adequately captures the nature of the skeptic's worry then their concern is misplaced, for this argument cannot possibly succeed as it stands. All it does, in this initial incarnation, is note the fact that our moral intuitions have their origin in a faculty which in turn has its origin in evolution. And that bare fact cannot suffice to undermine our trust in those intuitions, for the same thing is true for other mental faculties that we constantly rely upon as well.

It is, after all, also true that evolution built us to have the five senses that we do, and these in turn are the source of our various spontaneous beliefs about ordinary empirical objects, such as trees, rocks, rivers, and people. In effect, evolution shaped us to have beliefs like "here's a rock," or "there's a tree," or "that's water." Of course, it didn't implant these various beliefs directly in us. Rather, evolution built our eyes (along with our other senses), as part of a faculty (in this instance, vision) capable of generating observations about ordinary, everyday objects; and it is these observations that in turn ordinarily lead us to have the corresponding beliefs. Although the process is in this way indirect, it still seems appropriate to say that we have the empirical beliefs that we do (about ordinary everyday objects) because evolution built us to have them.

Yet no one thinks that recognizing this fact somehow shows that we shouldn't believe our eyes! No one concludes from the mere fact that the faculty of vision is the result of evolutionary shaping that this somehow shows us that vision is unreliable and shouldn't be trusted. Yes, vision is the result of evolutionary selection, but we rightly take it to be reliable for all that. (Not perfectly reliable, of course, but largely reliable.) No one concludes that we shouldn't trust the beliefs we arrive at in this way—that is, as a result of visual observations.

Similarly, then, the mere fact that the faculty that generates intuitions is the result of evolutionary shaping cannot suffice to give us a reason to be skeptical about that either. Even if our moral intuitions are the result of evolution, we can still take them to be reliable for all that. (Not perfectly reliable, of course, but largely reliable.) Our moral sensibility may be the result of evolutionary selection, but we shouldn't conclude from this that we shouldn't trust the moral beliefs we reach as a result of our intuitions.

I must confess, it is a bit of an exaggeration to say that *no one* concludes from the mere fact that evolution shaped our vision, that vision cannot be trusted. There are indeed those who think that discovering an evolutionary basis for a mental faculty really does call into question the legitimacy of making use of that faculty, whatever it is. If that's right, then evolution poses a threat to empirical knowledge as well as to ethics. But as usual, I am not attempting to reply to this sort of more general skepticism, only to the worry that morality is somehow in *worse* shape than other subjects. So if it turns out that evolution poses no greater an objection to relying on our moral intuitions than it does to relying on our visual observations, for our purposes, I think, that's good enough to put the worry to rest.

What all of this shows, I think, is this. If evolution really does pose some sort of threat to moral realism, the moral skeptic will have to work harder to show us just what it is.

8.2 A Second Try

The initial appeal to evolution failed. Perhaps that shouldn't surprise us, since it did little more than note the bare fact that our moral intuitions and beliefs have a basis in evolution. Without saying more about how evolution works, or what it responds to, it is difficult to see why merely noting evolution's role in shaping our moral beliefs should be particularly troubling. But the skeptic can do better. She might offer a second version of the argument, one which emphasizes the fact that evolution favors whatever tends to enhance reproductive success (or more precisely, propagation of the given gene). Roughly speaking, and skipping over a variety of details and qualifications, we can say that evolution gives us features that are evolutionarily *advantageous*. In particular, then, evolution will tend to give us beliefs (and faculties for generating them) when there is an evolutionary advantage in doing this, and not otherwise.

Let's think about the implications of this fact. First off, this means that if there were an evolutionary advantage in believing truths about morality (supposing that there are such) then we might well have evolved to believe them. But it seems equally true, second, that if there were *no* advantage in having correct moral beliefs then we might *not* have evolved to have true beliefs about moral matters (or any moral beliefs at all). Indeed, if certain *false* moral beliefs were advantageous, we might well have evolved to accept those false beliefs instead. In short, evolution would tend to give us whatever moral beliefs happened to be evolutionarily advantageous, regardless of whether they are *true* or not.

Here's an example to illustrate the point. Suppose (horrifically enough) that there is a standing, perfectly general moral obligation to kill any children one might have. Or imagine (a bit less horrifically) that there is a standing, perfectly general moral obligation not to have any children in the first place. Presumably, evolution would never favor our recognizing that fact, for any such belief would be tremendously disadvantageous from the evolutionary perspective. (Creatures with the ability to recognize either of these obligations would be less likely to have children, or, if they did have children, less likely to raise them to the point where those offspring could go on to have children of their own. Over the long run, then, any such creatures would be likely to go extinct.) Instead of evolving to recognize these moral truths, it is far more likely that we would have evolved to have the *false* beliefs that having children was permissible (or perhaps even obligatory) and that caring for one's children was morally required. We would have evolved to have the kinds of intuitions that we do in fact have, intuitions that it is obligatory to love and nurture one's offspring. Evolution simply wouldn't care about the fact that our intuitions in this instance would be—as we are imagining—false; it would only care about the fact that such intuitions would lead to moral beliefs that were evolutionarily *useful*.

But then why should we *trust* our intuitions, when they tell us that morality requires us to love and care for our children? We would have those same intuitions whether or not they were true! At best, all we can justifiably infer is that it is *advantageous* to have intuitions like these, not that they are especially likely to be correct. (No doubt, it would be more precise to talk about what *was* advantageous—that is, during the period when evolution was shaping our ancestors—rather than about what *is* advantageous, since the two needn't be the same. But almost nothing in our discussion will turn on this point, so I will allow myself some latitude on this score.)

Generalizing, then, the skeptic might conclude that given the role that evolution played in shaping our moral intuitions, the mere fact that I have a given intuition can provide no evidence at all for the truth of the corresponding belief. It only shows that it was advantageous to *believe* things like that. It tells me nothing at all about whether the belief in question is likely to be true.

To be sure, we may still want to insist, in keeping with the principle of phenomenal conservatism, that all appearances—including intuitions—really do provide at least *defeasible* evidence. We will then have to state the argument's conclusion this way: in the case of moral intuitions the force of this evidence is indeed *defeated*. From the skeptic's perspective, of course, that's just as damning a conclusion.

The underlying thought here seems plausible enough. If I would believe something whether or not it was true, then the fact that I do believe it provides no evidence for its truth. Similarly, if something would *seem* to me to be the case regardless of whether or not it was true, then the fact that it does seem to me to be the case cannot provide (undefeated) evidence that things are indeed as they appear to be. Yet isn't this the situation we are in with regard to our moral intuitions and the corresponding moral beliefs? They are selected for their advantageousness, not their correctness. So we have no reason to take them to be reliable representations of the underlying moral facts. (And at this point—as we have already noted—we might go on to wonder whether we have any compelling reason to believe that there are any moral facts at all.

Does our belief in such facts show us anything other than that it was evolutionarily advantageous for us to have such a belief?)

Presumably, one possible reply to this second version of the argument would be to accept its conclusion and agree that moral intuitions should not be taken to be reliable. Luckily (some moral realists might insist), we have *other* ways to gain moral knowledge. Even if our moral sensibility and the intuitions it generates have no particular epistemic value, why can't we simply use our *reason* to argue for various moral conclusions, and thus establish what the moral facts are?

One obvious difficulty with this proposal, however, is that ordinarily when we try to reason our way to moral conclusions, we do this by means of appealing to our moral intuitions! We treat those intuitions (in ways I described in the last chapter) as inputs to further theorizing. And while it certainly remains possible that the upshot of such reasoning might be a moral theory that rejects many of those initial intuitions as misguided or mistaken, it is hard to see why we would be justified in having any confidence in our *final* judgments if we were of the opinion that those initial intuitions have no force as evidence at all. (Analogously, empirical science can lead us to dismiss many of our initial observations as illusory; but we would hardly be justified in accepting those scientific conclusions if we were of the opinion that observations as a class have no force as evidence whatsoever.)

Admittedly, as I have previously noted (in 7.5), there are moral realists who offer arguments for moral conclusions that avoid appealing to particular moral intuitions—even as initial starting points. But these arguments still draw on a wide array of intuitions concerning other subjects (such as logic, or metaphysics, or the nature of rationality), and in the absence of a reason to find these other intuitions more reliable than our moral intuitions, it is hard to see what would justify our having greater confidence in these alternative arguments. Once we conclude that we would have the very same moral intuitions that we do, regardless of whether they are true or not, why wouldn't the same thing be true for our intuitions about other subjects as well?

Happily, there is a much more straightforward reply to the skeptic's argument, which is that it must go wrong *somewhere* since, if it were correct, then even in its revised form it would still undermine our claims to empirical knowledge. After all, if it really is the case that evolution cares *only* about what is advantageous, and not what's true, then won't this remain the case even when the subject matter of our beliefs is the external world rather than morality?

Imagine an argument parallel to the one that the skeptic has put forward, only this time let the target be our observations of the external world, rather than our moral intuitions. Such an argument might begin by agreeing that if it were advantageous to have true beliefs about the external world then we might well have evolved to have them. But similarly (it would continue), if it were advantageous to have *false* beliefs about the external world we might well have evolved to have those instead. Evolution doesn't care about the truth, it cares only about advantage. So we will tend to end up with whatever beliefs about the external world it is advantageous for us to have—regardless of whether or not they are true. Accordingly, the fact that I have a given empirical belief (for example, that there is a tree in front of me) gives me no particular reason to believe it. The fact that I seem to observe something (say, that there is a rock falling off a cliff) provides no (undefeated) evidence that what I seem to observe is really so. At best, given the various observations generated by my senses, I am justified in inferring only that it is advantageous to have the corresponding empirical beliefs, not that they are especially likely to be *correct*. (And if that's right, shouldn't we begin to wonder whether we really have good reason to believe in an external world at all?)

As I say, there are those who find these broader skeptical conclusions compelling. But most of us, I assume, will conclude instead that this argument must go wrong someplace. That doesn't yet tell us, of course, precisely where and how the argument goes wrong. But it does perhaps justify the thought that if the argument shouldn't undermine our belief in the reliability of observation it also shouldn't undermine our belief in the reliability of intuition. Somehow, despite the fact that all evolution really "cares about" is advantage, empirical knowledge remains possible. Similarly then, for all that we have been shown so far, moral knowledge may remain possible as well.

In principle, I suppose, we could now leave this second version of the argument from evolution as well, confident that it must be misguided. But I think it worth our while to see if we can figure out where exactly it goes wrong. (Somewhat surprisingly, getting clear on this point will ultimately point us toward a *third* possible version of the argument.) As it happens, thinking about the variant aimed against empirical beliefs may make it easier to recognize the crucial misstep. The mistake is this: the argument overlooks the possibility of there being a *connection* between truth and advantage.

We might put the point this way. Even though all that evolution cares about directly is giving us *advantageous* beliefs, nonetheless, if there is a link or connection between being a belief that is advantageous and being a belief that is *true*, then it will still be the case that evolution tends to give us true beliefs. For if beliefs in a given domain tend to be advantageous if and only if they are true, then it won't really be correct to say that evolution will give us beliefs *regardless* of whether they are true or not. Evolution will give us advantageous beliefs, to be sure. But if the advantageous beliefs are the true ones, then it is also the case that evolution will tend to give us *true* beliefs in that domain. So our beliefs in that domain (and the mechanisms that generate them) will tend to be reliable after all.

Now of course, we do believe that there is precisely this sort of connection between truth and advantage when it comes to empirical beliefs about the external world. It is evolutionarily advantageous to have a visual system that accurately portrays the world around me. If, for example, there is a tree in front of me, there is an evolutionary advantage in having a mental faculty (in our case, vision) that allows me to observe the tree and so come to have the corresponding belief. That way, I won't run into the tree when I am trying to escape a predator. Similarly, if there is *no* tree in front of me, there is an evolutionary advantage in not having the belief that there *is* one. That way, I won't waste time trying to run around a nonexistent tree. Generalizing, with regard to the ordinary everyday objects that surround me in the external world there is an advantage in having true beliefs. So even though evolution only directly cares about advantage, it will still have shaped me to have a largely reliable faculty capable of generating true beliefs about those objects. Accordingly, if I seem to see a tree in front of me, I am justified in inferring that there probably *is* a tree in front of me.

(On the other hand, it won't be true that there was an evolutionary advantage in having true beliefs about *all* aspects of the external world. There was advantage in knowing that there is a rock here, a tree there, a lion running way over there, and so on, but there was no advantage in knowing that there was a positive sodium ion here but not there. It shouldn't surprise us, accordingly, that we can't just see the presence or absence of sodium ions. Hence the need to talk about there being a connection between advantage and true beliefs with regard to a particular *domain*, or subdomain, or a particular range of facts, and so on. The requisite link between advantage and truth will only exist for some domains, or certain types of facts, and not others. More needs to be said about this point, however, and we will return to it below.)

We can, of course, imagine someone wondering whether it is really legitimate for us to posit this sort of connection between advantage and truth with regard to everyday empirical facts. Since the entire question is whether observation is reliable, isn't it question begging for us to assume that the empirical world works more or less as we take it to work (with trees getting in the way when one is running away from a predator, and its being useful to know whether the lion is near or far, and so on)? After all, we only have this picture of the world as a result of appealing to our observations. So isn't it circular to presuppose the accuracy of this picture of the world (one in which truth and advantage are correlated) as part of a *defense* of our reliance on observation?

But as always, our goal is not to defend common beliefs against this kind of *global* skepticism. In particular, then, our goal is not to defend the commonsense empirical worldview against general skeptical challenges, but only to make clear why, exactly, if that worldview is *correct* then evolution doesn't actually pose a particular threat to knowledge after all. Roughly speaking, all we are saying here is that if the commonsense empirical worldview is correct then it is indeed the case that truth and advantage are linked with regard to everyday empirical beliefs, and *if* they are linked—as we take them to be—then that suffices to explain why evolution is not a threat to empirical knowledge. Evolution cares only about advantage, but given the link between truth and advantage (accepted by those of us who believe in anything like the commonsense empirical worldview), evolution will still have built us to have largely reliable beliefs about the everyday empirical world.

Thus it is a mistake to say that since evolution only cares about advantage, it would give us the beliefs we actually have *regardless* of whether they are true or not. The former simply does not entail the latter. It can both be the case that, fundamentally, evolution cares only about advantage and yet, for all that, it built us to have largely reliable beliefs about a given domain. That's what happened with regard to observation and empirical beliefs, and for all that we have been shown so far, the same could have happened with regard to intuition and *moral* beliefs.

(For those who are curious, let me say a bit more about how the argument goes wrong. Given the way evolution works, we can indeed say, roughly, that if it is advantageous to have a certain belief we will likely end up with it, whether or not it is true. But that doesn't entail that it will *be* advantageous to have a belief regardless of whether or not it is true. Where there is a link between advantage and truth, if the belief isn't true it *won't* be advantageous to have it, so we won't end up with it. Here's an analogy. Imagine that I will vote for the more liberal candidate. This means, of course, that I will vote for the more liberal candidate *regardless* of whether they are a Democrat or a Republican. But that hardly shows that if I vote for someone this provides no evidence at all as to whether they are likely to be a Democrat or not. Given the link (imperfect, but real) between being a Democrat (rather than a Republican) and being the more liberal candidate, the people I vote for are much more likely to *be* Democrats. So it is at best distracting (and likely to mislead us) to point out that if a given candidate *were* the more liberal one but *not* a Democrat, I would nonetheless still vote for her. That's true, but for all that, given that there actually *is* a link, if I have voted for someone they are likely to be a Democrat.)

8.3 Truth and Advantage in Ethics

The second version of the argument from evolution failed because it overlooked the possibility of links between truth and advantage. Even though it is true that evolution only cares (or only cares "directly") about generating beliefs that are advantageous, nonetheless, if there is a connection in a given domain between being advantageous and being true, then evolution might still have shaped us to have faculties capable of generating beliefs concerning that domain that tend to be true. Since the second version of the argument overlooks this point, it fails to establish the unreliability of our moral intuitions.

But this suggests a further revision to the argument that might better suit the skeptic's purposes. The skeptic should concede that where there *are* such links between truth and advantage our beliefs and the mental faculties that generate them are likely to be reliable, but she should then point out that this doesn't show that there *is* such a link when the domain in question is morality. Indeed (the skeptic might continue), while it is clear that truth and advantage are connected when it comes to the external world (or, at least, the parts of it that we regularly "bump into" in our everyday life), it is implausible to believe that there is (or would be) such a link with regard to moral facts.

Ask yourself, just why is it that truth and advantage are connected when it comes to beliefs about the empirical world? The answer is obvious: advantageous empirical beliefs are advantageous precisely *because* they are true. For example, if it is advantageous in some situation to believe that there is a lion near me, this is because there *is* a lion near me, and believing this will help me avoid it! The belief is advantageous because it is *true*. More generally, if you have true empirical beliefs (about the presence and character of trees, rocks, streams, lions, other people, and so on) this means that you represent the relevant empirical facts accurately—the world really is the way you take it to be—and as a result you move around the world and negotiate its perils more effectively, all of which is clearly advantageous from the evolutionary standpoint. So the truth of the belief explains or *grounds* its advantageousness.

It isn't merely that there "happens to be" a link between truth and advantage here; it isn't that there is some sort of cosmic *coincidence*, where empirical beliefs just happen to be advantageous in all and only those cases where they are true. Rather, the link between truth and advantage holds precisely because the truth of the belief grounds the advantageousness of having the belief. (It is advantageous to have these beliefs *because* they are true; and were they not true, it would *not* be advantageous to have them.) It is our recognition of this fact that justifies our belief in the existence of the link in the first place.

But nothing like this is the case (the skeptic continues) when we are talking about *moral* beliefs. Consider, again, the question of the moral status of killing one's children, only this time suppose that it really is true (as we ordinarily believe) that killing one's children is indeed morally forbidden. Would this moral fact—supposing it to be one—somehow explain the advantage in having the belief that it is wrong to kill one's children? It certainly doesn't seem that it would.

After all, suppose we ask: what *is* it that explains the evolutionary advantage in believing that it is wrong to kill one's children? The answer, presumably, is that those who have this belief are less likely to kill their children (!), which means that their genes are more likely to be reproduced and spread (given that their children are more likely to survive and have children of their own). The advantage from having the belief is explained in terms of the impact this has on one's behavior, and thus on spreading one's genes. But the fact that it is *true* that it is wrong to kill one's children—supposing this to be the case—why, *that* fact plays no role in the explanation of the advantage at all!

This is a striking contrast with the case of empirical beliefs. When we want to explain why it is advantageous to have a given empirical belief, sooner or later we inevitably start talking about the *truth* of the belief in question. (If it is advantageous to believe that there is a lion nearby, that's because there *is* a lion nearby.) But nothing like this holds with regard to moral beliefs. When we want to explain why it is advantageous to have a given moral belief, we never end up talking about the *truth* of that belief. The *wrongness* of killing one's child, to stick to our example, plays no role at all with regard to explaining the advantage of having the corresponding belief.

In short, for empirical beliefs, truth explains advantage, and that is why the link between the two exists in this domain. But for *moral* beliefs, truth is *irrelevant* to advantage; it explains nothing. So there is no reason for us to believe there *is* a link between truth and advantage when it comes to morality. To insist that there is such a link nonetheless—to insist, despite all of this, that moral beliefs really are advantageous in just those cases where they are true—is to believe without justification in some inexplicable cosmic coincidence. So we should abandon the belief in a link between truth and advantage with regard to morality. Yet once we do this (and here the skeptic concludes), our belief in the reliability of our first-order moral beliefs can no longer be justified. Given the nature of evolution, we have no good reason to believe that our moral beliefs (and the mechanisms that generate them) are particularly reliable.

Note that someone putting forward this third version of the argument needn't hold (although they can hold) that moral facts (if such there be) are explanatorily impotent altogether. All that the argument insists upon is that the truth of a given moral belief plays no role in explaining one fact in particular: why it is *advantageous to have* the belief in question. And it certainly does seem plausible for the skeptic to hold that even if there are (or were) moral facts, they play (or would play) no part in explaining why true moral beliefs are evolutionarily advantageous. That more modest claim seems to be enough for the skeptic's purposes.

This means, I think, that the moral realist cannot evade the argument by positing, as some realists do, that moral properties are natural properties and moral facts natural ones. For even if we agree that natural properties have causal powers, and so (if naturalism about morality is right) moral facts have causal powers, that won't suffice to deflect the argument. After all, what the argument turns on is the thought that unless truth and advantage are linked when it comes to morality there is no good reason to think that evolution will have shaped us to have accurate moral beliefs. So even if moral facts (if such there be) do have causal powers, and so can sometimes play a role in explaining other facts, unless moral facts can help explain why it is *advantageous* to have true beliefs about morality the argument has not been met. And here I can only repeat that it does seem plausible for the skeptic to insist that the truth of a given moral claim seems to play no role at all in explaining why it would be advantageous to *believe* that claim. So the argument remains unanswered.

(Admittedly, it does seem just conceivable that there could be a version of naturalistic moral realism under which the truth of a moral belief does indeed somehow explain the advantage of having that belief. This strikes me as a rather unpromising line of thought, though I am not quite prepared to rule it out completely.)

Before considering other possible responses from the moral realist, it is worth noting that if the skeptic's argument succeeds it seems to support not only skepticism about our *moral* beliefs, but, more broadly, a more general skepticism regarding all of our normative beliefs whatsoever. Recall the position I dubbed *normative nihilism* (in 3.4). According to this view, not only are there no moral facts, there are no normative facts of any sort at all, no facts about what there is reason to do, no facts about what there is reason to believe. As I suggested when I introduced this view, it is almost impossible to believe. But as far as I can see, if the argument from evolution justifiably undermines our confidence in the reliability of our moral beliefs it should also undermine our confidence in the reliability of our beliefs about other normative matters as well (and this, in turn, might leave us wondering why we should believe in any sorts of normative facts at all).

Suppose, for example, that I put my hand over a flame, and it causes me pain. Suppose I realize that moving my hand will make the pain subside. These are just empirical facts, and they are not here in doubt. But imagine that I now conclude, on the basis of these facts, that there is a practical *reason* for me to move my hand, that there is a rational *justification* for moving it, that I rationally *ought* to move my hand. Is *this* belief to be trusted as well? I certainly have the *intuition* that there is a compelling reason for me to move my hand (since doing so will stop the pain). But what of it? No doubt there is a faculty which generates these intuitions and thus leads to my beliefs about what I have reason to do. But is it a reliable one?

We have of course already seen reason to think that my *empirical* beliefs are reliable (for example, my belief that moving my hand will stop the pain), but am I justified in thinking that my beliefs about *practical reasons* are reliable as well (for example, my belief that there is reason to *do* what stops pain)? Given what we have been saying about how evolution shapes our beliefs, we know that if there is a link here between truth and advantage we will be justified in relying on our beliefs about such everyday practical reasons. But is it at all plausible to think that such a link exists in cases like this?

Suppose we ask, why is it advantageous to believe that I have reason to move my hand? Details aside, I suppose the answer is that someone who believes that they have a reason to move their hand is more likely to *move* it, and moving one's hand when it is over a flame helps avoid damage to that hand, which in turn increases one's chance of successfully reproducing. Generalizing a bit, the advantage of believing that there is reason to move one's hand away from things causing it pain is explained in terms of the impact this belief has on one's behavior, and thus on the chances of spreading one's genes.

Notice, however, that the fact that it is *true* that there is a reason to move one's hand in such situations (as we normally believe) seems to play no role at all in explaining the advantageousness. The appeal to *normative* facts does no explanatory work here. The truth of my normative belief (that I *ought* to move my hand) is explanatorily irrelevant. And the same thing is clearly true as well for still other everyday cases involving normative beliefs about what I have reason to do. The truth of those normative beliefs won't help explain their advantageousness. So shouldn't the skeptic conclude accordingly that we have no good reason to posit a link between truth and advantage for normative matters? And shouldn't that lead to the conclusion (barring a cosmic coincidence) that our various beliefs about normative matters are, quite generally, unreliable?

(Although it can be a bit confusing when one tries to spell this out, the argument should also undermine our confidence in the reliability of our beliefs about what there is reason to *believe*, and not just our beliefs about what there is reason to do. Beliefs about theoretical reasons—beliefs about what there is *reason* to believe—can certainly be advantageous as well; but the *truth* of these normative beliefs (as opposed to, say, the truth of the underlying empirical beliefs themselves) plays no role in explaining the advantage of *having* these beliefs.)

In short, if the argument from evolution really did show that we are unjustified in taking our moral beliefs to be reliable, shouldn't it similarly show that we are unjustified in taking our various other normative judgments to be reliable as well? As we might put it in a slogan: if I can't trust my intuition that, morally speaking, I ought to take steps to save *your* life, why should I trust my intuition that, prudentially speaking, I ought to take steps to save my *own* life?

Clearly, the fact that the argument generalizes in this way should worry us. Few of us, I think, would be prepared to deny that our belief that there is a reason to move one's hand away from an open flame is an accurate one. Fewer still would be prepared to conclude with the normative nihilist that there are no such practical reasons at all! (Yet if our intuitions about such reasons are unreliable, why think that such reasons so much as exist?) All of this gives us reason to suspect that even this latest version of the argument from evolution must go wrong *someplace*. But as usual, this sort of observation doesn't yet tell us how and why, exactly, the argument fails.

How, then, should a moral realist reply to this third version of the argument? The crucial move, I think, is to agree that unless there is a link among our moral beliefs between truth and advantage there will be no good reason to believe in the reliability of those beliefs, but to insist nonetheless that the skeptic is working with an overly narrow view about how that link might be established. In particular, the argument assumes that unless truth grounds or explains advantage, the link must be an illusion (or a sheer coincidence). And that, I think, is an unwarranted assumption.

The skeptic is right to insist that it won't suffice to merely *posit* the existence of a link between truth and advantage for a given domain. We need an explanation of why the link holds. But there is more than one direction that such an explanation can go. (I made a similar point when discussing the correlation between truth and intuition in 7.4.) The skeptic is quite right that as far as empirical beliefs are concerned, the explanation runs from truth to advantage: empirical beliefs are advantageous *because* they are true. And it does seem that the skeptic is right as well when she insists that an explanation of the same sort (one going in the same direction) will strike us as implausible when we turn from empirical beliefs to moral ones. It simply doesn't seem to be true that moral beliefs are advantageous because they are true. But this still leaves open the possibility of explaining the link in some other way.

Suppose, for example, that we could make out the idea that when it comes to moral beliefs, the explanation runs in the other direction: that moral beliefs are true because they are *advantageous*. That too should suffice to establish the requisite link, even though the details of the explanation would be rather different from the ones we would offer in the case of empirical beliefs. For if it really were the case with regard to moral beliefs that the true ones are true by virtue of the fact that they are advantageous, then advantageous moral beliefs would be true, and nonadvantageous ones would not be. Thus, a moral belief would be true if and only if it were advantageous (or, what comes to the same thing, a moral belief would be advantageous if and only if it were true). So even if the skeptic is right, and when it comes to moral beliefs we cannot plausibly claim that truth explains advantage, the requisite link between truth and advantage would still be in place. And if it is, we will have reason to take our moral beliefs to be reliable after all.

That's all very well and good, one might reply, but can one plausibly suggest that something like this is indeed the case with regard to moral beliefs—that advantage explains truth? Although this might not seem a particularly promising idea, for some moral realists it may actually be fairly attractive. To see this, recall the point (explained in 7.4) that on certain constructivist views we can say that, roughly speaking, moral truths are true because we have the moral beliefs that we do (or because we have the intuitions and intuitive reactions that we do). That wasn't true for all constructivist views, but it did seem to be the case for some of them. But if that's right, then those who accept constructivist views of this kind now only need to add the further thought that we have the particular moral beliefs (and intuitions, and so on) that we do because it is advantageous for us to have them! For if moral truths are true because we have the beliefs and intuitions that we have, and we have the beliefs and intuitions that we have because it is advantageous for us to have them, then moral truths are true (ultimately) because it is advantageous for us to have the corresponding beliefs. Thus, constructivists of this sort can plausibly maintain that as far as morality is concerned true moral beliefs are true because they are advantageous! So there really is a link between truth and advantage for moral beliefs (despite being grounded in a different direction from the link for empirical beliefs). And this means, of course, that we are justified in taking our moral beliefs to be reliable.

That, at least, is a reply to the argument from evolution that seems available to realists who accept one of the relevant versions of constructivism. (And note, in particular, that the skeptic is hardly in a position to reject the "further thought" that we have our moral beliefs and intuitions because it is advantageous to do so. It is this thought, after all, that provides the heart of the argument from evolution in the first place.)

But what about those realists who accept other versions of constructivism (or, for that matter, realists who accept nonconstructivist versions of reductionism)? And what about those realists who are nonreductionists altogether and prefer simple realism? How are *they* to respond to the argument from evolution? Perhaps by identifying yet another direction through which a link between truth and advantage can be established.

8.4 Common Ground

If our beliefs concerning a given domain are to be reliable, then it must be the case that truth and advantage are appropriately "linked"; it must be the case that (roughly speaking) our beliefs about that domain are advantageous if and only if they are true. What's more, since it won't be credible to hold that it is simply a cosmic coincidence that such a link holds, something must explain *why* truth and advantage are connected in this way, *why* the linkage is in place.

As we have now seen, there are at least two importantly different ways in which one might try to explain any such purported link. First, and most obviously, it might be that in the relevant domain truth explains advantage. That's what we have in the case of empirical beliefs. But second, and less obviously, it might be that in the relevant domain advantage explains *truth*. That's what we may have in ethics if certain forms of constructivism are true. For constructivists of the right sort, the argument from evolution fails precisely because it overlooks the possibility of explaining the link between truth and advantage in this second way.

But there is, in fact, a *third* potential approach to explaining such connections as well, and it is even more easily overlooked than the second one. It might be that in some domains there is a *common ground* for both truth *and* advantage, something which explains both why the true beliefs about that domain are true and why it is advantageous to have them. This too should suffice to establish the relevant link. For when the common ground is in place, a given belief will be both true and advantageous; and when it is absent, the belief will be neither true *nor* advantageous. And this means, of course, that a belief will be true in just those cases where it is advantageous. Accordingly, when such a common ground account can be provided, the link between truth and advantage will be in place and our beliefs about that domain will be reliable.

It is this third possibility, I think, which is especially promising for moral realists (at least, those realists who cannot avail themselves of the second approach). To see how it applies to the kinds of beliefs that interest us, consider the plausible thought that when there is a reason to do something, this is so because of certain "underlying" facts about the act in question. These "lower level" or "base level" facts about the act *ground* the existence of the reason to perform that act—they explain why the reason to do the act exists. The existence of the reason *depends* on the presence of those base facts.

For example, why is there reason to move your hand away from a burning flame? Because doing so will stop the pain and avoid (or minimize) damage to your hand. These facts are what *make* it true that there is a reason to move your hand: the reason exists *because* these more base level facts obtain. If it weren't true that moving your hand would stop the pain and avoid the damage (and so on) there would be no reason to move it!

Notice, however, that these very same underlying facts are also, of course, the ones that explain why it is advantageous to *believe* that there is a reason to move your hand. These same base level facts explain why there is an advantage in *having* the normative belief in question. (Having the belief makes it more likely you will move your hand. But there would be no advantage in doing this if it weren't that doing so would stop the pain and minimize the bodily damage, thus enhancing your chances of reproductive success.)

Thus the very same set of underlying facts helps explain both why there *is* a reason to move your hand, and why it is advantageous to *believe* that there is such a reason. These facts act as a common ground, underlying both the truth of the relevant normative belief (that you ought to move your hand) and its advantageousness. And something similar holds, of course, in countless other everyday cases where one has a reason to do something: there are certain underlying facts about the acts which explain why one has a reason to act a certain way; and these same underlying facts explain why it is advantageous to have the corresponding normative beliefs (about what one has reason to do).

So the following holds: there is a range of facts about our everyday life such that when the appropriate underlying facts are in place it will be true both that there *is* a reason to do something and that it will be advantageous to *believe* that there is a reason to do this thing. But when these facts are not in place, it will neither be true that there is such a reason to act nor will it be true that there is any advantage in believing that there is. All of which is just to say: for everyday normative matters, thanks to the role these underlying facts play as a common ground for both truth and advantage, there is indeed a *link* between truth and advantage.

(Similarly, of course, if there is a reason to *believe* something—for example, a reason to believe there is a lion in front of me—this will be the case because of certain underlying facts (for example, the visible presence of a lion!), but these very same facts will also explain why it is *advantageous* to believe that there is a reason to have this belief. So here too, the underlying

8.4 COMMON GROUND 211

facts provide a common ground for both the truth of the normative belief (concerning what I have reason to believe) and the advantage of having that normative belief, thus establishing the requisite link between truth and advantage for normative beliefs about theoretical reasons, not just practical ones.)

In this way we can answer the threat of normative nihilism that would otherwise be generated by the argument from evolution. Truth and advantage are linked here thanks to their sharing a common grounding in relevant underlying facts.

A similar strategy should be successful for many of our moral beliefs as well. Why is there reason for you to help Smith harvest her corn? Because earlier she helped you harvest your wheat, and you reassured her that if she did this you would lend her a hand as well. These underlying facts about the pattern of past and potential future behavior are what ground the existence of a moral reason to help Smith. The obligation to help Smith exists *because* these underlying facts obtain; they explain why your belief that you ought to help Smith is *true*. But these very same facts also help explain why it is advantageous for you to *believe* that you have an obligation to help Smith. Among other things, those who believe there is reason to cooperate with those who have helped them in the past are more likely to actually *cooperate* in such circumstances, and such mutually beneficial practices have clear evolutionary advantages. So the underlying facts (about the pattern of behavior and assurances) ground both the truth of the moral belief *and* the advantage one gains from having it.

Or suppose that Jones asks you where to find the train to New Haven. Why is there reason for you to answer her, "It's on track 118"? Because that is indeed where the train can be found, and if you tell her she will know it too! That is to say, there are underlying facts about your knowledge of the truth and your ability to communicate that knowledge which ground your obligation to give this answer. The obligation exists *because* of these underlying facts, and so they help explain why your moral belief (that you ought to tell her it's on track 118) is correct. But these very same facts also help explain why it is advantageous for you to *believe* that you ought to answer her this way. For people who *believe* that they ought to tell the truth are more likely to *tell* the truth, and the disposition to tell the truth is (under normal circumstances) part of a mutually beneficial linguistic practice, one which leads to evolutionary advantages. So here too, underlying facts (about which answers are known to be true) help ground both the truth of the moral belief (about the answer one ought to give) and the advantage one gains from having that belief.

Other examples with a similar structure could easily be produced. After all, one striking accomplishment of contemporary evolutionary psychology is its having revealed just how much of our common moral outlook can be shown to be advantageous from an evolutionary perspective. The moral realist can accept these accounts of evolutionary advantage (or at least agree that adequate accounts can in principle be produced, whether or not we yet have them). They need only add that the very same underlying features which figure in these accounts—and which thus explain why it is advantageous for us to have the moral beliefs we do—also help explain why the moral beliefs in question are *true*.

In short, for a wide range of common moral beliefs, an appeal to the common ground strategy can help us see why there would be a link between truth and evolutionary advantage. And that in turn should help us see why we are justified in taking our moral beliefs to be reliable. In this way, I think, the moral realist may have a satisfactory answer to the argument from evolution.

To be sure, as always, this reply doesn't prove that moral realism is *correct*. All it does is defend realism against the *challenge* to it that is based on worries about evolution. It shows why, if one accepts moral realism, one shouldn't feel threatened by the thought that we (and our intuitions and our moral beliefs) have all been shaped by evolutionary processes. The moral realist can accept that thought and plausibly insist nonetheless that even if this is so, that shouldn't undermine our confidence in the overall reliability of those intuitions and beliefs. For if moral realism is correct there will be a link between truth and advantage, and that will explain why evolution would have shaped us to have moral beliefs that are reliable.

In effect, the realist's response takes the truth of moral realism for granted—takes it as a given—and then *uses* that perspective to explain why, according to that view, we will find a link of the sort needed. It doesn't establish the *truth* of realism, but rather shows why someone who *accepts* realism need not find evolution a threat.

This may seem suspicious to some, but it is actually perfectly parallel to what we did earlier when using the commonsense view of the external world to defend our empirical beliefs from initial versions of the argument from evolution. We didn't attempt to prove that there really are external objects that interact with one another in anything like the way we ordinarily think.

Rather, we simply took the commonsense view for granted as a given, and used it to explain why, according to that view, we will find the requisite link between truth and advantage. Our goal there was not to defend commonsense beliefs about the external world from those who would reject them outright, but only to show why if one does accept such commonsense views one won't be troubled by acknowledging the role that evolution has played in shaping our empirical beliefs. For our purposes, that sufficed, since it shows how the argument from evolution can be answered.

Similarly, then, we need not here try to prove that moral realism is correct. We need only show why those who accept that view can deflect any *further* threat that might be thought to emerge from recognizing the role that evolution has played in shaping our moral beliefs. If moral realism is correct, there will be a link between moral truth and evolutionary advantage, and that will help explain why, on the whole, our beliefs here will tend to be reliable. For the moment, at least, that answer should suffice as well.

(Let me close this section with a brief technical remark. It is tempting to wonder whether the defense of realism I have offered here is actually a version of the second approach, rather than the third. After all, couldn't one claim that, ultimately, the various "underlying facts" that ground our particular moral obligations all boil down to the fact that certain patterns of behavior can be mutually advantageous to the relevant individuals? So doesn't this show that, in the last analysis, advantage explains moral truth? There are various problems with this suggestion, but for present purposes the most important one is this. In thinking about the connection between truth and advantage, the relevant notion of advantage is *evolutionary* advantage—that is (when all is said and done), whether a given belief helps you increase the relative frequency of your genes in the gene pool. But it isn't at all plausible to suggest that the reason you have a moral obligation to keep your promises, or tell the truth, and so on, is because doing so helps you spread your genes! (Or rather, this isn't at all plausible if we have put aside the constructivist accounts of the sort already described.) At best, then, even if it really should turn out to be the case that all moral practices are grounded in mutual advantage and benefit to individuals—a controversial claim I won't explore here—it would still be true that this kind of mutual advantage remains distinct from and only helps to *explain* the evolutionary advantage of having the relevant moral beliefs. So this really would be a common ground account after all: *mutual* advantage would ground both moral truth and *evolutionary* advantage.)

8.5 The Continuity Problem

I have been arguing that where there is a link between truth and advantage, evolution will have shaped us to have beliefs that are largely reliable. Of course in many cases, perhaps most cases, evolution won't have "hardwired" the beliefs directly into us. Instead it will have given us a faculty capable of generating reliable appearances for the given domain, where normally we will then be disposed to tentatively accept the corresponding beliefs as true. That's what seems to have gone on in the case of vision and the other senses; and that, I have suggested, is what has gone on with moral intuition as well.

It is compatible with accepting this account to recognize that there may well be instances where some true belief would be (or would have been) advantageous for us to have, and yet, for all that, the faculty bequeathed to us by evolution doesn't generate a corresponding appearance. It may take intellectual work for us to figure out some advantageous truth, rather than simply having the facts more directly *appear* to us to be the case, right from the start.

Why, we might wonder, doesn't evolution give us a more forthcoming faculty (a more "obliging" one)? The answer, of course, is that evolution is limited to working with what is at hand and what shows up through random mutation, and so the faculty that emerges from evolutionary shaping simply may not be capable of generating appearances for *all* those truths it would be advantageous to believe.

None of this undermines the reliability of the faculty in question when it *does* generate appearances; it simply leaves gaps in our knowledge which we must then fill ourselves. That may be inconvenient, but it isn't a threat to the possibility of attaining knowledge—not even with regard to the questions where the faculty is silent.

How do we go about filling in the gaps? Through the process of inquiry and theory building familiar from both everyday reflection and scientific thought. We use the relevant appearances as inputs for our theories, working our way from these to more general principles and more systematic accounts of the given domain. And from these we then infer positions on the specific claims where the faculty was (as it happened) silent. The full story of how we do this is, of course, complicated, and we won't explore it here. For our purposes it is enough to remind ourselves of the familiar fact that we do routinely use this kind of systematic reflection to fill in the gaps, even when direct appearances are lacking. (And, of course, this process of systematic reflection can also lead us to *reject* some of the initial appearances—though that point isn't our particular concern right now.)

What's more, this same process of systematic inquiry can lead us to fill in gaps in our knowledge not only where it would be advantageous from an evolutionary perspective to have some particular set of beliefs, but also where evolution has no particular interest one way or the other as to whether we come to have beliefs about a given topic at all. The range of facts we might want to know about is limitless, and for much of that range—perhaps most of it—there would have been no particular evolutionary advantage in our ancestors having had beliefs of any sort on the subjects in question. (To take a few examples at random, there would have been no evolutionary advantage in their having had true beliefs about cosmology, quantum mechanics, multivariable calculus, cellular biology, or oceanography.) Accordingly, it is hardly surprising that the faculties that evolved leave us with gaps with regard to evolutionarily "useless" knowledge—even for countless local facts about my immediate environment (for example, the number of cells in the plant in front of me, or the presence of sodium ions in the water I am drinking, and so on).

No matter, we can still come to know things about such "useless" subjects, by using the inputs that we *have* been given. Roughly speaking, we can form hypotheses about these more exotic matters, and then confirm or disconfirm them by drawing predictions from them that can then be tested against the inputs we do have. (For example, we might confirm a hypothesis about something's chemical composition by seeing whether the contents in the test tube turn blue when heated.) The various techniques of abstract reflection and systematic inquiry allow us to move beyond those domains (and subdomains) where there was an advantage in having knowledge; we can come to have knowledge about matters where there was no particular evolutionary advantage in having such knowledge at all.

But there is a further complication that needs to be addressed. Often enough, the faculties that evolution gave us seem to generate appearances (and thus lead us to beliefs) not only for those domains and subdomains where this was advantageous, but also with regard to many domains or subdomains where, on the contrary, there was *no* evolutionary advantage in having beliefs on these subjects at all. For example, it isn't as though the faculty of vision is limited to generating observations—to seeing things—only in what we might call its "home range," where there was indeed an evolutionary advantage in having reliable appearances. We also see things that there was no advantage in being able to see at all. Thus, not only do we see falling trees, and running lions, and immobile boulders, and so on, we also see stars in the sky above us, solar eclipses, and (when looking through a suitable microscope) single cells and individual molecules. There was, we can presume, no particular advantage for our ancestors in having a faculty capable of seeing stars and individual molecules, but the faculty of vision as molded by evolution nonetheless does generate appearances (under the right circumstances) for these matters as well.

Is this a problem? It might not seem so. We might view these extra appearances—those that occur outside the home range—as "bonuses" or "unintended gifts" from evolution. Evolution didn't have any particular need to give us a faculty of vision that could generate true beliefs on such matters, it just turned out that way. What there was, rather, was a need to give us a faculty that was reliable for everyday empirical matters, and it just happened that the faculty we got—the faculty of vision we actually have—was also suitable for generating appearances (observations) about countless matters that go *beyond* the home range. That's a lucky break for us, we might say, since it gives us extra inputs to use in creating our overall theories, including theories about areas where there was no advantage in having true beliefs at all. As it turns out, we aren't limited to using abstract thought to extend our knowledge beyond the home range; the extra appearances help us to do that as well.

That's a tempting answer, but it isn't clear what justifies us in believing that the faculty of vision remains reliable when it comes to generating appearances on these further matters, aspects of the external world that go beyond the home range for vision. It is certainly true that our vision *generates* observations about stars and molecules (and not just trees, and rivers, and boulders), but what justifies our belief that these additional observations are *reliable*?

I have argued, of course, that a given faculty will be reliable for a given domain where there is a link between truth and advantage. That certainly is what we take to be in place with regard to vision for everyday empirical objects: there was an evolutionary advantage in our being able to see various facts about our environment (that the lion was running toward us, that the tree was in our way). For facts like these—what I am calling the home range of vision—we have reason to think our vision is largely reliable. But why should we think that vision *continues* to be reliable even when we use it on aspects of the external world that go beyond the home range? It is, after all, precisely these further areas where, by hypothesis, there was no evolutionary advantage in having true beliefs at all, so no link to be found between truth and advantage, so no reason to assume that vision will continue to be reliable. (This means, incidentally, that for our purposes perhaps we shouldn't think of the external world as simply constituting a single, undifferentiated "domain." Perhaps we should say that the external world divides into various "*sub*domains," and since the link only exists for some of them, the reliability of vision has only been established for some of them.)

We can call this *the continuity problem*, and of course it isn't at all limited to thinking about the reliability of vision. In effect, there are two rather different pictures we might have about any of our faculties. On one, we take the faculty in question to be reliable not only with regard to its appropriate home range, but beyond this as well. If we adopt this view with regard to vision, for example, then we think that not only is our vision reliable about whether trees have fruit on them, it is also reliable about the rough shapes of visible craters on the moon. There is a continuity of reliability as we move from the home range to other, more "exotic" subdomains. That's the first picture. But in principle we might take a quite *different* view with regard to any given faculty, one where we would take the faculty in question to be reliable *only* for the home range. Although the faculty may well generate appearances for subdomains that go beyond the home range, on this second picture we hold that the appearances are *not* reliable in this extended arena. There is a *discontinuity* of reliability.

We are of course inclined to think in terms of the first picture. To stick to the example of vision, we take our vision to be giving us defeasible evidence not only about the shape of a boulder in front of us, but also about the shape of the moon. But the mere fact that this is what we are ordinarily inclined to do doesn't yet show that we are justified in doing this. Since there is no link between truth and advantage beyond the home range, why should we think that vision and other faculties continue to be reliable there?

(Don't say: even when we have moved beyond the home range, appearances are appearances, and as such provide defeasible justification for belief. For while it is true that appearances provide defeasible justification, that justification can be appropriately undermined or undercut if we have reasonable grounds for worry. And that is what we have, I think, with regard to appearances that go beyond the home range. So although we have reason to think that evolution will have given us faculties that are largely reliable when operating *within* their home range, we also have reason to think that evolution would have been indifferent as to whether the faculties *remain* reliable when they are put to work further "abroad." That seems to me to constitute sufficient ground for worrying about the reliability of appearances in such cases—unless we can find further reason to be reassured.)

The continuity problem arises, of course, not only with regard to vision, or empirical observations more broadly, but for moral intuitions as well. (That's why it is worth mentioning in a discussion of evolution and moral knowledge.) Even if we accept that evolution will have shaped intuition to be largely reliable when it comes to situations where there is a link between moral truth and evolutionary advantage, why should we think that this faculty will *continue* to be reliable even when we are thinking about situations that go beyond the home range? Yet we certainly *have* intuitions about countless moral issues that do indeed take us beyond anything where we might expect there to be (or to have been) a link between truth and advantage. So we need to ask ourselves, are our moral intuitions reliable here as well, even when we move further afield and contemplate subdomains of morality that go well beyond the home range? No doubt most of us continue to rely on intuition here too, but what justifies our confidence that moral intuition remains reliable when we do this?

Since this is an issue that arises for vision (and other faculties), and not just for moral intuition, perhaps we can make progress in answering our question about moral intuition by asking how the continuity problem can be answered with regard to vision. Just how is it that we are justified—as I take it we all think we are—in believing that vision is indeed reliable even when it is applied to matters beyond its home range?

I presume the answer goes something like this. The belief that vision remains reliable even when used outside of its home range is simply one more hypothesis, to be tested and confirmed (or rejected) like others. In effect, we use the very same process of theoretical reflection that was briefly described above, only this time the particular question at issue is whether or not it is really true that vision remains largely reliable even when used outside of its home range. We test that claim by seeing whether the various particular judgments that correspond to our extra observations (those from *outside* the home range) are, on the whole, correct, and we test *those* judgments by drawing implications from them that can themselves be confirmed or disconfirmed on the basis of more "everyday" observations (those that fall *within* the home range). If those predictions are borne out—and they are—that justifies our belief that vision is reliable (not perfectly, but largely) both within and without the home range.

8.5 THE CONTINUITY PROBLEM

This is a bit like confirming the reliability of one instrument by means of a second one, one already known to be reliable. Here, we confirm the reliability of vision *outside* the home range by checking it against observations made *within* the home range, a subdomain where we already know it to be reliable.

We can, I think, do the same thing when it comes to moral intuition. We have intuitions about all sorts of moral questions where, it would seem, there was no particular evolutionary advantage in having the corresponding beliefs. But we can try to confirm these intuitions nonetheless—and thus confirm the reliability of moral intuition outside its home range—by drawing relevant implications for issues that do fall within the home range. In this way we can hope to show that intuition remains reliable on the whole. And if it is, then we can justifiably draw on moral intuitions here too, using them as further inputs for our theory building.

Admittedly, establishing this continuity involves far more moral theorizing than we can undertake here. Pursuing this task properly requires entering into the detailed investigations and systematic theory building of normative ethics; and that lies well beyond the scope of the present book. But perhaps we can at least see why, having once established the reliability of intuition in its home range, we can at least reasonably hold out the hope that moral intuition might prove reliable (not perfectly, but largely) even more broadly.

Note, in any event, that it isn't as though the skeptic has shown that moral intuition is in fact *unreliable* beyond its home range. All that the continuity problem does is raise the *question* of extended reliability; it doesn't create any *presumption* that intuition is reliable only within its home range. Arguing that intuition *ceases* to be reliable once we move beyond the home range is every bit as involved an undertaking as establishing its reliability would be. As far as I can see, then, there is simply nothing in the argument from evolution (including the continuity problem) that gives us reason to predict that the skeptic will emerge victorious on this score, once we undertake the detailed work of building and testing normative theories.

What's more—and it is important not to lose sight of this point—even if we ultimately did decide that discontinuity is the right perspective here, and intuition is not reliable once it moves outside its home range, that certainly would not be the same as showing intuition to be unreliable across the board. It would merely show that the only reliable moral intuitions are those that fall *within* the home range, and so moral theory confirmation would have to proceed on the basis of a more limited set of inputs than we might otherwise think. That would be inconvenient, to be sure, but it wouldn't come close to establishing the impossibility of moral knowledge.

8.6 Path Dependence

I want to close our discussion of evolution by considering a rather different skeptical argument from the one we have been examining (and modifying) up till now. This new argument from evolution turns on the idea of path dependence.

Imagine that you have been examining various bits of evidence, weighing them up, and you have come to a conclusion about some matter—for example, about whether Adam committed the murder or not. So far so good. But now imagine that you somehow come to the further realization that if only you had considered the very same bits of evidence in a different *order*, you would have reached the opposite conclusion (say, that Adam was innocent rather than guilty). You realize that your having reached the particular conclusion you did (that Adam is guilty) is an artifact of the "path" through the evidence that you happened to take. That would be a very troubling discovery indeed. Clearly, the truth of who actually committed the murder doesn't depend on the order in which we examine the evidence. So if our *judgment* about the matter does depend on the order, that would ordinarily undermine our confidence in our conclusion, and justifiably so. In a case like this, we have (somehow) discovered that our belief is *path dependent*, and except in rather special circumstances, that calls the validity of our judgment into question.

Here's a rather different sort of case. Imagine that you have driven from home to your science class at the university, and in class you were exposed to several arguments for or against a particular scientific hypothesis. Having thought them through, you accept the hypothesis. So far so good. But now imagine that you somehow come to the realization that if only you had driven to school along an alternative route you would have reached the opposite conclusion (that is, that the hypothesis is false rather than true). You realize that your reaching the particular conclusion you did is an artifact of the literal physical path you took to get to school. (Perhaps having gone a different route and seen different sights would have altered the ways in which you found yourself attending to the different considerations pro and con.) Here too we have a case of path dependence (though of a different kind), and here too, barring special circumstances it will appropriately call the validity of your judgment (that the hypothesis is true) into question.

Clearly, not all forms of path dependence are troubling. Suppose you realize that had you eaten pizza for lunch rather than the salad that you actually had, you would have believed the answer to the question on the math quiz was 27, rather than 17 (where 17 is the answer you actually accept)—but that the *reason* you would have thought this is because the pizza had psychedelic mushrooms which would have affected your ability to calculate. Obviously, this sort of realization will do nothing at all to undermine your confidence in your current judgments. But the first two examples I described are different. They do seem to be cases that raise legitimate concerns. Sometimes the discovery that your having the beliefs you do is an artifact of the path (literal or not) that you took to arrive at them is something that appropriately undermines your confidence in their validity.

Very well then, the skeptic now says, isn't it clear that our moral beliefs display path dependence of the troubling kind? Humans are primates, and so have a particular evolutionary history (a particular mammalian path along the evolutionary tree of life). Surely this has had an incredible impact on which moral beliefs we've ended up with. We can see this by imagining moral agents that had evolved from a completely different part of the animal kingdom (social insects, perhaps—for example, some ancient ancestor of modern bees or ants). "Ant people" or "bee people" (rational, moral agents descended from ants or bees, respectively) would clearly have quite different moral intuitions from our own. So here too we have an instance of path dependence of a sort that should trouble us. After all, it is absurd to think that by sheer luck we just happened to have the evolutionary path that was appropriate for arriving at *valid* moral intuitions, emotions, and beliefs, while other paths to moral agency would have left us unable to accurately discern the moral facts. ("How lucky we are that we are descended from mammals rather than insects or crustaceans!") Our moral beliefs are clearly path dependent (the skeptic concludes), and they are path dependent in a way that should undermine any confidence we might have in our various moral judgments, and in the intuitions and emotions that lead to them.

How might a moral realist respond to this argument? One way, I suppose, would be to embrace a new form of relativism—a version where the basic moral principles really do vary, but the variation depends on one's species rather than one's society. Perhaps moral agents descended from apes really are subject to one set of basic moral principles, while moral agents descended from insects would be subject to a rather different set of principles. And perhaps evolution would have seen to it that each such advanced species would have intuitions suitable for guiding them to the relevant, species-relativized moral truths. Such a suggestion may seem implausible, but perhaps that's simply because we humans have never yet encountered moral agents descended from utterly different parts of the evolutionary tree. (Alternatively, perhaps octopuses, say, *are* such moral agents, but we haven't yet managed to communicate adequately enough with them to realize it!)

Clearly, no suggestion like this will be acceptable to any moral realist who believes that basic moral truths are necessary. For if they are necessary, then the same basic moral principles will be valid for anyone—any moral agent at all—regardless of whether they are descended from mammals, insects, crustaceans, or something else. But if this sort of species-relativized morality is rejected, how else can the realist reply to the fact of path dependence?

My own view is that the realist should insist, rather, that there is actually far less path dependence in our moral beliefs than the skeptic would have us believe. For while it is easy to *assert* that moral agents descended from utterly different parts of the animal kingdom would have radically different moral beliefs from our own, and while this claim may well seem self-evident when you first consider it, on reflection, I think, it is far less clear that it is actually true. The skeptic's argument may not presuppose that *all* of our moral intuitions would be different had we been descended from other ancestors, but it does seem to assume that most, or at the very least a very large part, of our moral intuitions would be different. But is that right? Is it really true that ant people, say, would have radically different moral intuitions about most things?

I think not. I find it difficult—indeed, to be honest, impossible—to imagine an advanced, stable species of rational, reflective agents that didn't have moral principles (and intuitions supporting these principles) that supported telling the truth, keeping promises, avoiding gratuitous harm to one another, and aiding those in need, and so on. Indeed, when I try to think about the moral views that would be held by ant people, or bee people (or octopus people, or raven people, and so on) I find myself thinking that they would have basic moral views rather similar to our own. Contrary to what the skeptic claims, I find myself thinking that basic moral intuitions are not especially path dependent at all. (There may, of course, be differences at the *derivative* level, given the rather different forms of life that these different species would have. But intuitions about fundamental principles, I suspect, would be largely the same.)

This is only a conjecture on my part, to be sure, but I don't think it is a groundless one. Imagine that we land on Mars and discover (to our surprise) that there really are rational, thoughtful, intelligent agents there—advanced beings fully capable of reflecting on how they are to interact with one another. Don't they need to communicate with one another? But that will support a requirement of truth telling. Don't they ever need to cooperate? But that will support a requirement to keep promises and meet the reasonable expectations of others. Don't they need to be free from interference and harm if they are to accomplish their various goals? Don't they ever find themselves in need of aid? But these last two will support a prohibition against doing harm and a requirement to provide assistance. And so on and so forth. How could such beings ever have evolved to the point of being moral agents at all without having principles of these sorts (or principles very much like them) in place?

If I am right, then the core of morality (at the very least) isn't path dependent after all. Any creatures sufficiently evolved to *have* a morality will have one that is very much like ours. And if that is correct, then this last version of the argument from evolution fails as well. Our fundamental moral beliefs are not threatened by their path dependence, because it turns out that in the main these beliefs are not actually path dependent at all.

Of course, in saying this, I do not mean to be claiming that *all* of our moral intuitions are free from path dependence. That seems rather unlikely. But all along I have insisted that the moral realist need not (and should not) take moral intuition to be infallible. So if we find areas where intuitions seem likely to be the result of a troubling path dependence we will find ourselves with reason to worry about the validity of those particular intuitions. But that is a far cry from concluding that our intuitions need to be dismissed wholesale, as though they were nothing more than mildly interesting artifacts of our primate heritage.

Are there, indeed, areas where it is reasonable to worry that our intuitions may well have been "idiosyncratically" shaped by our particular mammalian origins? Perhaps. It doesn't seem implausible to suggest that some of our sexual mores (and the intuitions and emotions that support them) may be the result of our origins as primates rather than, say, bees. The same thing may be true for our views about the appropriateness of showing partiality for members of one's immediate family. Similarly—but coming at the question from the other direction—perhaps moral agents that had evolved out of *symbiotic* species would have less tribalistic intuitions than we humans seem to have.

If anything like this is right, then these are the sorts of intuitions that we might do well to worry about. These would be the ones that we should perhaps be most ready to reject if we find that we cannot provide them with an independent justification (finding a suitable place for them in our best overall theories of morality). And it is, I suppose, noteworthy in this regard that intuitions like these are among the ones where many have thought that there is indeed particular difficulty in providing larger theoretical justifications. So perhaps these really are intuitions that we should be prepared to dismiss as the moral equivalent of optical illusions, mistakes caused by accidents of our evolutionary path.

Obviously, to settle these questions, or even to pursue them further, would once again require immersing ourselves in the sort of detailed arguments that are the mainstay of systematic normative ethics. That lies well beyond the scope of the present work. I mention these examples only to illustrate what is, for present purposes, the more significant *metaethical* moral: that thinking about the nature of evolution, and its role in shaping our moral intuitions and beliefs, may lead us to reject, or at least question, certain of our beliefs; but at best it does this only in a piecemeal fashion. We can acknowledge the fact that our moral intuitions are the result of evolutionary shaping while still insisting that on the whole those intuitions are sufficiently reliable to be used as a source of moral knowledge.

9
Explanation

9.1 A Metaphysical Test

Here's a plausible thought about reality: things that are real make a difference to what is the case. They are explanatorily "potent." They help explain why things are the way they are.

Of course, no one real thing is likely to explain everything—but each and every real thing should help explain *something* or the other beyond itself. Otherwise we have reason to doubt whether the purportedly real thing is actually real at all.

That's a rather abstract claim, but a few examples should make the point seem obvious. Thus, for example, cars are real, and they explain, among other things, how Michael got to work last week, and why you might get injured if you cross the street without looking both ways. Trees are real, and they explain (among other things) why there are so many leaves on your lawn in the fall. The property of weighing more than a ton is a perfectly real property, and it explains (in conjunction with other things) why it is that you cannot lift an elephant, just as the property of having a negative electrical charge is a real property and helps explain why magnets attract one another, and why electrons don't all just float away from the atomic nucleus. Similarly, it really is a fact that pineapples have tough skins, which helps explain why we use knives to carve them before eating them. And the fact that I am trying to finish writing this passage explains why I haven't yet gone down for dinner. Finally—one last pair of examples—the truth of the claim that water freezes at around 32 degrees Fahrenheit helps explain why there are ice cubes in the freezer of your refrigerator, and the truth of the claim that your sister was pregnant last year helps explain why she went shopping for maternity clothes.

As I say, things that are real have an explanatory force: whether alone or in conjunction with other real things, they help explain still *other* things that are real as well.

But this thought points to a new argument for moral skepticism. For on the face of it, at least, it certainly doesn't seem as though moral facts—if there were such things—would explain anything at all. To put the point crudely but intuitively, there is a distinction between what is the case and what ought to be the case, and what ought to be the case simply doesn't play a role in explaining what *is* the case. Moral facts don't make anything happen. Moral properties—if there were such things—would be causally impotent. After all, nothing happens simply because it *ought* to happen. The purported moral goodness of some possible state of affairs doesn't bring that state of affairs into existence. So even if there were moral facts and moral properties (and so on), they wouldn't explain anything real. But if it truly is a condition on being real that you explain something real—if this provides a test which allows us to distinguish between what is genuinely real and what is mere phantasm—then moral facts, moral properties, and moral truths all fail the test. And this means, of course, that none of these things are actually real. There are no genuine moral facts, no moral properties, no moral truths. Which is to say: moral *realism* should be rejected.

The argument I have just sketched boils down to two simple claims. First, if there really were any moral facts, they would explain something. However, second, moral facts don't (or wouldn't) actually explain anything at all. So these supposed moral facts aren't genuine facts after all. The truth of the matter is, there *are* no moral facts. Moral realism is mistaken.

Given the simplicity of the argument, anyone wanting to defend moral realism must reject one or the other (or both) of its two premises. Either the realist must insist that moral facts really are explanatory after all, despite what we might initially think, or else they must reject the assumption that everything real will indeed have explanatory force of some sort.

Eventually, we will want to consider both possible replies. But first let's try to get clearer about the thinking behind the first premise of the skeptic's argument, the idea that a genuine fact must explain something (and so moral facts, in particular, will need to explain something if there really are to be such things).

Sometimes skeptics sympathetic to this argument focus, in particular, on the issue of whether moral facts or moral properties would help explain our various *beliefs* about those same facts and properties—whether, for example, the wrongness of killing an innocent person would help explain why we *believe* that it is wrong to kill an innocent person. And the skeptic's suggestion, of course, is that even if there were moral facts of this sort, they wouldn't play a role in explaining why we have the corresponding moral beliefs. That thought, in turn, might feed into an epistemological argument concerning whether those beliefs are *justified* or not.

We have, of course, already considered arguments that take this particular turn and found them wanting (see, in particular, 7.4 and 8.3–8.4). But in the present context our concern is with *metaphysics* rather than epistemology. We are exploring the more general idea that anything real must have explanatory force of some sort; and given this distinct, metaphysical focus, there is no particular reason to attend exclusively to the question of whether moral facts help explain *beliefs*, as opposed to something else.

After all, imagine that we somehow came to realize that the wrongness of killing explained something about the weather, or the behavior of turtles, or that the intrinsic value of giving people what they deserve explained something about the melting point of gold, or the color of roses. None of these "proposals" are remotely plausible, of course, but the point is that if anything like this *were* true, it would show that moral facts have explanatory force after all, and so moral facts would meet the metaphysical test we are currently exploring. Even if it is true that genuine facts must be explanatorily potent, it surely would suffice if the thing explained were a fact about turtles, the weather, roses, or gold.

So the relevant test should be construed broadly. A genuine fact—including moral facts, if such there be—must explain *something*. If not our moral beliefs, then something else.

Just *how* broadly should the test be construed? Must moral facts (or any facts, for that matter) explain *empirical* facts? Or would it suffice to explain anything at all? Suppose, for example, that moral facts, while explanatorily impotent with regard to the empirical world nonetheless somehow explained genuine facts of some other kind, perhaps something supernatural or theological (for example, something about God's nature). Wouldn't this really be good enough to count as far as the relevant metaphysical test was concerned? Wouldn't it suffice to show that moral facts were real?

Maybe. We'll come back to this question later. But for the time being let's assume that anything real must indeed help explain something about the *empirical* world. After all, even those who believe in a supernatural realm—positing, for example, the existence of a God—think that such facts in turn explain things about the empirical world. (That's part of why they feel entitled to claim the relevant supernatural facts are, indeed, genuine facts.) So if moral facts are real, let us tentatively suppose, they must explain something or the other about how things stand in the empirical world.

And what the skeptic claims, of course, is that this is a test that moral facts cannot pass, since moral facts are explanatorily impotent. Unlike light waves, or sound waves, or gravity waves, for example, there are no "ought waves," altering the world. Unlike X-rays or electronic charges or magnetic fields, there are no "value rays" or "justice charges" or "inequality fields." Moral facts don't explain anything. So there aren't really any moral facts at all.

9.2 Explaining Empirical Facts

How might a moral realist respond to this argument? As I have already noted, one possibility open to the realist is to try to argue that contrary to what the skeptic has suggested, moral facts actually do have explanatory force after all. Admittedly, there are no "ought waves" or "inequality fields," but that hardly shows that moral facts are indeed explanatorily impotent. There are no "car waves" or "lemonade fields" either, but facts about cars and facts about lemonade are perfectly real for all that, and they do indeed explain things about the empirical world (for example, facts about the thirst-quenching powers of lemonade help explain why sometimes there are lemonade stands across the street on hot summer days). Perhaps, then, we shouldn't be so quick to assume that moral facts lack explanatory force. When we look more carefully—the realist might insist—we may find that moral facts are explanatory after all.

This is not, as it happens, an answer that appeals to all moral realists, but it does appeal to some. Unsurprisingly, however, even among those realists who embrace this position there isn't always agreement about which particular empirical facts (or, more precisely, which *types* of empirical facts) are to be explained (at least in part) by reference to moral facts.

Some moral realists are prepared to claim that moral facts do indeed play a role in explaining our corresponding moral beliefs. That is to say, we have the moral beliefs we do (or at least many of the moral beliefs we do) precisely because those beliefs are true. Perhaps, for example, certain moral facts help explain why it is *advantageous* to have the corresponding beliefs. If so, then the facts may explain the beliefs. (If the moral facts explain the evolutionary advantage of having those beliefs, then they may help explain why evolution shaped us to have intuitions disposing us to accept those beliefs.)

As I have already explained, however (in 7.4 and 8.3–8.4), I don't myself find such accounts persuasive. I find it more likely that truth and advantage are jointly explained by relevant "underlying" facts that provide a common ground for both advantage *and* truth. And if that's right, then it isn't really true that moral facts are part of the best explanation of our having the moral beliefs that we do. So if moral facts do indeed explain something about the empirical world, we will need to look elsewhere to find it.

Still, there are many other cases where we do seem to appeal to moral facts as part of the explanation of empirical facts. In particular, we often explain the actions of individuals or groups by reference to moral facts of one sort or another. Perhaps the moral realist can meet the metaphysical challenge (of demonstrating the explanatory force of moral facts) by appealing to cases like this.

Here are some examples of the kinds of explanations that realists sometimes point to: Why did Hitler kill so many innocent people? Because he was *evil*. Why did Joanna pay for the candy bar? Because it was the *right* thing to do and she is a *good person*. Why will the socialist revolution come? Because capitalism is *unjust*. Obviously, examples like this could easily be multiplied.

It is important to note that you need not find all these particular explanations compelling. Indeed, my own view is that the example concerning the candy bar probably isn't one where moral facts are doing genuine explanatory work. For presumably Joanna paid for the candy bar because she *believed* it was the right thing to do; and if I am right that moral facts don't actually explain our moral beliefs, then it won't be true that moral facts explain Joanna's behavior. (In contrast, it wouldn't be especially plausible to suggest, similarly, that Hitler killed innocents because he *believed* it was wrong or evil to do so!)

But for the moral realist to rebut the skeptic's argument, it isn't necessary that every explanation of this kind be sound. It suffices if *some* are. That is to say, as long as *some* examples of this basic kind are compelling that seems sufficient to show that moral facts have explanatory force after all, thus defusing the skeptic's argument. And the fact remains, we do seem to regularly appeal to explanations of this basic type. So does that suffice to establish the explanatory force of moral facts?

Probably not. For what the skeptic may want to say, in response, is that for each such example, where moral facts purportedly explain some empirical fact, there are actually *nonevaluative* facts in the neighborhood as well, and it is these nonmoral facts that do the real explanatory work. We can illustrate this general idea by means of our same three examples: Why did Hitler kill so many innocent people? Because he was prepared to harm others to get ahead and maintain power. Why did Joanna pay for the candy bar? Because she was raised to pay the stated price for items she purchases. Why will the socialist revolution come? Because under capitalism workers do increasingly poorly, and so become increasingly unhappy with the status quo. Here too, the point is not whether you accept the specific details of these alternative, nonmoral explanations, but whether you agree that explanations *like* these—ones that make no appeal to supposed moral facts—are available, and indeed superior, to the moral ones.

It is this last bit that gives force to the skeptic's reply. For presumably the question is not whether we can dream up explanations of *some* sort or the other that appeal to moral facts, but whether the *best* explanations do this. Otherwise, the metaphysical test has no teeth! (Why did Hitler kill innocents? Because he was demonically possessed! Why will the revolution come? Because the rainbow fairies will grow tired of capitalism! Surely we don't want to say that the sheer availability of these silly explanations suffices to establish that such *supernatural* "facts" have genuine explanatory force!) So what the moral skeptic needs to claim isn't merely that these alternative, nonmoral explanations are available, but that they are superior to the moral ones.

I am confident, however, that many people will be inclined to agree with the skeptic about this. That is to say, many people will be inclined to agree with the skeptic that the *best* explanations of these sundry phenomena won't actually appeal to moral facts at all. It is these *other* facts, the nonevaluative ones, that really do the explaining here. And if that's right, of course, then it hasn't really been shown that moral facts do indeed have explanatory force. It will no longer be clear that they explain anything at all.

There is an interesting possible response to this claim, but it is only open to those moral realists who are reductionists. That is, the response is available to moral realists who believe that moral facts reduce to (or "boil down to") more basic facts of a nonmoral sort. In particular, the response is available to (at least some of) those reductionist realists who are *naturalists*, so that the more basic underlying facts are natural ones (see 2.3).

Realists of this naturalist reductionist bent can agree that the various nonevaluative facts—appealed to by the skeptic in the course of offering nonmoral explanations—do indeed explain the empirical phenomena in question. But the realists will simply go on to claim that this is still compatible with holding that the relevant moral facts *also* explain the empirical phenomena, precisely because the moral facts in question simply *consist* in these more fundamental nonevaluative facts. In effect, on this view, the moral facts just *are* the nonevaluative ones; that's what the moral facts *reduce* to. After all, if one is a reductionist about moral facts—and that's the position we are considering at the moment—then one thinks that moral facts ultimately reduce to nonmoral ones; that's just what the moral facts *are*. And so, in particular, if the existence of the relevant moral facts consists in the existence of the explanatorily potent nonmoral facts, then it turns out that the moral facts are themselves explanatorily potent after all.

Suppose, for example, that we agree that what explains Hitler's having killed millions of innocent people is (in part) the fact that Hitler was ruthless, unrestrainedly ambitious, and prepared to harm others to get ahead and maintain power, and so on. That doesn't in any way threaten the original explanation—the explanation that talked about the fact that Hitler was *evil*— if we are prepared to acknowledge the plausible reductionist suggestion that being evil simply *consists* in (among other things) being ruthless, ambitious, and prepared to harm others to get one's way. If being evil simply just *is* a matter of having a character like this, then if the latter explains Hitler's horrendous deeds, the former does so as well.

Similarly, if a social economic system's being unjust just consists in (among other things) needlessly impoverishing many of its citizens, leaving them miserable and bereft of satisfying life choices, with no legal means of significantly improving their lot, then if these latter facts explain why capitalism will be overthrown, so does an explanation that appeals to capitalism's being unjust.

In short, given suitable *reductionist* accounts of the relevant moral facts, it seems that if the skeptic's favored nonmoral explanations are good ones, so too are the corresponding *moral* explanations. So moral facts (of the right sort) will have explanatory force after all.

None of this, of course, yet tells us whether we *should* accept reductionist accounts of this sort. But it does suggest, at least, that realists who do accept such accounts may well be able to pass the metaphysical requirement central to the skeptic's argument.

To be sure, an answer along these lines will not be available to other forms of moral realism. A simple realist, for example—someone who denies the ultimate reducibility of moral facts to nonmoral ones—can hardly avail herself of the approach we've just mentioned. Indeed, even some of those who accept naturalist reductionism may be unable to appeal to the kind of answer we have just been entertaining, if they hold that moral facts reduce to the "wrong kind" of natural facts (that is, to facts that don't appear in the skeptic's favored explanations). Realists of these other sorts will have to find other empirical phenomena to explain, if they are going to meet the skeptic's explanatory challenge.

Still, can't we agree that, at the very least, the right *sort* of naturalist reductionist can indeed meet that challenge? If being evil, say, just *is* a matter of being ruthless, overly ambitious, and so on, isn't it plausible to hold that moral facts involving this property really do explain some things after all?

Even if it is conceded that moral facts of this sort really do have explanatory force (supposing, for the moment, that this type of reductionism is correct), several important questions remain unanswered. We might wonder, for example, how many moral facts are susceptible to being reduced in this way. Can *all* moral facts be shown to have explanatory force by means of arguments along these same general lines? If not, where does that leave morality as a whole? Must all moral facts pass the metaphysical test, if morality is to be acknowledged as real, or does it suffice if *enough* of them pass it? Just how many moral facts, and of what sort, would count as "enough" anyway?

I won't try to answer these questions here. Instead I want to turn to two other worries that the skeptic might raise concerning the argument we've just given. For the truth of the matter is that the skeptic may not be prepared to concede that the reductionist really has offered any examples at all where the supposed moral facts are genuinely explanatory. And if—as the skeptic is going to argue—even simple examples like the proposed account of what it is to be evil fail to establish the explanatory force of moral facts, then we hardly need to ask ourselves just how far that account can be extended. It cannot even get off the ground.

9.3 Reduction and Explanation

If reductionism is true, then moral facts reduce to underlying *non*moral facts that are more basic, more fundamental. Moral facts consist in, or are built up out of, these more basic facts. But if that's right, the skeptic may now suggest, then the *real* explanatory work is done by these underlying, more metaphysically fundamental facts. The moral facts just come along "for the ride"—and they don't really do any additional explanatory work. Which is just to say, these supposed moral facts aren't actually explanatory at all. And that means, given our assumption that real facts must be explanatory, that so-called moral facts aren't actually genuine *facts* after all. So, far from showing how moral facts can be explanatory, reductionism about morality threatens to guarantee that moral facts cannot actually have any explanatory force in their own right.

Or so the skeptic might argue.

This argument is tempting, but on reflection I imagine that most of us will rightly wonder whether it can really succeed. For we are indeed here supposing the truth of *reductionism* about moral facts, the thought that facts about evil, or injustice (or wrongness, or obligation, and so on) just *are* facts about the relevant underlying natural properties. So if the latter can explain things—as presumably they can—shouldn't we conclude, rather, that the former can too? After all, if the moral facts just *are* the relevant natural facts—if that's what they consist in—how could those natural facts have explanatory force while the moral ones lack it?

To get clearer about the various alternatives here, imagine an argument parallel to the one just offered by the moral skeptic, but this time aimed at showing that there are no *hearts*—because facts about hearts have no genuine explanatory force.

You are, I imagine, someone who believes in the existence of hearts. Hearts are, obviously enough, perfectly real. And if we ask whether facts about hearts explain anything, the answer is that of course they do. The failure of Beth's heart, for example, explains why Beth died! It is perfectly obvious that "cardiac facts" have explanatory force, and so facts about hearts pass our metaphysical test.

But we are, presumably, also *reductionists* about hearts and so reductionists about cardiac facts. Simplifying tremendously (but adequately for our purposes), facts about hearts presumably reduce to facts about how cardiac muscle fibers contract (or fail to contract) and thereby pump (or fail to pump) blood through a system of arteries and veins. These muscle fibers can fail to contract properly, and when they do, the person can die.

So imagine that a "cardiac skeptic" argues that it is actually these underlying, more physiologically basic facts about muscle fibers that do the *real* explanatory work in the case of Beth's death. Indeed, they argue, once we have given the explanation of the death in terms of the relevant muscle fibers, nothing gets added if we start to talk about hearts as well. So the appeal to supposed facts about hearts doesn't really add anything; such facts don't do any genuine explanatory work! And this means—the skeptic concludes—that there are no genuine facts about hearts at all, since these supposed facts don't actually explain anything.

Indeed, the skeptic might push further. Presumably these facts about muscle fibers themselves reduce even further, to complicated biochemical facts about complex organic molecules which undergo certain changes (in specified circumstances)—and so it is facts of these even more fundamental kinds that actually explain Beth's death. Talk of facts about muscles and fibers doesn't actually add anything to the explanation, so here too we should reject the idea that these are genuine facts.

And this same line of thought might be pushed even further. The skeptic might insist that ultimately only the basic particles posited by fundamental physics actually explain anything at all, since everything else reduces to facts about these particles. So shouldn't we conclude that there are no genuine facts of any sort at all, other than facts about the basic particles and their properties? Shouldn't we conclude that nothing is *real* at all, other than the basic particles of physics (and the properties ascribed to those particles by physics)?

Almost no one is prepared to follow this argument all the way to its sweeping skeptical conclusion. *Of course* there are hearts—as well as trees and rocks and books, and tables and alarm clocks! *Of course* facts about these things are perfectly genuine facts. There are facts about hearts and facts about trees—and for that matter there are facts about elections and facts about the ocean, facts about the history of France and facts about psychology, astronomy, and your tax bill. So the argument must go wrong somewhere. But if it does, then why shouldn't we agree that it goes wrong in the case of moral facts as well?

Admittedly, there are some philosophers who think that the argument I've just sketched does not actually go wrong at all. That is, there are those who conclude that it is indeed the literal truth that the only things that truly exist are the basic particles of physics, and the only genuine facts are facts about those particles. All other purported facts are mere fictions—convenient fictions, perhaps, useful for various everyday purposes, but strictly speaking nothing more than illusions and phantasms.

As usual, it is not my goal here to try to refute broad skeptical positions like this one. My aim is the more limited one of arguing that belief in morality is in no worse shape, philosophically speaking, than countless other beliefs we never have serious doubts about (like beliefs about trees, or astronomy, or income taxes). So while I do believe that this kind of sweeping skeptical argument is mistaken, I won't try to establish that here.

Still, supposing we agree—as I imagine that almost of us will want to do—that there are indeed facts about countless matters besides ultimate particles, how might we best respond to the sweeping skeptical argument? What are our choices for identifying where exactly it goes wrong? Let me quickly mention three possibilities.

First, we might agree with the skeptic that the only things that ever actually explain anything at all are facts about ultimate particles. But we might then insist (in light of this realization) that we should reject the metaphysical claim that something must have explanatory force if it is to be real. To be sure, up to this point we have taken this claim as a given—we have accepted the idea that anything real must have explanatory force—but perhaps we have now reached a stage where we might decide instead to reject it. If something does not actually need to be explanatory to be *real*, then we can concede, if we are so inclined, that facts about hearts and bridges and the Treaty of Versailles don't actually explain anything, and yet insist, for all that, that these facts are perfectly genuine facts. In short, we can reject the metaphysical test that we have been exploring, thus opening the door once again for accepting the reality of things that lack explanatory force. And of course, if we do go this route, then morality is no longer threatened by the skeptic's argument. Even if it turns out to be true that moral facts don't actually explain anything at all, they might still, for all that, be perfectly genuine facts. I'm not myself inclined to take a position like this, but some may find it attractive.

Alternatively, second, we might insist against the skeptic that reduction does not actually entail explanatory impotence. While it is true, let us suppose, that facts about hearts really do reduce to facts about muscle fibers of the right sort (which reduce, in turn, to facts about complex molecules, which reduce to facts about basic particles), in and of itself this doesn't actually entail that facts about hearts lack explanatory power. Perhaps we should insist instead that when one kind of fact reduces to another more fundamental set of facts, then the first ("reduced") fact actually has all the explanatory force of the facts to which it is reduced. After all, if the reduction is correct, and the first fact simply consists in, or is constituted by, the second set of facts, then perhaps by virtue of the truth of that very reduction, the first fact "inherits" (as we might put it) the explanatory force of the underlying facts. So even if ultimately everything reduces to facts about basic particles, it won't really be true that the things that are reduced are explanatorily impotent. If that's right, then even if the metaphysical test is legitimate, the sundry familiar facts we ordinarily believe in can still pass that test, and so can still qualify as real. And this means, of course, that the reductionist moral realist may escape the skeptic's argument as well. If being evil, for example, really just is a matter of being ruthless, ambitious, and so on, then if the latter (nonmoral) properties are explanatory, the former (moral) one is also. And so moral facts—like the fact that Hitler was *evil*—can be perfectly genuine facts as well.

There is a third possible position that is also worth mentioning. Perhaps the skeptic is too quick to assume that if one set of facts reduces to a second, more basic set of facts, the fundamental explanations will always be in terms of that second set of facts. Perhaps, instead, in some cases it is actually only a higher-order explanation (one that is couched in terms of the first type of fact) that genuinely gets things right.

Suppose we ask, for example, why the bridge fell. The answer might well be that it fell because the bomb on it exploded. (A bit more fully: because the bridge was made of such and such materials, with such and such an overall structure, and the bomb exploded with such and such force, and so on.) Now I imagine that it is true that facts about bridges reduce to facts about the types and positions of the various subatomic particles that make them up, just as it is true that facts about bombs reduce to facts about the various subatomic particles that make *them* up. But for all that, it doesn't seem right to say that the reason the bridge fell is precisely because subatomic particles P_x, P_y, and P_z and so on (composing the bridge) were in locations L_x, L_y, and L_z and so on, when they were hit by particles B_x, B_y, and B_z from the bomb, and so on. For normally the bridge would *still* have fallen even if particle P_x had actually not been part of the bridge at the crucial moment, or had P_y been in a slightly different location, or had P_z been hit by B_q rather than B_z. And so on and so forth.

Intuitively, the trouble with any explanation that is offered at the level of subatomic particles is that it is way too specific to actually properly demarcate the circumstances which explain the bridge's having fallen. Countless other nearby arrangements of microparticles would have resulted in the bridge falling too, and the best explanation of why it fell is that it was in one or the other of the relevant alternative arrangements. But to adequately pick out that range, we are probably going to need to start talking about the shape and structure of the *bridge*, and the nature of the *bomb*, and so forth. Arguably, then, the real explanation of the bridge's falling will be one that talks about macro features of the bridge and of the bomb; that's where the real explanatory work takes place. But if something like that is right, then it isn't so much that the reduced facts "inherit" their explanatory force from the facts to which they reduce, but rather something more like the reverse: although facts about bridges reduce to facts about basic particles, explanations that explicitly refer to bridges may still have explanatory *priority*.

This last position, like the two that came before it, is controversial, and though I am sympathetic to it I won't argue for it further here. Note, however, that if something like this is right, then it isn't necessary to claim that facts about bridges (and hearts, and psychology, and the French Revolution) pass the metaphysical test by virtue of "inheriting" explanatory force from the underlying facts to which they reduce. On the contrary, they will be straightforwardly explanatory in their own right and pass the test directly. Similarly, then, the reductionist moral realist might want to claim that moral facts pass the test directly as well.

Return, yet again, to the question of why Hitler killed so many innocents, and the suggested explanation that he did this because he was evil. The reductionist suggested that being evil might simply consist in being ruthless, ambitious, prepared to sacrifice others for the sake of gaining power, and having other character traits of a similar sort. But notice that it might be that no one of these characteristics (or sets of characteristics) is essential for explaining what Hitler did. Even if he was ruthless, say, it could still easily be the case that he would have behaved just as he did if he hadn't been; it would have sufficed if he had been a sadist, or callously indifferent to the suffering of others, and so on. There is presumably a range of nearby—but not identical— character traits any of which would have sufficed to lead Hitler to kill innocents as he did. So arguably what really explains what he did is the fact that he had one or another of the traits in this range. And if we want to pick out that range of underlying traits, to demarcate its boundaries, perhaps there is no better way to do this than to appeal to the concept of being *evil*. If so, then an explanation of what Hitler did that refers to the fact that he was evil may well have explanatory priority, and so moral facts may well pass the test directly.

I won't here try to adjudicate between these three different proposals about how to avoid the sweeping skeptical conclusion that the only real facts are ones about ultimate particles. The topic of reduction and explanation is a controversial one, and it would take us too far afield to consider it further. For our purposes it suffices to note that there are at least these three different ways for reductionists to resist skepticism about ordinary, familiar facts. And so, for all we have seen so far, there is no obvious reason why someone who is also a reductionist about *moral* facts should not appeal to one or another of these three proposals as well.

9.4 The Normative Aspect of Moral Facts

Unfortunately for the reductionist moral realist, however, the skeptic may be able to press their argument further, in a way that threatens belief in moral facts without similarly threatening ordinary, familiar facts across the board. The problem is this. It seems plausible to suggest that there is something more to being a moral fact than what the reductionist has so far pointed to. Moral facts—if such there be—have an essential *normative* aspect, and this is something that hasn't yet been brought into the picture. In particular, it hasn't been shown that the normative aspects of moral facts do any explanatory work; and if not, then it seems reasonable to wonder whether it is truly the case that full-blown *moral* facts—as opposed to their nonnormative, merely descriptive contents—explain anything at all.

For example, even if we were to agree that being evil consists, in part, in being ruthless, sadistic, or callous, and so forth, there is more to the notion of what it is to be evil than the mere having of one or more of these character traits. That merely captures what we might call the *descriptive* component of what it is to be evil. But there is also an evaluative or normative component as well, the idea that one should not *be* this way, that one should not *have* these traits.

Similarly, even if we were to agree that being a good person consists, in part, in being prepared to pay for the items one takes in stores, being disposed to keep one's promises, being someone who avoids harming others, and so on, there is more to the notion of what it is to be a good person than this, for that merely captures the descriptive aspects of the idea. It doesn't yet bring in the normative aspect, the thought that one *should* be someone like this, that it is *better* to be that way.

Or suppose we come to accept the constructivist proposal that an act's being right is a matter of its conforming to the rules that would be favored or endorsed by the relevant minds. That too points to a descriptive property, but doesn't yet bring in the evaluative aspect of the concept of rightness—the thought that there is a compelling *reason* to perform such acts (and to avoid those acts which *lack* this property).

In all of these cases, for a given moral fact to hold it doesn't suffice that the descriptive component of the fact be in place, it also seems necessary for the normative aspect to be in place as well. Arguably, unless one shouldn't be evil, unless one ought to be good, unless there is reason to act rightly, it just isn't true that there are *moral* facts at all. There may be descriptive facts about how people act, or what people are disposed to do, but these won't be *moral* facts unless it is also true that they *should* or should *not* act in these various ways.

The objection, then, is this: at best the reductionist moral realist has shown that the descriptive components of moral facts are explanatory, but not the normative components. So at best the realist will have shown that the descriptive facts in question are genuine facts. But since there is more to the existence of a moral fact than its descriptive component, the realist hasn't really shown the moral fact itself—that "larger" fact consisting of both the descriptive and the normative elements—has explanatory force. And if not, the existence of genuinely *moral* facts hasn't been defended after all.

To see the force of this objection, imagine someone trying to argue that facts about *demons* are explanatory. Imagine, in particular a "demonic reductionist" who says, for example, that being demonically possessed just is a matter of behaving in certain characteristic ways (screaming at night, behaving erratically, shrinking away from religious symbols, and the like). Behavior like this can certainly be explanatory (it might, for example, explain why the neighbors have moved away), so doesn't this suffice to show that demonic facts have explanatory force?

In response, we would reasonably insist that an essential part of being a genuinely *demonic* fact involves having some connection to the right sort of supernatural being (such as the devil or one of his minions), so that unless *that* aspect of the supposed demonic fact is doing explanatory work as well, it isn't really correct to say that the purported demonic fact is truly explanatory. As we might put the point, even though the behaviors in question are certainly explanatory, the supposed demonic fact isn't really explanatory *qua* demonic fact. So we don't really have reason to agree that demonic facts have explanatory force.

Similarly, then, if we agree that an essential part of being a genuinely moral fact involves having a normative component, then unless that aspect of the supposed moral fact is doing explanatory work as well, it isn't really correct to say that the purported moral fact is truly explanatory. So even if it is true that the various descriptive facts appealed to by the reductionist are indeed explanatory, the supposed *moral* facts haven't really been shown to be explanatory—they haven't been shown to be explanatory *qua* moral facts. And this means that we don't really have reason to agree that moral facts have explanatory force.

Clearly, this new argument will only trouble those realists who accept the thought that genuine facts must indeed be explanatory. Those realists who prefer the first of the three possible replies that we canvassed above—the one according to which countless everyday, familiar facts lack explanatory force, so the test should be rejected—won't need to search for a further reply. But what of those realists who agree that genuine facts are explanatory?

One possibility, presumably, would be to reject the assumption that a genuinely moral fact must indeed have a normative component. Perhaps there really is nothing more to any given moral fact than the merely "descriptive" elements to which it reduces. Perhaps the normative element is really nothing more than a logically distinct "add on," and not something essential to the presence of a genuinely moral fact. If something like this is right—if moral facts really can be reduced to the relevant descriptive facts without remainder—then it won't matter that the realist hasn't demonstrated the explanatory force of these normative elements, for they won't really be part of the moral fact after all. Admittedly, we may have to conclude that there are no genuine facts about *normativity* (no facts, for example, about what we have reason to do or believe), but at least we won't have to agree that there are no facts about *morality*.

While this is, I know, a position that may appeal to some moral realists, it is not one that I find congenial. To deny the existence of normative facts is to embrace normative nihilism (3.4) and as I have already explained, this is a position which I find I cannot seriously entertain. But be that as it may, even if the threat of normative nihilism could somehow be avoided, I am not attracted to the idea that moral facts do not themselves involve normative ones. It does seem to me to be the case that if an act is truly morally required, this involves, in part, the existence of a reason to do that act. Similarly, if a certain character trait is evil, this involves, in part, the existence of a reason to not be someone like that. And so on, and so forth, for other moral facts. In effect, this is just to acknowledge that I am attracted to the position we are calling *reasons internalism* (see 1.2), according to which morality provides reasons for action. For me, that's part of the very job description of morality, and not a part I am prepared to abandon. So if there really are to be moral facts, there had better be reasons to act accordingly.

Suppose then that we accept reasons internalism (or some other view close to it that similarly requires moral facts to have a normative component), and suppose, as well, that we continue to embrace the metaphysical test, so that genuine facts must have explanatory force. It does seem, then, that if the realist is to maintain that moral facts are real facts, not only must the relevant descriptive components of moral facts explain things, the normative

9.4 THE NORMATIVE ASPECT OF MORAL FACTS 241

components must do so as well. Roughly speaking, the fact that there is a *reason* to do what morality requires of us must itself explain something about the world.

Can the realist plausibly assert that this too is the case? Conceivably a reductionist approach might be helpful here as well. Imagine that the realist argues that what it is for there to be a reason to do something reduces to more basic underlying facts of a nonnormative sort. That is, suppose that the realist offers a reductionist account of normativity itself, so that the very fact that there is a reason to act in a certain way reduces in turn to a further set of more basic, nonnormative facts. In principle, at least, it might not then surprise us if it turned out that these underlying facts had explanatory force. Perhaps we would conclude that normative facts "inherit" the explanatory force of these underlying nonnormative facts. Or perhaps we would conclude, instead, that in at least some of the relevant cases it was the normative fact that actually had explanatory priority over the underlying facts. Either way, a suitable reductionist account might show normative facts could be explanatory.

(What might such a reductionist account of normativity look like? The most natural suggestion to make here is a constructivist one, where normative facts boil down to relevant facts about relevant minds. Perhaps, for example, the fact that there is a reason to do something ultimately consists in the fact that a mind that is reasoning in certain specified ways would decide to perform that act. This is certainly too crude a proposal as it stands—it doesn't even allow for the possibility of reasons that are outweighed—but it may suffice to illustrate the rough idea. See 12.6 for more on this suggestion.)

What sorts of things might normative facts explain? The obvious proposal is that they sometimes explain our behavior, by way of explaining our normative beliefs. That is to say, we have the beliefs that we do, concerning what there is reason to do, because of the *truth* of those beliefs—because it is a *fact* that we have reasons to do these things. So normative facts explain our normative beliefs, and our normative beliefs explain our behavior. If this is true, then normative facts are explanatory after all, in a fairly straightforward way. And once this idea is in place the realist can go on to claim, once again, that moral facts—those complete larger facts, consisting in part of normative elements—are indeed explanatory as well.

Unfortunately, I do not myself think that proposals of this particular kind are correct. Although it would be satisfying if it were true, as I have already explained (in 8.4) I do not actually believe that normative facts explain our normative beliefs. (Nor, for that matter, do I believe that our normative beliefs explain the normative facts.) Rather, my own view is that there is a common ground that underwrites both the facts and the beliefs. So if normative facts really are explanatory, there will have to be something else that they explain; and it is far from obvious what that might be.

So should we conclude with the skeptic that moral facts, and normative facts more generally, are not genuine facts at all? That would be a very distressing conclusion indeed, but one that I think it would be premature to embrace. Perhaps it really can be shown that normative facts (and thus moral facts as well) have the relevant kind of explanatory force. If so, then the skeptic's argument will be answered on its own terms. But even if not, there is a second possible reply to the skeptic's argument, one that we have not yet considered except in passing. Perhaps the metaphysical test underwriting the skeptic's argument should be rejected.

9.5 The Unrestricted Test

The skeptic's argument against moral realism turns on the thought that genuine facts must be explanatory. But we should not lose sight of the fact that we have been interpreting this thought in a particular, narrow way—as the thought that genuine facts must explain something about the *empirical* world. That is, we have been interpreting the skeptic as holding that only explanations of *empirical* facts count as meeting the relevant metaphysical test. Unsurprisingly, this makes the test a more difficult one to pass, and so poses a more difficult challenge to the moral realist: if moral facts are to count as genuine facts it has to be shown that they can explain empirical facts of one sort or another.

Can the moral realist meet this challenge, so construed? That's the important question we have been exploring over the last few sections. But it is even more important to step back and ask whether we really should accept the test, once restricted in this way, in the first place. Should we indeed agree that unless a purported fact can explain something empirical it cannot be a genuine fact at all?

To be sure, it does seem as though explanatory potency is a common mark of reality. Indeed, often enough the very reason we believe in something that we don't directly see is precisely because positing such a thing helps us explain something else. We believe, for example, in subatomic particles that we cannot see, because doing so helps explain chemical changes that we all agree are taking place (for example, the fact that the liquid in the test tube just turned blue). We believe in exoplanets—planets orbiting other stars—even though we cannot see the planets themselves, because doing so helps explain the flickering of the remote star's light (and the slight wobble in the star's location). Such instances of inference to the best explanation (as philosophers call it) are a ubiquitous part of our reasoning, and in many such cases it is precisely because the things being posited would have explanatory force (in the right ways) that we feel justified in believing in them as real.

And of course, even for countless facts that we already believed in anyway—familiar, uncontroversial facts about trees, fences, accordions and squirrels, and so on—it also seems patently clear that these facts also have explanatory force as well. It seems a straightforward part of the nature of such facts that they help explain still other facts. So it certainly isn't a strange or outlandish thought to suggest that any genuine facts will indeed help to explain *something* or the other. Reality isn't a mere heap of unconnected, isolated facts. Rather, part of what it is for a fact to be part of reality is for it to have a place in a vast web of interconnected facts, explaining (and sometimes being explained by) still other parts of that web. Accordingly, I am inclined to agree with the skeptic that any genuine fact will have explanatory force.

However, even if we grant all of this—that is, even if we grant that any genuine fact must have explanatory force of *some* sort—there is no clear reason why we should insist that a genuine fact must explain something about the *empirical* world.

To see this point, imagine, first, that a candidate fact couldn't explain anything about the weather, say, but only something about Egyptian history. It would obviously be absurd to insist that genuine facts must explain something about *meteorology* as opposed to something else. Similarly, it would clearly suffice if a supposed fact could explain something about human behavior, say, but nothing at all about cosmology. It would be unreasonable to insist that all genuine facts must indeed explain something about cosmology, or—for that matter—something about photosynthesis, or jet engine mechanics, or Russian history. What matters, presumably, is only that any genuine fact must help to explain some other genuine *fact*.

But once we grasp this initial thought, it is hard to see why it should matter whether the fact explained is an *empirical* fact at all, as opposed to a fact of some other kind. As long as we agree that the fact being explained is indeed a genuine fact—something *real*—that should suffice. There is no obvious justification for restricting the set of facts to be explained to empirical ones.

Admittedly, in the various examples listed above, the facts that get explained are indeed all empirical facts. But what of it? If some candidate fact explained something that we all agreed was a genuine fact, albeit not an empirical one, why wouldn't that be good enough to count as passing any reasonable version of our test? So while it does seem reasonable to assume that any genuine fact must help explain other genuine facts, I see no good reason to insist that the facts explained must be empirical ones.

Suppose, then, that we embrace the test, but in an unrestricted form. If moral facts are to be genuine, they must explain something or the other, but it needn't be the case that they explain something empirical.

Yet once we adopt the test in this unrestricted form, it seems plausible to suggest that moral facts pass it easily and obviously. For moral facts help to explain other *moral* facts!

For example, why was Jeff morally required to come to the concert? Because he promised that he would do so, and one must keep one's promises. Why was Frank's killing of Laura wrong? Because killing is normally wrong except in self-defense, and Laura hadn't attacked him. Why was giving the prize to Amos the right thing to do? Because he deserved it, and justice is in part a matter of giving people their due.

For our purposes, of course, it doesn't matter whether you agree with the specifics of these particular explanations. What matters is only that you agree with the thought that moral facts would indeed explain still other moral facts. And this certainly seems plausible, indeed undeniable. At least, it will seem that way to anyone not already skeptical about the very existence of moral facts. So unless you were *already* inclined to accept moral skepticism, you have no reason to agree that moral facts would lack explanatory force. Putting the same point the other way around, the skeptic's argument—now interpreted without the unjustified restriction—should have no force in persuading us to *abandon* moral realism if we were otherwise inclined to *accept* it.

To be sure, one might well wonder whether the test, as we are now construing it—that is, in an unrestricted form—has any real bite at all. Someone might reasonably worry that any set of purported facts—no matter how fanciful and ungrounded in reality—can now be shown to pass the test of explaining facts of *some* sort or the other, for all one needs to do now is to claim that these purported facts help explain further facts of the same (unreal) sort! For example, can't the fan of demonic facts claim that they too explain things, namely, other demonic facts? Why did the demon get angry? Because Gina was playing classical music, and demons *hate* classical music!

Surely we don't want to agree that supposed demonic facts have explanatory force, merely because they would—if any of them *were* real—help explain still other demonic facts.

Agreed. If these sorts of pseudo-explanations sufficed to establish the explanatory force of a given class of candidate facts, then we would be justified in abandoning the test altogether as having no real bite. But I don't think this extreme response is necessary. Even in its unrestricted form, the test we are examining still does have some teeth, for the requirement is that the candidate facts help explain *genuine* facts. So before declaring that a given type of fact has real explanatory force we will want to make sure that the purported facts that they would help explain are indeed genuine facts. Since I don't think it a genuine fact that there was a demon that got angry (since I don't believe in demons), there is nothing here to explain, and so the supposed candidate explanation (that demons hate classical music) has not been shown to have real explanatory force after all.

In contrast, however, I do believe it to be a fact—a genuine fact—that Jeff was required to go to the concert, or that killing Laura was wrong, or that giving the prize to Amos was the right thing to do. So when more fundamental moral facts are appealed to by way of explaining these more derivative moral facts, I believe that genuine facts are being explained, and so genuine explanatory force is being displayed. Generalizing, then, if moral facts are genuine facts—as moral realists believe—then the explanatory challenge is trivially met: moral facts have explanatory force, because they help explain still other moral facts.

Of course, none of this shows that moral facts *are* genuine facts. Just as I would remain unmoved by someone insisting that demonic facts are genuine facts (someone who believes, accordingly, that certain demonic facts explain still other demonic facts), nothing I have said here should persuade the moral skeptic of the reality of moral facts. Moral skeptics don't concede the reality of such facts, just as I don't concede the reality of demonic facts, and so they won't concede that moral facts have been shown to have explanatory force.

But my goal here is not to establish the truth of moral realism. It is only to show how a moral realist can plausibly respond to the challenge raised by the skeptic's argument. *Given* the truth of moral realism, moral facts have explanatory force, and so any reasonable version of the metaphysical test will be met. This means that unless you *already* deny the existence of moral facts, nothing in the current argument gives you any reason to do so.

No doubt, some will want to complain that the reply that I have just laid out begs the question. Isn't it unacceptably circular to assume the existence of moral facts as part of a response to an argument that challenges the very existence of such facts? Notice, however, that we wouldn't ordinarily be moved by a similar complaint about our belief in the explanatory power of *empirical* facts! If someone claimed that it begs the question to try to establish the explanatory force of empirical facts by showing how such facts can help to explain still other empirical facts, we would rightly dismiss this challenge as needlessly restricting the candidate class of facts to be explained. We would insist, rather, that since empirical facts are *among* the genuine facts, showing how a purported fact would help explain some empirical fact is indeed an acceptable way of establishing that purported fact's explanatory force. But if such an answer is legitimate—and unless we are global skeptics we will certainly take it to be—then a similar answer is available to the moral realist as well. The moral realist can simply say that since moral facts are among the genuine facts, explaining such facts is indeed one acceptable way of establishing a purported fact's explanatory force.

Again, my goal right now is not to establish the *truth* of moral realism. It is only to show why, from the standpoint of the moral realist, the current skeptical argument should not be seen as an especially troubling one. Anyone who already believes in moral facts should think it a relatively trivial matter to demonstrate their explanatory force.

Of course, if we ask, instead, what reason do we have to *believe* in the existence of moral facts in the first place, then my answer is that we are justified in doing this by virtue of our having the moral intuitions that we do. It *seems* to us that certain acts are morally required or morally forbidden, that certain states of affairs are morally good ones or morally bad ones, that certain character traits are morally virtuous or morally vicious, and so on. Such appearances justify our tentative belief that there are indeed moral facts, just as there appear to be.

To be sure, the justification provided by intuition is defeasible, as I have repeatedly noted. It will be undermined if we find compelling reason to dismiss our intuitions as mistaken or illusory. That is why we have an obligation to examine the skeptic's sundry arguments with care. If any were successful, that would indeed give us reason to dismiss our intuitions as misguided, to reject moral intuitions as being unreliable as a class. The argument for moral realism would be overthrown. That is why one cannot simply note the existence of our moral intuitions and then dogmatically refuse to consider arguments that aim to challenge their validity.

But that doesn't mean that when we are examining those arguments we need to put aside or bracket the various beliefs we are defeasibly justified in accepting. In answering skeptical arguments we are entitled to say something like the following: *given* what we defeasibly believe, the skeptic's questions can be answered this way, their challenges met that way. All of which is just to say: if the skeptic's arguments can be answered *provided* that the world is the way we are defeasibly justified in taking it to be, then the skeptic's arguments can indeed be *answered*.

And that, I believe, is the situation that the moral realist is in with regard to the skeptical argument that we have been examining in this chapter. Given our moral intuitions, we are defeasibly justified in believing in moral facts. And if the world really is the way we are defeasibly justified in taking it to be—if there really are moral facts—then the skeptic's argument can be straightforwardly answered, since those facts will indeed help explain other perfectly real facts. Accordingly, if we are to be given a compelling reason to abandon moral realism, we will have to look elsewhere.

10

Motivation

10.1 Motive Internalism

Morality has an intimate connection to action. In part, of course, this is because morality is—or would be, if there were such a thing—action guiding, both directly (telling us which acts are required, which forbidden) and indirectly (telling us what kind of person to be—honest, trustworthy, benevolent, and so on).

But more than this, morality is also connected to action because moral values *move* us to action. They push or pull us to act in keeping with those values. Morality doesn't merely tell us *what* to do, it *motivates* us to act accordingly. Or so it has seemed to many people. Morality has a kind of internal motivational power. That is part of its very nature.

Of course, not everyone believes in the reality of objective moral facts. But even those who deny their existence often believe that if there really *were* such a thing as morality, it *would* have this kind of motivating force.

At the same time, however, many people—including some of the very same people—think that morality couldn't possibly *have* that kind of intrinsic motivational power. So this suggests, in turn, yet another skeptical argument, this one focused on morality's supposed connection to motivation. Although we will need to refine it, as a first pass we can state the argument like this: the moral realist's conception of morality requires it to have an intrinsic motivating power that it could not possibly have. So the realist's account of morality should be rejected.

To develop this argument more carefully, we have to start by getting clearer about the disputed motivating power that lies at the argument's heart. We have to clarify the nature of the supposed connection between morality and motivation.

The view that there is (or would be) some kind of intrinsic connection between morality and motivation—that this is part of the very nature of what it is to be morality—is sometimes called *motive internalism*. Those who accept this idea (introduced in 1.2) are motive internalists.

Although many find this an attractive and compelling position, not all accept it. Those who deny it are motive *externalists*.

Of course, it isn't as though motive externalists deny that we *can* be moved to do what morality asks of us. Many of us care about right and wrong, doing good and avoiding evil, and so—unsurprisingly—we often find ourselves motivated to act rightly. But according to the externalists there is no *necessary* connection between morality and motivation. It is one thing to say what we are obligated to do, or what we take ourselves to be obligated to do; it is quite another thing to say whether we are in any way moved to act accordingly.

Indeed, the externalist might hold (though she certainly need not hold) that all people raised decently—with a loving upbringing and a proper moral education—do in fact care about acting morally. So it could be that for such people there is always at least some motivation to act in keeping with our obligations. Or, more boldly still, the externalist might even hold (though she certainly need not hold) that, as it happens, it is a fact about human nature (given the particular evolutionary heritage of our species) that we always care about morality at least *somewhat*, regardless of our upbringing. But the externalist insists that even if either of these things is true, it is still the case that morality is only able to move us by virtue of our having these "extra" desires (whether as a matter of our upbringing, or as a matter of human nature). Morality alone cannot suffice to move us; it cannot move us in the absence of something *additional* (a desire of the relevant sort). Thus, regardless of whatever moral desires we *happen* to have, moral values—perfectly objective moral values—could have existed even if we had *not* had those desires, in which case morality would be unable to move us. Morality has no *intrinsic* motivating power; motivation always requires something more.

In contrast, motive *internalists* insist that there is indeed a necessary connection of *some* sort between morality and motivation. That's part of the very job description of morality. If there is to be such a thing as an objective morality, they say, it must be more than a mere (motivationally inert) list of requirements and prohibitions. Somehow the contents or bases of our various obligations must be capable of reaching us—of reaching *into* us—and moving us, pulling us to act appropriately. If there is to be such a thing as morality then it cannot be the sort of thing that could in principle fall upon completely deaf ears. On the contrary, if we are genuinely *bound* by morality then we must be capable of being *moved* by it; recognition of a moral obligation must be sufficient to move us, all on its own, without requiring an additional "something extra." The motivation to act morally cannot be a merely contingent addition to whatever it is that generates the obligation in the first place. Rather, if there is truly to be such a thing as *morality*, then morality itself must somehow be enough to move us.

That's the view of the motive internalists. I suspect that it is the majority view. In particular, I suspect that it is the majority view among moral realists. But the skeptic insists that the purported connection between morality and motivation could not possibly hold. And if that's right—if we agree with the skeptic that the relevant connection between morality and motivation is actually impossible—then anyone who includes that connection as part of the very job description of morality will also have to agree with the skeptic that moral realism must be rejected.

As I say, that's the rough idea. But we haven't yet tried to pin down the precise nature of the connection posited by internalists. And that's a crucial point. For if the skeptic's argument is going to have any real force against the realist, then when the skeptic insists that morality couldn't possibly have the imagined connection to motivation, the specific connection denied by the skeptic had better be one that internalist realists actually believe in. Otherwise there is no genuine threat to realism at all.

After all, imagine that the skeptic convinces us that for some conceivable motivational power, nothing at all could actually have that particular power. But imagine as well that realists had never thought that morality had that precise power in the first place. Clearly, if that were the situation we found ourselves in, the skeptic's argument wouldn't pose any sort of genuine challenge to the realist. For it is not at all damaging for the realist to agree that nothing can have some particular power, if having that *particular* power was never actually taken to be part of morality's job description.

Thus, if the skeptic is going to argue that nothing could possibly have the particular connection to motivation that motive internalism posits of morality, the version of motive internalism that is under discussion—the precise connection being discussed—had better be one that motive internalists genuinely accept. Otherwise, the skeptic will be attacking a position that realists don't actually hold, and their argument will miss the mark.

Suppose, for example, that the skeptic's argument turned on a version of motive internalism that asserts the following: if there *were* moral facts, then any time at all that someone had a duty to do some act, they would necessarily be so strongly motivated to do that act that they would always in fact (try to) *perform* the act in question.

10.1 MOTIVE INTERNALISM 251

Pretty clearly, there are no moral facts with that sort of infallible, overriding connection to motivation. We all know that people sometimes fail to act on their moral duties.

(Of course, even someone overridingly motivated to perform an act might still fail to pull it off—despite it being within their abilities: they might stumble or fall at a crucial moment, or simply slip up in one way or another. Overriding motivation simply doesn't guarantee success. That's why, in formulating this version of internalism, I've included the parenthetical remark about *trying*. But for present purposes this distinction—between trying to act and succeeding in acting—isn't an important one, and so in what follows I won't be careful about observing it. The crucial point is that sometimes people don't even *try* to do what they are required to do.)

So does that show that there are no moral facts? Of course not! For no realist ever claimed that the connection between morality and motivation was of this inescapable, unfailing sort. Accordingly, even when the realist concedes—as surely they must—that moral facts lack, and could not have, that kind of infallible connection to motivation, they won't find this concession especially troubling. The connection the realist meant to posit was presumably of a more modest sort.

I take it to be obvious that there are various things that can keep someone from acting on their moral duty in any given case. After all, the person may not even *realize* that she has the duty in question. Why not? Well, for starters, the person may not know some of the relevant (descriptive) facts of the situation—the facts which together make a given general principle relevant to the particular situation at hand. Or they might be aware of the facts but not recognize the moral *relevance* of the facts. Perhaps they are, for example, too distracted to put two and two together, and so they fail to realize that in their particular situation the general principle applies and so they have the particular (derivative) duty in question. Or perhaps they don't accept the underlying moral principle at work here (the one which applies to situations like this), mistakenly rejecting the principle in question. We can't expect people to act on principles they mistakenly reject! And so on and so forth.

As I say, there are various things that could keep someone from recognizing their duty, in which case it will hardly surprise us if they aren't motivated to act in the requisite way at all. None of this should give the realist pause, not even those realists who embrace motive internalism. So if the skeptic is going to genuinely threaten the realist, it won't do to appeal to a version of internalism like the one described above—a version so implausibly strong that no realist actually accepts it.

Here's another try. Perhaps the internalist accepts something like this: if an agent *believes* that they have a duty to do some act, then they will necessarily be so strongly motivated to do that act that they will always in fact (try to) perform the act in question.

This version of motive internalism is more plausible than the first, insofar as it posits a weaker and more indirect connection between morality and motivation. Here it isn't so much the very existence of the moral facts themselves that are supposed to guarantee the presence of motivation, but rather the agent's *beliefs* about the moral facts. Thus this second version of internalism recognizes that motivation may be lacking if the agent fails to realize that she has a relevant duty; it recognizes that the link between morality and motivation may exist only when the agent has the relevant beliefs.

Indeed, strictly speaking, on this second version of internalism it isn't the moral facts themselves that motivate, but rather our *beliefs* about morality that do so. Notice, in particular, that this new version of internalism doesn't actually require that the moral beliefs in question be *true*. What is being posited here is the motivational force of moral beliefs per se, whether they are mistaken or not. Obviously, this constitutes an important shift from the version of motive internalism with which we began—where it was the moral facts themselves that had the power to motivate, rather than our beliefs about those facts. But for our purposes we can still count this as a version of internalism, since it holds that it is indeed our beliefs about *morality* that are sufficient to guarantee motivation.

This second version of motive internalism is, I think, more plausible than the first. But it, too, is too strong to be plausible. For it still insists that if someone believes something to be their duty, they will necessarily be motivated enough that they will at least *try* to do the act in question. And that still doesn't seem right.

If our second version of internalism were true, no one would ever deliberately fail to perform an act they thought was morally required. No one would ever deliberately do an act they believed to be wrong. And that certainly doesn't seem to be the case. We all know of situations where someone fails to do what they sincerely believe they are morally required to do. (Haven't you ever told a lie, for example, even though you thought it was wrong to do so?) Internalists will certainly recognize this fact as well. Not only do we sometimes *unwittingly* fail to do what we are required to do, sometimes we fail to do what we *take* ourselves to be required to do. I may know that an act is morally required; but this doesn't guarantee that I will try to do it.

Here, the problem isn't that morality may not motivate us if we don't recognize what it asks of us. Rather, the problem is that even when we *believe* that some act is morally required, we may not always be *sufficiently* motivated to try to perform the act. Other motives may get in the way, pulling us away from our duty, and these other motives may win out, so that we do not even *try* to do what we are required to do.

Internalists ordinarily recognize all of this as well. So here, too, any skeptical argument that turns on this second version of internalism is likely to leave the realist unconcerned. Few if any realists will think the motivating force of our moral beliefs is *so* strong that it always wins out.

These thoughts suggest, in turn, an even more modest version of internalism: if an agent believes that they have a duty to perform a given act, then they will be at least *somewhat* motivated to do that act.

This third version of internalism readily accommodates the idea that people sometimes knowingly fail to do what they are morally required to do. Even if you believe some act to be your duty, you may still fail to be *sufficiently* motivated overall to try to do it. Still, if this third version of internalism is correct you will necessarily have at least *some* motivation to do the act in question. Beliefs about morality cannot leave you altogether unmoved. Admittedly, the motivation provided by your moral beliefs may be outweighed; you may not even *try* to do the act that you take to be morally required. But at the very least there will be *some* motivational force arising from your moral beliefs; there will be *some* pull toward doing what you think is required.

In many cases, no doubt, the motivation to do what you believe is required of you will indeed be strong enough to win out overall, so you will in fact try to do what you are required to do. But in contrast to the second version of internalism, this third version doesn't insist that your motivation to do what you think you are required to do is *always* overriding and dominant. More modestly, it only insists that where there is a moral belief there will always be a corresponding motivation of *some* sort—*some* kind of pull to do what you believe you ought to do. In short, regardless of whether this motivation wins out or not, moral beliefs can and do *motivate* us. The mere thought that I have a duty can suffice to move me at least somewhat.

Here at last, I think, we have a version of motive internalism that many realists would accept. Not all of them, of course, since not all realists are internalists. But for those realists who are indeed drawn to an internalist position, this third version—unlike the first two—is likely to be one that they will be hesitant to dismiss. So if the skeptic can show that even this minimal connection between morality and motivation cannot obtain, many realists will agree that moral realism is in danger after all.

(As it happens, there is an even milder version of internalism that is not without interest as well. Instead of saying that moral beliefs *always* provide motivation of some sort, the internalist might claim only that moral beliefs *can* provide such motivation. even if they don't always do so. I believe that even this extremely minimal version of internalism would suffice for the skeptic's purposes. But we can focus on the somewhat bolder third version.)

We can spell out the internalist picture a bit more fully. Although it is often convenient to say that according to internalism moral beliefs can motivate on their own—that they necessarily provide at least *some* motivation—typically it would be more accurate to say that moral beliefs motivate only when combined with relevant background beliefs. For example, the mere belief that I ought to keep my promises will not motivate me to be at the shopping mall at 4:00 P.M. unless this is combined with the relevant background belief that I promised you that I would indeed be there at 4:00. Similarly, the belief that I ought to be in my classroom in time to teach my class will not motivate me to leave my office and start walking across campus unless this belief is combined with relevant background beliefs—beliefs concerning the current time, the time my class starts, the length of time it takes me to walk to the classroom, and so on. So in most cases it would be an exaggeration to say that moral beliefs can motivate all by themselves; usually, they only do this when combined with relevant background beliefs. (The exception, of course, is when you have a *derivative* moral belief about the *particular* act you are contemplating doing.) Still, except when this complication is important, we can summarize the internalist position—evocatively, if sometimes a bit misleadingly—by saying that moral beliefs can motivate on their own, all by themselves. This internalist view provides the first premise of the skeptic's argument.

10.2 An Argument for Noncognitivism

The next premise of the skeptic's argument is based on what philosophers call *the Humean theory of motivation*. (It's called that because it finds a classic presentation in the writings of the 18th century philosopher David Hume. But we won't be concerned here with Hume exegesis.) The basic idea is really quite simple: motivation requires a combination of belief and desire. It takes *both*. A bit more precisely, when we want to explain how it is that someone was motivated to do some particular act, we need to ascribe to the person both a belief and a desire, where the belief and the desire "hook up" in the relevant way.

Here's an easy example to make the idea clear. Suppose we want to explain why I put a few dollars into the vending machine. How is it that I was motivated to do this particular act? Consider the sort of explanation we might give: perhaps I wanted a candy bar, and I believed (correctly, as it happens) that putting the money into the machine would help me get the candy, satisfying my desire. Here we have a perfectly good explanation of why I was motivated to perform the act in question: I had a desire for something (candy) and a belief about how performing the given act would help me satisfy my desire.

Note that in explaining motivation in this way, we have to appeal to the existence of *both* a belief *and* a desire. Neither one would do the trick on its own, in the absence of the other. Suppose, for example, that I wanted the candy, but I simply had no idea at all how vending machines work. Then we wouldn't really have an explanation of why I put the money into the machine after all. In such a case, we would have a desire, but we wouldn't have an appropriate belief (roughly speaking, a belief to the effect that performing the act in question would satisfy the desire in question), so we wouldn't really have explained why I did what I did at all.

Similarly, suppose I understood perfectly well how vending machines work, but I didn't actually want any candy. Here too we would have no real explanation of why I did what I did. In the absence of a desire for candy, my action remains mysterious. No mere belief that putting money in the machine will produce candy can explain why I did what I did—if I don't want candy!

So it takes *both* to explain why I am moved to act: I need to have a desire for something or the other, and I need to have a belief about how acting in that way will help satisfy the desire.

Of course, the actual explanation may turn out to be more surprising than we were supposing. Perhaps I didn't want candy at all, but wanted instead to appease the vending machine gods. And perhaps I believed (incorrectly, no doubt) that putting money in the slot would do this. Maybe that's the *actual* explanation of why I did what I did! Notice, however, that even here we have appealed to the presence of both a belief and a desire. After all, a desire to appease the gods wouldn't explain my motivation if I didn't also have a belief about what the gods want, and my belief about *how* to appease the gods wouldn't explain my behavior either, if I didn't actually *want* to appease the gods! It takes *both* to have motivation.

(In addition, as I have already suggested, the belief and the desire also have to "hook up" in the relevant way. If I want to appease the gods, but don't care for candy, and I believe I can get candy by putting money in the machine, but I don't have views about how to appease the gods, we *still* don't have an explanation of why I did what I did! Being moved to perform an act requires a desire for something and a belief about how acting in that way helps you to satisfy that very same desire. But this complication won't be important in the argument that follows.)

That's the Humean theory of motivation, and it obviously isn't an obscure philosophical doctrine that only a philosopher would ever accept. It is something closer to common sense. We use this idea all the time when explaining the behavior of ourselves and others, both in everyday life and in the social sciences. The Humean theory of motivation is an extremely plausible, widely held view.

But when we combine Humeanism with internalism we seem to have the materials necessary to produce an argument against moral realism, because the skeptic is now in a position to offer an argument for *noncognitivism*—the view that moral claims are not genuine assertions at all. Since moral realists are cognitivists about morality (see 2.2), if there is indeed a compelling argument for noncognitivism, moral realism has to be rejected.

Here is the core of the skeptic's argument: According to cognitivism, moral claims are genuine assertions, and so the mental states that we ordinarily take to be moral beliefs—let's just call them moral "opinions"—are genuine beliefs. But moral opinions can *motivate* (when combined with relevant background beliefs), something they *wouldn't* be able to do if they really were genuine beliefs. So moral opinions are not genuine beliefs after all. Rather, moral opinions are, or presuppose, *desires*. That is, to have a moral opinion is to have a desire, and making a moral utterance is simply a matter of *expressing* that desire (as noncognitivists claim), not a matter of expressing a belief (as cognitivists, including realists, have thought). So noncognitivism is true, and realism has to be rejected.

Even in its current form, of course, the argument is still compressed. Let's unpack it slowly.

10.2 AN ARGUMENT FOR NONCOGNITIVISM

First, then, and perhaps most obviously, if the argument is right then it is a mistake to talk about our having moral *beliefs*. The mental states we normally *take* to be moral beliefs aren't actually beliefs at all. They might be better referred to as our "so-called moral beliefs." That's why, for the purposes of the present discussion, it's useful to have a different way of referring to them. As I just explained, I'm going to refer to them—these mental states that we actually do have, whether they are beliefs or not—as our moral *opinions*.

Admittedly, even this label is far from perfect, insofar as an opinion just seems like a kind of belief. Perhaps it would be better still, from the noncognitivist's point of view, to call the relevant mental states moral *views*, or moral *perspectives*, or something like that. But having now noted this point, I think there is no real danger in framing the debate the way I will—as being over whether our moral *opinions* are genuine *beliefs* or not.

Second, relatedly, if the argument is sound, then it turns out to have been a mistake (though an easily corrected one) to state motive internalism as the claim that our moral beliefs can motivate—for strictly speaking, we don't actually *have* any moral beliefs! We have moral *opinions*, to be sure, and perhaps *those* can motivate, just as internalists claim. But if noncognitivism is correct then those opinions aren't really beliefs. So it would be more accurate—in light of the argument's conclusion—to say that what internalism holds is that our moral *opinions* can motivate.

Of course, in light of an observation we made previously (now suitably restated, so as to use the language of moral "opinions"), it would be even more accurate to say that what internalism holds is that moral opinions can motivate *when combined with* the relevant background beliefs. That internalist thought appears as one of the premises in the argument sketched above.

But why should we believe as well that if moral opinions *were* genuine beliefs they would *not* be able to motivate (not even when combined with relevant background beliefs)? This is where the Humean theory of motivation comes in. According to that theory, after all, it takes both beliefs and desires to motivate. So if—as internalism claims—moral opinions really *can* motivate when combined with relevant background beliefs, we are going to need to find both beliefs and desires when this happens. Otherwise the motivational power posited by internalism will be impossible.

Suppose, for example, that I remember having made a promise to meet you at the mall, and I realize as well that unless I get going I won't be there in time. It is a familiar experience that these thoughts can get me moving, given my "belief" (that is, my *opinion*) that I ought to keep my promises.

According to internalism, that's all it takes to have at least *some* motivation to start going. The moral opinion that one ought to keep one's promises and the relevant background beliefs suffice. But given the Humean theory of motivation, if these thoughts really do suffice to move me, there must be both a belief and a desire (related in the relevant ways) that are present in this case. Can we locate them?

Obviously, it isn't at all difficult to find the relevant beliefs, since we have stipulated that in the case at hand I do indeed have various beliefs that seem well suited to fit into a Humean explanation. I know, for example, that I have made a promise. And I also know that unless I get going I won't be able to keep my promise. But where are we to find the *desire* that the Humean theory says must be present as well?

Pretty clearly, we aren't going to be able to find the requisite desire if we continue to focus on the background beliefs. These are, after all, simple beliefs about straightforward matters of fact. There is, for example, nothing desire-like going on in the mere thought that if I don't leave now, I won't make it to the mall on time.

So where is the desire? It must be located in the moral opinion itself! It must be that despite *looking* like a belief, a moral opinion actually just is a desire or consists in a desire (here, the desire to keep one's promises), or perhaps it presupposes a desire, or something desire-like. If the moral opinion really were a *belief*—as the cognitivists claim—then all we would have here are beliefs and more beliefs. There would be nothing desire-like in the neighborhood. That's why, given the Humean theory of motivation, it simply cannot be true that moral opinions are genuine beliefs. If they really *were* beliefs then the motivational power posited by internalism could not exist.

But if moral opinions are not beliefs, then cognitivism is false. We must accept, in its place, some version of noncognitivism. When I tell you that one ought to keep one's promises, I am not actually making any kind of assertion at all; I am not expressing a belief about some supposed moral fact. Rather, I am expressing a desire, the desire that we all keep our promises. I am revealing my dislike of promise breaking, my approval of promise keeping, and so on. I am expressing attitudes of approval and disapproval (and perhaps issuing corresponding commands), but I am not *stating* anything. So when cognitivists tell us that moral claims are genuine assertions, and moral opinions genuine beliefs, they are wrong. Cognitivism about ethics is mistaken and so moral realism must be rejected.

(What if a cognitivist insisted that the argument only shows that moral opinions must *presuppose* desires—that they need not actually *be* desires? Wouldn't this allow for a subjectivist view, according to which "one ought to keep one's promises" just means "I approve of promise keeping"? The latter *is* a genuine assertion, though it will only be true if I have the relevant desire. Doesn't this accommodate the Humean requirement, while managing to do so within a cognitivist framework? I don't think so. For the internalist view under discussion holds that moral opinions can motivate even when those opinions are *mistaken*—hence, on this subjectivist view, even when one lacks the desire in question. In such cases, it seems, subjectivism fails to guarantee the existence of the desire required by Humeanism.)

One final observation. If the argument we are discussing succeeds, then it provides a defense of noncognitivism, and moral realism must be abandoned. But moral realism isn't the only form of cognitivism. *Nihilists* are cognitivists as well. After all, nihilists share with realists the thought that our moral claims are genuine assertions and our moral opinions genuine beliefs. It is just that nihilists believe that all of these assertions and beliefs are false!

This means, of course, that if the argument we are examining succeeds, it is a threat not only to the realist, but to the nihilist as well. Moral skepticism will have been established, but in a way that rules out nihilism along with realism. Accordingly, finding a suitable reply to this argument will be a matter of interest not just to realists but to nihilists as well. The argument doesn't so much pit realists against skeptics as it does cognitivists against noncognitivists.

10.3 Rejecting Motive Internalism

The argument for noncognitivism depends on two crucial premises: motive internalism and the Humean theory of motivation. Consequently, there are two obvious ways for a cognitivist to try to resist that argument. They can reject motive internalism, arguing with the externalists that moral opinions alone are insufficient for motivation. Or they can reject the Humean theory of motivation, arguing that in certain cases it doesn't actually take both a belief and a desire to have motivation; in certain cases beliefs alone can suffice.

If the cognitivist takes the first path, they can concede that beliefs alone cannot motivate, but having rejected the internalist claim that moral opinions (along with background beliefs) guarantee the presence of at least some motivation, there will no longer be a barrier to the cognitivist claim that moral opinions are indeed genuine beliefs. Alternatively, if the cognitivist takes the second path, they can agree that moral opinions can motivate, but having rejected the Humean claim that motivation always requires desires, there will still be no barrier to the claim that moral opinions are genuine beliefs. Either way, the noncognitivist's argument will have been disarmed, and the cognitivist will be able to retain their view that moral opinions are indeed genuine beliefs, just as they appear to be.

(There is also, of course, the possibility of rejecting both internalism *and* Humeanism—that is, insisting that moral opinions cannot motivate, but even if they could, this wouldn't stand in the way of their being genuine beliefs. Since the relevant arguments here are similar to those for the first two replies, I won't consider this position separately.)

Since our concern in this book is with the defense of moral realism, in examining these potential replies to the noncognitivist I will present them from the perspective of the realist. Of course, as we have already noted, noncognitivism is incompatible with nihilism and not just with realism. So it may also be worth noting, in passing, that similar replies are also available to the nihilist: they can either reject internalism or reject the Humean theory of motivation. Nonetheless, I will be examining these replies from the standpoint of the realist.

Let's start, then, by considering the possibility of resisting the argument for noncognitivism by rejecting motive internalism.

Although I imagine that most moral realists actually accept internalism rather than externalism, not all do. Some realists are indeed motive externalists. And obviously enough, if externalism is true, the argument for noncognitivism fails. For even if the Humean theory of motivation is true, and it takes desires along with beliefs to motivate, as long as we agree with the externalist that there is actually no *necessary* connection between moral opinions and motivation (not even when combined with other background beliefs), we will no longer have any reason to deny that moral opinions are genuine beliefs. Instead we can simply hold that moral opinions really are beliefs after all and, like other beliefs, they cannot motivate in the absence of a relevant desire (not even when combined with other beliefs).

That's not to say, of course, that we are never motivated to act morally. On the contrary, the externalist might suggest that many of us, perhaps almost all of us, have standing desires to be good people and to do what morality asks of us. These general desires to act morally can certainly combine with our various moral beliefs, in just the way the Humean theory suggests, with the result being that we are at least somewhat motivated (often, indeed, sufficiently motivated) to act as morality requires. But it isn't as though moral beliefs can actually motivate all on their own (in combination with relevant background beliefs). Rather, they can only do it by virtue of our *also* having the desire to be moral. (We might, of course, also have more "specific" moral desires as well, such as a desire to help others or to show them respect. These too can combine with relevant moral beliefs to generate motivation.)

To be sure, the externalist might suggest, we do often talk as though we have been motivated by our moral beliefs alone, but that is because for most of us the various desires to act morally are always with us, waiting in the background. What changes, from moment to moment, are our various beliefs about just what it is that morality *asks* of us in the given situation. So when those largely unchanging desires to act morally combine with the newly acquired beliefs about what morality asks of us here and now, we point to those moral beliefs as the explanation of our being motivated, even though—strictly speaking—the moral beliefs do not actually motivate us all by themselves, but only by virtue of being combined with the easily overlooked background desires. (A loose analogy: we typically just point to the lit match as an explanation of why the paper caught fire. We don't usually bother to mention the presence of oxygen, even though it is equally essential, since oxygen is almost always there, while a lit match is not.)

That's the externalist's position: moral opinions *are* beliefs, but they *cannot* motivate by themselves; they can only do this in combination with (easily overlooked) background desires that almost all of us have. Take away the background desires and there will be no motivation to act.

This certainly seems to be a coherent view. And if we accept it the argument for noncognitivism no longer goes through. But should we believe it? It is easy enough to *insist* that moral opinions cannot motivate in the absence of moral desires that are distinct from and additional to those opinions. But is that, in fact, the truth? After all, it does *seem* to many of us as though we can be motivated by our moral opinions alone, without bringing in anything further (beyond relevant background beliefs). Why think that this isn't really the case?

The most common argument for motive externalism appeals to the possibility of an "amoralist"—someone who is simply unmoved by moral considerations. The thought is that if there could indeed be such a person, someone who has all the relevant moral opinions but who is not at all moved to act on those opinions, then that shows that moral opinions are insufficient for motivation. Only those who have the *extra* ingredient—a *desire* to act morally—will be moved. The amoralist, lacking the relevant desire, remains unmoved, thus demonstrating the truth of motive externalism.

A common externalist example involves imagining a hit man, a professional killer, on his way to murder his innocent victim. The externalist asks us to recognize that in principle at least such a person might have perfectly correct beliefs about morality. He might readily acknowledge that killing his victim is morally wrong, without being *moved* by that thought. "*Of course* killing is wrong," we are to imagine the hit man telling us. "But so what? I just don't *care* about being moral. I only care about getting ahead in the Mob."

If such a character is possible, the externalist argues, then that shows that moral opinions cannot motivate by themselves. They only do so when one also has a relevant desire as well, something that the hit man lacks. So internalism is mistaken and we should be externalists instead. It may well be that most of us do have the requisite additional desires, but the mere possibility of such a person as our imaginary hit man suffices to establish the truth of externalism.

(Let me mention a small complication. As I noted previously, it is actually compatible with motive externalism to hold that it is a fact about human nature that *all* of us have the relevant moral desires, so that no *human* could be like our imaginary hit man. If so, we would then need to resort to an even more fanciful example—perhaps one involving an alien from outer space who has perfectly correct opinions about the contents of morality, but who simply remains unmoved by those opinions. As long as the possibility of such an amoralist seems coherent and intelligible—whether human or not—that should suffice for the externalist's purposes.)

Do examples like these establish the truth of motive externalism? The answer, I think, is less clear than it might initially seem. The first thing to remember is that the version of internalism that plays a role in the argument for noncognitivism is a fairly modest one. It doesn't assert—implausibly—that one always *acts* on one's moral opinions. It only says that one will be at least *somewhat* moved by those thoughts—that there will be at least *some* pull or tug toward doing what one thinks one ought to do. So in refuting the internalist it will be irrelevant to point out that the hit man may well go ahead and kill his victim, despite his realizing that it is wrong to do this. That could be true even if the hit man does have *some* moral motivation as well. If it is simply the case that other motives *outweigh* his moral motivation, then the possibility of a hit man doesn't really establish the truth of the externalist's position.

Thus, to make their case, the externalist has to claim that our hit man feels no compunction at all, no pull at all toward doing the right thing, no inner conflict, however minimal. It is only if we imagine the hit man in this way as being utterly unconflicted that we have the kind of example that the externalist needs. And speaking personally, at least, I find it far less obvious whether someone like this is indeed genuinely possible.

Suppose, however, that for the sake of argument we agree (as, no doubt, some will) that it is indeed possible to have such a hit man, someone with no inner motivational conflict here at all. There remains a second question: does the hit man *really* think that it is wrong to kill innocent people? Is that *genuinely* his opinion? Or is that merely something he is telling us?

Perhaps all that is really going on here is this. Perhaps the hit man is using what are sometimes called "scare quotes," and what he really means is that he realizes that killing innocent people is "wrong"—that is, it is the sort of thing that people ordinarily *say* is wrong. Perhaps what the hit man really thinks, however, is that what is genuinely wrong is disrespecting the Mob, or failing to do the job one has agreed to do, however unpleasant it may be, and so on. Or perhaps he thinks his victim deserves it, having insulted the crime boss, or whatever. He recognizes, however, that people ordinarily *view* the sort of deed he is about to do as being immoral, and that's all he meant when he said that he just doesn't care about "morality": he just doesn't care about the misguided values that society generally accepts.

If anything like this is what is actually going on, then of course we still don't have the kind of example the externalist needs. We still don't have a case of someone who truly thinks that what he is about to do is indeed *genuinely* wrong (not just thought to be wrong) while still being, despite this, utterly unmoved by this thought.

Or perhaps the hit man doesn't completely grasp the concept of being morally *wrong*! Perhaps the hit man has only a partial and incomplete notion of what it is for an action to be morally unacceptable, and thinks of morality simply as a somewhat arbitrary set of rules, nothing that one need have any particular reason to attend to. So when the hit man says that he recognizes that killing his victim is wrong perhaps he means what he says, but he doesn't really grasp everything that is involved in an action's being wrong! If something like this is right, then it isn't really true that he has a (full-blown) moral opinion that killing is *wrong*; in which case we still don't have a counterexample to the motive internalist's view that where there are moral opinions—the real deal—they necessarily motivate at least somewhat. (Perhaps the hit man is a bit like a man who has been blind from birth, and so has only an incomplete concept of what it is for something to be red, since he himself has never so much as experienced the color red. Such a person may well be aware of the fact that tomatoes, say, are red, without fully grasping what it *means* to be red.)

If any of these concerns are well placed—if the hit man has only an inadequate grasp of the concepts of duty and moral obligation, if he is speaking in scare quotes, or if he is feeling at least some qualms about killing his victim—then the example doesn't do the work that the externalist needs it to do. In short, it doesn't suffice to paint a quick sketch of an amoralist and conclude on the basis of that sketch that internalism is false. We need to be confident that there really can be the kind of individual the externalist needs to posit, someone who fully grasps what's involved in an act's being wrong, who genuinely thinks that the act he is about to do is wrong—morally unacceptable in reality, and not just in common opinion—and who is, despite all this, utterly unmoved by that thought.

No doubt there are realists who think it clear that people like this are indeed possible, and so externalism is the right position to embrace. If so, the argument for noncognitivism can be answered (relying, as it does, on the assumption of internalism). If moral opinions cannot motivate by themselves, there is no reason to deny that they are genuine beliefs.

However, I imagine that many realists—perhaps most—will find the matter far less obvious. That's certainly how I view the issue myself. Speaking personally, when I think about our imagined hit man I am far from confident that there really could be someone like this. Once we have filled in the picture of what the hit man would need to be like to establish the truth of externalism, I am not at all confident that such a person could actually exist. Indeed, I find myself strongly inclined to think that if a hit man doesn't feel any compunction at all about killing his victim, then either he doesn't really believe that killing is wrong, or he doesn't fully grasp what it is for something to *be* morally wrong.

(There is an additional possible response to the example of the hit man that is worth noting: the internalist might insist, plausibly, that moral beliefs only motivate agents who are sufficiently rational, and then insist—more controversially—that our hit man demonstrates, in his failure to be moved by morality, that he is *not* in fact sufficiently rational. I think there is a great deal to be said for this view, but as it might be considered question begging in the present context, I put it aside.)

All of which is just to say, I remain inclined to accept internalism rather than externalism. And I suspect that many, perhaps most, realists will agree with me on this score. But since doing this grants the noncognitivist the first of the two premises of their argument, we now need to ask whether perhaps it is the *second* premise—the Humean theory of motivation—that can plausibly be rejected instead. We turn to that question next.

(What if an internalist concedes the possibility of the externalist's hit man, but notes that strictly speaking this only shows that moral opinions *need* not be able to motivate—but that it still might be the case that some moral opinions *can* motivate all by themselves? This would involve moving to an even more modest version of internalism, one which admits that not all moral opinions are sufficient for motivation, but which holds nonetheless that moral opinions *can* be capable of motivating, even in the absence of any separate moral desires. Note, however, that when it is combined with Humeanism even this stripped-down version of internalism would still imply that the moral opinions that *do* motivate in this way are not genuine *beliefs*— a conclusion that the realist won't find congenial. So even those realists who are minimal internalists of this sort have reason to reject Humeanism.)

10.4 Rejecting the Humean Theory of Motivation

At first glance, the prospects for denying the Humean theory of motivation seem dim. After all, it really does seem as though we typically need to appeal to both beliefs and desires when we want to explain why someone was motivated to act in a certain way. Your belief that starting on your road trip early in the morning will get you to your destination sooner doesn't explain why you are at least somewhat motivated to get up early unless we add that you also have a desire to reach your destination sooner rather than later. My belief that criticizing your work in front of your boss will embarrass you doesn't explain why I am motivated to avoid offering those criticisms unless we add that I have a desire to avoid embarrassing you. And so on and so forth. Isn't it a simple commonplace that motivation requires not only beliefs but also desires?

Perhaps, however, the situation is more complicated than this. Couldn't it be that even though in *many* cases there is no motivation in the absence of desire, nonetheless this isn't true across the board? That is, even if it is true that many beliefs, perhaps most beliefs, are incapable of motivating on their own, couldn't it be the case that some beliefs *are* capable of motivating even in the absence of anything more? Perhaps the Humean theory is guilty of overgeneralizing. Although *most* beliefs cannot motivate in the absence of desires, some *can*.

If we then ask, what sorts of beliefs could possibly have this power, this ability to motivate even in the absence of some separate desire, the answer might well be the obvious one: *moral* beliefs might well be like this, just as they often seem to be! Or, more broadly, perhaps we should say that evaluative beliefs more generally have this power. Or, perhaps, more broadly still, that normative beliefs of all sorts have it, including beliefs about what one has reason to believe or do.

Suppose, for example, that you realize you have a good reason to believe some proposition, say, that Abraham Lincoln was taller than Thomas Jefferson. Can't your belief that you have a reason to believe this proposition move you to believe it, all on its own? Wouldn't it be silly to insist that your normative belief (about what you have reason to believe) will be "inert" unless you also have a *desire* to believe what you believe you have reason to believe? On the contrary, it seems clear that your (second-order) beliefs about what you have reason to believe can have an impact on those (first-order) beliefs all on their own, without requiring some additional, extraneous desire.

Similarly, then, why not also say that your beliefs about what you have reason to *do* can have an impact on what you do, all on their own, without requiring any further, separate desire? Suppose, for example, that you realize that you have a good reason to perform some act—say, to eat some food before it spoils. Can't your belief that you have a reason to eat the food sooner rather than later move you all on its own? *Must* we insist that your normative belief (about what you have reason to do) will be inert unless you also have a *desire* to do what you believe you have reason to do?

Thus, the realist might argue that normative beliefs can motivate, all on their own (or in conjunction with relevant background beliefs), contrary to what the Humean theory says. And while the Humean might insist that this only shows that our normative "opinions" are not, in fact, the genuine beliefs we take them to be, but must themselves be (or consist in) desires of some sort, we might well wonder what this assertion is, other than a dogmatic insistence that Humeanism *must* be right.

10.4 REJECTING THE HUMEAN THEORY OF MOTIVATION

So suppose we decide that the Humean theory is an overly hasty generalization. Thanks to an understandable but misguided initial focus on *non*normative beliefs—beliefs about how to get from one place to another, or what happens if you put money in a vending machine, and so on, beliefs that *do* require desires if motivation is to be generated—we mistakenly concluded that *all* beliefs require desires if there is to be any motivation. But in fact, we might now prefer to say, some beliefs—and in particular, normative beliefs—can indeed motivate, even in the absence of a separate, added desire.

With the rejection of the Humean theory the moral realist has a second possible answer to the argument for noncognitivism. The realist can insist that moral opinions are indeed genuine beliefs, just as they appear to be; and yet, for all that, they can motivate—since Humeans were wrong to insist that beliefs can never motivate in the absence of desire. Normative beliefs can motivate, and since moral beliefs are among our normative beliefs, moral beliefs can motivate as well. (Indeed, on one possible realist view, moral beliefs just *are* beliefs about what we have reason to do—albeit reasons of a special kind.) Humeanism is wrong, and so the argument for noncognitivism fails.

(The proposal sketched here is a pluralist one, in that it allows that both desires *and* normative beliefs can motivate. An even more radical rejection of Humeanism might hold that it is *only* normative beliefs that can motivate. On this more radical view, a mere desire for something cannot in fact motivate at all—not even when combined with a belief about how to satisfy that desire—unless that desire is combined with (or partially consists in) the belief that one has *reason* to act on that desire. For the purpose of defending moral realism the more conciliatory, pluralist view suffices; but this more radical view would certainly work as well.)

How might a Humean respond to the realist's claim that desires aren't actually needed for motivation? Conceivably, they might start with the simple observation that if someone freely performs some act, if no one is literally forcing them to act that way, then it is obviously the case that they *want* to do it (in some suitably broad sense of the term "want"). After all, if they didn't want to do it, why did they do it? So they do have a desire after all (using the term "desire" broadly as well). So whenever someone is sufficiently motivated to do an act, it is clearly correct to say that they want to do it, that there is a desire of some sort to do the act in question. And even if the person is only *somewhat* motivated to perform an action, it must still be the case that they want to do that act at least a little. So it seems a virtually undeniable truth that where there is motivation, any motivation at all, there must be desire.

But the realist can acknowledge this point—that where there is motivation, there is desire—without it really damaging their position. That is, they can acknowledge that there is a notion of want and desire sufficiently broad and thin so that it is indeed a trivial truth that if you are freely doing something then you want to do it (and if you are struggling over whether to do something or not, you want to do it at least a little). The crucial question, however, is whether some desire had to be there from the *start*, whether desire must occur as one of the initial ingredients necessary to *generate* motivation in the first place, or whether, alternatively, desire might simply *emerge* in the course of the process of deliberation and reflection that *results* in motivation.

In effect, we need to distinguish between two different versions (or interpretations) of the Humean theory, one less demanding, the other more so. The less demanding version of the theory holds that although motivation requires both beliefs and desires, the desires needn't be there from the start; beliefs alone might suffice to generate motivation, with relevant desires being created along the way. In contrast, the more demanding version of the theory holds that motivation is only possible if desires are there from the very beginning of the process, as no mere set of beliefs alone could ever suffice to generate motivation.

The less demanding version of Humeanism poses no threat to the realist—not even if the realist is an internalist. The realist can insist that moral opinions are indeed genuine beliefs, just as they appear to be. Those beliefs can then combine with relevant background beliefs to generate motivation. To the extent that motivation gets created it is now true that there is a corresponding desire to act accordingly; so where there is motivation, there is indeed desire. But the desire gets created along the way, it is the result of *seeing* that one is morally obligated to act in a certain way. One need not have *started out* with any particular desire (not even some generic desire to act morally); rather, the desire simply emerges in the course of realizing what one is obligated to do.

So if the Humean is merely putting forward the more modest version of their theory the argument for noncognitivism no longer goes through. Realists can agree with both internalism and the modest version of Humeanism, all the while insisting that moral opinions are genuine beliefs.

It is only the more demanding version of Humeanism that raises problems for the realist. For if desires must be present from the beginning if there is to be motivation—if desire must be one of the initial ingredients—then if moral opinions really can motivate (as the internalist claims), it certainly does seem

10.4 REJECTING THE HUMEAN THEORY OF MOTIVATION 269

to follow that such opinions cannot be genuine beliefs after all. It looks like anyone committed to both internalism and the *bolder* version of Humeanism must embrace noncognitivism.

Of course, having distinguished between the modest and the bold versions of Humeanism, it isn't at all clear why we should *accept* the more demanding, rather than the less demanding, version of the theory. Certainly, as we now realize, the mere commonplace that where there is motivation there is desire does not suffice to establish the claim of the more demanding theory, that motivation requires that some desire be present from the beginning, rather than sometimes being generated by one's beliefs along the way. So until some more compelling argument for the demanding version of Humeanism is offered I think the realist may be on reasonable grounds in holding, instead, that the demanding theory is at best a hasty overgeneralization, overlooking the many cases in which motivation can be created even in the *absence* of an independently existing desire.

Still, suppose one finds the demanding version of Humeanism compelling nonetheless. Suppose one simply finds it overwhelmingly plausible to hold that motivation can *never* exist unless a suitable desire of some sort was present from the beginning. Can we at least agree that anyone committed to the more demanding version of Humeanism—who *also* accepts the internalist idea that moral opinions can motivate—must accept noncognitivism as well? After all, if moral opinions and background beliefs *can* motivate by themselves, there is nowhere else to locate the requisite desire *other* than in the moral opinion itself. So having a moral opinion will have to be a matter of having a relevant *desire*, rather than a matter of having a genuine belief.

In fact, however, there remains one further way for the realist to avoid this noncognitivist conclusion. Strictly speaking, all that the argument establishes (given the assumption of internalism and the bold version of Humeanism) is that moral opinions must be desires (or must be constituted by desires). But the intended noncognitivist conclusion, that moral opinions are not in fact *beliefs*, only follows if we add an extra premise to the argument, namely, that no mental state can be both a belief *and* a desire at the same time. And while this is itself a common enough assumption—so seemingly obvious that I didn't bother to explicitly note it until this very moment—the truth of the matter is that it might not be correct.

Suppose for the moment that this common assumption is actually mistaken, and that a given mental state could be both a belief and a desire. And suppose, more particularly, that this is what our moral *opinions* are like. This would mean, first, that our moral opinions are indeed genuine beliefs, and our moral claims genuine assertions—straightforward assertions attempting to describe the moral dimension of the world. But at the same time, if beliefs can also be desires and if moral opinions have the kind of "double nature" we are here considering, then those very same moral opinions would also be desires. And so, in addition, even if we were to grant the truth of the bolder version of Humeanism, where motivation requires that desires be among the initial ingredients, it could still be the case that moral opinions can indeed motivate, just as internalism claims. In short, if moral opinions can be both beliefs *and* desires, then internalism and the demanding version of the Humean theory could both be true, and yet, for all that, cognitivism could still be true as well.

From the standpoint of the moral realist the resulting picture would look like this. There are moral facts, and under appropriate circumstances we can come to recognize them, resulting in our having various moral beliefs. But since those very beliefs are also *desires* they can combine with relevant background beliefs to generate the motivation (admittedly, sometimes only inadequate motivation) to act in keeping with those beliefs. Thus, even if we grant the demanding version of Humeanism and retain a commitment to internalism, moral realism could *still* be true—*provided* that a single mental state could be both a belief and a desire.

Admittedly, we don't normally allow for this possibility. We normally think of belief and desire as forming mutually exclusive categories: a mental state can be a belief, or it can be a desire, but it can't be both. (We don't, of course, think of these as being *exhaustive* categories: a mental state might be neither a belief *nor* a desire.) But perhaps this is simply another case of an overly hasty generalization. Perhaps it is only the case that many or most beliefs are "pure" beliefs (as we might call them), and not also desires. (Or perhaps it is only the case that many or most desires are "pure" desires, and not also beliefs.) Perhaps we normally simply fail to notice that some mental states—including our moral opinions—are indeed both.

Indeed, once we so much as consider the possibility of something's being both a belief and a desire, that may strike us as a fairly reasonable thing to say about our moral opinions (or about our normative opinions more generally). For example, when I find myself thinking that one ought to keep one's promises, it does often seem as though this thought is both a genuine belief

(I take it to be a *fact* that one ought to keep one's promises) and a genuine desire (I *want* people to keep their promises). So the suggestion that our moral opinions are both beliefs and desires may well be one that realists will find attractive. And while some people will doubtless insist that there must actually be two *distinct* mental states here that I am describing rather than just a single one—a belief on the one hand, and a desire on the other—it isn't clear that this assertion is based on anything other than the dogma that no single mental state *can* be both.

So let us ask, is there any good reason to dismiss the possibility we are considering here? Is there good reason to agree that nothing can be both a belief *and* a desire?

10.5 The Direction of Fit

The best argument I know of for the claim that no single mental state can be both a belief and a desire (indeed, the only argument that I know of) turns on what philosophers sometimes call "the direction of fit."

Here's the basic idea. Both beliefs and desires have *representational content*—that is, they involve a representation or picture of the world, portrayed as being some way that it is or could be. Thus, for example, your belief that snow is white involves a representation of the world as one in which snow is, indeed, white. Similarly, my belief that I teach philosophy involves a representation of the world as one in which I am, indeed, a professor of philosophy. These two beliefs both happen to be true. But, of course, beliefs have representational content even when they are mistaken. If I mistakenly believe that I am over six feet tall, for example, then my belief involves a representation of the world (an inaccurate representation, as it happens) as one in which I am over six feet tall. And so on.

Desires have representational content as well. Thus, for example, if a college student wants to have over a million dollars before they turn thirty, then their desire involves a representation of a possible state of the world, one in which they have that much money but haven't yet turned thirty. If, on a hot summer day, you want a lemonade, then your desire involves a representation of (a possible state of) the world, one in which you are drinking a lemonade. And if I want to avoid embarrassing myself, then my desire involves yet another representation, this one of a world in which none of my actions cause me embarrassment. And so on.

As I say, both desires and beliefs involve representations of the world. They have representational content. But this representational content functions in quite different ways in the two cases. Roughly speaking, beliefs purport to picture how the world *is*, while desires picture how the world "should" be, how we want it to be or what we wish it were.

In both cases, ideally there is a match between the world and the representational content. Things are as you believe them to be, or things are as you want them to be. Such perfect matches occur with varying degrees of frequency, of course, but they do happen: sometimes our beliefs are correct and sometimes we have what we want. So beliefs and desires are similar in that we strive to attain a match between their content and the world. But sometimes there is no such match, and in those cases there is a crucial difference between beliefs and desires. Roughly speaking, when we discover that we have a belief that doesn't match the world we change our beliefs. But in contrast, when we discover that we have a *desire* that doesn't match the world, we don't normally change our desires—we try to change the *world*! The difference is straightforward: We alter our beliefs so as to fit the world, but we don't do that with desires. Rather, we strive to alter the *world* so as to fit our *desires*.

Of course, we don't always do that. Sometimes changing the world in keeping with one desire will interfere with satisfying some other desire that we care about more. And sometimes we realize that there is simply nothing we can do to make the world one in which our desire is satisfied. But still, the mere discovery that the world doesn't match the content of our desire doesn't in and of itself tell us that there is something wrong with that desire. But a similar discovery about a belief—that it doesn't match the world—does indeed indicate a flaw in that belief.

So there are two completely different "directions of fit" that are relevant when we are dealing with beliefs and desires. And this suggests that nothing can be both. If the discovery of a lack of match leads us to change the mental state in question, it is a belief. If the discovery of a lack of match leads us to (try to) change the world, the mental state is a desire. So something can be a belief, or it can be a desire, but it can't be both.

That, at least, is how the argument is supposed to go. But the obvious question to raise is this: why can't a single mental state have *both* directions of fit?

At first glance, this may seem impossible. If we discover a mismatch between the world and the representational content of the mental state in question, which one will we consider defective or inadequate—the mental state or the world? And if one tries to resolve the puzzle by answering "both," that hardly makes things clearer: are we to now start trying to change the world on the basis of a mental state that we have simultaneously declared defective? That hardly seems sensible.

Nonetheless, I do think we can make perfectly good sense of the idea of a mental state with both directions of fit. The basic idea is that the mental state in question will have *two* representational contents, one embedded or contained *within* the other, with one of the contents having one direction of fit, while the other content has the *other* direction of fit. Since it has both directions of fit, this mental state—this single mental state—will be both a belief and a desire.

The technical details get somewhat complicated, so I won't try to spell them out here, but we can get an intuitive feel for the idea by thinking about what is involved in having a belief that a certain state of affairs would be morally good. This belief represents the world as being a certain way—in particular as being such that a certain possible state of affairs (the one that would be good) would have a certain property (the property of goodness). If we were to discover that we were mistaken about this moral belief—if we were to decide that the state of affairs in question wouldn't actually be good after all—then we would of course revise that belief. So the belief is indeed a genuine *belief*: if it doesn't match the world properly, if it misrepresents the particular moral aspect of the world that it attempts to describe, then it is defective and needs to be replaced. But at the same time, this belief is also a *desire*. For the belief also contains within it a representation of a particular possible state of affairs (the state of affairs that we believe would be good), and if we discover that this state of affairs does not actually exist we will then strive to alter the *world*, so as to bring about a match between the world and that representation. So this mental state is indeed a genuine desire as well: we try to alter the world when we discover that the world doesn't match (the relevant part of) the mental state's representational content.

Thus, the mental state in question looks to be both a belief and a desire; it has both directions of fit. If the world doesn't match the relevant (embedded) part of the moral opinion's representational content, we change the world. So it is a desire. But if the world doesn't match the opinion's larger overall content, we change the opinion. So it is a belief. In effect, by virtue of being a belief about the *goodness* of a *possible state of affairs*, we have a mental state with one content embedded within the other—and this allows the single mental state to involve *both* directions of fit, thus constituting both a belief and a desire.

Something similar happens when I have moral opinions about right and wrong. To see this, however, we first need to note that sometimes desires don't actually lead me to try to *change* the world, but rather lead me to *refrain* from changing the world in relevant ways, or lead me to *prevent* relevant changes (changes that would *create* a mismatch between the world and my desires). Suppose, then, that I have the moral opinion that telling white lies is wrong. Here I represent one aspect of the moral dimension of the world in a particular way: I represent a certain type of action (telling white lies) as having a certain moral property (being wrong). If I discover that I am mistaken about this, if I discover that acts of this sort aren't actually wrong at all, then I will revise my view. So this is a genuine belief. But at the same time, this very same moral opinion may keep me from *telling* such a lie (since if I do, this will create a mismatch between my activities and my moral opinion). So this is a genuine desire as well: I refrain from altering the world in certain ways because of the mental state in question. So my moral opinion is both a belief and a desire; it has both directions of fit.

As I say, the details get rather complicated. But I hope I have said enough here to show why no simple-minded appeal to ideas about the direction of fit can suffice to rule out the possibility that some mental states, and in particular our moral opinions, can be both beliefs and desires. If this is indeed an impossibility, it will take a more complicated argument to show this.

(Imagine a critic who says that since the moral opinion has two representational contents—one contained within the other—there must actually be two distinct mental states here after all, one a belief, the other a desire, rather than a single mental state that is both. This suggestion has some breezy plausibility, but only until we remember that there is no way to express the *content* of the belief without bringing in the embedded (desire-like) content as well. So there is no way to separate out the two purportedly distinct mental states. And if the critic then suggests that at best this shows that having the moral opinion is more like having a belief *about* a desire, rather than having something that is both a belief *and* a desire, they will then be conceding that the bold version of Humeanism is mistaken. For if this belief can indeed lead one to change the world (or refrain from changing it), then it isn't really true after all that motivation requires desires as well as beliefs: beliefs of the right sort—*this* sort—can suffice.)

There is, as always, more to say about all of this, but at this point perhaps it is clear that the possibility of mental states that are both beliefs and desires is one that should not be dismissed out of hand. And if this is indeed a possibility, then the realist may choose to embrace it as a way of responding to the argument for noncognitivism. If she takes this last approach, the realist can accept internalism and accept as well the Humean theory of motivation, even in its more demanding form. For even if it takes a desire to get motivation going, if moral opinions can be beliefs as well as desires then moral opinions can motivate (by virtue of being desires) and yet still be beliefs as well, just as the realist claims.

So we now actually have *three* different replies that the realist might offer to the noncognitivist's argument. First of all, as we have seen, some realists will be happy (or at least willing) to accept motive externalism. If moral opinions cannot actually motivate on their own, then nothing stands in the way of treating them as the genuine beliefs that realists take them to be. On the other hand, second, realists may prefer to challenge the Humean theory of motivation. Perhaps certain beliefs—including moral beliefs—really can motivate, even in the absence of an initial desire that is present at the outset. Here too, then, there will be nothing standing in the way of moral opinions being genuine beliefs. Finally, third, some realists may accept both motive internalism *and* the demanding version of Humeanism. Such realists may prefer to argue that certain beliefs—including moral beliefs—really can motivate, but that they do so precisely by virtue of being both beliefs and desires. If a single mental state can indeed be both a belief and a desire, then recognizing the motivational powers of moral opinions, as well as accepting the need for initial desires (if there is to be motivation), will still be compatible with also taking those moral opinions to be the genuine beliefs that they seem to be.

Unsurprisingly, realists will differ among themselves as to which of these three replies they find most attractive. The choice depends in part on one's other philosophical commitments, including what you want to require as part of the job description of morality. Speaking personally, I have of course already expressed my inclination to accept motive internalism. So I am not personally attracted to the first of these three replies. I remain unsettled, however, about the choice between the second and the third. While I do believe that moral opinions can motivate, I am unsure whether this is because they are desires as well as beliefs (the third reply), or because desires are not actually needed for motivation (the second). But no matter. *Any* of the three replies will allow the moral realist to escape the argument for noncognitivism.

Returning now to an earlier point, recall that if the argument for noncognitivism had been successful it would have undermined not only moral realism but moral nihilism as well, since the nihilist, like the realist, is a cognitivist. As it happens, however, nihilists can avail themselves of the same three replies. That is, the nihilist can reject internalism, reject the bold Humean theory, or reject the claim that nothing can be both a belief and a desire. Nothing in any of these replies makes use of the realist's further claim that moral facts do indeed exist.

So the situation is this. Consideration of the motivational powers of morality provided the materials for an important argument for noncognitivism, but that argument can be answered without yet telling us whether we should be realists or nihilists. *That* choice must be made on other grounds.

Of course, as I have already argued (in chapter 7), intuition provides us with defeasible justification for *believing* in moral facts. So the burden is still on the nihilist to give us compelling reason to deny the reality of such facts while remaining within a cognitivist framework. And there is nothing in the argument we have been examining that provides such a reason.

One final point. Given the failure of the argument for noncognitivism we can now drop the practice we adopted earlier—of avoiding talk of moral beliefs and restricting ourselves instead to talking about our moral opinions. I introduced that latter term, of course, merely as a convenient way of referring to the things we normally *take* to be beliefs, while at the same time avoiding commitment to the cognitivist claim that this is what they really are. But given the failure of the argument for noncognitivism, we have no compelling reason to deny that moral opinions are indeed the genuine beliefs that they appear to be. Accordingly, we can revert to referring to the mental states in question in the simple, familiar way that we normally do—that is, as genuine moral *beliefs*.

11

Reasons

11.1 Reasons Internalism

If morality requires you to perform some act, then there is something to be said in favor of doing that act. There is a *reason* to do what morality asks of you; there is a justification of some sort for doing what morality requires you to do.

Virtually all moral realists, I imagine, believe something like this. Moral requirements aren't mere bluster, empty commands which one has no reason to obey. On the contrary, there is something about morality—whether due to its content, or its basis, or both—that guarantees that if you do indeed have a duty to act in a given way, then there is at least *some* reason for you to act accordingly.

To be sure, we do seem to have a notion of "requirement" that is sufficiently "thin" that nothing at all like this follows from the mere fact of something being a requirement in that minimal sense. Imagine that you find a copy of *A Guide to Ritual Practice* for some long-forgotten religion. Suppose it says that everyone is to shave their head each year on the summer solstice. Given that the solstice is rapidly approaching, you may recognize that the rule book requires you to shave your head; but you certainly won't take yourself to have any genuine reason to do so.

But morality seems different. If you realize that you are morally required to do some act—perhaps because of a promise you made earlier—then you will now indeed take yourself to have a reason to do the act you are required to do. This is unlike your situation with regard to the ancient rule book, where—except in extraordinary circumstances—you have no reason at all to do what the book asks of you. But in contrast, you do have a reason, a justification, for keeping your promises—just as there is a justification for telling the truth, acting justly, helping the needy, and refraining from harming the innocent. The requirements of morality are valid and binding—genuine and legitimate—in a way that the requirements of the forgotten ritual handbook are not, and one way in which this seems to be true lies in the fact that the requirements of morality are backed by reasons, in a way that arbitrary requirements (such as those in the book) are not.

Some might prefer to capture this idea in a slightly different way. They might prefer to say that the rules listed in the handbook are not genuine requirements at all (even if people once took them to be such), precisely because there is no reason to do what they ask of you. Genuine requirements, it might be suggested, are indeed backed by *reasons* of some sort. Where there is no reason to do what you are being told to do, there is no real requirement at all, only empty commands. Accordingly, those who prefer this alternative way of talking might insist that there are no genuine requirements in the handbook at all; there are merely *purported* requirements. Or they might use scare quotes, and say that while there are "requirements" listed in the book (meaning only that the rules listed there are things that certain people presumably *took* to be requirements), there are no genuine requirements.

On this second approach, then, something isn't actually a requirement at all, unless it is backed by reasons. The "requirements" listed in the handbook fail this test, and so are not genuine requirements. But the requirements of morality are different—they are indeed *genuine* requirements—precisely because it does seem as though there is reason to do what morality asks of us. I am not merely "required" to keep my promises: I am *required* to do so.

Of course, not everyone believes in the reality of moral facts; not everyone accepts the existence of moral requirements. But even those who are moral skeptics typically will agree that if there *were* moral facts, if there *were* moral obligations, then there *would* be reason to do what morality asks of us. That is to say, even moral skeptics agree that it is part of the job description for morality that it entails the existence of corresponding reasons. If there is to *be* such a thing as morality—if morality is to be more than another empty list of commands—then its "requirements" must indeed be genuine requirements: its demands must be backed by reasons. Skeptics of course deny that there *are* any moral requirements in this robust sense, but they generally agree that this is indeed part of what it would take for there to *be* such a thing as morality.

We can call the view that if there are such things as moral requirements then they are backed by reasons of an appropriate sort *reasons internalism* (see 1.2). Those who accept this view—and that is almost all of us, I suspect—are reasons internalists.

(Like *motive* internalism, reasons internalism posits an "inner" or "internal" connection between morality and something else. But in contrast to motive internalism, where the connection being posited is one between morality and *motivation*, reasons internalism posits a connection between morality and the existence of *reasons*. The two views are logically distinct and independent, in that someone could accept either one without the other, accept neither, or accept both.)

Those who reject reasons internalism, the reasons *externalists*, certainly need not hold (implausibly) that one *never* has reason to do what morality requires of us. But this is always a further matter. Suppose, for example, that I offer to pay you $1,000 if you keep the promise you made to our dying mother. Even the externalist will acknowledge that you now have a reason to keep your promise (to wit, the chance of gaining the money). But the existence of a reason wasn't guaranteed by your having made the promise (and your being morally required to keep your promises). On the contrary, the reason is something extra, external to the obligation itself. Similarly, it might be that your friend Sheila cares enough about helping others and respecting their interests that she always has a reason to do what morality asks of her. But here too, the reasons externalist will insist, the mere existence of these various moral requirements does not by itself suffice to guarantee that Sheila has a reason to do what morality requires. That was due to a mere further accident of her upbringing. As far as externalists are concerned, the existence of a moral requirement is one thing; the existence of any sort of reason to act on that requirement is quite another. The former simply doesn't guarantee the latter.

But reasons internalists view the matter rather differently. According to the internalist, if it really is a fact that you are morally required to keep the promise you made to our mother, then you really do have a reason to keep that promise, whether or not I offer you a payment on the side. (At best that provides a *further* reason.) And while the fact that Sheila cares about others may give her some additional reason to do what morality asks of her, there would still be at least *some* reason to do this, even if she didn't. Where there is a genuine moral requirement, there is always at least *some* rational justification for doing what is required, there is always *something* that speaks in favor of acting as one is required to do.

Unsurprisingly, reasons internalists may disagree about the details. Some think any reason provided by morality must have at least some (specified) minimum strength. Perhaps these reasons can be outweighed, but they're never weak or trivial. Others, more boldly, think that moral reasons must be overriding, so that one would always have *more* reason to do one's duty than to fail to do so. Some think (perhaps a bit more strongly still) that the reason one has to do what morality requires must be rationally *decisive*, so that the only rationally permissible course of action is to do one's duty. And many think the reason must be *categorical*, a reason one would have regardless of the various desires one happens to have. But the fundamental thought is simply this: if there truly are moral requirements—if it really can be the case that some action is morally required—then there must be reasons to act in keeping with those requirements, reasons of the appropriate *sort*.

This in turn points the way to yet another argument for moral skepticism. The basic idea of the argument is this: If there really were moral facts then moral duties and obligations would always be supported or backed by reasons of the relevant sort. But there cannot be reasons of the kind in question (alternatively, there can be no guarantee that a reason of the relevant sort will always *accompany* the existence of a moral requirement). So there cannot be any moral facts. Moral realism must be rejected.

Strictly speaking, this argument may show only that there cannot be any moral *requirements*. Conceivably, then, it could still be the case that everything is morally *permissible*, since even a reasons internalist need not think that one necessarily has a reason to do a given act simply because one is *permitted* to do it. Presumably, however, few if any moral realists will be attracted to a view according to which there are and can be no moral requirements and nothing is morally forbidden. So for simplicity I will assume that if moral realism is true—if there are any moral facts at all—then there are at least some acts that are morally required. Accordingly, if there cannot be any moral requirements, there cannot be any moral facts.

This new argument will be our concern in the present chapter. But before turning to it more directly, we first need to get clear about what is involved in saying that there is a reason to do something. What exactly do we have in mind when we talk about something being a *reason*?

11.2 Reasons

The term "reason" can, it seems, be used for two rather different things. On the one hand, sometimes when we talk about reasons we merely mean to be making a claim about (or asking a question about) the *cause or explanation* of why something happened. But, on the other hand, sometimes when we talk about reasons we mean instead to be making a claim about (or asking a question about) whether something (an action, perhaps, or a belief) is *justified, rationally supported, or appropriate*.

Consider some examples. Suppose we ask, what's the reason that the old oak tree fell over? The answer might be (in part): it had died, and the roots had decayed. That's the reason why it fell. Obviously, in a case like this, no one is saying that the tree is somehow *justified* in doing what it did, or that this was an "appropriate" thing for it to do. Such an idea doesn't even make sense in this context. We are, here, just talking about the cause or explanation. Similarly, it might well be true that the reason the milk curdled was because it had spoiled, and the reason the car started running again is because the battery had been replaced. In all these cases, talk of reasons doesn't imply anything at all about justification, or being a rational response to the circumstances, and the like.

Unsurprisingly, we sometimes use this first notion of reason even when we are talking about various human actions. Why did Larry growl at the radio? Perhaps he was angry at the news that his favorite team had lost their most recent game. That's the reason he did it. Here too, we need not be making any claim at all about whether there was any sort of justification for doing what he did. We are simply trying to *explain* Larry's behavior; we are not trying to justify it, or suggest that this was in any way an appropriate response.

Sometimes, however, we *do* want to say of a certain action that there is (or was) a justification for doing it, that there is (or was) a kind of rational support for acting that way. Here we are making a *normative* judgment, we are claiming that something in the given situation *speaks in favor* of performing the act in question. Here too, we may use the language of reasons.

For example, we might tell Betsy that there is a reason for her to slow down while driving: otherwise she might hit that deer. Or we might tell Laurel that there is a reason to stop smoking: otherwise it will ruin her health and shorten her life. Similarly, there might be a reason for you to try the casserole: it's delicious! In all of these cases there is something about the situation that makes a given action rationally appropriate. At the very least, there is something to be said in favor of acting in the way in question. There is some sort of rational justification or rational support for acting in the specified way. As we might put the point: there is a *reason* to do this act, rather than that.

Note, however, that the mere fact that there is some sort of rational support for doing something doesn't in any way tell us whether the person does, in fact, do the act in question. It might be, for example, that although there is *some* reason to act in a given way, there is even greater reason not to. (Perhaps the casserole, though delicious, is fattening, and you are on a diet.) Or it might be that even though there is on balance far *greater* reason to perform the act than not, the person simply fails to act rationally. Whatever the explanation, the point is simply that the existence of a reason in this second sense doesn't in any way guarantee that the relevant act will be done. And if the act isn't done, then of course there is no reason of the first sort why it happened, since it *didn't* happen—though there may well be a reason of the first sort why it didn't, despite there being a reason of the second sort about why it should have.

Of course, often we do in fact do what we have reason to do. Then, presumably, there will be both an explanation and a justification. In such cases, the two types of reasons may be very closely related. For sometimes a person does a given action precisely because there was a good reason to do it! In such cases, the two types of reason come together: there is good rational support for doing the act, the person realized it, and that explains why he did it. The existence of the reason (or, perhaps, his recognition of the reason) is the reason why he did what he did.

But in some cases, it seems, the explanation of why the person did what he did may have little or nothing to do with the justification that existed for doing what he did. There may have been good reason for doing something, and he may even have done that thing, but that doesn't necessarily mean that that's why he *did* it. The explanatory reason may have nothing to do with the justifying one. In cases like that, there is a danger that simple-minded talk about reasons may mislead or confuse us, as it won't always be clear what kind of reason we are talking about.

The danger is especially sharp given the possibility that someone may act because of something that they *take* to be a (justifying) reason, even though it is not, in fact, a good reason at all. Here, the explanatory reason will involve reference to something that the person mistakenly takes to be a *justifying* reason, even though it isn't one. Or it might be that the person acts on something that they correctly take to be a justifying reason, but they do this despite the fact that the justificatory force of this reason is outweighed, all things considered. Here too, the (explanatory) reasons why the person acts as he does will fail to correspond—at least in part—to the (justificatory) reasons there are for acting one way rather than another.

Of course, in the more ideal cases, the person acts on reasons that he rightly recognizes as being genuine justifying reasons overall, and so the explanatory reasons will indeed correspond exactly to the justifying ones.

But even here, it is analytically useful to distinguish between the explanatory reasons and the justifying ones, even though the former will involve reference to the latter.

In light of all of this, philosophers sometimes distinguish between *motivating* reasons and *normative* or *justifying* reasons. The motivating reasons are those things that the agent takes to be reasons, which he acts upon: these are the reasons (genuine or not, outweighed or not) which help explain why the agent was moved to act as he did. The normative reasons, in contrast, are those considerations which genuinely support performing the act in question, speaking in favor of doing it, regardless of whether, in the case at hand, the agent is moved by these considerations at all.

The distinction between motivating reasons and normative reasons is clearly an important one. It is especially important to keep it in mind when thinking about moral realism and moral skepticism, as even the skeptic about morality is ready to agree that people are often *motivated* by moral concerns. The skeptic simply insists that there are no moral facts to provide *justification* for acting as we do. In terms of the vocabulary just introduced, we can say that the skeptic recognizes that moral reasons are among our *motivating* reasons, but she insists that moral reasons are not among the genuinely *normative* reasons, reasons which can potentially justify our actions. In contrast, moral realists—or at least, those realists who are reasons internalists—think that moral requirements are indeed backed by normative reasons; they are backed by reasons that provide rational support for acting in keeping with those very requirements.

Nonetheless, having drawn the distinction between motivating and normative reasons, for our purposes it will now be simpler if we hereafter restrict unspecified talk of "reasons" to the normative sense of the term. Going forward, let me simply stipulate that unless context suggests otherwise, if I speak of a reason—without classifying it further—I mean a *normative* reason. After all, if moral realism is susceptible to an attack from the skeptic by virtue of embracing some version of reasons internalism, what the skeptic is skeptical about is whether it can really be the case that moral requirements are always backed by a *normative* reason of the relevant kind. Since it would be tiresome to be forever flagging all our talk of "reasons" with the qualifying labels "normative" or "justifying," I will typically leave the qualification implicit. (This has, in fact, been my practice in the previous chapters as well. When talking about the existence of a reason I have usually had *normative* reasons in mind, not motivating or explanatory ones.)

A few additional clarificatory remarks may be helpful. First, as I have already suggested in passing, to say that there is rational support for an action merely means that there is *some* justification for doing the given act. The existence of a reason needn't imply that the act is justified all things considered. There might be competing reasons which bear on the subject as well, and they may provide stronger support overall for an alternative course of action. Still, where there is a reason there is at least *something* that speaks in favor of doing the act in question. Second, although people do sometimes talk about "reasons" without thereby committing themselves to whether the purported reason is genuine or not, when reasons internalists claim that moral requirements are backed by reasons they do indeed mean that these requirements are (or would be) backed by *genuine* reasons. The idea isn't merely that morality *claims* that there are reasons to do what it asks, or that people who believe in morality *think* that there are reasons to do what it asks, but rather the bolder thought that if there really are moral requirements then there are indeed genuine reasons to do what it asks.

Third, in many contexts it is useful to distinguish between the question of whether something truly does provide rational support for a given course of action and the question of whether the relevant agent *realizes* this. It is one thing for the reason to *exist*, it is another thing for the agent to *recognize* that fact. For example, if drinking this liquid will cure Miriam's cough, there is a reason for her to drink it. But if Miriam doesn't know about the medicinal virtues of the cough syrup she may not realize this. In cases like this, people sometimes mark the distinction by saying that although there *is* a reason for Miriam to drink the medicine, she doesn't yet *have* a reason to drink it—meaning only that she doesn't yet recognize all the reasons there are. But we don't always follow this convention, and many people will be perfectly comfortable saying of this example that Miriam *has* a reason to drink the syrup, though she doesn't yet realize it. At any rate, regardless of how we mark the distinction, presumably when the internalist says that moral requirements are backed by reasons, the claim is only that such reasons *exist* (or would exist, if there really were moral requirements); no claim is being made that everyone will necessarily *recognize* the existence of those reasons. (After all, sometimes people don't even realize that they are under a given obligation; why, then, would they recognize the existence of a reason to act in keeping with it in the situation in question?)

Next, let's try to get a bit clearer about a metaphysical point. What exactly is it for a reason to exist? For that matter, when a reason exists, what exactly constitutes the reason? Suppose, for example, that moving your hand off the hot stove will stop the pain. Clearly, there is a reason to move it: the fact that moving your hand will stop the pain provides *rational support* for the action of moving your hand. More generally, whenever there is a reason there is an underlying fact (or set of facts) by virtue of which there is rational support for performing the action in question. Typically, I think, we say that this underlying fact *is itself* the reason for performing the given act. For example, if we were to ask, what is the reason to move your hand, the answer we would normally give is this: that doing so will stop the pain. On this way of talking, the reason simply *is* the underlying fact. And in our example, of course, that fact is a straightforwardly empirical one (in particular, the existence of a causal relation between a certain bodily motion and a change in your unpleasant mental states). Still, to say of that empirical fact that it is a *reason* is to ascribe to it a *normative* property—the normative property of providing rational support for some action. Thus, although the underlying fact which *is* the reason may be an empirical one, the fact that it is a *reason* is actually a *normative* fact: it is the fact that the underlying fact provides rational support for moving your hand.

This brings us to a fourth point. Although, as I just suggested, we typically talk as though the reason itself in any given case is the underlying fact (or set of facts) which provides rational support for the given action, we do not always talk that way. Sometimes we talk as though the reason is actually something *distinct* from that underlying fact. For sometimes we say that the underlying fact creates or generates or *gives you* a reason to perform the act in question. And when we talk this second way, it seems as though we are distinguishing between the underlying fact, by virtue of which there is a reason to perform a given act, and the reason itself, which exists *because of* that underlying fact. On this second way of talking, the underlying fact provides the basis or grounding for the reason, but it isn't the reason itself. Rather, it might be more accurate to say that the existence of the reason to perform the act consists in the "purely normative" fact that the act in question has rational support. It is this *normative* fact that is the reason, not the underlying empirical fact by virtue of which this normative fact obtains.

Metaphysically speaking, I suppose, these two different accounts are incompatible. Is the reason the *underlying* fact which provides the rational support for the given action, or is it the *normative* fact that the action in question does indeed have rational support? It doesn't seem as though it can be both. Happily, however, for our purposes there is no need to resolve this bit of metaphysical controversy. For our purposes, nothing turns on whether we talk the one way or the other. Accordingly, I will help myself to both types of locutions, sometimes saying the underlying fact *is* the reason, sometimes that it provides or *generates* a reason. What is important, either way, is recognizing that reasons inevitably involve something *normative*—the fact that a given action is rationally supported.

One final point. Although I have been focusing on reasons for action, it is of course true that reasons can support things that don't involve bodily motion. For example, there are reasons to have particular beliefs, where this too is a normative notion, the idea that there is some sort of rational support for *having* the beliefs in question. Admittedly, sometimes in asking the reason why someone believes something we are indeed merely asking for an explanation, without thereby assuming that there is anything at all to be said in favor of the given belief. But we also accept the idea that there can be justifying reasons as well, reasons *to* believe something (for example, reasons to accept one hypothesis rather than another). It is, accordingly, important to recognize the fact that reasons to believe are every bit as normatively infused as reasons to act.

11.3 Refining the Argument

Although we have only described the skeptic's argument in the thinnest of terms—to date it is more of a promissory note than an actual argument—one natural thought is that this argument, whatever its details, can be sidestepped altogether if the moral realist simply denies reasons internalism. For what the skeptic wants to convince us of is the claim that the reasons posited by the realist cannot exist (or perhaps, would not always exist). But if the realist indeed rejects the assumption that moral requirements must be backed by reasons of the relevant sort (whatever precisely that turns out to be), then it looks like it shouldn't really matter whether reasons of that kind are possible or not. The skeptic will be denying the existence of something that the realist isn't committed to! So it is worth asking whether the rejection of reasons internalism is indeed a position that the realist should seriously consider adopting.

My own view is that it is not. In saying this, I don't merely mean to indicate that I personally find reasons internalism a more plausible view than reasons *externalism* (although that is certainly true). I mean to suggest something stronger—that reasons externalism is likely to be unappealing to anyone genuinely drawn to moral realism. To be sure, it isn't that reasons externalism is somehow incoherent or self-defeating; it is simply that anyone who truly believes in the existence of moral facts is likely to believe that where there is indeed a genuine moral duty to perform a given act, there is always at least *some* justification for *meeting* that duty—some rational support for doing the act that morality requires. That is part of what it is, the realist is likely to think, for moral requirements to be genuine requirements; it is part of what differentiates moral requirements from the various other "requirements" (requirements in name only) that might otherwise be made up out of whole cloth. Moral requirements are backed by *reasons*. Of course, they are hardly unique in this regard; there are plenty of other genuine requirements besides moral ones. But this is at least part of what makes moral requirements genuine *requirements*.

Again, it isn't as though there is any logical *inconsistency* in combining moral realism with reasons externalism. One can simply insist that it is one thing for a given act to be morally required, and quite another thing—an utterly distinct thing—for the agent to have any *reason* to do that act. One can claim that whether an agent has any reason at all to do what he is required to do is always a *further* question.

But why should a realist be attracted to such a position? I suppose the argument would be that it is an easy enough matter to imagine someone of whom it is true that they simply have no reason to do what they are required to do. Consider once again the example (from 4.2 and 10.3) of a hit man on his way to kill his assigned victim. Imagine that the hit man cares not at all for his intended target, that he simply isn't concerned about respecting the interests of others (and so on), and that he knows as well that there is no serious chance of his getting caught. Isn't it clear, the externalist may ask, that such a person has no reason at all to refrain from killing his victim? Yet won't the realist want to insist, for all that, that our hit man is, just like the rest of us, under a moral obligation to refrain from killing innocent people? So doesn't the possibility of a case like this show that moral requirements need not be backed by reasons for acting on those requirements? Perhaps then the realist really should be a reasons externalist after all.

Although an example like this may be initially persuasive, on reflection it is far from clear what it actually shows. Our current question, after all, isn't whether the hit man is in any way *moved* to meet his moral obligations, or whether he *believes* he has reason to refrain from killing. (To simplify the current discussion we can stipulate that he isn't moved, and that he *doesn't* believe this.) Our question, rather, is whether there is a *reason* for the hit man to refrain—whether such a reason *exists* (whether or not he realizes it). So we need to ask, is there anything at all that would justify a decision to refrain from killing, anything that *speaks in favor* of not killing his victim?

I find it hard to believe that there are many realists who think the answer to that question is no. From the perspective of the moral realist, after all, moral requirements aren't simply arbitrary rules, commands which one has no more reason to attend to than any alternative rules which someone might arbitrarily propose in their place. On the contrary, there are facts about the contents of these rules and their ultimate basis or justification that make it true that there are indeed reasons to *obey* these rules—facts that make it true that there is at least *some* justification for doing what morality asks.

Just to be clear, we are not currently asking whether the reasons posited by the realist really do exist. The point is simply that from the perspective of the realist it will probably seem obvious that they do. Almost all realists, I think, will want to insist that wherever there is a genuine moral requirement there are reasons to do what one is required to do.

Indeed, on a view that many moral realists will find attractive, the fact that there is a moral requirement to act in a given way may simply *consist* in the fact that there is a reason (of the right sort) for acting in that way (see 12.5). It isn't so much that there is a requirement, on the one hand, and the relevant reasons to act accordingly, on the other. Rather, the existence of the requirement simply consists in the fact that the right sorts of reasons exist. (On such a view, of course, talk of requirements being "backed" by reasons of the right kind may be slightly misleading. Rather, requirements just *are* reasons of the relevant kind.) But in any event, whether or not the realist takes this extra step—of reducing requirements to reasons—reasons internalism is likely to remain extremely compelling for the realist.

I conclude, accordingly, that the vast majority of moral realists will decline the option of evading the skeptic by embracing reasons externalism. If I am right, then most realists remain vulnerable to an argument that claims that the sort of reasons that they posit can't or don't exist.

Of course, to concede this point is not yet to have been given any grounds for agreeing with the skeptic that there is indeed something *problematic* about belief in the reasons that realists accept. It is hardly surprising to learn that moral skeptics deny the existence of all sorts of reasons that moral realists believe in. But can the skeptic offer us any reason to join her?

It would not, I think, be promising for the skeptic to proceed piecemeal, challenging the reasons corresponding to individual moral requirements one at a time (or one set at a time), requirement by requirement. For this is unlikely to ever lead us to the general skeptical conclusion about morality that the skeptic hopes to establish. Suppose, for example, that the skeptic convinced us that there is no compelling reason (special circumstances aside) to avoid white lies. Even if so, there might still be good reason to avoid telling other kinds of lies. Or suppose the skeptic somehow convinced us that there is no compelling reason (special circumstances aside) to keep one's promises. Even if so, there might still be good reason to avoid harming people, or to help the needy, or to promote justice, and so on. Engaging in this sort of piecemeal debate would fall short of the skeptic's aim of offering general reasons to reject moral realism altogether. The skeptic would, instead, simply be participating in the familiar first-order substantive debates that fall *within* normative ethics, part of the ongoing attempt to identify the genuine moral requirements and to determine their precise contents. Arguing about this or that particular purported moral fact provides no reason to think there are no moral facts at all.

Instead, what the moral skeptic needs to do, it seems, is point to something more general, something that would undermine belief in moral requirements *across the board*, by challenging the realist's belief in the corresponding *reasons* across the board. Presumably the way to do this would be to challenge the existence of the *kind* of reasons posited by the moral realist. That way, instead of being engaged in a piecemeal debate about whether this particular requirement or that particular requirement is genuinely valid or binding, the skeptic would have given us reason to reject the very idea of moral requirements altogether.

Very well, but what is it about the sorts of reasons posited by moral realists that seems unacceptable from the perspective of the moral skeptic? Presumably, it isn't that the skeptic holds that there are no normative reasons at all. Even moral skeptics believe that if I am thirsty, for example, the fact that drinking this glass of water will quench my thirst provides at least some justification for drinking it. Similarly, the fact that moving my hand from a hot stove will end the pain provides rational support for doing just that. So what is it about moral reasons in particular that the skeptic finds questionable?

I suspect that the answer is this: moral realists typically think of moral requirements as being backed by *categorical* reasons, where these are reasons that provide rational support for a given action *regardless* of the particular desires that the agent happens to have. A categorical reason is one whose justificatory force doesn't depend on whether the given agent has some particular desire—and as such one cannot escape its force by proclaiming that one doesn't care about this, or that one isn't concerned about that. If there is a categorical reason to keep one's promises, for example, then this is a reason that everyone has, regardless of whether they care about disappointing others or are concerned about frustrating the reasonable expectations they have deliberately created. If there is a categorical reason to keep one's promises then the fact that you have made a promise provides a reason to keep that promise *regardless* of whether you happen to care about respecting the interests of others or promoting their welfare, and so on. But the idea of a reason like *that* is something that is likely to strike the skeptic as unacceptable. It isn't merely that they are dubious about whether there are categorical reasons to keep one's promises, or categorical reasons to tell the truth, or categorical reasons not to kill; rather, they typically reject the very idea of categorical reasons altogether.

Think again about our imaginary hit man. A skeptic is likely to think that although you or I may well have compelling reason to refrain from killing innocent people—whether because we care about others, or want to show them due respect, or because we feel squeamish about the prospect of killing someone, or we are afraid of getting caught and going to jail—these reasons only exist because we have one or another of the desires I just listed (or others like that). It is only because of the presence of desires like these that most of us do indeed have reason to refrain from killing. But in the absence of any of these desires, they may hold, there is no reason to refrain from killing. The existence of a reason essentially depends on the existence of an appropriate *desire*, and so, in the absence of some relevant desire there is no reason to act one way rather than another. Accordingly, unlike the rest of us, our hit man may well have no reason to refrain from killing.

But if there were such a thing as a *categorical* reason, then it would be irrelevant whether you had or lacked any given desire; you would have at least some reason to act in the relevant way regardless of what you happened to want. And if, in particular, there were a categorical reason not to kill, then even our hit man would have a reason to refrain from killing. But how, the skeptic may ask, could there possibly be a reason to do something (or to refrain from doing something) that didn't essentially depend on our having a desire or preference of the relevant sort? Aren't all genuine reasons for action conditional on the agent's having a desire with relevant content?

Moral realists may well believe in the existence of categorical reasons, but the very idea of such a reason is likely to strike the skeptic as unacceptable. So here at last we have arrived at a further possible argument for moral skepticism: If there were any genuine moral requirements, there would have to be categorical reasons; but there are no categorical reasons, so there are no moral requirements. Thus moral realism must be rejected.

Admittedly, sometimes skeptics focus their attacks instead on other features of the reasons posited by moral realists. For example, sometimes it is claimed that what is problematic is the thought that there can be reasons that are *other* regarding, or the thought that moral reasons must always *override* other reasons. But most skeptics wouldn't be troubled by the possibility of other-regarding reasons that are overridingly strong if, say, the person in question happened to care most strongly about helping others. It is only the claim that such reasons would exist *regardless* of what the person happens to want that is likely to be objectionable to the skeptic. So the truly central question remains whether *categorical* reasons are indeed possible.

11.4 Hypothetical Reasons

The skeptic argues that there are no moral requirements because there are no categorical reasons. How might a realist respond? One possibility, easily overlooked, is for the realist to insist that a perfectly adequate defense of moral realism is available even if there *are* no categorical reasons.

After all, it isn't as though the skeptic denies the existence of normative reasons altogether. It is simply the existence of categorical reasons that are being called into question. So if the realist can show why moral requirements can always be backed by reasons to meet those requirements, then even if those reasons aren't categorical ones, that may suffice for the purpose of deflecting the skeptic's argument.

Let's consider this possibility further. The key distinction here (among normative reasons) is that between categorical reasons, on the one hand, and what philosophers call *hypothetical* reasons, on the other. In contrast to categorical reasons, hypothetical reasons are reasons that exist by virtue of the agent having a relevant desire—roughly speaking, a desire that the agent can satisfy (or help to satisfy) by performing the act in question. Many instances of everyday, uncontroversial reasons are hypothetical ones. Thus, to revert to an earlier example, if you are thirsty you may have a reason to drink the water. That's a hypothetical reason, because the very existence of the reason depends on the underlying fact that you want your thirst to disappear. Similarly, if you want to make a million dollars before you are thirty, you may have a reason to start your own business. That too is a hypothetical reason, for you only have that reason given your desire to make so much money. (If you would rather think about the meaning of life, you might have a reason to become a philosopher instead!)

In our everyday life our decisions are constantly guided by our recognition of a wide variety of hypothetical reasons; but the present point of course is that these reasons exist precisely because acting in the relevant ways will help us to satisfy our various desires and preferences. If we lacked those desires, and had others instead, then there would be different reasons in their place, directing us to perform other actions. But those too would be hypothetical ones, insofar as their existence would also depend on our having the relevant (alternative) desires. Hypothetical reasons thus stand in contrast to categorical ones, for the latter—if there were such things—would exist regardless of what desires the agent happened to have.

I trust it is clear that despite the standard philosophical label, hypothetical reasons are perfectly real reasons for action. (A better label might be *conditional* reasons, or *desire-based* reasons, but the use of the term "hypothetical" is probably too well entrenched to change.) The crucial point is that when you have a hypothetical reason to perform a given act there is indeed rational support for doing that act—there is something to be said in favor of doing it—but the ground or *basis* of your having that reason lies in the fact that you have a desire with the appropriate content. Change the desire—take it away, or replace it with a different desire with a different aim—and you will find yourself with different reasons for action. And of course if you never had the desire in the first place, then you will never have had that particular hypothetical reason at all. (If you want to get into medical school, you may have a reason to take organic chemistry. But if you have no desire to go to medical school then you have no reason to take it. Or at least, you don't have that *particular* reason to do so.)

It may also be worth pausing to note that talk of hypothetical reasons shouldn't be confused with talk of motivating ones. As always, to talk of a motivating reason is to talk about why the given individual acted the way they did: it is to say something about what motivated them. But although hypothetical reasons are based on desires, they need not motivate us, if for no other reason than that we may not realize that the act in question will help us satisfy the desire in question. And even if you do realize it, you still might not act on it, perhaps because you see that there are even stronger reasons to perform some other action instead. To be sure, often we do act on our hypothetical reasons (you drink the water, you start the business, you take organic chemistry), and in such cases our hypothetical reasons may well be among our motivating ones. But even then it is crucial to remember that in saying that something is a hypothetical reason we are saying that it has genuine justificatory force. Hypothetical reasons are *normative* reasons—they provide rational support for performing the action (or actions) in question.

Suppose for the moment that hypothetical reasons are the only reasons there are. That is, suppose the skeptic is correct and there are no such things as categorical reasons (reasons whose existence does not, in this way, depend on the agent having some appropriate desire). It is easy to see why the skeptic might conclude that, given the assumption of reasons internalism, this suffices to undermine moral realism. After all, if reasons internalism is true, then genuine requirements must be backed by reasons; and if the only reasons are hypothetical reasons, then unless the agent happens to have a relevant desire (some desire or preference that would be satisfied by acting on the requirement) there will be no such reason. But given the tremendous variation in the desires we find as we move from one person to the next, it seems quite implausible for the moral realist to claim that everyone will always have a desire of the right sort, for any given purported moral requirement. (Think again about the hit man, who seems to have no desires at all that would provide him with a hypothetical reason to refrain from killing his intended victim.) In short, if the only reasons are hypothetical ones, then while it may be true that most of us often have reasons to refrain from killing, or to keep our promises, and so on, it cannot be true that *everyone always* has such reasons. And so—again, given the assumption of reasons internalism, the assumption that genuine requirements are always backed by reasons—it turns out that there are no genuine moral *requirements* after all.

That, at least, is the skeptic's thought, and it must be conceded that it seems plausible. If there are only hypothetical reasons then it certainly looks like moral requirements couldn't have the normative backing that reasons internalism posits. So how then can a moral realist hope to defend morality without insisting upon the possibility of categorical reasons?

The answer, of course, is that the realist must claim that we were too quick to assume that some people lack desires that would provide them with *hypothetical* reasons to conform to their moral obligations. Even if it is true—as it would be, if there are only hypothetical reasons—that one has a reason to obey morality only given that one has a desire of the right sort, moral requirements could still be real and still be backed by reasons if everyone does in fact *have* a desire of the right sort.

If that seems an implausible suggestion to pursue, it may be because we have an overly narrow notion of what the relevant desires would have to look like. We may be assuming that if an agent has a hypothetical reason to perform an act, then they must have a desire either to do that very act itself, or at the very least a desire that would be fairly directly satisfied by performing the act in question. But while some hypothetical reasons are like this (drinking water, for example, more or less directly quenches your thirst), others are not: if you want to get into medical school, for example, then you really do have a reason to take organic chemistry, even though the connection between taking organic chemistry and getting into medical school is long, indirect, and not guaranteed to succeed in every case.

Suppose, then, that there were a connection between morality and the various desires that people really do have, such that conforming to morality made it more likely overall that those desires would be satisfied. This connection too could be long and indirect, and it might not be guaranteed to succeed in every instance, but so long as there was a broad, general connection between morality and satisfying your desires, it might well turn out that everyone really does have a reason to obey morality after all.

Is any view like this at all plausible? There certainly have been moral realists who thought so. For example, there are contractarians who emphasize the fact that all of us are vulnerable to being harmed by others and are extremely limited in our abilities to accomplish our various goals on our own. Pretty much regardless of what it is that you want, you are almost certain to be unable to get those things without the regular and ongoing cooperation of others. (If you want to play the piano, for example, you need others to build pianos, sell them to you, tune them, compose music, teach you how to play, and so on; and you need everyone else to refrain from stealing the piano, setting it on fire, or otherwise damaging it.) Without morality in place, virtually nothing that any of us want can be attained. (You wouldn't even be able to take a peaceful nap, for example, for fear that someone might kill you or steal your food.) These contractarians suggest that we think of the requirements of morality as constituted by the terms of an overall social agreement, under which each of us agrees to abide by morality in exchange for the similar agreement of others. This leaves all of us ahead, on the whole, and so provides all of us with a reason to conform to morality, even the hit man. (The hit man may not *realize* that there is a reason for him to obey morality, but it is there, nonetheless.) And the reason in question is a *hypothetical* reason, since it is a reason whose very existence is conditional on the fact that each of us does indeed want a host of things, large and small, that we could not achieve without the moral cooperation of others.

I will not here try to lay out this view in any greater detail than this. To investigate suggestions like this, or others that might similarly attempt to base morality on a system of hypothetical reasons, would be to engage in the detailed work of normative ethics, where these and various rival theories of the foundations of morality are discussed, refined, and evaluated, and that lies well beyond the scope of our discussion. But I mention this sort of view to make it clear that the possibility of defending morality, even if the only reasons are hypothetical ones, is not one that should be dismissed out of hand. So even if the skeptic is right, and categorical reasons simply do not exist, it might still turn out that moral requirements can be provided with the kind of normative backing that reasons internalism demands.

At the same time, it must also be admitted that many moral realists think that approaches like these are unlikely to be adequate in the end. Like the skeptic, many realists will agree that if moral requirements are really going to have the requisite normative backing—where *everyone* has a genuine reason to act on their obligations, regardless of whatever else is true about what they do or don't desire—then the only way to provide this backing is if there are categorical reasons to obey morality. And for many realists, in any event, nothing short of an appeal to categorical reasons will seem fully satisfactory as a *defense* of morality. After all, if I have an obligation to keep the promise I have made to you, it does seem as though the reason I have to do this has nothing to do with my having this or that desire. It seems, rather, like it is a reason I would have regardless of *what* I happen to desire, or whether indeed I have any desires at all! Similarly for the obligation to refrain from hurting others, or the obligation to tell the truth, or the obligation to help the needy, and so on.

In short, many moral realists will agree with the skeptic that we will have an adequate account of moral requirements only if such requirements can indeed be backed by categorical reasons rather than merely hypothetical ones. So such realists, at any rate, will want instead to press the question, why should we agree with the skeptic that there is something dubious and unacceptable about the very idea of a categorical reason?

11.5 Rational Support

Moral skeptics are not alone in finding categorical reasons troubling. Although almost everyone takes the idea of a *hypothetical* reason to be straightforward and clear, many people think that the idea of a categorical reason is, in contrast, problematic and implausible. It isn't, of course, that people have trouble understanding (in broad strokes) what it would take for something to *be* a categorical reason; rather, they cannot see how such a thing could possibly exist.

But what, exactly, is the problem with categorical reasons supposed to be? One common source of worry, I think, is this. The existence of a categorical reason (if there were such a thing) would be a *normative* fact of a particular kind. It would be the fact that there was rational support for performing a given act (or for having a certain belief, and so on), independently of whatever desires the agent happened to have. But what kind of fact could possibly be like *that*? It is, of course, easy enough to *say* that there is a categorical reason to do something, but what kind of property could categorical normative support possibly be? Categorical normative support doesn't seem like any other, more familiar, property. As the point is sometimes expressed, it seems "spooky" or "weird" or "queer"—something altogether too strange to admit into our metaphysics. Perhaps this metaphysical misgiving should lead us to reject the very possibility of categorical reasons altogether.

As I say, worries about categorical reasons along these general lines are common enough. But it is less than clear what exactly is supposed to be troubling here. Perhaps the issue is this. To make sense of the idea of a categorical reason, we have to be able to make sense of the underlying idea of rational support, of it being the case that something speaks in *favor* of acting in a given way. And this idea, the idea of it being "appropriate" or "justified" to act in a given way can seem troubling and opaque. To say that there is a categorical reason to perform an act is to say that there is an "ought-to-be-doneness" about the act, and the very idea of a property like *that* can seem perplexing. Perhaps then the thought is that we do well to rid ourselves of the belief in the existence of properties anything like this, and with it rid ourselves of the very idea of a categorical reason.

But if this is indeed the source of skepticism about categorical reasons, then it is essential to notice that *this* idea—the idea of rational support or justification—is one that is common to both categorical *and* hypothetical reasons! After all, even those who believe only in hypothetical reasons appeal

11.5 RATIONAL SUPPORT

to the notion of rational support. They simply disagree with those who also believe in categorical reasons over what it takes for an act to *have* that kind of support. Those who believe only in the existence of hypothetical reasons think that an act cannot have rational support unless it helps satisfy one of the agent's desires. Those who believe in categorical reasons think that *other* things besides this can help make it true that an act has rational support. This is, of course, an important debate, but right now the point is that the idea of rational support figures in the concept of a hypothetical reason every bit as much as it does in the concept of a categorical one. For hypothetical reasons are still reasons—and the very idea of a reason is that of something which speaks in favor of, or rationally supports or justifies, acting (or believing, and so on) one way rather than another. So we cannot dismiss the idea of rational support—as somehow "spooky" or "weird"—without simultaneously threatening the possibility of hypothetical reasons too, and not only categorical ones.

Sometimes friends of hypothetical reasons deny this. They say that to posit the existence of a hypothetical reason is to do nothing more than to note that a certain kind of means-end relationship holds between a given act and a given desire. For example, they might claim, to say that there is a hypothetical reason to move your hand from a flame is to say nothing more than that doing so will serve as a means of achieving your end of making the pain stop. And since such means-end claims are simple empirical claims, there are no "spooky" or "weird" properties being brought in at all. The existence of the hypothetical reason simply consists in the metaphysically untroubling empirical fact that such and such an act will help to satisfy such and such a desire. Nothing more.

But to say this is to misunderstand what it is to assert that there is a hypothetical reason. If we say that there is a *reason* to move your hand (so as to make the pain stop) we are not merely pointing out that a certain act stands in a certain means-end relationship to your goal. Rather, we are saying that *because* of all of this—because you have this goal (making the pain stop) and because this relation holds between moving your hand and this goal— there is *rational support* for moving your hand. The means-end relationship explains *why* the act is supported, but we are doing more than merely noting the *existence* of that relationship: we are saying that it is (normally) rationally *appropriate* to take the means to one's ends: other things being equal, such acts *ought to be done*! In short, when we assert the existence of a hypothetical reason we are not *avoiding* appeal to the idea of rational support. Rather, we are simply helping ourselves to the thought that (other things being equal, and putting aside details that needn't concern us here) acts that are means to satisfying one's desires are rationally *supported*. So, initial appearances to the contrary notwithstanding, even hypothetical reasons involve the notion of rational support.

Thus categorical reasons are not at all unique in involving the supposedly "spooky" property of rational support; hypothetical reasons do this as well. So we cannot appeal to the purportedly metaphysically troubling nature of this property as grounds for dismissing categorical reasons. To do this would be to simultaneously provide grounds for dismissing hypothetical reasons along with the categorical ones!

Admittedly, some philosophers do indeed conclude that we should dismiss the very idea of hypothetical reasons along with that of categorical reasons. What is truly troubling, they insist, isn't the idea of a categorical reason per se, but the entire notion of rational support of any sort. *All* such talk should be abandoned.

We have, of course, seen this view before: it is *normative nihilism* (3.4). Those who accept this sweeping form of nihilism reject not only moral facts, but *all* normative facts whatsoever, across the board. And precisely for this reason, this view is virtually impossible to take seriously. For if normative nihilism were true, it would follow that there is no reason to do anything at all! There would be no reason to take one's hand from the flame, even though moving it would stop the pain. There would be no reason to eat, even though you realized full well that eating is the only way to keep yourself alive. There would be no reason to get out of the way of the oncoming car, even though you didn't want to die. There would be no reason to do *anything*.

Indeed, if normative nihilism were true, there would be no reason to *believe* anything either! For if there are no reasons, there are no reasons to believe one thing rather than another. (Reasons to believe, after all, are just another case of something being rationally supported—in this instance, some particular belief or set of beliefs.) There is no reason to believe that $1 + 1 = 2$. No reason to believe that the sun will rise tomorrow. No reason to believe that you are reading this book. I could go on, but I trust it is apparent just how implausible a view like this really is.

(Well, maybe just a bit more. Note, in particular, that if normative nihilism is true, there is no reason to believe the various arguments that might be put forward on its behalf! There is no reason to believe that these arguments are any better than any other arguments, or that there even *is* such a thing as an argument for normative nihilism. There is no reason to believe anyone actually *endorses* normative nihilism. And so forth and so on.)

As with the other highly general forms of skepticism that we have encountered previously, I will not try to argue further here against normative nihilism. As always, my goal is not to provide replies to these sweeping forms of skepticism, but only to defend the more modest thought that belief in morality is intellectually respectable, in no worse shape than countless other beliefs we are not prepared to dismiss. I assume that, like me, you believe that there is reason to get out of the way of oncoming cars (at least, given that you don't want to die). I assume you believe there is reason to move your hand from a hot stove, and reason to study for your exams (assuming you want to pass the class), and so on. In short, I assume you believe in hypothetical reasons. But this means that you believe in—and are rightly unwilling to abandon—the idea of rational support. And that being the case, you cannot dismiss the idea of categorical reasons either, at least, not on the mere ground that it too involves the idea of rational support.

Better, I think, is to say this: the idea of rational support—the idea of something constituting a reason—is a perfectly acceptable one. Instead of being persuaded by the skeptic's assertion that the idea is spooky or weird, unfamiliar or strange, we should simply remind ourselves of the fact that the notion of rational support—the notion of something being a reason—is in fact an utterly familiar one to all of us, one we make use of constantly, in every aspect of our lives. The property of providing rational support may well be different from various other properties, but what of it? Being different is not at all the same thing as being suspect in some way. To take a simple example, we would never dismiss the property of being a prime number, say, on the mere ground that this property is rather unlike most others. Similarly, then, there is no reason to dismiss the property of providing rational support, simply because this too differs in various ways from still other properties. (Similarly, of course, for the property of being rationally *supported*.)

But once we recognize that the idea of rational support is one we have no reason to abandon, we no longer have a convincing reason to dismiss out of hand the idea of a categorical reason. Just as hypothetical reasons are simply facts that provide rational support for acts (or beliefs, and so on) by virtue of one's having some relevant desire, categorical reasons—if such there be—will also be nothing more than facts that similarly provide rational support for acts (or beliefs, and so on). It's just that *categorical* reasons—unlike hypothetical ones—will be facts which provide their rational support *independently* of the particular desires that the agent happens to have.

Of course, to say all this is not at all to say that there is anything inappropriate about asking, what exactly *is* this property of rational support? Can we be reductionists about reasons, or have we here reached bedrock? Should we perhaps be simple realists when it comes to reasons, or can we offer another account? These are all questions to which we can still turn. But for now the important point is simply this. If the skeptic hopes to convince us that there is something unacceptable about the idea of a categorical reason, they'll need another argument.

11.6 Categorical Reasons and Motivation

Talk of categorical reasons shares with talk of hypothetical reasons the idea that certain acts are rationally supported by virtue of the existence of relevant underlying facts. The two types of reasons simply differ in terms of what those underlying facts must be like, what the ground or basis of that support can be. One way, presumably, that there can come to be rational support for performing an action is if it will promote (directly or indirectly) one or more of the agent's desires. But why think that this is the only way? Those who believe in categorical reasons do nothing more than add the thought that there are, in addition to this first way, still other ways that reasons can come into being, other things that might speak in favor of performing an act besides its helping to satisfy one's own desires. That certainly seems to be an intelligible claim, if nothing more. Why then think that it cannot be true? Why should we think that the *only* possible ground for a reason for action is that the act in question will satisfy one or more of the agent's desires?

The only promising argument, as far as I can see, turns on the idea that reasons can motivate. More particularly, if you realize that you have a reason to do something, then that very fact—in and of itself—can move you to perform the act in question. Of course, if you think this reason is outweighed, you may not be moved to act on that reason after all. But if you think that the balance of reasons *favors* some action, this thought does seem capable, at least in principle, of moving you (at least somewhat).

This view—that our beliefs about reasons can motivate—is of course similar to a claim we have previously discussed concerning the motivational powers of our *moral* beliefs (see, in particular, 10.1 and 10.3). We called that earlier view motive internalism, though in light of the introduction of this new view it might be better to rename that earlier view motive internalism about *morality*, so as to distinguish it from the new view, which we might then dub motive internalism about *reasons*. Both views ascribe motivating power to a particular class of beliefs, but where motive internalism about morality ascribes this power to our moral beliefs, motive internalism about reasons ascribes it, rather, to our beliefs about reasons.

(To be sure, on some views moral beliefs just *are* beliefs about a particular class of reasons—moral reasons, perhaps of a decisive sort. If that's right, then the two versions of internalism will be connected. But even if that's so, logically speaking it remains important to distinguish them. It is also, of course, important not to confuse motive internalism about reasons with the view we are calling *reasons internalism*. Reasons internalism is the claim that moral requirements are backed by reasons; motive internalism about reasons, in contrast, is the logically distinct claim that our beliefs about reasons can *motivate*.)

Suppose we combine this idea—that beliefs about reasons can motivate—with the bolder, more demanding version of the Humean theory of motivation (introduced in 10.4). According to that theory, recall, motivation requires that there be desires among the initial ingredients as well as beliefs. It seems to follow, then, that categorical reasons would be problematic in a way that hypothetical reasons are not. After all, if it really is true that the realization that you have a reason (or reasons) to do something can suffice to motivate you (which is what motive internalism about reasons asserts), and it really is true that motivation requires starting with both beliefs and desires (which is what bold Humeanism holds), then you can have a reason to do something only if you start out with an appropriate *desire*.

Obviously, the skeptic may claim, that's not a problem when it comes to positing the existence of *hypothetical* reasons—for such reasons exist precisely when you have a desire of a relevant kind. When there is a hypothetical reason to perform some act, your performing that act will help to satisfy one or more of your desires. So if you *realize* you have a hypothetical reason, you will correctly believe that performing the act in question will be connected in the relevant way to the satisfaction of your desires. Thus the two ingredients required for motivation according to the Humean theory will both be in place: you will have both a belief and a desire (connected in the right way). And so, it might be suggested, there is nothing particularly mysterious about how hypothetical reasons can have the motivating power which is ascribed to them by motive internalism about reasons.

In contrast, the argument continues, categorical reasons could not possibly have the motivating power in question. For the very idea of a categorical reason is of a reason that would exist regardless of what desires the agent happened to have. So if beliefs about such reasons really could motivate, then it would have to be the case that motivation was possible even in the absence of any corresponding initial desires. And that is precisely what the (bold) Humean theory of motivation rules out. According to Humeanism, after all, motivation requires desires and not only beliefs. Since categorical reasons would not require the existence of desires (on the part of the agent), mere beliefs about such reasons could not suffice for motivation, contrary to the claims of motive internalism about reasons. Thus categorical reasons simply cannot exist. When combined with the Humean theory of motivation, motive internalism about reasons entails that categorical reasons are impossible.

I imagine that at least some of those who are skeptical about the very possibility of categorical reasons can trace their skepticism to something like this line of argument. Nonetheless, moral realists have a number of different replies available to them. Unsurprisingly, these replies are similar to those already canvassed in the previous chapter (in 10.3–10.5), where we examined the strikingly similar argument against moral *beliefs*, since that too was grounded, as here, in a joint assertion of motive internalism and Humeanism. Since the possible replies are similar, we can be briefer here in rehearsing them.

First of all, then, it is conceivable that some moral realists will want to resist the argument by denying motive internalism about reasons. Perhaps beliefs about reasons cannot actually motivate after all—in the *absence* of an appropriate desire. To be sure, *hypothetical* reasons can normally motivate (since they presuppose the existence of a relevant desire). But perhaps for *categorical* reasons, precisely because the existence of such reasons does not presuppose any desires on the part of the agent, our beliefs about these reasons *cannot* motivate, unless we happen to have some further desires of the appropriate sort. Perhaps motive internalism about reasons is nothing more than an overly hasty generalization from the particular case of hypothetical reasons. In short, perhaps categorical reasons are perfectly genuine reasons, but our beliefs about them simply cannot suffice for motivation.

Although this certainly seems to be a logically coherent position, I suspect that few realists will find it an attractive one. For suppose we try to imagine an individual who acknowledges that he has a categorical reason to perform an act, who nonetheless remains completely unmoved by that thought. Consider our imaginary hit man, once again, on his way to kill his victim, only this time picture him agreeing that he has a categorical reason not to kill, a reason not outweighed by other, potentially competing reasons, and yet insisting all the while that this thought simply doesn't move him in any way. He acknowledges that the balance of reasons favors refraining from killing his intended victim, and yet he feels no motivation at all to act in keeping with the balance of reasons. Is such a person indeed possible? I don't think it at all obvious that he is.

As usual, we have to be sure to assume that the hit man is sincere. He isn't speaking in scare quotes, merely reporting the fact that "most people" think there is a categorical reason not to kill (though he himself doesn't actually believe this). Similarly, it isn't that the hit man has only a "partial" or "incomplete" understanding of the concept of a categorical reason. On the contrary, he fully understands what it is to have an undefeated reason to behave in a certain way, he knows how to engage in practical reasoning, he sincerely acknowledges the fact that he *has* such a reason in this case, and yet, for all that, this belief does nothing whatsoever to pull him toward acting in the relevant way.

Speaking personally, I am far from confident that such a person can really exist. I am drawn to the thought that anyone who truly understands the *concept* of a reason—the idea that when one has a reason to do something then there is something that *speaks in favor* of doing the given act—will be at least somewhat moved when he has the belief that he *has* such a reason (at least, given the supposition that the reason in question isn't outweighed by still other reasons). So if the hit man genuinely believes he has a (categorical and undefeated) reason to refrain from killing, this thought will move him at least somewhat. And I imagine that most realists will agree with me: if there really *are* categorical reasons, then they too will necessarily have the power to motivate (or rather, our beliefs about them will have this power).

Suppose then that the realist does indeed embrace motive internalism for *all* reasons, including categorical reasons. How else can they resist the skeptic's argument that categorical reasons are impossible?

One way, of course—and this is the second possible reply to the skeptic—would be to reject the other main premise of that argument, the (bold) Humean theory of motivation. The argument assumes that motivation requires that desires be among the initial ingredients of motivation, that beliefs alone cannot suffice to motivate. But perhaps the Humean theory should simply be rejected as itself being the result of an overly hasty instance of generalizing. While it may well be true that many beliefs cannot motivate on their own (in the absence of a desire), it could still be true that there are *exceptions* to this generalization, and certain beliefs *can* motivate, even if there is no relevant desire present at the start. And once we allow for this possibility, once we allow for the possibility that certain beliefs can suffice to motivate (perhaps by generating derivative desires along the way) then it seems likely that *normative* beliefs—including our beliefs about what there is reason to do—will be like this. If any mere beliefs can motivate on their own, then it certainly seems plausible to hold that the belief that I have *reason* to act one way rather than another will be among the beliefs with the motivating power in question. Thus the realist can defend the possibility of categorical reasons, even while embracing motive internalism for *all* reasons, so long as they insist that the Humean theory is mistaken and that certain beliefs—in particular, normative beliefs—can suffice for motivation.

It is, of course, easy to imagine someone *insisting* that normative beliefs per se can motivate only if we also assume that the agent has a background *desire* to be rational, a desire to act on reasons. Absent such a desire, they claim, there can be no motivation. But the realist needn't be impressed by this dogma. Why not similarly (and equally implausibly) insist that a mere desire to be rational cannot suffice for motivation either? Why not also require a desire to *act* on that desire? Or a desire to act on that desire to act on that desire—or a desire to act on that desire to act on that desire to act on that desire, and so on, forever! If the Humean can plausibly reply that a mere first-order desire suffices for motivation (when combined with relevant background beliefs), even without the positing of further desires, why can't the realist say the same thing about normative beliefs? Perhaps they too suffice for motivation (when combined with relevant background beliefs). Perhaps in such cases we can have motivation without positing any desire at all.

Alternatively, some realists may prefer to retain the Humean theory of motivation and agree that beliefs cannot motivate in the absence of desires. But here too the skeptic's argument can be resisted (even while accepting motive internalism about reasons), by challenging the argument's easily overlooked assumption that nothing can be both a belief *and* a desire. Arguably—and this is a third possible reply—some mental states are both; and in particular perhaps our normative beliefs—including our beliefs about reasons—are both fully beliefs and fully desires. If this is a possibility (see 10.5) then the realist can affirm that the conditions laid down by the Humean theory of motivation are met after all, even when it comes to categorical reasons: beliefs about such reasons can motivate by virtue of the fact that when you believe there is a categorical reason to do something, that very belief is, at the same time, a *desire* as well. So even if we accept the Humean theory, and motivation requires both beliefs *and* desires, beliefs about categorical reasons can suffice for motivation.

(Should one worry that if beliefs about reasons are also desires, this would show that all reasons are actually hypothetical ones after all, since they would necessarily involve desires on the part of the agent? Not at all: for even if our *beliefs* about a given reason necessarily involve desires, that doesn't mean that *the reason in question* only exists by virtue of our having that desire. The reason *itself* can still be a categorical one—something whose existence doesn't depend on the particular desires of the agent—even if our *belief* in that reason necessarily involves desire.)

Thus there are at least three possible replies to the skeptic's argument for the impossibility of categorical reasons. And while I am not myself attracted to the first of these, both the second and the third remain available to realists who share my skepticism about the first. In any event, any of the three should make it possible for the realist to retain their commitment to categorical reasons.

One final point. Earlier the skeptic claimed that there is nothing puzzling about how our beliefs concerning hypothetical reasons could motivate, given that hypothetical reasons presuppose the existence of appropriate desires. A problem arises, the skeptic claimed, only if we posit categorical reasons as well. But this claim about hypothetical reasons should not, in fact, be so readily granted. Imagine a case where you mistakenly believe that you *want* something, and then come to correctly believe that doing some particular act will help bring that thing about. In such a case you might well (mistakenly) believe you have a hypothetical reason to perform the relevant act, and it certainly seems as though you could be *motivated* by that belief to act accordingly. But if Humeanism is correct, what could possibly explain the power of that belief to motivate you? By hypothesis, you don't actually have the desire in question; so if motivation requires not only beliefs but desires as well, how can your mistaken belief motivate you?

Presumably the skeptic does not want to conclude that *hypothetical* reasons are impossible as well! But then just what is it that they should say here? One possibility, of course, would be to insist that one simply cannot be mistaken about one's desires, so cases like this just cannot arise. But positing such infallible insight into our own desires seems highly implausible. Alternatively, the skeptic might decide to *reject* the thought that motive internalism about reasons holds across the board. Perhaps you cannot actually be motivated by this kind of mistaken belief about hypothetical reasons. But that claim seems implausible on the face of it as well. And at any rate, if there really *can* be beliefs about hypothetical reasons that cannot motivate, why can't the same be true for beliefs about *categorical* reasons as well—even when they are true—in which case the skeptic's entire argument against categorical reasons will collapse at the outset.

Suppose, then, that the skeptic concedes that such mistaken beliefs about hypothetical reasons really can arise, and that they really can suffice for motivation. But then it seems as though the skeptic must concede as well that either Humeanism is wrong, and normative beliefs can suffice for motivating, even in the absence of any initial desire, or else that normative beliefs can be desires as well as beliefs, in which case Humeanism might be right, but normative beliefs will still be capable of motivating on their own. Either way, in the course of giving one or the other of these two answers the case for skepticism about *categorical* reasons will be undermined as well.

The bottom line is this. Although some may be led to skepticism about categorical reasons as a result of reflecting on the motivating powers of our normative beliefs, such reflections do not actually provide us with a compelling reason to deny the possibility of such reasons after all.

Of course, that doesn't yet show that there *are* any categorical reasons. But arguing that, and in particular arguing that there are categorical reasons to obey morality, is a subject for the substantive debates that fall within normative ethics. Some theories of normative ethics do take up this challenge (though not all of them, of course, as some view ethics in terms of hypothetical reasons, rather than categorical ones), but it would take us too far afield to lay out these theories and assess them here. Our aim was only the more limited one of showing that even if the moral realist does indeed think of moral requirements as backed by categorical reasons, in and of itself that does not give us reason to embrace moral skepticism. We can reasonably disagree about what particular categorical reasons exist (or whether indeed there are any at all). But we have no reason to dismiss the very idea of categorical reasons out of hand.

What's more, the simple fact of the matter is that many of us do have intuitions that there are indeed categorical reasons to obey this or that moral requirement. For example, we have the intuition that there is reason not to kill innocents (extraordinary circumstances aside) no matter what desires you happen to have, or that there is reason to keep your promises (special circumstances aside) no matter what your desires may be, and so on. And although such intuitions provide only defeasible evidence for the existence of such reasons, they are indeed *evidence*. In the absence of some compelling reason to dismiss these intuitions as being illusory we are justified in believing them.

Admittedly, if we found that we could not adequately combine these various intuitions into a coherent overall account of morality, that would be troubling. But it is precisely the task of normative ethics to determine to what extent this can be done, and that lies beyond the scope of the present discussion. For present purposes it suffices to have argued that there is no good reason for general skepticism about the very *idea* of categorical reasons. And so the skeptic's attempt to reject moral facts on the ground that they would need to be backed by something that simply cannot exist—categorical reasons—remains, I think, an unsuccessful one.

12

Reductionism

12.1 The Appeal of Reductionism

By this point we have considered a number of different arguments for moral skepticism. I have argued that none of them are successful. But we have yet to consider what may well be the most common source of skepticism about morality, the thought that if there really were moral facts there would have to be something deeply mysterious about them, metaphysically speaking. After all, what kind of a fact could a moral fact possibly be? To take the existence of moral facts seriously seems to require positing the existence of something inexplicably strange and different from all other facts with which we are familiar. We are all, of course, perfectly comfortable positing the existence of *empirical* facts, and some are even prepared to posit the existence of supernatural (or theological) facts as well. But what in the world (or out of it!) could a *moral* fact be? How could such a thing so much as exist?

So this points the way to yet another skeptical argument, perhaps the most common one of them all. It holds, simply, that no satisfactory account of the metaphysics of moral facts can be provided. And if that's right, obviously, we have compelling reason to reject moral realism.

Of course, as I have previously noted (in 2.3), if we are puzzled by the metaphysics of moral facts the odds are that what we are truly puzzled about is the metaphysics of moral *properties*. The moral fact (supposing that it is a fact) that killing innocents is wrong seems to amount to the fact (supposing that it too is a fact) that a certain type of action (the killing of innocents) has a certain moral property—the property of being *wrong*. So if we had an adequate account of the nature of that property, wrongness, it would eliminate the air of metaphysical mystery surrounding the moral fact in question. Similarly, the moral fact (supposing it to be a fact) that inequality is bad seems to amount to the fact (if it really is one) that certain states of affairs (those with inequality) have a different moral property—the property of having an aspect that is intrinsically bad. So if we had an adequate account of that second property, badness, that too would eliminate any residual metaphysical mystery concerning what that moral fact in question could consist in.

Accordingly, in examining worries about the metaphysics of moral facts we can focus on questions about the nature of moral properties, properties that an act might have (if moral realism is true) in being required, permissible, or forbidden, or that an object or state of affairs might have in being good, or bad, and so on. Clear up the metaphysical mysteries surrounding the nature of moral properties—if we can—and we are likely to have cleared up whatever metaphysical qualms we may initially have had about moral facts as well.

But while this point seems correct, it doesn't actually to take us very far. For moral properties do indeed strike many of us as troubling and mysterious.

Suppose, for example, that we are naturalists, and we believe that the only objects that exist are empirical objects and the only properties that exist are natural ones. If, as it seems, moral realism requires the existence of *moral* properties, how could we possibly find a place for such properties in a scientific worldview? After all, basic moral properties—like being good, or right—simply don't seem to be empirical ones. How then can they be metaphysically acceptable? Doesn't a scientific worldview require us to embrace moral skepticism?

For that matter, even if we reject naturalism, and allow for the possibility of a God (or gods) standing outside the natural order, how exactly does that help? A worldview like this may allow for the existence of various *theological* properties (like the property of being loved by God), but how, exactly, would *moral* properties fit into such a picture?

It is because of worries like this that many moral realists are attracted to the idea of moral reductionism, the view that *moral* facts reduce to facts of a more basic, *nonmoral* sort. Given our focus on moral properties, this becomes in turn the claim that moral properties boil down to, or can be reduced to, some suitable set of more basic or fundamental properties, where these more fundamental properties are not, in themselves, moral ones.

The crucial thought here, of course, is that if the various underlying properties to which the moral properties are reduced are themselves familiar, or at least metaphysically unobjectionable ones, then the metaphysical mystery surrounding moral properties (and thus, moral facts), will have been eliminated. If there is "nothing more" to the presence of a given moral property than the presence of the relevant complex of underlying properties, and if those underlying properties are not themselves metaphysically troubling, then the moral property in question won't be metaphysically troubling either.

Note that the proposed reduction might be a fairly complicated one. Some contractarians, for example, have suggested that moral permissibility reduces to the property of being an action that conforms to the rules that would be agreed upon by a suitable set of rational bargainers, bargainers who are ignorant of their actual place in society but eager to settle upon rules that would be mutually beneficial. That's hardly a *simple* reduction, and it may or may not be a correct one, but the relevant point right now is that there is nothing metaphysically mysterious about any of the elements that show up in the proposed reduction. If this really *were* an adequate account of what permissibility consists in, then the skeptic's *metaphysical* worries would be laid to rest.

To be sure, whether you find any particular proposed reduction metaphysically reassuring or not will depend on the nature of the more fundamental properties incorporated into the proposed reduction, and whether you are prepared to embrace properties like *that*. Still, putting aside concerns about the *plausibility* of the contractarian account that I just described, I assume that no one is *metaphysically* troubled by talk of what rational bargainers would agree to, or what it would be to be ignorant about one's place in society, or what it is for an agreement to be mutually beneficial, and so on. On the other hand, if it were proposed, instead, that permissibility is a matter of an action's conforming to God's will, then although theists might find such an account metaphysically acceptable, atheists (and more generally, all those who deny any sort of supernatural realm) will not.

Unsurprisingly, then, even those moral realists who are reductionists differ among themselves with regard to which sorts of candidate reductions would be metaphysically acceptable. For those with naturalist leanings in metaphysics quite generally—so that the only genuine properties are natural ones—the only forms of moral reductionism worth considering will, of course, be naturalist reductions (reductions where all the relevant properties are themselves natural properties). In contrast, those realists willing to entertain a wider set of properties, including perhaps theological ones, have a correspondingly wider array of reductionist proposals that they can entertain (though it is perhaps worth noting that even a theist could, in principle, accept a naturalist reduction of morality).

So people will disagree with one another about which particular reductionist proposals are metaphysically reassuring. But none of this should keep us from appreciating the appeal of moral reductionism in itself. If a candidate reduction is offered that you find otherwise plausible, and the relevant underlying properties are ones you find metaphysically acceptable, then you will be in a position to answer the skeptic's worries about the metaphysics of moral facts. Moral facts will reduce to still more basic facts, facts which are not themselves particularly metaphysically troubling. And this will mean, in turn, that positing moral facts will not actually raise any special metaphysical difficulties.

It is not surprising, then, that many moral realists have embraced one or another version of reductionism. What we still need to ask ourselves, however, is whether any such reductionist programs have a serious chance of succeeding.

In answering this question, we should begin by recognizing that insofar as the moral realist is drawn to reductionism as a way of answering the skeptic's metaphysical challenge, it is essential that the reduction leave us with no irreducible moral properties at all. For if all that has happened is that certain moral properties are reduced to other properties, but that the process of reduction comes to a halt with a list of basic moral properties that cannot be reduced further, that won't really suffice to vindicate the realist. If there are any moral properties at all that cannot be reduced in turn to nonmoral ones, then the worry that moral facts are somehow metaphysically dubious will not have been put to rest, only temporarily put off. Realists will still need to face the skeptic's charge that these basic moral properties—those that cannot be reduced further—remain metaphysically unacceptable.

It is because of this concern that for our purposes the truly interesting forms of reductionism are those that are "fully" reductionist, reducing *all* moral properties to nonmoral ones—eliminating any appeal at all to moral properties that cannot be reduced further. That is the form of reductionism that we will be considering in this chapter, and so talk of "reductionism" or "reductionists" will be limited to referring to those positions that involve, or those people who embrace, this kind of complete reductionist program.

For similar reasons, however, we should probably also limit our examination of reductionist theories even further, to those that avoid positing irreducible normative properties of *any* sort at all (a point noted in 2.3). Suppose, for example, that all moral facts could indeed be reduced to nonmoral ones, but that among the nonmoral facts that could not be reduced further there were facts about the existence of *reasons*. Imagine, in particular, that the property of being *supported by a reason* was one that could not be reduced further, or at least, could not be reduced all the way to properties none of which were normative ones. Or imagine that the property of *providing rational support* (for an action, say, or a belief) could not be fully reduced to any set of exclusively nonnormative properties. Where would that leave us?

It seems likely that anyone troubled by the metaphysical status of irreducible *moral* properties is going to remain troubled if this is indeed the best that we can do—that is, if we still find ourselves positing some irreducible *normative* properties. So for present purposes the most important forms of reductionism are those that are more ambitious still, proposing reductions for all normative properties whatsoever, and not only the moral ones. Accordingly, when talking about "reductionist" theories, we can limit our attention to theories that are reductionist in this more ambitious way.

Suppose for the moment that such thoroughgoing reductionist approaches to morality (and normativity, more generally) can somehow be shown to be unsuccessful. Would that force us to abandon moral realism? Not necessarily. In principle, at least, there remains the possibility of being a *simple realist*, someone who unabashedly accepts the existence of irreducible moral (or normative) properties. Perhaps—such realists say—we should never have been troubled by the positing of such properties in the first place.

A view like this will no doubt strike many as unappealing. But it deserves to be examined carefully (something we will do in the next chapter). Perhaps irreducible normative properties will turn out to be less metaphysically worrisome than they might initially appear.

Still, even if not all moral realists are reductionists, many are. And it certainly seems as though a reductionist account of morality would suffice to answer the skeptic's metaphysical worries. It shouldn't surprise us, then, that many moral *skeptics* have argued that such reductionist programs are guaranteed to fail. Examining that claim will be our concern in the rest of this chapter.

But it is worth noting explicitly—what may be less obvious, although already implicit in these last few remarks—that skepticism about *reductionism* isn't at all limited to those who are skeptical about the existence of objective morality altogether. After all, simple realists are precisely those realists who have concluded that it is impossible to completely reduce morality to the nonmoral (or the nonnormative). That's why they assert the existence of irreducible moral or normative properties—so as to retain the possibility of moral realism in the face of what they take to be the failure of reductionism. Accordingly, simple realists have often joined with moral skeptics in denying the possibility of a successful reductionist approach. *Antireductionists* can be either moral skeptics or simple realists.

12.2 The Nature of Reduction

The general concept of reduction is, I assume, a familiar one. For often enough we find ourselves thinking that one sort of fact (or one sort of property) reduces to a set of underlying facts (or properties) that are, in an important way, more basic or fundamental. In such cases we may say, for example, that the facts of the first sort "just consist in" facts of the second sort, that there is "nothing more" to there being a fact of the first kind than whatever is involved in there being a fact (or set of facts) of the second kind, that facts of the first kind "boil down to" facts of the second kind, and so on and so forth for other, similar, locutions. Similarly, of course, we may say that one kind of *property* reduces to a more basic kind of property (or set of properties), when having the first type of property simply "consists in" having the second, or when there is "nothing more" to having the first property than having the second, and so on.

For example, most of us agree that in some important sense chemistry reduces to physics. Modern science seems to have shown us that chemical facts ultimately consist in facts about physics and nothing more. There is nothing more to chemical reactions than physical reactions, nothing more to the chemical properties of atoms and molecules than the underlying physical properties, and so on. For that matter, modern science also seems to have shown us that biological facts ultimately reduce to facts about chemistry (and so, in turn, can be reduced, even further, to facts about physics). In broad strokes, at least, we are familiar with the idea that entire scientific disciplines may ultimately reduce to more fundamental, underlying ones.

That's not to say, of course, that the concept of reduction is a simple one, easy to analyze. On the contrary, as with many interesting concepts, getting clear about the *precise* nature of reduction—what *exactly* is involved when one thing reduces to another—is a difficult undertaking. There are important and difficult debates in metaphysics and the philosophy of science about how best to understand the nature of reduction. Happily, however, I think we can largely avoid entering into these debates. I imagine that anyone reading this book has at least a rough and ready handle on the concept of reduction, one that should be adequate for our purposes.

After all, I presume that you would certainly understand me (and would also agree with me) if I suggested that the property of being a mother simply consists in the property of being a female parent. That's just what it *is* to be mother—to be a female parent. The one property (motherhood) reduces to a set of properties that are arguably more basic or fundamental (the properties of being a female and of being a parent).

Here's a second example, equally familiar. Water is H_2O. There is *nothing more* to being water than being H_2O. That's what being water *consists* in. The one property (being water) *reduces to* a complex of more basic physical properties (being composed of hydrogen and oxygen atoms in the right ratio, where the hydrogen and oxygen atoms have combined in the right structure). There is nothing more to the property of being water than that.

What do we mean by calling the one set of properties (the ones to which the others are reduced) more *basic* or fundamental? This is, perhaps unsurprisingly, one of the philosophical controversies I alluded to above. Spelling out the idea precisely is not a simple matter. But intuitively, at least (and this should suffice for our purposes), the thought is that when one property is reduced to another (or to a set of such properties), the more basic ones deserve that title by virtue of the fact that they are the grounds or the basis of something having the "reduced" property. Thus, for example, a person is a mother *because* they are both female and a parent. It is by *virtue of the fact* that one is a female parent that it is true to say that one is a mother. (It certainly isn't as though Sally is female, say, *because* she is a mother!) Similarly, the given liquid's being composed of hydrogen and oxygen atoms (in the right combination, and so on) *explains* or is the *basis* of the fact that the liquid is water. The fact that this liquid is water is *grounded* in the fact that it is made up of hydrogen and oxygen atoms combined in the right way. It is water by virtue of the fact that it has the relevant chemical composition (and not the other way around).

But it is important not to be misled when using locutions like this. The mere fact that something has one property by virtue of having a second does not necessarily mean that the first property *reduces* to the second. For example, it seems correct to say of some lustrous gold coin that it is shiny *because* it is gold (or *by virtue of* being gold), or that its being gold *explains* its being shiny, and yet, for all that, we certainly don't think that the property of being shiny *reduces* to, or somehow *just consists in*, the property of being gold. Indeed, even if golden objects were the only shiny things in the entire world, it still wouldn't be plausible to say that the property of being shiny *just is* the property of being gold. There is more to reduction than that.

Still, when we do think that one property reduces to others, it does seem to be correct to say that the former property holds, when it does, by virtue of the other properties—the "reduction base"—holding. That's what makes the latter properties more basic. That's why we say that the first property reduces to the others, rather than the other way around.

And of course if it really is the case that one property reduces to other more fundamental ones, then if there is nothing metaphysically troubling about the more basic properties, there should be nothing metaphysically troubling about the reduced property either. After all, if the reduction is a genuine one, then there is nothing more to having the reduced property than having the more basic ones, and by hypothesis, there is nothing metaphysically troubling about the latter. And that, of course, is why moral realists reasonably believe that if reductionism in ethics can be defended, and moral properties can all be reduced to nonnormative ones, then any metaphysical worries one might have about morality will have been answered.

Although it would take us too far afield to say much more in a general way about the nature of reduction, I do think it will be helpful to distinguish between two importantly different *kinds* of reduction. In some cases, a proposed reduction is *analytic*; it purports to be true by definition. In other cases, however, the reduction is *synthetic*; it is a substantive truth that cannot be established simply on the basis of the meaning of the relevant terms, or the contents of the relevant concepts, alone.

Consider again the two familiar examples of reduction that I mentioned above, the reduction of the property of being a mother and the reduction of the property of being water. Suppose, as certainly seems plausible, that to be a mother just is a matter of being a female parent. If being a mother really can be reduced to being female and being a parent in this way, that surely isn't a substantive *discovery* about the nature of motherhood. On the contrary, this just seems to follow directly from the meaning of the word "mother" or perhaps from the *concept* of motherhood. The claim that there is nothing more to being a mother than being a female parent looks to be what philosophers call an "analytic truth," something whose truth can be worked out a priori, simply through thinking about the logical connections between the relevant concepts.

In contrast, the fact that being water just is a matter of being H_2O is not at all the sort of thing one could discover a priori, through thought alone. It is, rather, what philosophers call a "synthetic truth," a substantive claim about the nature of the world, something that can only be known a posteriori (roughly, only as a result of examining the *world*). Mere knowledge of the relevant concepts could never suffice to establish the truth of this second reduction.

So it looks like reductions can be usefully sorted into two different kinds, those that are true by definition, and those that are not. And while the precise nature of this distinction is itself a philosophically contentious topic, I think it likely that we have a sufficient feel for it that we can make use of it in the discussion that follows.

It is probably worth noting, however, that not everyone believes that both forms of reduction are truly possible (not just with regard to morality—I mean more generally). Some, for example, deny the very possibility of *analytic* reductions, because they deny the existence of any genuine analytic truths. Nothing at all (they may say) can really be true by *definition alone*, true *simply* by virtue of the meanings of words (or the contents of concepts). On the contrary, examples of what seem to be analytic reductions are actually substantive *synthetic* ones, appearances to the contrary notwithstanding. On this view, even the claim that being a mother is just a matter of being a female parent is indeed a *substantive* claim about the world, albeit one that is so familiar, so obvious and so commonplace, that we easily fail to recognize it as the substantive truth that it is.

Similarly, but in contrast, some deny the possibility of *synthetic* reductions (or at least, synthetic reductions of properties), because they think that unless the supposed reduction is an analytic one, true by virtue of the very meaning of the terms (or concepts), there can't be a genuine reduction here after all, only the establishment of a *connection* between *distinct* properties. Although (they may say) we have cases where it seems natural to say that we've discovered that some property *reduces* to another (or to a set of others), all that is really going on in such cases is that we have discovered that these properties are *linked* in important ways, so that, necessarily, we always have one of these properties in just those cases where we have the other. After all, as I have already noted, even if being gold and being shiny were somehow always co-instantiated (so that nothing had either property without also having the other), that would hardly show that shininess reduces to being gold. Similarly then, it isn't really true that we have discovered that the property of being water is *nothing more* than the property of being H_2O. Rather, these remain distinct properties, and all we have actually learned is that something with one of these properties will necessarily have the other one as well, and—more particularly—that it will have the former property *because* it has the latter one. But that's not the same as *reduction*.

Obviously, to further pursue either of these lines of thought would take us very far afield. To lay them out properly would require entering into complex debates within metaphysics, philosophy of language, philosophy of mind, and more; and all of that is well beyond the scope of our discussion. So I will content myself with the thought that virtually everyone believes in *some* form of reduction or the other. Some will happily allow for both analytic and synthetic reductions; others, for only one or the other of the two. Since I don't want to take a stand here on which forms are genuine, I will proceed on the assumption (which seems prima facie plausible, if nothing else), that both forms of reduction are possible, at least in principle. For our purposes, the truly important question is whether reduction—of any kind at all—is indeed possible for *ethics*.

12.3 The Open Question Argument

Although reductionists, as we are understanding them, share the conviction that moral facts can all be reduced to nonmoral ones (indeed, to nonnormative ones), they differ, unsurprisingly, about the details of their favored reductions. Moral philosophy is filled with rival proposals about how best to reduce one or another moral fact or moral property, and any given proposal may be subject to a variety of telling criticisms that nonetheless leave other proposals altogether untouched. Because of this, the failure of any particular reductionist proposal may show us little or nothing about whether other proposals—differing in large or small ways—will do any better. (Analogously: had someone proposed that the property of being a mother reduces to the property of being an *unmarried parent*, the utter inadequacy of such an account would hardly establish the impossibility of finding a more successful reduction of the property in question.) This means that the moral skeptic would be ill advised to focus on "local" criticisms, objections that at best are telling only against this or that particular reductionist account. They will never succeed in establishing the impossibility of reductionism that way. Thus, while moral realists can happily debate the merits and shortcomings of various specific reductionist proposals, the moral skeptic, in contrast, needs a way to rule out all reductionist proposals whatsoever—a way to convince us that the very project of finding a successful reductionist account is misguided, doomed to failure.

Is there a way to do this? The most popular attempt to argue against all forms of reductionism is by means of something that has come to be called *the open question argument*. Here's how it goes. (Although the basic idea is simple enough, I'm going to spell it out at some considerable length.)

Imagine that someone puts forward a reductionist proposal concerning some fairly basic moral property, like the property of being good, or being permissible. Why a "basic" property? Because even the skeptic is likely to concede that *some* moral properties can be reduced to other, more basic, *moral* properties. (For example, perhaps the property of being morally permissible can be reduced to the property of not being morally *forbidden*.) Controversy emerges only over whether even the most basic moral properties can be reduced in turn. Suppose, then, for the sake of concreteness, that the property of (moral) *goodness* is a member of this final set, the set of the most fundamental moral properties. And now our reductionist offers to reduce the property of goodness as well.

Presumably, any such account will look like this: being good is just a matter of being XYZ—where the dummy variables, "XYZ," will be replaced by the particulars of the specific reductionist proposal. Thus, to throw off a few random possibilities, the suggestion might be that being good just consists in (1) being *desired*, or (2) being the sort of thing I *want to want*, or (3) being *favored by rational bargainers*, or (4) being *loved by God*, and so on.

Somewhat arbitrarily—and again, for the sake of concreteness—let's suppose that the proposal in question is the third one, the suggestion that there is nothing more to being good than being favored by rational bargainers. Now compare two questions:

1. Such and such a state of affairs is favored by rational bargainers, but is it good?
2. Such and such a state of affairs is good, but is it good?

The first question certainly seems to be "open" in the following sense: whatever the answer might be—indeed, even if you think the answer to the first question must be yes—it seems perfectly coherent and intelligible to *ask* this question.

In contrast, the second question is clearly "closed." No one who speaks English could possibly sincerely be asking this question. There is no room whatsoever for uncertainty or doubt about the answer to the second question. If someone asked it, you would have no idea at all what they were trying to get at.

But this seems to show that the two questions are asking different things! And doesn't that show that being good does not actually reduce to being favored by rational bargainers after all? For if there really were nothing more to being good than being favored by rational bargainers, then in saying of the given state of affairs that it was favored by rational bargainers we would be saying that it was good, and so the two questions would really have to be asking the same thing after all. Since the second question is clearly a closed one, the first should be closed as well. But it obviously isn't a closed one, and that shows that it simply isn't true that there is nothing more to being good than being favored by rational bargainers—that the former simply consists in the latter. So the proposed reduction must be mistaken.

We would get a similar result if we asked the first question the other way around. "Such and such a state of affairs is good, but is it favored by rational bargainers?" This too seems to be an open question—one can intelligibly ask it. But if there were truly nothing more to being good than being favored by the rational bargainers, shouldn't this actually be a *closed* question? (Shouldn't it be like raising the second question, where we wonder whether something that is good is good?) So the proposed reduction must be mistaken.

Contrast this situation with what we find when we try a reductionist proposal that we know to be correct, say, the reduction of the property of being a mother to the property of being a female parent. Imagine that we try to pose the analogue of our first question and ask: such and such a person is a female parent, but is she a mother? This question too is—obviously enough—a *closed* one. No one could intelligibly raise it. Precisely because there is nothing more to being a mother than being a female parent, to say of someone that they are a female parent just *is* to say of them that they are a mother. And so to ask of such a person whether they *are* a mother—once we have specified that they are a *female parent*— is to ask a closed question (exactly like stipulating that someone is a mother, and then asking whether they are a mother).

In short, when a proposed reduction is correct, the relevant version of our first question will be closed. But the relevant question *isn't* closed for the proposed reduction of being good as simply consisting in being favored by rational bargainers. So that reduction can be rejected.

But as a little reflection suggests, no real work was done here by the details of the particular proposal we happened to be looking at. Suppose we had tried a different reduction of being good instead, asking, say, whether something that I want to want is good, or whether something loved by God is good, or whether something desired is good, and so on. It certainly seems as though all of these questions would be open as well.

Again, it isn't that one cannot have a favored answer to one or more of these questions. It might be, for example, that you confidently believe that if God loves something, it must be good. But that isn't the relevant issue. The issue is whether the given question would be an *open* one, in the sense that someone could intelligibly raise it. And even if you are confident that if God loves something it must be good, it is surely the case that you would understand someone who wonders whether that is so or not. Whereas, in contrast, you would be utterly baffled if someone wondered whether something good was good or not.

So all of these questions are open ones, and that means that all of these reductions must be failures as well. And once we see this, we can presumably see that *any* proposed reduction of the property of being good will also be a failure. For no matter *how* we fill in the details, *whatever* our XYZ might be, provided that XYZ are indeed genuinely nonmoral (and nonnormative) properties, if we ask whether something that is XYZ is good, the question will always be an open one. So XYZ *cannot* be an adequate reduction of the property goodness, no matter what reduction we propose. All such reductions must fail.

Here's a slightly different way of making this same point. If I tell you that all good things are favored by rational bargainers, I am saying something *informative*. Similarly, of course, if I tell you that all things favored by rational bargainers are good. But in contrast, if I tell you that all good things are good, I am not telling you anything informative at all.

What follows from this? That it can't be true that there is *nothing more* to being good than being favored by rational bargainers. For if that were true, then in telling you, say, that all things favored by rational bargainers are good, I would not be telling you anything informative. But I *am* telling you something informative. So the proposed reduction cannot be correct; being favored by rational bargainers can't be what being good simply *consists* in. And of course, as before, the point generalizes. No matter what our proposal, XYZ, if these are truly nonnormative properties then it seems very informative indeed to be told that everything that is XYZ is good, or that everything that is good is XYZ—from which it seems to follow that being good cannot simply be reduced to being XYZ. Any such reduction must fail.

It is of course important to remember that the claim is only this: that reduction cannot be carried through all the way to the point where *no* moral or normative properties remain. For all we've seen, it might well be possible to reduce the property of goodness to some other *moral* properties (or to other *normative* ones), properties that are even *more* basic. Maybe yes, maybe no. For our purposes we needn't take a stand on this issue; we needn't try to determine what the most basic moral (or normative) properties would actually be. But *once* we have arrived at the most basic moral or normative properties—*whatever* they turn out to be—it will be impossible to reduce them any further, all the way to some set of *non*normative ones. For if there *were* such a reduction, then to ask whether something that has the relevant nonnormative properties also has the relevant moral or normative property would be to raise a closed question. But this question would *not* in fact be a closed one. It would *always* make sense to ask whether something with the relevant nonnormative properties also had the relevant *moral* property as well. So no such reduction can succeed.

That's the open question argument. Philosophers who offer it have often taken it to show that any (thoroughgoing) reductionist program in ethics must fail.

As we will see, that's probably too hasty a conclusion. But suppose for the moment that the argument could indeed show this, what remaining options would there be? If the open question argument really did establish the impossibility of reductionism, what should we conclude?

There are, I think, two main possibilities. First, it might show nothing more than this: that the property of goodness (or rightness, or whatever our candidate basic moral or normative property turns out to be) is indeed *irreducible*. That is, it might simply show that among the fundamental, simple properties that need to be given a place within our metaphysics there are certain basic moral or normative ones that should be included as well. It isn't that we have been given a compelling reason to reject moral realism; we have only been given a reason to reject *reductionist* forms of realism. We should, instead, embrace *simple* realism.

Second, however, and more radically, one might think that the open question argument supports moral *skepticism*. To the extent that we find the idea of irreducible moral or normative properties metaphysically worrisome, if we really do conclude that there is no way to avoid positing such properties if we are going to continue to talk about the existence of moral facts at all, then perhaps the right conclusion to draw is that there simply are no such properties after all, and so we should abandon the belief in moral facts.

Note, in particular, that *all* moral facts will be threatened by this second line of thought. For even if certain moral facts could be reduced to more basic ones (if only such basic moral facts were to exist), if we abandon belief in the more basic ones then the entire edifice collapses. In particular, then, without basic moral properties there is no room for any moral facts at all. We must become moral skeptics.

This second approach would still leave unresolved the debate between nihilists and noncognitivists. On the one hand, nihilists might continue to insist (in keeping with their cognitivism) that when we make moral claims, we are indeed making assertions. Those assertions ascribe moral properties (to actions, or outcomes, and so on). But since there *are* no such properties, all such claims are *false*.

But on the other hand, noncognitivists might argue, instead, that it was a mistake to take our first-order substantive moral claims to be genuine assertions in the first place. Indeed, if we cannot offer a reductionist account of supposed basic moral properties like good or right (and so on), this is because we have misconstrued what terms like "good" and "right" are being used to *do*. It is a mistake, the noncognitivist might claim, to think that such terms are being used to refer to (obscure) properties at all; rather they are doing a completely *different* linguistic job. In particular, these are simply terms we use to express our attitudes of approval and disapproval and to give commands. No wonder, then, that these supposed properties cannot be made metaphysically respectable: we were never using these terms to refer to any such properties in the first place. (And no wonder that the various open questions remain open: how could any merely descriptive set of properties guarantee the attitude that is involved when one calls an outcome "good," for example, or an action "right"?)

Accordingly, if we agree that the open question argument really does establish the impossibility of reductionism we will need to decide between moving to some version of moral skepticism or defending simple realism.

Nonetheless, I think that this choice is not really forced upon us since, as far I can see, the open question argument doesn't actually *establish* the impossibility of reductionism. There are, I believe, at least three different replies to the argument that the reductionist might offer.

First, the reductionist might point out that the impossibility of reduction will only follow if all candidate proposals will leave us with an open question.

12.3 THE OPEN QUESTION ARGUMENT

That is, the claim must be that no matter what properties XYZ we appeal to, provided that the only properties used are nonnormative ones, questions like "such and such is XYZ, but is it good?" will be open ones. But is this really the case? That does seem true for the particular proposed reductions we considered (for example, that being good reduces to being favored by rational bargainers). But what of it? Perhaps there is some other reduction that does better! Maybe we simply haven't yet considered an appropriate proposal, and if only we were to do that, we would find ourselves thinking that the relevant question was indeed a closed one (just as the question "is Sally, who is a female parent, a mother?" is a closed one). In short, even if this or that particular proposal fails, what could possibly justify our concluding that *all* reductionist proposals will fail as well?

Sometimes those putting forward the open question argument confidently proclaim that we can just *see* that any reductionist proposal whatsoever must result in an open question. To this claim I can only reply that I don't myself think I am able to see anything remotely like this. I have no confidence at all that *no* candidate reduction whatsoever would result in a closed question. For all I know, we simply haven't yet considered the right proposal.

A rather different reply—the second—begins with the observation that sometimes reductions are trivial and obvious, but sometimes they are not. It is pretty uncontroversial, indeed it is utterly obvious, that there is nothing more to the property of being a mother beyond that of being a female parent. But in many other cases it is far more difficult to figure out what an adequate reduction will look like. In many cases, perhaps most cases, even though we may well believe that some reduction is possible, it may still be the case that the reduction is difficult to figure out, and sufficiently nonobvious, so that even the correct reduction will remain controversial—or at least, nonobvious—even when we finally arrive at it. (Philosophers will be familiar with many such examples: What is it to know? What is causation? What is it to be an action?)

Suppose, then, that we have such a nontrivial reduction for a basic moral property—let's stick with the property of being good—and imagine that we ask ourselves the question whether something that has the relevant underlying properties is, indeed, good. Couldn't it be the case that even though this really is the *correct* reduction, it simply isn't *obvious* that it is the correct reduction, and so the question remains open for all that?

As it happens, this seems like it should be possible even if we are aiming to provide an *analytic* reduction. Recall that the idea here is that an analytic reduction is one that can be figured out a priori, simply by sufficiently thinking through the meanings of the relevant terms or concepts. "Mothers are female parents" is an analytic reduction, and one that is obviously correct (which is why the relevant question is a closed one). But it certainly looks as though there might be analyses or analytic reductions for *other* properties where the truth of the given reduction simply is not obvious and it takes a tremendous amount of thought to grasp, even though it is true by definition. (As an analogy, think of how certain complicated logical tautologies are analytically true, but far from obvious.) But if we had such a reduction and asked whether it was correct, the question would certainly remain an open one—in that we would understand what someone would mean in raising it. Precisely because the account isn't an *obvious* one, it will be intelligible to ask whether things that have the relevant more basic properties really do necessarily have the property we are trying to reduce. That is to say, the question will remain open, even though the reduction is correct—and even though the reduction is an *analytic* one, true by virtue of the very meanings of the terms and concepts involved.

If this second approach can be made out, then the reductionist can concede (if they want to) that when it comes to basic moral properties there may be no account that generates a closed question. And yet for all that, such reductions might still be true, and even analytic. So the open question argument cannot so much as establish the impossibility of even analytic reductionism.

Finally—and this is the third possible reply—we should remember that some reductions are not analytic at all, but synthetic. "Mothers are female parents" is an example of an analytic reduction, but "water is H_2O" is not; it is an example of a *synthetic* reduction. This means that the truth of the reduction doesn't follow from the mere meanings of the relevant words or concepts. It is a substantive truth about the world, something that has to be discovered a posteriori. Mere thought cannot suffice to establish its truth.

But when we have examples of synthetic reductions, we do not expect the relevant questions to be closed! Rather, we expect them to be *open*. After all, it is precisely because synthetic truths are not analytic ones that we cannot hope to establish them via thought alone. (Discovering a synthetic reduction is a bit like discovering that two distinct names pick out the very same person. That's something that can't normally be done by thought alone.) And that means that it will always be *intelligible* to ask whether any proposed synthetic reduction is correct. The question will always be an open one. Water really *is* H_2O—there is nothing more to being water than that—and yet we understand perfectly well what someone would *mean* if (not realizing this) they ask, "Yes, this liquid is water, but is it H_2O?" or "Yes, this liquid is H_2O, but is it water?"

Telling us that water is H_2O is telling us something *informative*. And yet, for all that, being water really does seem to reduce to being H_2O. So if there really are synthetic reductions—and this example from chemistry certainly seems to show that there can be such—then it seems as though the open question argument will simply have to leave them untouched. Yes, the reductionist can say, the relevant questions remain open, and yet, for all that, the proposed reductions may well be correct, for they are *synthetic* reductions, not the sort of reductions that should ever have been expected to generate closed questions in the first place. Accordingly, if the reductionist account that gets offered of some basic moral property is a *synthetic* one, then an open question argument will have no force against that account at all.

So there are, it seems, at least three different replies that can be made by the reductionist. It might be that eventually we will find an analytic reduction that generates appropriately closed questions, it might be that we will find an analytic reduction that is sufficiently complicated and nonobvious that it won't be at all surprising if the relevant questions remain open, or it might be that we will decide that the appropriate reductions are synthetic, rather than analytic, and so we shouldn't be looking for closed questions in the first place. Unsurprisingly, reductionists differ among themselves as to which of these replies is the most plausible one, but we need not try to settle that question here. For our purposes the crucial point is this: despite initial appearances, the open question argument cannot actually establish the impossibility of reduction.

12.4 Properties of the Wrong Kind

There is a second general antireductionist argument that some people have also found appealing. In some ways it is similar to the open question argument, but it is considerably simpler.

As we know, the aim of reductionism in ethics is to provide accounts of moral properties according to which they ultimately reduce to nonnormative ones. If such accounts really are correct, then there is nothing more to having a given moral property than the having of the underlying nonnormative ones; being something with the given moral property *simply consists in* being something with the relevant nonnormative properties. However—and this is where the new argument comes in—we can easily see that nonnormative properties are simply of the *wrong kind* for anything like this to ever be true. So reductionism *must* be false.

Here's the argument spelled out a bit more fully. Moral facts are normative ones. They involve truths about what ought to be the case, or what one should think or do or feel, or what there is reason to favor, and so on. In contrast, nonnormative facts are normatively inert: they tell us what *is* the case, but—by their very nature—they tell us nothing about what *should* be the case, or what one *ought* to think or do, and so on. So how could it possibly be true that a moral fact would simply *consist* in some set of nonnormative facts? How could it possibly be the case that there was simply *nothing more* to the possession of some moral property than having the right sorts of nonnormative properties? Obviously, nothing like that could possibly be true, so reductionism must be mistaken.

It is important not to misunderstand the thought at work here. The objection isn't that if any such reduction were true this would be a very surprising discovery indeed. For as we should all readily acknowledge, the details of *synthetic* reductions can certainly be surprising. Prior to the relevant discoveries in chemistry, for example, who would ever have imagined that being water would turn out to just be a matter of being composed of hydrogen and oxygen combined in the right way? Similarly, it was surprising to learn that being lightning is just a matter of being a massive electrostatic discharge of the right sort, or that being hot is just a matter of having a higher than average mean kinetic energy. And for that matter, it is arguable that even *analytic* reductions can be surprising as well. Prior to one's introduction to Euclidean geometry, for example, one might well be surprised to realize that there is nothing more to the property of being a circle than that of being a collection of points on the plane all of which are equidistant from some single designated point (the center). As I say, reductions can be surprising.

So imagine that—or remember when—you were being presented with these various reductions for the first time, before you had considered the evidence for their truth or even understood the details of how the proposed reductions would work. You might have been skeptical of one or more of the proposals, dubious whether anything like that could really be true. Still, for all that, there would have been nothing about the various proposals that would have allowed you to simply dismiss them out of hand, nothing that would have justified your rejecting the proposed reductions altogether without even examining the relevant arguments. In particular, in none of these cases would you ever have been in a position to simply dismiss the proposed reduction on the grounds that you could just *see* that there was an insurmountable *mismatch* between the kind of property being reduced and the supposedly underlying ones. On the contrary, to settle whether one of these proposed reductions held or not, you would have had no alternative but to investigate the matter. It would have been completely inappropriate to simply rule them out from the start.

But in contrast, it seems, we *are* in a position to rule out the sort of reductions being proposed for morality. There is no need for detailed investigations. We can simply *see* that nonnormative properties are of the wrong kind for it to ever be the case that there is nothing more to having a moral property than having some set of nonnormative ones.

That, at any rate, is what this new argument claims.

One might, of course, wonder: are we ever *really* in this sort of epistemic position—able to simply see that one sort of property is the wrong *kind* to provide a reduction base for some other particular type of property? Are we ever entitled to simply rule out a proposed reduction immediately, right from the start, without so much as investigating the matter?

Interestingly enough, it does seem plausible to think that this can sometimes happen.

Suppose, for example, that someone proposed that the property of being a planet reduces to (is nothing more than) the property of being a piano concerto! It is hardly as though we need to give this proposal any serious thought. Rather, all of us can see at once that nothing like this could conceivably be correct. Why? Because we all already know enough about astronomical properties and musical properties to see—straightaway and without further ado—that it simply could not be the case that the former property reduces to the latter. On the contrary, we can just see that the property of being a piano concerto is simply of the wrong *kind* to so much as leave open the *possibility* of it being true that the property of being a planet reduces to the property of being a piano concerto. It is *inconceivable* that there is nothing more to being the former than being the latter. More generally, we can simply see that *any* attempt to reduce such astronomical properties to musical ones is doomed to failure. There is no need to examine the details.

The suggestion, then, is that something similar happens when we contemplate the very suggestion that moral properties might reduce to nonnormative ones. Surely, the claim goes, we can simply see that nothing like this could conceivably be the case. The two types of properties are too different in kind. There is an unavoidable mismatch between the normative (including the moral) and the nonnormative. So we can simply see that any attempt to reduce moral properties to nonnormative ones is similarly doomed to failure. Here too, then, there is no need to examine the details.

How might a reductionist respond to this new argument? The critical point to grasp, I think, is this. If we really are going to dismiss a proposed type of reduction immediately, out of hand, this can only be justified if we are indeed able to see that the proposed underlying properties are of a kind that could not *conceivably* provide a reduction base for the property being reduced. We must be able to *see* the unavoidable mismatch, the unbridgeable difference in kind of the two types of properties. It will not nearly suffice if all that is going on is that we *cannot yet see* how a reduction of the proposed sort could possibly work. After all, this mere *failure* to see will frequently occur with reductions of new and unfamiliar kinds, cases where we haven't yet come to understand how the reduction works. So a mere failure to see is not enough; dismissing the very possibility of a given type of reduction takes more than a mere *inability* to see how a reduction of the given kind might go. Rather, it must be the case that we can actually *see* that *no* reduction of that kind could possibly work at all. This is what distinguishes the case of water from the imaginary proposal about being a planet. With regard to water being H_2O, all that anyone might have had, at best, is a mere *failure to see* how such a reduction might work. That's why it would have been illegitimate to simply dismiss the very possibility of such a reduction. But in contrast, when it comes to the proposal that being a planet might simply be a matter of being a piano concerto, we can actually *see the impossibility* of anything like the proposed reduction holding. It is only because of this that we are entitled to dismiss the idea immediately.

But if that's right, then the obvious question becomes, is it really the case that we *can* see that it is indeed utterly impossible to reduce the moral to the nonnormative? Even if—in the absence of detailed proposals—it is difficult to see how such a reduction might work, are we really justified in making the requisite bolder claim, that we can actually *see* the sheer *impossibility* of any such reduction? It is easy enough for the critic of reductionism to make a claim like this. But is it really true?

Speaking personally, I don't think that I *do* see anything remotely like this. I will readily admit that I am far from confident as to whether the reductionist program can succeed. It certainly does often seem difficult to see how a complete reduction of the moral and the normative would go. But as I have just pointed out, this mere failure to see how a suitable reduction could work is a far cry from what is needed if the antireductionist conclusion is to follow. A mere failure to see does not suffice; what we would need, rather, is sufficient insight into the very nature of moral and normative properties, on the one hand, and nonnormative ones, on the other, so that we could simply see the sheer impossibility of any conceivable reduction of the former to the latter. We would need to be able to see that the seeming difference in the two types of properties is literally insurmountable. And all I can report is that I do not myself seem to have anything like this kind of insight. I may not be able to see how an adequate reduction here would go; but that is a far cry indeed from being *able* to see that *no* such reduction could possibly succeed. So in my own case, at least, I find that even this new attempt to argue against the very possibility of reduction in ethics is an unsuccessful one as well.

Admittedly, there are some people who confidently claim to be able to see what I do not. They insist that they can indeed simply see that normative and nonnormative properties are too dissimilar, so that any proposed reduction of the former to the latter must inevitably fail. I can only reply that I have no such insight myself, and that I am, in fact, skeptical of their own claims to see this. (The situation often reminds me of an earlier episode in the history of thought. Many people used to claim to be able to see that *biological* facts—facts about *life*—could not possibly reduce to facts about inorganic matters like mere chemistry. In fact, however, they were mistakenly ascribing to themselves insight that they did not actually possess. I suspect something similar is happening in the present case.)

In short, as far as I can tell, the possibility of reducing moral properties to nonnormative properties remains a live one. Reductionism may or may not succeed, but we've yet to see any compelling reason to believe that it must, inevitably, fail.

12.5 The Significance of Reasons for Reduction

To say that two arguments against the very possibility of reductionism are unsuccessful is, of course, not at all the same thing as saying that a reductionist account of morality can indeed be provided. For all that we have seen so far, it could still turn out that some moral or normative properties are metaphysically basic or simple and cannot plausibly be reduced further. If that's the case, of course, then morality cannot be reduced to the nonnormative after all.

Ideally, therefore, what I would do now would be to systematically lay out and evaluate the leading reductionist accounts of morality, or, at the very least, describe in detail the particular reductionist account that I find most plausible. But I am not going to do that. There are far too many different types of moral facts that in principle we would need to take a look at, and far too many different suggestions about how the most fundamental moral properties might be reduced. Indeed, there isn't even agreement about what the most basic moral or normative properties might be. And even if we had such agreement, we would first need to show how all other moral facts could be reduced to ones involving only these more basic properties. Only then could we try to complete the reductionist project by showing how these most basic ones could be reduced, in turn, to nonnormative ones. To do this properly would require our getting immersed in detailed debates from across the whole of moral philosophy; and that is well beyond the scope of our discussion.

I do, however, want to make two related points. First, I take it to be the case that any complete account of morality will eventually (or perhaps immediately) include a variety of claims about what there is reason to do (or feel or prefer, and so on). For example, if, as most of us believe, killing is (normally) morally forbidden, then a complete account of the contents of morality will assert that there is a *reason* to refrain from killing. Similarly, if (as most of us believe), honesty is a virtue, then a complete account of the contents of morality will hold that we have a reason to be disposed to tell the truth and avoid lies. If equality is intrinsically good, then each of us has a reason to prefer outcomes with less, rather than more, inequality. And if (as many consequentialists believe) the morally right action is the one that produces the best outcomes, then I have at least some reason to do such optimizing actions. And so on.

I assume that my saying all of this will come as no surprise, since I have several times indicated my sympathy for reasons internalism, according to which morality provides reasons for action (see, in particular, 9.4 and 11.1). If there are moral facts, then there are reasons to act (and feel, and so on) in keeping with those facts.

But this means that an adequate account of moral properties will eventually need to say something about the property of being a reason (the property of providing rational support for something).

12.5 THE SIGNIFICANCE OF REASONS FOR REDUCTION

Why do I say this? It surely isn't as though metaphysical accounts of morality are responsible for describing the nature of *all* properties to which they are committed. Honesty is a virtue, after all, and explicating the nature of that virtue requires reference to the notion of truth, but we would hardly think that the moral realist owes us a philosophical account of the nature of truth! So even if it is the case that moral facts entail the existence of facts involving various kinds of reasons, why should the realist owe us an account of the property of being a reason?

The answer, of course, is that normativity is so central to the idea of morality that unless the property of being a reason (or of providing rational support, or some other, similar property) can be shown to be a metaphysically acceptable one, then it won't just be this or that particular moral claim that will be endangered, but all of morality, the very idea of moral facts altogether. (Admittedly, reasons externalists might deny this; but as I have previously noted, I suspect that very few moral realists are reasons externalists.)

It is for this reason that I have suggested that if the moral realist is going to try to dispel the worry that moral facts are somehow metaphysically suspect by means of an appeal to a reductionist approach, then it won't suffice if they merely reduce moral properties to nonmoral ones, but allow themselves to appeal to the property of being a reason and then avoid saying anything further about this basic *normative* property. That's hardly likely to allay whatever metaphysical worries one might have had about morality in the first place. Thus, while it is perfectly *coherent* to argue that moral properties can all be reduced to nonmoral ones, including the property of being a reason, while still insisting that the property of being a reason cannot itself be reduced further (to something nonnormative), to the extent that the reductionist is motivated by the desire to put to rest metaphysical concerns about morality they will likely want to offer a reductionist account of being a reason as well. That's why for our purposes it makes sense to classify anyone who posits any irreducible normative properties at all as a simple realist. We will examine simple realism in the next chapter, but for now the point is simply that any moral realist who is a thoroughgoing reductionist will want to offer a reductionist account of *reasons* as well.

Suppose, however, that we had an acceptable account of the normative property of being a reason—whether a reductionist one or not. It does seem to me plausible to hold—and this is my second point—that this property, along with a suitably rich set of nonnormative properties, should suffice to provide an adequate reduction base for all *moral* properties. That is, whether or not all moral properties can be reduced to nonnormative ones, I do think it likely that we can reduce all moral properties to non*moral* ones, provided that we are in fact permitted to appeal to the property of being a reason as well.

To make good on this claim would require a far more detailed discussion than we have room for here. And many of the details, in fact, cannot be fully provided until other debates within moral philosophy have been resolved as well. After all, until we have agreed about what the various moral facts *are*—which deeds are required, which character traits are virtuous, and so on—we can hardly be in a position to spell out how all the actual moral facts are to be reduced. We can't even say what the basic categories of moral facts in need of reduction will look like. Still, considering a few examples may give you a feel for why I find this second suggestion an attractive one as well.

Many moral claims say of particular acts (or act types) that they are permitted, forbidden, or required. Arguably, however, if we are allowed to appeal to the property of being a reason, reductionist accounts of all three of these properties quickly fall into place. We can say, for example, that an action's being morally *required* simply consists in there being a decisive reason of the right sort to perform that action. Similarly, we can say that its being *forbidden* is just a matter of there being a decisive reason of the right sort to *refrain* from performing it. And that its being *permissible* is nothing more than the *absence* of a decisive reason (of the right sort) to refrain. (Meanwhile, to be *wrong* is just a matter of being forbidden, and to be *right* is just a matter of being permissible or required.) Thus, once we are given the property of being a reason, a reductive account of a central group of basic moral properties can readily be provided.

To be sure, some might prefer an alternative account of what it is to be required, according to which an act's being required simply consists in it being the case that if you fail to do the act in question it is appropriate for you to feel guilt or shame and for others to feel anger and resentment. (Correspondingly, for an act to be forbidden is for these emotions to be appropriate if you *perform* the act in question, while its being permissible is simply a matter of these emotions being *inappropriate* if you perform it.) And what is it for such emotions to be "appropriate"? Perhaps nothing more than that there is a *reason* (of the right sort) for the relevant individuals to feel these various emotions in these circumstances.

As it happens, I prefer an account of the first kind rather than the second. But either way, several central moral properties can again easily be reduced, once we are allowed to appeal to the property of being a reason.

In offering these proposals, I've repeatedly made reference to there being a reason "of the right sort." I've included this qualification, of course, because not any old reason will suffice to ground (or constitute) a moral requirement or prohibition. Your having a *moral* obligation to keep your promise, for example, presumably cannot simply consist in your having a reason to do so—not even a decisive reason—if your reason for keeping your promise is that I will pay you a thousand dollars if you do. Rather, the reason must be based on the *relevant* sort of facts.

And what sort of facts are those? Roughly speaking, they are facts connected to the central content of morality or its foundation. That is, the reason that constitutes your having a moral requirement, say, must be a reason that is based on facts appropriately connected to morality's content or basis.

To say anything much more specific than this requires taking a stand on unresolved debates within normative ethics. But some hypothetical examples should make the basic idea reasonably clear. (For simplicity of exposition, I'll leave aside some of the details.)

Suppose—if only for the sake of illustration—that contractarianism is correct and an act is permissible if and only if it conforms to the rules governing social interactions that suitably specified rational bargainers would agree to. Then we could say that your being morally required to keep your promise consists in the fact that you have a (decisive) reason to keep it, where that reason exists *by virtue of the fact* that rational bargainers would indeed agree to a rule demanding that one keep one's promises. Or suppose—again, for the sake of illustration—that utilitarianism is right and an act is permissible if and only if it results in the greatest possible total amount of well-being (counting everyone equally). Then we could say, instead, that your being morally required to keep your promise essentially consists in the fact that you have a reason to do so, where that reason exists *by virtue of the fact* that your keeping it would result in the greatest possible amount of overall welfare. Or suppose—one last illustration—that a universalization approach to ethics is correct, and an act is permissible if and only if there is a possible rule permitting such an act that you can rationally will to be universally valid. Then we could say that your being morally required to keep your promise consists in the fact that you have a reason to keep it, where that reason exists by virtue of the fact that you cannot rationally universalize any rule that would permit the *breaking* of such promises. (As you can now see, still other normative theories would point, in turn, to still other specifications of what it takes for the reason in question to be a reason of the *right* sort.)

In all three of these cases, of course, there are further questions we would inevitably want to ask as well. Why, for example, should the fact that promise keeping promotes the overall welfare provide you with a *reason* to keep your promise? Why should the fact that rational bargainers would agree to a rule requiring promise keeping generate a reason for you to *follow* such a rule? Or why would the fact that you cannot universalize a rule permitting promise breaking give you a reason to *keep* your promise?

If it really is the case that the existence of a moral requirement boils down to the existence of a reason of the right sort, then the full defense of a given normative theory will inevitably have to include showing that the reasons that it posits really do exist (in the circumstances that it claims, and for the reasons that it claims). But to examine and evaluate the various answers that might be provided on behalf of these or other theories would be precisely to enter into the detailed normative debates that I have been deliberately avoiding throughout this book. Our goal here, recall, is not to decide between rival normative theories, but only to show what a reductive account of morality might conceivably look like. And the point that I have been trying to make, with the help of these few rough and ready examples, is that many moral properties (including right, wrong, permitted, forbidden, and required) can arguably be reduced to nonmoral ones, *if* we are indeed allowed to make use of the property of being a *reason*.

There are, of course, still other moral properties, beyond those we've been discussing. But they too seem capable of being reduced to the nonmoral, if we can include the property of being a reason in the reduction base. We might, for example, want to say that honesty is a virtue. But what does it mean to say this? What *is* it to be a virtue, anyway? Perhaps nothing more than to be a character trait that one has a reason to have—a reason of the right sort. Or we might want to say of inequality that it is *bad*, while equality is *good*, and this might ultimately consist in the fact that we have a reason (as always, a reason of the right sort) to promote and care about equality while disapproving of inequality and striving to eliminate it.

Examples like these could easily be multiplied, and I certainly don't mean to insist on the details of any of these specific candidate reductions. (In many cases, indeed, more precise and accurate reductions would be more complicated than the quick examples I've mentioned.) But I hope I have said enough to allow you to see that it is, at the very least, not implausible to suggest that moral properties can indeed be reduced to nonmoral ones, provided that the property of being a reason is one that is allowed to appear in the reduction base.

If I am right about all of this, then the question of whether the property of being a reason can *itself* be reduced to some suitable set of nonnormative properties is central to determining the prospects for a complete reduction of moral facts to nonnormative ones. On the one hand—and this was my first point—unless the reductionist can offer an account of reasons which reduces the normative property of being a reason to a set of nonnormative ones, she won't yet have put to rest worries about the metaphysical status of morality. Or rather, more precisely, reductionism alone will not have managed to put such worries to rest. And on the other hand—and this was my second point—suppose I am right that once we are allowed to appeal to the property of being a reason, the goal of providing reductive accounts of the rest of morality may well be within reach. Then we have reason to think that if we *can* provide a reduction of being a reason to some set of nonnormative properties, then it should be possible to reduce all of morality to the nonnormative. Speaking loosely but intuitively, if we can reduce moral facts to facts about reasons, and facts about reasons to nonnormative facts, then we can reduce morality to the nonnormative. And doing *that*, presumably, really would answer any qualms we may justifiably have had about the metaphysical status of morality.

Thus, if either of my two suggestions is correct, and especially if both are, we have particular reason to wonder whether we can indeed reduce the property of being a reason to a suitable set of more fundamental, nonnormative properties. If we can, then the prospects for a complete reduction of morality to the nonnormative look very promising indeed. But if we cannot, any such reduction of morality to the nonnormative is, I believe, almost certainly going to be unsuccessful.

12.6 Reducing Reasons

It is sometimes suggested that it is a trivial matter to reduce facts about reasons to nonnormative facts—or rather, it is a trivial matter if the sort of reasons we are trying to reduce to something more basic are *hypothetical* ones. After all, the suggestion goes, what is it for an action to have the property of being backed by a hypothetical reason? Nothing more than that the act is a means to satisfying some desire of the agent's. But the fact that someone desires something is not, in itself, a normative fact, and neither is the fact that the act in question will help satisfy that desire. So the property of being a hypothetical reason, at the very least, can be readily reduced to something nonnormative.

But as we have previously noted (in 11.5), this thought is mistaken. It fails to take into account the crucial point that even hypothetical reasons involve the idea of there being *rational support* for the act in question. When you assert the existence of a hypothetical reason you are doing more than merely noting of some possible act that it will help satisfy some desire that the agent has. Rather, you are saying that, *by virtue of* that fact, there is some rational *support* for doing that action. The fact that the act will satisfy the desire *speaks in favor of* doing it, it *justifies* it (at least somewhat).

It is this *further* property—the property of providing rational support—that we should be wondering about. To be sure, ordinarily when an act has the right causal connection to satisfying some desire this does indeed ground that act's also having that further property as well. But to note all of this doesn't yet tell us what this further property consists in; it doesn't tell us whether the property of *providing* rational support can be reduced further. It is only if this further property can be reduced to something nonnormative that the reductionist approach to morality can be completely carried through.

We can express the essential point here in either of two different ways, depending on what view we accept concerning which precise facts constitute reasons themselves (see 11.2). On the one hand, some might prefer to say that even if the *grounds* for there being a reason consist in nonnormative facts alone (whether the reason is a hypothetical one or, for that matter, a categorical one), that doesn't yet tell us whether the reason itself—the *distinct* fact that these underlying grounds provide rational support for the given act—can be reduced further. On the other hand, some might prefer to say that the grounds themselves simply *are* the reason—though only by virtue of the fact that they have the further property of providing rational support. But even on this second view the question remains: can this *further* property be reduced to some suitable set of nonnormative ones?

The most promising suggestion for doing this—for reducing the property of providing rational support to something nonnormative—appeals to the idea of an ideal deliberator (or ideal reasoner), someone ideally suited to reason from relevant facts to conclusions about what to do (or believe, or feel, and so on).

What might such an ideal deliberator be like? The precise list of characteristics might be debated, no doubt, but if we tried to do this in nonnormative terms, we might want to include things like knowing all the facts, reasoning without bias, thinking logically, and the like. Next, we are invited to imagine such a person engaged in a bit of practical reasoning. They might, for example, reason from the fact that they are hungry, along with the realization that eating a sandwich would satisfy their hunger, to a decision to eat a sandwich. Or perhaps they would reason from the fact that they had made a promise to meet a friend at the library, and the realization that they wouldn't be there in time to keep their promise unless they left home now, to the decision to leave for the library. For present purposes the details of these instances of practical reasoning needn't detain us (and, of course, any particular example might be controversial). What's important is simply that we have this picture in mind, of the person reflecting on various facts, and making decisions in light of them.

The suggestion, then, roughly speaking, is that for a given fact to provide rational support for an action is nothing more than it being the case that such an ideal deliberator would decide to do the act in question partly on the *basis* of their belief in that fact. A given fact's being a reason simply consists in the fact that an ideal deliberator would make the decision that they do *because* of their belief in the fact in question.

This proposal inverts the way we might ordinarily think of what's going on in practical deliberation. According to this proposal, it isn't—as we might normally think—that an ideal deliberator *recognizes* some fact as (already) *being* a reason (or grounding one) and then acts accordingly. Rather, the suggestion is that the fact's being a reason simply *consists in* the fact that the deliberator will make the decision that they do *because* of their belief in that fact. That is, speaking a bit loosely, to say of a given fact that it *is* a reason to perform an act is simply to say that the belief in that fact would figure in a piece of ideal practical reasoning that culminates in a decision to do the act in question.

Thus, the fact that eating a sandwich will make your hunger go away will indeed be a reason to eat the sandwich. But what makes this fact *constitute* a reason—what it comes to for this fact to provide rational support for eating the sandwich—is nothing more than the fact that even if you were an *ideal* deliberator you would decide to eat the sandwich, and you would do so (in part) *because* of your recognition of this fact (that eating it will end the hunger). It is only because facts like these play this role (or would play this role) that they *are* reasons—that's what rational support *consists in*. In contrast, the fact—let us suppose it to be one—that the radio is playing Mozart while you decide whether to eat a sandwich is *not* a fact that would influence the decision of an ideal deliberator (extraordinary circumstances aside). So that fact does *not* provide any rational support for eating a sandwich (nor does it provide any support for *not* doing so); this fact is not a *reason*, precisely because it would play no role in the deliberations of an ideal reasoner.

Similarly, your having made a promise gives you a reason to leave for the library, but what makes this fact *be* a reason is that even if you were deliberating perfectly you would still make the decision to leave now, and would do so (in part) precisely because of your remembering that you had indeed made such a promise. It is by virtue of playing this role in practical deliberation—or rather, more carefully, by virtue of the fact that it *would* play this role even in the reasoning of an ideal deliberator—that it is true to say that the given fact provides rational support for going to the library. (In contrast, the fact—suppose it to be one—that the library is in the oldest part of town would ordinarily play no role whatsoever in an ideal deliberator's thinking about this case; so *that* fact is no reason at all, one way or the other.)

If an account along these general lines can be defended, then perhaps the reductionist's project really can be successfully completed. After all, as I've already suggested, it is plausible to think that moral facts can be reduced to facts about reasons. So if facts about reasons can, in turn, be reduced to facts about what would or would not play a role in the practical reasoning of an ideal deliberator (where the latter idea can itself be spelled out in completely nonnormative terms), then perhaps morality really can be reduced all the way to the nonnormative, finally putting to rest the skeptic's worries about the metaphysical status of moral facts. When all is said and done, the reductionist will say, moral facts are simply facts about what we would decide to do, were we deliberating with sufficient care.

However, I think it must be conceded that, as it stands, the proposal I've been describing is really too simplistic to constitute an adequate theory of what it is to be a reason. For example, at best it points us toward an account of what it is to provide *overriding* rational support, support strong enough to outweigh the competing considerations, if any, that happen to exist in the given case. Intuitively, after all, what we are doing is looking to see whether the ideal deliberator would decide to perform an act on the basis

12.6 REDUCING REASONS

of recognizing certain facts. If so (the suggestion goes), those facts provide rational support for the act in question. But this only covers the case where the facts provide *sufficient* rational support so that, on balance, they outweigh any opposing considerations. (At best, then, the proposal provides only the beginnings of a general account of reasons.)

What then should we say about rational support that, though genuine, is nonetheless *outweighed*? We obviously cannot say that for a fact to provide such outweighed rational support is for it to figure in a piece of ideal deliberation that culminates in a decision to *perform* the act in question. For by hypothesis, in such cases the rational support, though real, is outweighed by *other* considerations, so an ideal deliberator would certainly *not* decide to perform the act supported by the original, weaker reasons.

Thus the reductionist needs a way to extend the basic account, so as to cover cases of genuine but *defeated* rational support. However, I am not going try to spell out what a more fully developed account might look like. To be sure, an initially promising idea might be to ask what the ideal reasoner would do in the *absence* of countervailing considerations. But the details rapidly become rather complicated, and I won't try to explore them here—especially since there are other, similar, problems that would ultimately need to be resolved as well, before we had a sufficiently adequate proposal in place. My own impression is that reductionists rarely offer more than a few quick gestures in the direction of that more adequate theory. That's not to say that a suitable reductionist account of reasons cannot be completed. But I do think it fair to say that no such complete account has yet been provided.

Although I don't want to consider the various potential revisions to the basic account that might be called for, there is nonetheless a more general worry about this entire approach that it is important for us to acknowledge. The reductionist hopes to reduce the normative to the nonnormative by means of the idea that a fact's being a reason is basically just a matter of it playing a particular role in the deliberations of an ideal reasoner. Obviously enough, however, for any account like this to actually accomplish what the reductionist is asking it to do, it had better be possible to characterize the ideal deliberator (or, alternatively, to characterize an ideal process of deliberation) in strictly nonnormative terms. But is this truly possible? Or must any solely nonnormative description inevitably fall short of capturing a genuinely *ideal* deliberator?

We can get at the worry this way. Suppose we really do restrict ourselves to describing "ideal" reasoning and an "ideal" deliberator solely in terms that are uncontroversially nonnormative—for example, in terms of knowing all relevant facts, and never making a logical error, and so on. Can we really be confident that reasoning so described will always be appropriately sensitive to *all* those facts that we (intuitively, and pretheoretically) think of as *reasons*? If even an "ideal" reasoner might in principle fail to respond to a genuine reason, then the attempt to characterize reasons in terms of the deliberations of such a reasoner will inevitably be inadequate.

We could of course make this worry disappear if we were to simply describe the ideal deliberator as someone who always appropriately recognizes and responds to rational support, wherever it arises. But to do so would be to abandon the goal of characterizing the ideal deliberator in *nonnormative* terms. And that, of course, would amount to abandoning the reductionist project. So in describing the ideal reasoner, particular care must be taken to avoid inadvertently smuggling in any essentially normative properties.

Some antireductionists claim that, if we think about it, we will all realize that *no* approach along these lines can possibly succeed. With a little thought, they say, we can all just see that if we limit ourselves to describing the supposedly ideal deliberator in *nonnormative* terms we cannot truly eliminate the possibility that such a reasoner might sometimes fail to deliberate soundly. In principle, they claim, any such deliberator might sometimes fail to decide to do the act that is best rationally supported by the facts. And if this is indeed always a possibility then the attempt to reduce facts about reasons to facts about the decisions of a (nonnormatively characterized) ideal deliberator cannot possibly succeed.

Speaking for myself, however, I can only reply once again that I do not myself see what these others claim to be able to see. While I do not know whether an adequate reductionist account of reasons in terms of the deliberations of an ideal reasoner can be developed or not, that is not remotely the same thing as being able to see that any such account is doomed to failure. My own view, in any event, is that the jury is still out on this matter—or, at least, *should* still be out—and that a more informed judgment must await the further development of this general line of thought.

Where, then, does that leave us? A moral skeptic might try to argue that in the absence of a fully developed and independently plausible account of how to reduce reasons to the nonnormative, it is reasonable to conclude that reductionism cannot succeed, and that this conclusion, in turn, supports skepticism about the reality of moral facts, since they remain metaphysically suspect. But a moral realist needn't be overly impressed by this argument. It

12.6 REDUCING REASONS

is just as reasonable to conclude, instead, that since the intuition that there are moral facts is so very robust (consider, for example, the intuition that it is morally wrong to torture babies for fun), it is far more likely that there are moral facts than not—and if this truly requires the successful reduction of the normative to the nonnormative, then so be it: the odds are that such a reduction can indeed be completed.

Alternatively, the realist might wonder whether it really is true that moral facts can only be metaphysically respectable if facts about reasons can be reduced to something even more fundamental. Perhaps the realist need not embrace thoroughgoing reductionism after all. Maybe the realist should insist instead that the property of being a reason is one that need not be reduced any further—that there is nothing metaphysically problematic about embracing simple realism with regard to the normative. That is the view, of course, of the simple realist. It is time for us to examine that view more carefully.

13

Simple Realism

13.1 Simple Normative Realism

Simple realists share the conviction that some normative facts cannot be reduced further. Or, a bit more precisely, that some normative *properties* cannot be reduced to nonnormative ones. While it may be possible to carry out reductionist programs to various degrees, sooner or later we arrive at normative properties that cannot be reduced; they are, in this sense, basic or fundamental.

Of course, simple realists can and do differ among themselves as to which normative properties are the irreducibly basic ones. Some simple realists believe that certain specifically moral properties—like being permissible, or right, or good—belong on our list of irreducible ones. If that's right, obviously, then the moral cannot be reduced to the nonmoral. (Even here, though, there can be disagreement about how *many* basic moral properties there are, and what they might be.)

As we have seen, however, it's not implausible to think that all particularly moral properties actually *can* be reduced further—that is, reduced to *nonmoral* ones—provided that we are allowed to include in the reduction base properties that while not specifically moral are nonetheless still *normative*, such as the property of being a reason. Since the notion of rational support isn't limited to moral contexts—one can, after all, have a reason to be afraid of an escaped lion, or a reason to believe that 27 + 14 = 41, and so on—if facts about morality can indeed be reduced to facts about reasons of the right sort, then morality will have been reduced to the non*moral*, even if it hasn't been reduced to the non*normative*. Suppose, however, that facts about reasons cannot be reduced further, that the property of providing rational support cannot be reduced to something even more basic, something nonnormative. That will still be a version of what I am calling simple realism, since we will still need to include some normative properties on our list of metaphysically simple ones.

Should we be troubled by a view like this—a view we might call *simple normative realism* (to distinguish it from those views that posit irreducible moral properties)? No doubt, many people will be inclined to believe that we should be. Moral skeptics, at the very least, may want to insist that it is by virtue of this commitment to something irreducibly normative that morality ultimately reveals itself as metaphysically unacceptable. For how can the irreducibly normative find a place in a scientific worldview? (It is one thing to posit an array of scientific properties, but how can one possibly make sense of irreducibly normative ones?) But the truth, of course, is that even moral *realists* may feel uncomfortable at the thought of embracing irreducibly normative properties. It is precisely that discomfort that drives many realists to more thoroughgoing forms of reductionism, according to which normative properties, though real, are not metaphysically simple but can in fact be reduced even further, to suitable complexes of nonnormative properties. To many people, then, simple normative realism has seemed to be a view that one should not be prepared to take seriously.

Suppose, however, that it were to turn out that all *reductionist* approaches to normativity proved *unsuccessful*. That is, imagine that all the most promising proposals for reducing reasons to the nonnormative ended up in failure, or that some more general antireductionist argument proved compelling, so that the only reasonable conclusion to reach was that the attempt to reduce the normative to the nonnormative had to be abandoned. I am not at all suggesting, of course, that this is what we should ultimately conclude. But I do want to consider what the implications of our reaching such a conclusion would be. At this point, it seems, our choices would be limited: either we could embrace simple normative realism, or we could reject belief in the normative altogether. Which choice would be preferable?

I hope it is clear that despite whatever it is that one might initially think, the option of abandoning all belief in the normative is something that it is virtually impossible to accept. Doing this would constitute embracing normative nihilism, and as I have previously noted, embracing this form of nihilism is incredibly costly. Not only would we have to abandon any talk of what we are morally required or permitted to do, we would have to give up all talk of reasons whatsoever. We would have to insist that there is no reason to believe that $2 + 2 = 4$, no reason to believe that fish can swim, no reason to be careful near hungry lions, no reason to move one's hand off the hot stove, no reason to drink when thirsty. There would be no reason to think or do or feel or imagine or want or hope for anything at all. A position like this may not be literally incoherent, but it is, I trust, one that almost no one is prepared to accept.

Rather, we are confident of the existence of reasons. And presumably those reasons are either reducible or not. So although we may not be (and need not be) certain about what the best metaphysical account of reasons will turn out to be, we can still reasonably insist that if it *does* turn out that the property of being a reason is not reducible any further, then the right conclusion to draw is not that there are no reasons at all, but only that the property of being a reason is an irreducible one after all. Simple normative realism may not strike you as an especially attractive view considered on its own, but surely it is a more attractive view than normative *nihilism*. So if reductionism turns out to be false, a suitable version of simple normative realism should still be preferable to the skeptical alternative.

Of course, even if all of this is right, in and of itself this does nothing to reduce any initial resistance to the idea of simple normative realism that one may have had. That view may well be better than the alternative, once we suppose reductionism off the table, but don't we still have to admit that we are right to be *troubled* by the idea of irreducible normative properties? Isn't simple normative realism at best a view that one should embrace only out of necessity? Even if we should, in fact, prefer it to normative nihilism, shouldn't we also agree that a reductionist view would be better still (assuming one can be worked out)—that there would indeed be something deeply unsettling if we had to posit the irreducibly normative?

I do think it likely that many will agree with this thought. But to acknowledge the existence of this sort of unease with the idea of irreducible normative properties is not yet to concede that it is warranted. It is easy enough to express discomfort with a view like simple normative realism on the grounds that it is (somehow) metaphysically objectionable. But it is another matter altogether to say what, precisely, the objection actually comes to—precisely what it is about the idea of irreducible normative properties that is supposed to make the belief in them so very troubling.

My own view is that all or almost all of this discomfort is misguided, that if we think carefully about the matter it turns out to be surprisingly difficult to find anything at all that should trouble us about the belief in irreducible normative properties. That's not to say, of course, that such a view will turn out to be correct. Perhaps a reductionist program really can be carried through to a satisfying conclusion. I don't think we are yet in a position to say, one way or the other. But I do think we should get over the thought that there would necessarily be something deeply disquieting or unsatisfying about a simple realist position if we were led to that result instead. On the contrary, my own view is that if we ultimately conclude that some normative properties are ultimately irreducible, then all that has happened is that we have learned something interesting about the nature of normativity; there is nothing in this hypothesis that should especially trouble us.

In a moment we will take a closer look at a few attempts to move from the vague notion that simple realism would be somehow metaphysically problematic to specific proposals about what, exactly, the problem might be. Before doing this, however, let me say a bit more about the particular simple realist position we will be examining.

First of all, as I have already noted, I think the most promising version of simple realism is simple normative realism. It does seem to me plausible to think that claims about moral facts can indeed be reduced to claims about more basic, nonmoral facts—facts with no intrinsic moral content per se—provided that we are allowed to include facts about *reasons* (see the examples offered in 12.5). Accordingly, I see no compelling reason to think that there are any irreducible *moral* properties. The harder question is whether facts about reasons can be reduced as well. So the version of simple realism that we are most likely to end up with—if thoroughgoing reductionism is false—is simple normative realism.

In addition, it seems likely that if we are given the property of being a *reason*, then *other* general normative concepts (like "ought," as in "you ought to get gas now, as the next gas station is 100 miles away") can probably be accounted for as well. So we can restrict our attention to simple realism with regard to reasons.

Both of these things being the case, however, there will normally be no further need for us to continue to talk, as we've been doing here, about simple *normative* realism, or simple realism with regard to *reasons*. We can drop the various explicit qualifications and restrictions. Hereafter, then, unless context suggests otherwise, when I refer to "simple realism" it is this particular version of simple realism that I have in mind.

Second, I will often talk, a bit loosely perhaps, about whether "reasons" or "facts about reasons" can be reduced or are irreducible, even though what I really mean is whether the *property* of being a reason can be reduced. What we are wondering about is the property of rational support, and whether it would be troubling if it cannot be reduced further. But there is no need to always use the same precise locution when referring to the intended subject of our discussion.

Indeed, on some views, if we were being fastidious it might be more accurate still to say that the object of our inquiry isn't a property at all, but rather a *relation*. This is a point that I have deliberately disregarded until now. But consider the following. Sometimes I have talked about the property that a fact might have of providing rational support for something (an act, say, or a belief). At other times, however, I have talked instead of the property that something might have (an act, say, or a belief) of being rationally *supported*. Both locutions, I assume, have been readily understood, and I trust that no one has been confused as to what the property was that I meant to be discussing. Note, however, that strictly speaking these two locutions actually pick out different properties! (It is, after all, one thing to *provide* support, and quite another thing to be *provided with* support.) The reason there has likely been no confusion is that in both cases the same underlying *relation* is in play, though it can be described from either of two directions. If a given fact provides rational support for, say, some particular action, then there is a certain *relation* that holds between that fact and that action, and for our purposes it has mattered not at all whether we describe it as the fact supporting the action or the action being supported by the fact. What we really want to know, of course, is whether this *relation* is itself basic, or whether it can be reduced further, to something nonnormative.

(To be sure, on some metaphysical views, it would be more accurate still to say that there are actually two *distinct* relations at work here—the relation of A's providing support for B, and the relation of B's being supported by A—though if one of these holds then necessarily the other does so as well. But this complication needn't detain us. Anyone attracted to this alternative picture could simply settle on a single relation as the favored one, reduce the other to it, and then think of our question as being whether the *favored* relation is reducible or not.)

If we wanted to, no doubt, we could regiment our discussion. We could focus on one of these two (distinct but related) properties, and take care to always ask about the very same one. Or, alternatively, we could explicitly focus instead on the underlying relation itself, always being careful to make it clear that it is the relation that is being discussed and not the distinct (but closely related) properties. Similarly, we could limit ourselves to talking only about reasons, or limit ourselves to talking only about rational support, or normativity, and so on. But for our purposes, I think, there would be no real advantage in rigorously regimenting the discussion in any of these ways. Accordingly, I'll continue to help myself—as I've been doing all along—to the entire range of similar (though not quite identical) locutions. Roughly speaking, our question is whether it would be metaphysically troubling if rational support were something that couldn't be reduced further. But as far as I can see, we needn't especially worry about always expressing that question in precisely the same way; so I won't particularly try to do that.

There is one final preliminary issue that should be mentioned. Is this property that we are wondering about—the supposedly irreducible property of providing rational support—to be thought of as being a *natural* property or a *nonnatural* one?

It is important to see that there is nothing in the idea of being irreducible *per se* that forces us to hold that if there really were such an irreducible property it would have to be a nonnatural one. Presumably, after all, even among natural properties the process of reduction comes to an end eventually, leaving us with a set of simple natural properties that cannot be reduced any further. So in and of itself, irreducibility is compatible with something being a natural property.

For all that, I think it fair to say that most simple realists are indeed nonnaturalists. They posit an irreducible property—that of being a reason—and then they claim, further, that this irreducible property isn't a natural one. Thus, the most common form of simple realism, I think, is one according to which the irreducible property of providing rational support, though a perfectly genuine property, is nonnatural. But this further claim is one that we needn't yet incorporate into our understanding of simple realism. To evaluate it properly we'll first need to ask what it *takes* for a property to be a natural one (or a nonnatural one), and that's an issue to which we can return later. For the time being, then, let's remain uncommitted on this point.

Simple realists hold that the property of being a reason is one that cannot be reduced to anything more basic. Obviously, one need not agree that a view like this is *correct*. But why should this proposal be thought especially *unattractive*?

13.2 Objections to Irreducible Normativity

I take it that few if any of us are troubled by the mere idea of there being irreducible properties of some sort or the other. To be sure, specific proposals—claims to the effect that this or that particular property is a simple one, incapable of being reduced further—may well be controversial. But that there are simple properties of *some* sort is an idea that most of us will find metaphysically untroubling (indeed, most of us will think the existence of such properties obvious and inevitable, on pain of infinite regress). So what, exactly, is it that is supposed to be troubling about the idea that *being a reason* is one such irreducible property?

Plausible answers are hard to come by. One initially tempting thought, I suppose, might be this: if rational support is an irreducible property, it would have to be "free floating" in the sense that nothing at all could explain why this or that particular act (or act type), would be rationally supported. We might, conceivably, be able to identify which acts *had* such rational support, but there would be nothing that could be said about *why* those acts that had such support had it, and why those that lacked it lacked it. And that, arguably, would be an intolerable situation, or at least a troubling one. So simple realism is not a position we could ever be altogether comfortable with.

In point of fact, I'm actually not at all confident that it really would be troubling to posit properties that were free floating in this way. Happily, however, I need not argue the point here. For the truth of the matter is that there is no need at all for the simple realist to think of reasons as *being* free floating. (It certainly wouldn't follow from the mere irreducibility of rational support.) Indeed, this picture is one that the simple realist is almost certainly going to reject. Normativity is not free floating, inexplicably attaching itself now to this act, now to that one. On the contrary, for each reason that exists there is a basis or a ground for the existence of that reason, an explanation of *why* there is a reason to perform the act in question. If, say, there is a reason for you to move your hand from the hot stove, there will be some underlying fact that explains or grounds the existence of this reason—for example, that doing this will stop the pain! Similarly, if there is a reason for you to believe that it is snowing outside, there will be an underlying fact or set of facts that explains or grounds the existence of that reason as well—perhaps the fact that you've just heard a weather report to this effect, or that you've just glanced out the window and seen snowflakes falling. Even if the *property* of being a reason cannot be reduced to anything more basic, it can still be the case that each time that there *is* a reason there is an underlying explanation of why that is so.

One might still worry: if reasons are irreducible, couldn't there still be *some* free-floating cases of rational support, at least in principle? And isn't that mere possibility problematic? But the simple realist can reply that it is a *necessary truth* that each reason has a basis. That's an essential fact about the nature of rational support—a fact about how reasons "work," if you will: there is a basis for each reason that exists. The irreducibility of normativity is perfectly compatible with it being the case that something (an act, say) can be

13.2 OBJECTIONS TO IRREDUCIBLE NORMATIVITY 349

rationally supported *only* when there is an underlying fact that grounds or explains the *presence* of that support.

As it happens, I don't imagine that this initial train of thought leads many people to reject the idea of an irreducible normative property. Far more common, I suspect, is the simple thought that normative properties inevitably strike us as being weird and unfamiliar. They seem spooky and strange, utterly unlike anything else with which we are acquainted. That alone, it may seem, is sufficient reason to be suspicious about them.

Admittedly (one might continue), any such initial suspicion would be satisfactorily answered if reductionism proved successful, for then normative properties would themselves reduce to more familiar and uncontroversial ones. If reductionism were correct then in talking about normative properties we wouldn't be committing ourselves to anything strange or new. We would see that normativity reduces to things that are simpler and more familiar, and so our initial suspicion about it would be allayed. But when we are entertaining the possibility of *simple* realism about the normative there is nothing to make the air of weirdness dissipate. We are left positing properties that are different and strange, unlike any others with which we are familiar. That leaves us with nothing to eliminate or even lessen our initial sense of unease.

An initial response to an argument like this might be as follows. There is actually nothing unfamiliar at all about normative properties! Indeed, there are few properties that are more familiar from our daily life. We regularly find ourselves with thoughts to the effect that there is reason to perform some act, or that there is reason to avoid doing some other act; that one ought to believe this, or feel that; that pursuing this goal would make sense; that there is something to be said in favor of thinking or doing or feeling or wanting or being this or that. What's more, countless other, similar thoughts hover silently, just below the surface, brought to consciousness only when we are challenged to justify ourselves. Whenever the need arises to consciously reflect on whether anything justifies our actions and beliefs, relevant explicit judgments are forthcoming. So the simple fact is, our lives are utterly infused with normative judgments, conscious or implicit; normative properties are a regular part of our everyday life.

Thus, any suggestion to the effect that the property of being a reason is somehow an unfamiliar one, strange and unknown, is a claim that should be dismissed immediately. Contrary to what's being suggested, the simple realist is not introducing a new property into our thinking at all. She is simply offering a particular hypothesis about the *nature* of that already familiar property, to wit, that it cannot be reduced to anything even more basic.

Suppose, however, that we were to agree that at the very least simple realists are adding something new to our metaphysical *theories* (insofar as they are suggesting an addition to our catalog of basic, irreducible properties). Even if so, what of it? It can hardly be unacceptable to add something new to our list of fundamental properties if doing so helps us to better understand the world and our experience of it. (When electromagnetic charges were first introduced into our physics, it surely wouldn't have been appropriate to reject them on the mere ground that doing this was introducing *new* properties into our theorizing.) So if positing the property of rational support helps us to better make sense of our familiar experience that some things ought to be done—or ought to be believed, or felt, or preferred—how can the mere act of introducing such a property be found objectionable?

But if the concern isn't with the introduction of what is (arguably) a new property into our theorizing, or an unfamiliar one, or an irreducible one, what exactly is it that might make us anxious? What is it about the suggestion that being a reason is an irreducible normative property, that might leave one ill at ease?

I suspect that the real complaint isn't so much that the notion of rational support is strange in the sense of being *unfamiliar* (since it isn't unfamiliar), but rather that it is strange in the sense of inevitably being *weird*—bizarre— utterly unlike any *other* properties with which we are acquainted. Rational support (supposing it to be irreducible) just seems so very, very different from other properties (other than, of course, other normative properties) that it is disconcerting to contemplate simply dropping it into our metaphysics "whole," as it were—without reducing it to other, more familiar, components.

But if that really is the complaint—that normative properties, as a class, are quite unlike other properties—then there is a straightforward answer available to the simple realist, namely, that this may well be true, but the very same thing is true for other families of properties as well. Properties often come in groups (think of colors, for example, or temporal properties, or mathematical ones), and the simple truth of the matter is that the members of any given family or group typically seem to be utterly unlike the members of other families. Color properties, for example, really aren't very much like economic ones at all; and economic properties aren't at all similar to the properties posited by fundamental physics; and so on. Indeed it isn't much of an exaggeration to say that most broad families of properties are quite unlike all of the other broad

13.2 OBJECTIONS TO IRREDUCIBLE NORMATIVITY

families of properties. Any given family will be unique—strange and weird—when compared to the other types of properties that we accept, but there is nothing remotely unique about *being* unique in this way. So even if it is true that normative properties are quite different from other types of properties (the properties of physics, say, or mathematics), once again we should just ask, what of it? *Most* types of things are rather different from other types of things. (Consider, for example, just how different substances, space, time, numbers, and mental states all are from one another.)

I can think of one other way in which a given property might strike someone as disconcertingly weird or strange, and conceivably some of the resistance we might have toward positing irreducible normativity might be because we find ourselves thinking that the property of rational support would be troubling in this final way. I have in mind the quality that we sometimes mean in calling something "spooky"—the thought that some phenomenon is mysterious and beyond our ability to truly understand. Many of us, for example, are dismissive of supposed parapsychological or paranormal phenomena for just this reason. It isn't merely that we feel that the evidence doesn't yet support the belief in these purported facts. Rather, more than that, we may resist the very idea of accepting a belief in such phenomena precisely because it seems that believing in these things would require us to accept the existence of matters that by their very nature would elude understanding, things that would remain mysterious to their very core. Conceivably, then, some may feel that something similar would have to be true if there really were such a thing as the irreducible property of being a reason. The very thought generates resistance because it seems that irreducible normativity would inevitably remain mysterious, incapable of truly being understood. In a word, it would be spooky.

I don't actually know, of course, how common this last feeling is, and how big a role it plays in explaining the unease that some have when so much as contemplating the mere possibility of positing irreducible normativity. Still, I suspect that something like this may well be at work—often, no doubt, behind the scenes.

To the extent that this is so, however, it is worth asking whether normativity really would be *inevitably* mysterious in this way. And again, the analogy to parapsychology may be helpful. Imagine a possible future in which evidence for ESP (extrasensory perception) or telekinesis (the ability to move objects through thought alone) or precognition (foretelling the future) became commonplace, readily replicable and familiar. Indeed, imagine that we were eventually able to work out laws which spelled out the precise conditions under which each of these phenomena would occur. Doing this, of course, might well require positing new properties or new entities—"psi waves," perhaps, or the property of "telesensitivity," or what have you. But suppose that, having done this—having posited the new properties, and having explained how, exactly, these new properties interacted with one another and with other more familiar properties—we were able to view parapsychological phenomena as law bound and predictable. Initially, no doubt, this would all continue to seem a bit strange and weird, but eventually, I think, the feeling of weirdness would diminish. We would have "domesticated" the parapsychological, and it would then simply be one more part of our (now expanded) theory of the world. (Indeed, something like the process that I just described is what happened over time with electromagnetism. What was once strange and spooky became "tamed," as the relevant laws were worked out and more fully understood. But doing this required positing new properties, properties that initially seemed distressingly weird and unfamiliar.)

I certainly don't expect anything like this to happen with regard to the paranormal. But the crucial thought here is that the difference between something feeling "spooky" and its seeming ordinary and familiar is to a considerable extent a matter of whether we take the properties and phenomena in question to be rule bound, governed by laws that we can articulate and understand. So the relevant question for us might be whether something like this could happen with regard to *reasons*. Might we eventually arrive at general rules or laws stating precisely what reasons exist, under which circumstances, and how these various reasons interact with one another and with still other properties? If so, wouldn't any initial feeling that irreducible normativity was spooky or weird be something that would recede, if the relevant laws governing normativity were spelled out and well understood?

To test this hypothesis, of course, we would first need to discover and defend the relevant laws. It won't surprise you to learn that I am not going to try to do that here. Doing it properly would require settling numerous debates that fall well outside the bounds of our present discussion. First of all, and most obviously, since moral requirements entail (or are constituted by) reasons, to lay out the precise laws governing the existence and behavior of those reasons we would have to take a stand on any number of substantive first-order questions from normative ethics. And that—to repeat a familiar refrain— lies beyond the intended scope of this book. Indeed, second, developing the relevant laws would also require exploring any number of issues that lie *beyond* normative ethics. After all, as I have repeatedly noted, normativity arises in countless other areas besides ethics (there are, for example, questions about what to do in *non*moral contexts, and questions about what to believe and, even more generally, questions about what to feel or want or prefer or be). So adequately capturing the laws of normativity would not only require detailed investigations within normative ethics but also parallel investigations within epistemology, moral psychology, action theory, decision theory, and more. Offering a comprehensive treatment of the laws of normativity would be a complicated—and controversial—affair indeed.

(There are also questions about what we might call the "logical form" of those laws. Would they be universal and exceptionless? Or might they, instead, be mere generalizations, liberally strewn with ceteris paribus clauses ("other things being equal")? There is an ongoing debate within normative ethics about this issue; and corresponding questions arise in other areas of philosophy as well.)

Suppose, however, that I am right, and if only we had a suitable set of basic normative laws any residual worry about irreducible normativity would lose its force. I'm certainly not in a position to state and defend those laws—but is there any good reason to believe that an appropriate set of laws could never actually be produced? I find it difficult to see what that reason might be. As I've already suggested, the experience of normativity is an everyday, familiar one, and we are certainly used to recognizing (even if only in a sporadic and piecemeal fashion) how specific reasons are generated by relevant underlying facts. So it is hard to see what would justify the pessimistic conjecture that this familiar array of normative phenomena could never be systematized and brought under suitable laws.

As far as I can see, then, there is nothing in the very idea of irreducible normativity that would warrant our dismissing this possibility out of hand. Simple realism may or may not be the truth, but we've seen no compelling reason to deny that it is a view that deserves to be taken seriously.

13.3 Nonnatural Properties

Actually, there is probably one more line of thought that may play a significant role in leading people to be wary of the idea of an irreducible normative property. It starts with the thought that any such property would have to be a *nonnatural* one, and it then combines this thought with the suggestion that, for all that, the very idea of nonnatural properties is one that we should all be wary of.

Obviously, no simple realist will accept both premises of this argument. If they accept the first premise, and agree that the property of being a reason is a nonnatural one, they will reject the second, and deny that there is something unacceptable about positing the existence of nonnatural properties. Alternatively, if they agree with the second premise, that positing nonnatural properties is objectionable, they will presumably deny the first premise, insisting instead that the property of being a reason is actually a natural rather than a nonnatural one. These are, it seems, the two main options available for resisting the argument, and in principle, at least, both appear to be available to the simple realist. (Beyond this, of course, there is also the alternative of rejecting *both* steps of the argument, insisting that although the property of being a reason is in fact a natural one, nonetheless there wouldn't have been anything wrong with it being a nonnatural property either.)

Still, I think it must be conceded that the argument has a certain amount of intuitive force. For as I have already remarked, most simple realists do seem perfectly prepared to agree that the irreducible normative property they are positing would be a nonnatural one. So in putting forward the first premise of the argument, the critic of simple realism can hardly be accused of interpreting that view in a hostile or uncharitable way. (In contrast, most contemporary reductionists aim to reduce the normative to nonnormative *natural* properties. Thus we get a striking sociological contrast: in broad terms, reductionists tend to be naturalists, simple realists tend to be nonnaturalists.)

That leaves only the question of whether we should indeed be open to the existence of nonnatural properties, or whether, instead, as the second premise claims, we might rightly insist that an intellectually respectable metaphysics will restrict itself to positing natural properties alone. And here too it must be admitted that although there are those who *reject* a naturalistic worldview (theists, for example), a great many people find it implausible to posit anything that takes us beyond, or outside of, the natural world. No doubt, they may claim, we are free to posit various *natural* properties as we see fit, when doing this leaves us better able to explain the world; but to introduce *nonnatural* properties, the thought goes, is to jettison any pretense of offering a scientifically acceptable worldview. It is to abandon science for mysticism.

So the second premise will be widely endorsed (especially by those with a scientific bent), and the first premise appears to be one even simple realists typically accept. Taken together, however, they spell trouble for simple realism. Simple realism appears to be positing a *kind* of property that the scientifically inclined will be strongly disposed to find problematic.

In fact, however, even those who *reject* a naturalistic worldview may think it important not to be overly profligate with the positing of nonnatural properties. It is one thing, they may say, to believe in a God who stands outside of the natural order, and whose interventions into that world are literally miraculous and supernatural. But it would be implausible, they might suggest, to think that every single occurrence of *normativity* stands outside the natural order in a similar way. It cannot be that every single time one has a reason to think or feel or do something, there is something that stands outside of the natural world. So even if it would be a mistake to dismiss the very category of nonnatural properties, it may still be plausible to insist that *reasons* cannot be something nonnatural. If positing irreducible normativity really would be positing something nonnatural—as simple realists seem to be conceding—this remains a problematic metaphysical position.

As I say, I think it possible that thoughts like these may play a role in explaining why many people are uncomfortable with the very idea of simple realism. The view seems committed to positing nonnatural properties, and it is easy to believe that the existence of such properties should either be rejected altogether, or, at the very least, appealed to sparingly, used only in ways that simply don't seem relevant when thinking about normativity.

But what exactly *is* it for a property to be a nonnatural one? If we imagine, if only for the sake of argument, that there really is an irreducible property of rational support, by virtue of what would it be correct to classify this property as a nonnatural rather than a natural one? Why can't the simple realist just insist that the property that they posit is indeed a natural one after all, and thus completely sidestep whatever problems might attend the more typical suggestion that the property is actually nonnatural? What exactly does it *take* to be a natural property anyway?

It actually turns out to be difficult to draw the distinction between natural and nonnatural properties in a clear, intuitive, and uncontroversial way. I do have a suggestion, though I am not wed to it, and I certainly recognize that others may prefer to draw the line in a different way.

First, though, here are two initially plausible but inadequate proposals. One might initially be tempted by the thought that a natural property is a property that can be had by a natural object. To be sure, this just puts off the day of reckoning, as we would still need to know what it takes to be a natural object. But no matter, for the proposal is clearly too wide. Imagine that God exists and especially loves rivers. Rivers are, presumably, natural objects, and so the property of *being loved by God* would be a property that could be had by a natural object. But I presume that this property—being loved by God—is, for all that, a paradigmatic example of something that would be a *nonnatural* property, rather than a natural one. So this first proposal fails.

Second, one might propose that a natural property is one that is directly observable, through one or more of the five senses. But that's clearly too *narrow* a criterion, since having a negative electric charge is presumably a natural property, yet it's not something that we can directly see (or taste or smell, and so on). Of course, we could *widen* the test, so as to include as natural properties all those that we might conceivably learn about *indirectly*, via empirical investigation. But while this now correctly includes electric charge as a natural property (since we learn about electric charge by drawing inferences from the evidence of our senses), the revised criterion now becomes *too wide*, since those who believe in a supernatural God might think it possible to infer things about supernatural matters by studying the empirical world. Some have argued, for example, that we can infer that the world was *created by God*, since life itself would have been impossible had any of a small number of physical constants had somewhat different values from their actual ones (this is the so-called fine-tuning argument). Yet even if this were true, and the inferences sound, it still would not seem plausible to classify being created by God as a *natural* property.

Rather than continuing to consider other, similarly unsuccessful, attempts to demarcate the difference between being a natural and a nonnatural property, I'll simply offer my own tentative proposal: natural properties are those that (1) have causal powers and (2) are governed by laws. Both features are necessary for being a natural property, and together they are jointly sufficient.

The causal powers condition is intended to cover the thought that a natural property will be part of the causal nexus. On the one hand, the occurrence of a natural property can cause other properties to obtain, and on the other hand, the occurrence of a natural property can itself be the causal result of the obtaining of still other properties. Something like this thought may lie behind the earlier suggestion that natural properties—and more generally, I suppose, natural phenomena—are those that can be studied empirically (in effect, studied by science, broadly construed), since studying something empirically is basically a matter of investigating it through its causal powers (what it causes and what it is caused by). If a property lacks causal powers it cannot be studied empirically; and if it cannot be studied empirically then arguably it is not a *natural* property.

Of course, the causal condition cannot be sufficient on its own. A supernatural God might well be part of the causal nexus, creating the world and responding to it, but for all that, divine properties (like omnipotence or omniscience, or, for that matter, infinite goodness) do not seem to be natural ones. It's not merely that no natural object happens to have these properties, but rather that there is something about the *kinds* of properties these are that seems to take them outside the natural order altogether. But that's where the second condition comes in: natural properties (and, more broadly, natural phenomena) are *governed by laws*. A natural property is one that is connected in lawlike ways to still other properties.

It is this second condition that allows us to accommodate the thought that divine attributes (like omnipotence) and other supernatural properties (like being created by God) are nonnatural rather than natural ones. For despite the causal character of these properties, intuitively we do not think of them as governed by lawlike regularities. God is not bound by *laws*; that's precisely what we have in mind in thinking that a god would be something *super*natural, rather than being a part of the natural order. Similarly, demonic possession, if there were such a thing, would involve a number of properties that we would rightly think of as nonnatural if, as might be the case, there were no laws governing possession's onset, its attributes, or its termination.

Imagine, however, that we actually *discovered* laws governing "demonic possession." Suppose there were causal regularities that explained the onset of the condition, indicated clearly what would happen to the victim during the course of the possession, and showed how to bring that condition to an end. Then we might well come to think of "demonic possession" as a natural phenomenon after all (and give it a new name). We would, in effect, have come to think of possession as a *disease*, rather than being something supernatural or nonnatural.

In the same vein, recall the example of parapsychological phenomena, discussed in the previous section. It is precisely to the extent that we think of such things (supposing them to be real) as eluding lawlike regularities that we find ourselves viewing them as something that stands *outside* the natural order—despite being part of the causal nexus. Nonetheless, as I have already suggested, if we ever did work out laws governing telekinesis, say, or clairvoyance, then parapsychology would simply take its place as the newest of our empirical sciences, and the relevant newly introduced properties (whatever they might be) would be ones we would rightly view as *natural* properties, rather than nonnatural ones.

So that's the suggestion. Natural properties are those with causal powers but subject to laws. No doubt, the proposal could be refined (at the very least, each of the two conditions could stand to be made more precise), and I doubt it will capture everyone's intuitions. But let us suppose that something like this account is on the right track. We can now ask: if there really were an irreducible property of rational support, would it be a natural property or not?

I am inclined to think that the answer is that it would *not* be. That is, if these really are the relevant requirements for being a natural property, then rational support—conceived of as simple and irreducible—would not be a natural property but a nonnatural one. For it seems to me likely that although irreducible normativity would meet the second condition—it would be law bound—it would not meet the first; it would lack causal powers.

I won't argue for the claim that even an irreducible property of rational support would be governed by laws. As I have already suggested (in 13.2), although I believe we are not yet in a position to state a suitable set of general principles spelling out all the various conditions under which reasons get created and how they interact with one another, I see no good reason to think that facts about normativity are weird—spooky, or supernatural, in the sense of being ungoverned by lawlike regularities. If there is a reason to do something (or think something, or feel something), then this is because an underlying fact of the right sort generates that reason, and I see no compelling reason to think that the relevant explanations cannot be brought together in a systematic fashion, subsumed under a suitable set of general principles. The same thing is true, I think, with regard to the various ways in which reasons interact with each other, sometimes reinforcing one another, sometimes opposing one another, all the while generating facts about what one has most reason to do (or think, or feel); these facts, too, I believe, are governed by general principles or laws. Moral theory attempts, in part, to state some of these laws, and the same thing is true for decision theory, and epistemology, and so on. So while I readily admit that we cannot yet produce a complete and adequate set of laws concerning rational support, it still seems to me plausible to maintain that normativity is rule governed. And if the simple realist is right and normativity is irreducible, nothing on that score changes. All that follows is that the *irreducible* property of being a reason is governed by laws.

Still, it does seem to me plausible to think that this irreducible property would not be a *causal* one. Normativity per se doesn't cause anything,

I think, and strictly speaking it isn't *caused* by anything either. To be sure, as I have repeatedly insisted, when a given act is rationally supported there is a *reason* why this is so, there is an underlying fact that generates or grounds the rational support. But these underlying facts do not literally cause the rational support to come into existence. The rational support exists *by virtue of* these underlying facts, but the coming into existence of the reason is not the result of a *causal process*. Similarly, while it is certainly true that your beliefs concerning reasons are part of the causal nexus—your belief in the existence of a reason can cause you to act, for example—it is only the *belief* that has this causal power, not the reason itself. My own view (for reasons closely related to those given in 8.4) is that the existence of a reason doesn't actually cause the *belief* in that reason. Nor, I think, do reasons cause anything else. Reasons have justificatory powers, not causal ones.

That last point should probably be stated a bit more cautiously. After all, if *reductionism* about reasons is true, and in particular if reasons can be reduced to more basic *natural* properties, then reasons will turn out to have causal powers after all, by virtue of being nothing more than those underlying natural properties. On this sort of reductionist account, therefore, the causal condition actually would be satisfied (and the property of being a reason would be a natural one).

But suppose simple realism is right, and the property of being a reason is irreducible. Then it seems to me plausible to believe that reasons will lack causal powers altogether. To be sure, there is nothing in the idea of being an irreducible property that rules out having causal powers (there are, I presume, any number of basic natural properties—irreducible, but causally efficacious.) But for all that, it seems to me plausible to hold that if *normativity* is irreducible, it will, in fact, be causally inert. Irreducible normativity would justify; but it wouldn't *cause* anything.

If that's right, then the basic property posited by simple realists—the irreducible property of being a reason—does indeed turn out to be a nonnatural one. That, as I've suggested, is the dominant view among simple realists, and we can now see why it is a plausible position for them to take when describing their view.

But this only serves to bring us back to the skeptical worry from the start of this section: don't we have good reason to reject a belief in any kind of *nonnatural* property of rational support? As we have already noted, the scientifically minded may feel that the only rationally respectable position is one that rejects all nonnatural properties altogether; and even those who reject a naturalistic worldview and embrace belief in the supernatural may feel that there is something objectionable about the suggestion that a commonplace property like being a *reason* could be a nonnatural one.

In short, simple realism may well be committed to the claim that being a reason is an irreducible nonnatural property. But doesn't that fact actually just give us reason to *reject* simple realism?

In fact, however, no such conclusion would be warranted. For if the account I've given of what it takes to be a natural property is correct, then *non*natural properties are, it turns out, far more common than we might otherwise have thought; they are, indeed, an uncontroversial and ubiquitous occurrence. Consider, for example, the property of *being self-identical*. Every single object in the world has this property, and yet it certainly seems to be a causally inert one: nothing *causes* you to be self-identical; and the fact that you are self-identical certainly doesn't seem to cause anything *else* either. So the property of being self-identical is not, by the proposed test, a natural one. Yet it would be absurd to dismiss it as somehow illegitimate or suspect. Similar remarks apply to countless other properties, like the property of *being red or not*, or the mathematical property of *being divisible by itself*. These properties lack causal powers, so they are nonnatural; but it would be silly to find any of them objectionable.

These examples suggest that being a nonnatural property—even a commonplace one—isn't something that anyone should find especially troubling. So even if it is true that simple realism is committed to the existence of a property like that, that isn't actually a good reason to reject simple realism. Simple realism may or may not be true, but we should not dismiss it simply because it is committed to the existence of a (commonplace) nonnatural property.

Of course, some may find themselves thinking that the properties just mentioned—being self-identical, being red or not, and being divisible by itself—should actually all be classified as *natural* properties rather than nonnatural ones, despite being causally inert. Presumably, anyone wanting to say this will need to reject the causal condition for naturalness. Perhaps, then, we should accept only the *second* condition, holding that a property is natural just in case it is governed by laws (as all these properties certainly are). Note, however, that if we do revise the test for naturalness in this way, and if I am right that even irreducible normativity would be law governed, then despite what many have thought, irreducible normativity will turn out to be a natural property as well, and not a nonnatural one. Either way, then—whether because being a nonnatural property isn't problematic, or because being a reason isn't actually a nonnatural property after all—the thought that we should reject simple realism because of its (supposed) commitment to nonnatural properties will be misguided.

I realize, of course, that despite everything I have said, the feeling that there is something unavoidably disreputable about simple realism may still persist. When all is said and done—some may say—isn't it clear that nothing like irreducible normativity can find a place in a scientific worldview? Certainly empirical science is incapable of establishing the existence of anything remotely like that. And isn't it clear that the only truths are those that can be established by science?

In fact, however—the simple realist should reply—it isn't *at all* clear that the *only* truths are those that can be established by empirical science. Indeed, this can't possibly be the case. For that very claim—that the only truths are those that can be established by science—is not itself the *sort* of claim that could ever be established by science! It is a *philosophical* thesis (about the kinds of truths there are), not a scientific one. Suppose, then, though only for a moment, that it were true, and the only truths were those that could be established by science. It would immediately follow that this very claim was actually false (since it cannot be established by science, and so, by its own lights, cannot be true). That is to say, if the claim *were* true, it would have to be false. So it cannot actually be true at all; it *must* be false. But if it is false, then there are truths that go *beyond* those that can be established by science. There is more to reality than what science alone can establish.

This retort, to be sure, doesn't tell us what those additional truths might be. So it certainly doesn't establish the truth of simple realism. But it does show that it must be a mistake to dismiss simple realism on the grounds that it goes beyond anything that science might hope to establish. There are truths that are not scientific truths, facts that go beyond anything that can be proven by empirical science alone. And it could well be the case that among those facts is the existence of an irreducible property of being a reason.

13.4 The Metaphysics of Morals

Over the course of the last two chapters we have examined possible replies to what may well be the most influential argument for moral skepticism, the claim that it is impossible to provide an acceptable *metaphysical* account of morality, that moral values could never be given a place in a plausible account of the sorts of things that there are. The skeptic argues that the world contains rocks and trees and people and books, as well as molecules and atoms, photons and neutrinos. But no values. There is a place for facts about love and sunspots, reading the newspaper and calling your mother. But there is no place for *morality*. No respectable metaphysics can find a place for moral facts. That's the thought.

In response, the moral realist points out that there really would be nothing especially puzzling or problematic about the metaphysics of morality, provided that we are allowed to ascribe moral properties to various familiar objects. If *acts* can be right or wrong, *outcomes* good or bad, *character traits* virtuous or vicious, and so on, then there can be moral *facts*. So the crucial question is whether there is something metaphysically troubling about positing moral *properties*.

And what is the right account of the metaphysics of moral properties? There are two basic possibilities: reductionism and simple realism. Each has its advocates. Of course, virtually all moral realists believe that *some* moral properties can be reduced to others, so the real question is whether *all* moral properties can be reduced to nonmoral ones, or whether there are some simple, basic moral properties that cannot be reduced any further. My own view, as I've explained, is that we can indeed reduce moral properties to nonmoral ones, provided that we are entitled to appeal to the more general normative property of *being a reason*. So the question then becomes whether this property too can be reduced even further, or whether reduction comes to an end at this point, with the positing of an irreducible property of rational support.

Unsurprisingly, opinions differ. Some moral realists are thoroughgoing reductionists, holding that reasons can indeed be reduced to something even more basic, so that morality can in fact be reduced all the way to the nonnormative. But others—the simple realists about reasons—think that reduction comes to an end with normativity. Clearly, that's an important distinction among moral realists, but for our purposes the essential point is that *either* position would provide an answer to the skeptic's objections—provided of course that the position could be plausibly maintained.

In our discussion I have not taken a stand as to which of these two approaches to answering the skeptic is to be preferred. What I have tried to do, instead, is to show why *both* of these are positions that one might reasonably embrace. Of course, any given moral realist may have convictions on this point, with some finding reductionism the more attractive of the two theories (or perhaps the only attractive theory), while others think that it is, rather, simple realism that we should favor.

But there is a third possibility as well, one we shouldn't overlook. A moral realist might be uncertain as to *which* of these two views is the more plausible one, confident only that one or the other of the two must be correct. Such realists are content to say that *either* view is more plausible than the option of rejecting *both* alternatives, since that would be tantamount to accepting normative nihilism, an utterly implausible view. Thus, a moral realist need not commit herself as to which of reductionism and simple realism is the more plausible position; she need only insist that *one* of them must be true.

This third stance is the one that seems right to me. I do not know if reductionism is correct, though it might well be. If it is, of course, then the skeptic is answered, and moral realism is shown to be metaphysically respectable. But if, on the other hand, the reductionist project proves unsuccessful, so be it, that merely shows that we should be simple realists rather than reductionists. That too would be fine with me, since despite whatever misgivings one might initially have about it, simple realism is a perfectly respectable alternative. And obviously enough, if simple realism does turn out to be the truth, then the skeptic is once again answered and moral realism remains metaphysically acceptable.

So while I remain uncertain as to which of these two views—reductionism or simple realism—is correct, I am confident that one or the other is the truth. It would be absurd to suggest that no metaphysically acceptable account of normativity could ever be provided, and that we must abandon all talk of having reasons to act, or think or feel or want. Yet once we acknowledge that there are indeed reasons to act, the metaphysical challenge to morality is disarmed, for the moral realist can plausibly maintain that moral facts are simply facts about reasons—reasons of a particular kind, reasons with a particular basis. In sum, the assault on morality by way of metaphysics is one more skeptical challenge that we can reasonably take to have been answered.

14

Moral Realism

14.1 Answering the Moral Skeptic

What would it take for there to be such a thing as morality? What exactly would need to be the case for it to be correct to say that there are objective facts about right and wrong, objective moral truths about what we are morally required to do?

As I noted in the first chapter, people disagree. It isn't merely that they disagree about *what* the particular moral facts are. Nor is it merely the case that they disagree about whether there *are* any moral facts at all. They disagree as well about what would need to be true for it to be appropriate to say that there *were* moral facts, what would have to be the case for there to be something that genuinely deserved to be *called* "morality," or "objective moral truth."

Still, suppose there were a rule or perhaps a set of principles that required certain actions, while forbidding still others. Suppose that it was possible for us to figure out the contents of those rules, and that in principle at least we could guide ourselves by them, trying to do the actions that were required and to avoid those acts that were forbidden. Suppose that it was possible to know not only what the principles were (in a general way) but also how they applied to particular cases, so that although people might disagree about any of these matters, there were objective answers about who was right, correct views about what was actually required, and so on. Suppose that, although the principles sometimes generated different specific requirements in different circumstances, the same *basic* principles applied to everyone—they were equally *binding* on everyone—no matter what the given person's particular group or society. What's more, suppose that having figured out what one was required to do, whether generally or in particular instances, one would then be moved by those beliefs, so that one was always motivated, at least somewhat, to act in keeping with what one took to be the various requirements and prohibitions. And suppose as well that there was always at least some justification for doing this, that the requirements were backed by reasons, perhaps even of a categorical sort. Finally, suppose that what these various principles required of us were different ways of protecting and promoting the interests of oneself and others, along with ways of showing everyone due respect.

If all of this were true, if there really were principles with all of these features, I take it that almost all of us would readily agree that these principles were *moral* principles, and that all of this constituted something worthy of being called an objective morality. A list of the relevant rules would be an objective moral code, and the sundry facts about what the principles required of us (or permitted, and so on) would be objective *moral* facts. There would be objective moral truths.

Of course, some might think it a mistake to emphasize rules and principles, as I have just been doing, with their corresponding focus on actions as being permitted, required, or forbidden. They might think it preferable to focus instead on virtues and vices, with objective facts about what sort of person one should be, positing as well the existence of reasons and motivation to act and think and feel as the virtuous person would act and think and feel, and so on. But for present purposes this would be to quibble over details. Presumably, if it really were the case that certain character traits were objectively preferable, so that one had reason to be such a person and to deliberate and act accordingly, and so on, then here too it would be appropriate to talk about the existence of an objective morality with corresponding moral facts. (For simplicity of exposition, however, I will continue to talk primarily in terms of rules and principles.)

Admittedly, some might ask for more. Perhaps some would want to be assured that the basic principles are not merely universally binding in the actual world, but necessary truths, holding in all possible worlds. Or perhaps they will want to be assured that the validity of these rules, what makes them binding, is essentially a mind independent affair, or that the reasons justifying conformity to the principles are sufficiently strong to always override any competing considerations. And so on. As I say, people disagree about what precisely would need to be the case for it to be appropriate to affirm that there really is such a thing as morality (or objective moral truth). So no single list of features like this is likely to satisfy everyone. (And for that matter, of course, many people would be satisfied with somewhat *less* than what I have just described.) Still, there is a cluster of features—if not exactly the list I gave, then something in the neighborhood—that would satisfy all or almost all of us. If there really were requirements (and prohibitions, and so on) more or less of the sort I described, then the moral realist would be vindicated. There would be such a thing as objective morality. There would be moral *facts*.

To which the moral skeptic will of course respond: That's all well and good, but what of it? The question was never whether we could *describe* something, such that if only it were to exist, it would constitute objective morality, but only whether such a thing actually exists. We might well agree that if something like the story just told were true (putting aside questions about which precise features of the story are essential), then the moral realist would be right, and moral facts really would exist. But again, what of it? There is no good reason to believe that anything remotely like this really is the case. And there is, in fact, plenty of reason to think that it might even be true that nothing like this *could* be the case. Indeed, describing in detail just what it would take for there to be such a thing as morality makes it all the easier to see why we are right to *deny* the existence of moral facts. There is compelling reason to believe that the moral realist's picture (whatever the precise details) simply does not correspond to reality. To believe in morality is to believe in a *fiction*.

I imagine that few, if any, of us are altogether immune to the moral skeptic's taunts. Even if we find ourselves thinking that skepticism is misguided and that there really is such a thing as morality, it is easy, I think, to fall prey to the thought that belief in morality is a less than fully respectable matter, that there is something intellectually suspect or second rate about believing in the reality of moral facts. At the very least, we may still worry about how best to respond to the skeptic's specific challenges—wondering whether there really are compelling answers to their objections, and if so, what those answers might look like.

That's why it is important to take the skeptic's challenge seriously. Each of us should want to see whether plausible answers to the skeptic can be given. But doing this, of course, requires moving beyond vague skeptical worries to the effect that there is something or the other implausible about the moral realist's position. Rather, answering the skeptic requires that we spell out and pin down specific criticisms, separating each one from the next, so as to hold them all up to the light and subject them, each in turn, to critical scrutiny. We need to see exactly what it is that might trouble someone about accepting the realist's position. If there are features of realism that are problematic, what exactly are they? If there are reasons to think that belief in the existence of moral facts is a less plausible position to take than the skeptical alternative, what precisely are those reasons? It is only after we equip ourselves

14.1 ANSWERING THE MORAL SKEPTIC

with a more fine-grained understanding of why one might be led to deny the existence of morality that we can be in a good position to judge whether one's confidence in the truth of moral realism is something that should grow weaker. That's why we needed to distinguish and examine a series of specific arguments—so as to properly understand and evaluate the specific concerns that might lead one to embrace moral skepticism (or, at a minimum, leave one worried about the overall *plausibility* of realism).

Some of these arguments have aimed to show that nothing could actually have one or another of the features that anything worthy of being called *morality* would need to have. We have, for example, considered arguments to the effect that there could be no such thing as moral knowledge, that moral beliefs couldn't properly motivate us, or that the very idea of a categorical reason is problematic. Other arguments claimed to show only that moral realism is a less plausible *hypothesis* than moral skepticism is, given, for example, the presence of widespread moral disagreement, or realism's purported inability to offer an acceptable account of the metaphysics of moral properties. And all of these arguments—including, of course, others that I haven't explicitly mentioned here—come in various forms, or can be revised in response to initial replies on the part of the realist.

Of course, any given skeptic might not put forward all of these arguments, just as any given moral realist might not be troubled by all of these objections. But each of them, I think, represents a genuine and reasonable question to raise about morality, in the sense that each gives voice to a concern that might well occur to a thoughtful and open-minded person impartially reflecting on the legitimacy of believing in morality.

In each case, however, I have argued that there are plausible answers available to the moral realist. Often enough, there is more than one possible answer (though whether any given answer will be acceptable to any given realist may depend in part on what, exactly, the realist wants to include in the "job description" for morality). Sometimes, in such cases, I've merely laid out the various alternative replies that the realist might offer, without choosing among them. In other cases, however, I have indicated which particular answer strikes me as most plausible. And in still other cases I have presented only a single answer, the one that seems to me uniquely promising.

Sometimes, I realize, providing a careful statement of a possible answer turned out to be a disappointingly complex affair. That's unfortunate, I know. But as I warned in the introduction, even the simplest of questions can require complicated answers.

In any event, the crucial claim I want to make is this: there are indeed plausible answers to each of the arguments we've discussed.

That's not to say, of course, that there is nothing more that the skeptic can say about any of these issues. There are further replies that could be made by the skeptic—responses to my responses, as it were (or, more accurately in many cases, responses to my *responses* to their responses to my responses). For as I also noted in the introduction, philosophical debates rarely come to an end; they mostly just get deeper, as each side tries to strengthen their arguments, sharpening and revising their objections and replies. So it should not be thought that I have said the last word on any of the topics that we've examined. Indeed, philosophers working in moral philosophy will already know of various ways in which each debate could easily be carried on for at least several more rounds.

However, I do hope that I have said enough to make it plausible to think that there is nothing intellectually disreputable about believing in morality. No one drawn to moral realism should think of himself or herself as being philosophically naive, as though it is just obvious that moral skepticism has the dialectical upper hand. On the contrary, my own view is that it is the realist who has the upper hand, and it is the moral skeptic, not the moral realist, who is in the argumentatively weaker position.

But even if I am wrong about this last claim, it is *far* from being the case that any objective reviewer of the arguments on both sides would have to conclude that skepticism is in the obviously stronger position—as though it were much more likely to be true, or is clearly the more plausible of the two competing views. Even if I am wrong to think that moral realism has the *better* of the argument, we should agree, at a minimum, that it does not clearly have the *worse* of it. Skeptical arguments can be satisfactorily answered—or so I have tried to show. But at the very least, there are answers to those arguments that are sufficiently plausible so that one needn't worry that believing in moral realism is somehow adopting a view that is philosophically dubious or shoddy.

There are, of course, still other skeptical arguments, different from the ones we have analyzed here. But it isn't as though what I have done is avoid the most compelling arguments for moral skepticism, presenting and criticizing only what anyone knowledgeable would immediately recognize as constituting the weaker portions of the skeptic's attack. On the contrary, I have tried to discuss the arguments that seem to me the most plausible and difficult to respond to. (I have also tried to focus on arguments that threaten moral realism broadly, rather than on ones that raise problems only for this or that particular *account* of morality.)

I realize that some of these arguments (or some versions of these arguments) are more "philosophical" than others, in that they may turn on abstract points that philosophers will be particularly concerned about. But I have tried to discuss arguments with wide intuitive appeal as well. In effect, in choosing the arguments to discuss I have tried to take account of the main worries that I thought should trouble thoughtful and reflective individuals. I have laid out and responded to the skeptical misgivings that seem to me the most important and worthy of our attention.

Thus, the arguments that we have examined represent the deepest and most significant challenges to morality of which I am aware. So if I am right in thinking that, despite their initial appeal, they can be given plausible answers, then this goes very far indeed in suggesting that moral realism remains a defensible view.

14.2 Systematic Moral Theory

Suppose I am right, and the various skeptical challenges to morality can all be answered—if not decisively, at least satisfactorily. Where would that leave us? Would that show that the belief in morality is a justified one?

Not quite, or rather, not all by itself. For even if a variety of potential objections to morality are unsuccessful, that doesn't yet provide us with any positive reason to *believe* in morality. (The lack of a compelling objection to a given view doesn't tell us whether we have any reason at all to *accept* that view.) So it might seem that we still need to ask, is there indeed any positive justification for believing that morality exists? Or should we, instead, declare the matter a standoff, with no compelling arguments on either side?

In fact, however, as we have already seen (in chapter 7), there is indeed a prima facie justification for thinking that there really is such a thing as morality, that there really are objective moral truths. For we all have *intuitions* about an endless array of moral matters. It seems to us that certain actions are right or wrong, morally required or morally forbidden. It seems to us that certain states of affairs are intrinsically good, while others are intrinsically bad. It seems to us that some character traits are virtuous while others are vicious. We have intuitions about rights, justice, promise keeping, and lies; about consent, self-defense, inequality, and compassion; about harm, fairness, self-respect, and gratitude. We have intuitions about the moral status of particular actions, in real and in imaginary cases, intuitions about the moral relevance of various factors, and how they weigh against one another, intuitions about general principles and potential exceptions to those principles. We have intuitions about all of these matters—and a great deal more besides. And each one of these intuitions is a piece of evidence, a prima facie reason to believe that there are indeed moral facts, that there is a way things are, morally speaking—in short, that there *is* such a thing as morality.

To be sure, the justification provided by all these intuitions is *defeasible*. Had we discovered compelling reason to think that there simply could not be such a thing as morality, then we would have had no choice but to conclude that our intuitions are mistaken and that the moral facts seemingly revealed by intuition are all phantasms and illusions. But of course if I am right in thinking that the various skeptical challenges to morality are unsuccessful, then we do not yet have reason to doubt that things really are, on the whole, more or less as they appear to be. Admittedly, any given intuition may yet be proven wrong or unreliable (just as any given empirical observation can be in error), and conceivably we might yet discover reason to be suspicious of entire classes or particular types of moral intuitions (just as we are rightly suspicious of empirical observations made while inebriated). But none of this will give us reason to reject wholesale the evidence provided by moral intuitions—that there are indeed moral facts, facts whose nature we can study and investigate.

So epistemically speaking, it isn't a standoff at all. We have striking evidence for the existence of morality, and while in principle the force of that evidence could have been undermined or defeated, we have no compelling reason to think that this is the case. We are left, then, with the evidence of our intuitions, which constantly attest to the existence of moral facts. We are, therefore, justified in believing there is indeed an objective moral reality, captured in the various moral truths revealed by those intuitions.

Accordingly, the moral realist is in a dialectically stronger position than the moral skeptic. Since it *seems* to us that there are moral facts, we are justified in believing that there *are* such facts, unless the skeptic can convince us that these intuitions are misleading us. Thus the burden of proof is on the skeptic to show us either that there *cannot* be such a thing as morality, or that belief in morality is a *significantly less plausible hypothesis* than its denial. If I am right in thinking that the skeptic hasn't come close to doing either one of these, then it remains more plausible, on balance, to hold that the various moral appearances really do justify our belief in a corresponding moral reality.

There is, however, one final way in which moral skepticism could conceivably be established. Imagine that it turned out to be impossible to construct a systematic moral theory, that there was no way to combine our various moral intuitions into a coherent overall picture of a corresponding moral domain. Then we would have good reason to believe that our intuitions were illusory after all, akin to dreams or hallucinations in that they could no longer be taken to (directly) reveal anything about reality. If we could not turn our moral intuitions into moral theory, then perhaps the best explanation would be that this is because there are no moral facts after all, no moral truths waiting to be systematically described.

The situation here would thus be similar to what we would have had to conclude had we found that it was impossible to use our various empirical observations to form a coherent overall theory of the external world, one which vindicates and supports many (though not all) of those very observations. What we find, of course, is that we *are* in fact able to offer such a picture—a picture of a world with people and things moving around in space and time, causally interacting with one another in countless ways. Crucially, this is a picture that not only hangs together, it is a picture which largely (though not totally) vindicates the observations we used to construct that very picture. But imagine that it had been impossible to construct a systematic theory of an external world that corresponded to and matched (the bulk of) our observations. Then we would have had to dismiss the belief in an external world as an illusion, and our observations of it mere hallucinations. Indeed, this is precisely what we do with the "observations" made during dreams, and this is the reason we dismiss the "dream world" as an illusion: things certainly *seem* to us to be various ways when we are dreaming, but since there is no way to combine these various seemings into an overall systematic picture of a corresponding "dream reality," we rightly deny the very existence of a genuine dream world.

Suppose then that something like this had happened when we began to move from our various particular moral intuitions as well. Imagine that although we are all bombarded by a panoply of moral appearances, we had discovered that there was simply no way to combine those appearances into a picture of a moral domain that hung together coherently and that could be described systematically. Imagine that despite our best attempts to describe moral facts in a systematic fashion, we always came up short, so that every attempt to describe this apparent moral reality was invariably fragmented and incoherent, where each attempt forced us to dismiss the vast bulk of our moral intuitions as failing to correspond to anything real. If we had found ourselves in such an unhappy situation, then here too we would ultimately have had to conclude that moral intuitions are illusions after all, that "moral facts" are no more real than "dream facts."

But to concede all of this—to concede that morality would be justifiably rejected as an illusion if it could not be coherently described in a way that also vindicated most (though not all) of our moral intuitions—is not, of course, to suggest that we do indeed find ourselves in this situation. Just as most of us have a rough, commonsense theory of the external world, one which upholds as accurate most though not all of our observations—this is a world with rocks and trees, people and clouds—most of us have a rough, commonsense theory of the *moral* world as well, one which upholds most though not all of our moral intuitions: this is a world with rights and duties, virtues and vices. And just as the commonsense picture of the world is one that can be refined, modified, and improved upon, thanks to the systematic reflections that constitute the natural sciences, our picture of the moral world can be refined as well—modified and improved upon—through the systematic reflection that constitutes moral philosophy.

And what does this systematic reflection reveal about the exact contents and basis of morality? What is it, exactly, that we are obligated to do? What do we actually owe to one another, and why? These are questions I have not tried to answer in this book. Doing justice to them would require our immersing ourselves in the ongoing debates of normative ethics.

But this much we can say, based on what we have seen here. These are questions we are justified in approaching in the same way we would approach any other vitally important questions: with our minds open, looking for objective answers.

Notes

The notes that follow include suggestions for other books and articles that the interested reader might want to look at next. They also discuss a handful of complications that I deliberately avoided introducing into the main body of the book. Most importantly, they identify the places where I am directly indebted to the writings of others.

General: This book is a defense of moral realism. Three other books with the same overall aim are Shafer-Landau, *Whatever Happened to Good and Evil?*, Shafer-Landau, *Moral Realism*, and Enoch, *Taking Morality Seriously*. The first of these is a short and highly accessible defense of moral realism; the second, a significantly more advanced treatment of the same basic set of issues by the same author. The third is particularly engaged with the contemporary philosophical literature, in a way that this book is not, making it easy to find references for further reading (though Enoch's constant references to the philosophical literature may sometimes make for slow going for nonphilosophers). Finally, Huemer, *Ethical Intuitionism*, covers much of the same ground that I do, and while I don't always agree with his particular replies to skeptical arguments, many of his points are quite incisive. I am directly indebted to it at a number of points.

Although this book attempts to avoid substantive debates within normative ethics, I do periodically refer, in passing or by way of examples, to a variety of normative theories, including rival accounts of the foundation or basis of morality. Those wanting to learn more about these theories might have a look at my *Normative Ethics*.

Basic Positions: Two helpful introductions to metaethics are Miller, *An Introduction to Contemporary Metaethics*, and Darwall, *Philosophical Ethics*. The first of these, as the title suggests, is focused on contemporary views; the second, on important examples from the history of ethics.

It is important to realize that philosophers don't always agree about how best to carve up the space of alternative metaethical views, and they differ as well about what names to use for the different positions and how best to define them. Indeed, two philosophers will sometimes use the very same label for different views. So consider yourself warned: not everyone uses labels the same way I do. In particular, I use the term "moral realism" more widely than some other authors. Some limit "moral realism" to views according to which moral facts are mind independent; others, to views that avoid reductionism altogether; still others, to views that are nonnaturalist; and still others, to views that combine all these features. Similarly, the term "constructivism" is often used far more narrowly than I use it here; it is often restricted to a particular *type* of mind dependent reductionism.

I have drawn the distinction between cognitivism and noncognitivism in terms of whether substantive, first-order moral sentences are truth apt or not. But on some views in the philosophy of language, strictly speaking it isn't sentences that can be the bearers of truth values, but rather the *propositions* that some of them can be used to express. On such views, then, we would need to distinguish between cognitivism and noncognitivism somewhat differently, perhaps in terms of whether moral sentences can be used to express propositions. But for simplicity I have disregarded this complication in the text.

Nihilism: Chapter 1 of Mackie, *Ethics: Inventing Right and Wrong*, is an extremely influential defense of a nihilist view; it was, I believe, Mackie who introduced the term "error theory" into this debate. Mackie famously claims that objective moral values would be "queer" and "utterly different from anything else in the universe." Since the rest of Mackie's book is, a bit surprisingly, devoted to working out a suitable ethics, perhaps Mackie was what I here call a *revisionist* nihilist. A more recent defense of revisionist nihilism can be found in Joyce, *The Myth of Morality*. (Warning: much of the central argument in Joyce's book—chapters 2–5—will be difficult to follow for those without a significant background in contemporary philosophy.) Another recent defense of nihilism is Olson, *Moral Error Theory*. Olson's book contains a careful analysis of possible interpretations of Mackie's arguments in chapters 5 and 6.

A classic statement of the suggestion that we inadvertently "project" our preferences onto the world and then mistake these as objective values can be found in Hume, *A Treatise of Human Nature*, Book I, Part III, Section XIV. The idea is explored in Blackburn, *Essays in Quasi-Realism* and in Olson's *Moral Error Theory*.

For detailed arguments to the effect that the most natural interpretation of first-order moral claims is along cognitivist lines, see Enoch, "Why I Am an Objectivist about Ethics (And Why You Are, Too)," and Joyce, *The Myth of Morality*, pp. 9–16.

The suggestion that nihilism can be rejected on the grounds that we are far more confident of the truth of any number of moral claims than we are of the truth of the abstract philosophical premises that figure in arguments for moral skepticism can be found, among other places, in Huemer, *Ethical Intuitionism*, pp. 115–117. Arguments of this sort—where we reject skepticism about some subject because we find the threatened first-order claims more plausible than the philosophical premises required to mount the skeptical challenge—are sometimes called "Moorean" arguments, after the philosopher G. E. Moore, who sometimes explicitly argued in this way.

I have presented the nihilist as holding that all substantive moral claims are *false*, since they all presuppose something, the existence of objective morality, which—the nihilist claims—isn't so. There is, however, an alternative view in the philosophy of language concerning "presupposition failure" according to which sentences with false presuppositions are not false per se, but rather lack a truth value altogether; they are neither true *nor* false. Obviously, if this second approach to presupposition failure is correct, nihilism should be described in slightly different terms: instead of holding that moral claims are all *false*, nihilists would only assert that although moral claims are indeed genuine *assertions*, they aren't *true*. Presumably, that is still sufficient for the nihilist's purposes, since she can still insist that there are no moral facts and there are no substantive moral truths. For simplicity of exposition, however, I have disregarded this complication in the text. This second approach to presupposition failure would also require tweaking the definition of truth aptness.

Defenses of full-blown normative nihilism are rare; but if I interpret him correctly that's what Olson means to defend—without using that label—in *Moral Error Theory* (see, especially, chapter 8). Interestingly enough, however, Olson is neither an abolitionist nor a typical revisionist; rather, he believes we should simply continue making false normative claims. Arguably, this shows that abolitionism and revisionism do not literally exhaust the alternatives open to nihilists. Alternatively, however, it might be suggested that continuing to make and believe normative claims which we nonetheless know to be false really would constitute a *revision* to our current use of normative language.

Noncognitivism: Darwall provides a quick overview of noncognitivism in *Philosophical Ethics*, chapter 8. A more thorough discussion of noncognitivism and objections to it can be found in Schroeder, *Noncognitivism in Ethics.*

Classic defenses of noncognitivism can be found in Ayer, *Language, Truth and Logic*, chapter 6, and Stevenson, "The Emotive Meaning of Ethical Terms." More recent and more sophisticated contributions include Gibbard, *Wise Choices, Apt Feelings*, and Blackburn, *Essays in Quasi-Realism*. A version of noncognitivism that especially emphasizes the imperatival aspect of moral claims is Hare, *The Language of Morals.*

Critical discussions of noncognitivism can be found in Shafer-Landau, *Moral Realism*, pp. 22–37, Huemer, *Ethical Intuitionism*, chapter 2, and Miller, *An Introduction to Contemporary Metaethics*, chapters 3–5, as well as in Schroeder's *Noncognitivism in Ethics*. The challenge of providing noncognitivist accounts of moral claims in contexts that are more complicated than that of simple atomic assertions (more complicated than, for example, "lying is wrong") is known as the "Frege-Geach problem," after two philosophers who first emphasized it; Miller and Schroeder provide especially full discussions of this issue.

A brief discussion of subjectivism and its relation to noncognitivism can be found in Rachels and Rachels, *The Elements of Moral Philosophy*, chapter 3.

I have characterized noncognitivism in terms of the thesis that substantive, first-order moral sentences like "lying is wrong" are not truth apt—not the sort of thing that can be true or false—and thus that such sentences are not in the business of trying to describe or state purported moral facts and therefore not the sort of thing that one can literally believe. There are, however, philosophers who endorse "minimalist" or "deflationary" accounts of truth, according to which to say of a sentence that it is true is (roughly) to do nothing more than to indicate one's assent to it, one's willingness to endorse it. Accordingly, some noncognitivists are actually prepared to say that moral sentences can be used to express moral truths after all, and indeed—given similarly minimal accounts of "belief," "facts," and "describing"—that there really are moral facts (those that the "true" moral sentences "describe"), and that moral beliefs are genuine beliefs. Of course, if the noncognitivist does go this route, it becomes rather difficult to say precisely how, if at all, noncognitivism still differs from moral *realism*! (Perhaps some "noncognitivist" theories are really just metaphysically minimalist forms of constructivism?) It is noteworthy, for example, that Blackburn's preferred name for his own view is "quasi-realism." A fuller discussion of the issue can be found in Dreier, "Meta-Ethics and the Problem of Creeping Minimalism."

Examples like that of the hit man have been discussed in numerous places, including Harman, "Moral Relativism Defended," Brink, *Moral Realism and the Foundations of Ethics*, chapter 3, Shafer-Landau, *Moral Realism*, chapter 6, and Smith, *The Moral Problem*, chapter 3. I believe it was Harman who first introduced this particular example to the literature.

Disagreement: The claim that the existence of widespread moral disagreement supports moral skepticism is made by Mackie, *Ethics: Inventing Right and Wrong*, pp. 36–38. The argument from disagreement is criticized by Shafer-Landau in *Whatever Happened to Good and Evil?*, chapter 14, and *Moral Realism*, chapter 9. The issue is given a particularly detailed analysis in Huemer, *Ethical Intuitionism*, chapter 6. Both Shafer-Landau and Huemer note that the skeptic's claim that disagreement within a given domain supports skepticism about that domain is especially problematic given the existence of widespread disagreement in philosophy quite generally and in metaethics in particular. A similar point is made by Enoch in "Why I Am an Objectivist about Ethics (And Why You Are, Too)," p. 202. Enoch critically examines a number of different versions of arguments from disagreement in *Taking Morality Seriously*, chapter 8.

Explanations of moral disagreement that are compatible with moral realism are discussed by Brink in *Moral Realism and the Foundations of Ethics*, pp. 197–209, and by Huemer, *Ethical Intuitionism*, pp. 132–141. Sinnott-Armstrong, *Moral Skepticisms*, pp. 197–202, discusses the nature and extent of moral disagreement.

The argument from disagreement is also discussed at length in Parfit, *On What Matters*, chapter 34. Parfit pays particular attention to the question of whether disagreement about moral claims would remain even under ideal conditions, as does Shafer-Landau, *Moral Realism*, pp. 221–227.

Relativism: A brief discussion of moral relativism can be found in Rachels and Rachels, *The Elements of Moral Philosophy*, chapter 2. A helpful though sometimes difficult collection of essays is *Moral Relativism*, edited by Moser and Carson.

For a fuller introduction to the foundational theories briefly mentioned in the discussion of foundational relativism, see Part II of my *Normative Ethics*.

I have focused on versions of relativism according to which one is obligated to obey the moral code of the society of which one is a member. But there is an alternative version of relativism according to which, rather, what one is obligated to do is to conform to the moral code that one sincerely accepts and intends to obey. (Since different people do or could accept different moral codes, this would of course still be a form of relativism.) Harman argues for a view like this in "Moral Relativism Defended." His argument presupposes that the only genuine reasons for action are desire-based reasons (hypothetical reasons), an idea I examine in chapter 11.

Relativism stands in contrast to the view that the basic moral rules or principles are universal or absolute—applying to everyone, regardless of society. This particular notion of what it is to be an absolute moral principle should not to be confused with a different one, where we call a principle "absolute" only if it is exceptionless, holding regardless of the circumstances. (A rule against killing, for example, would be considered absolute in this second sense only if one must not kill even in self-defense, and no matter how much good one could bring about if one did, and so on.) It's important not to conflate the two notions. Thus even a relativist—who denies the existence of absolute moral rules in the first sense of the term—can agree that the particular moral code that is valid for a given society might contain some moral prohibitions that are absolute in the second sense (that is, they don't allow for exceptions). Similarly, even if you believe that all moral principles can be outweighed or are limited in relevant circumstances—and thus believe that no principles are absolute in the second sense of the term—you might still reject relativism, holding that the very same basic principles are indeed valid for everyone. The truth of relativism turns only on whether moral principles are absolute in the *first* of these two senses.

Knowledge: My discussion of moral knowledge is particularly indebted to the defense of intuitionism to be found in Huemer, *Ethical Intuitionism*, especially chapter 5. The name "phenomenal conservatism" comes from Huemer, as does the basic approach to distinguishing and comparing intuitive appearances and sensory ones.

Intuitionism is criticized by Sinnott-Armstrong in *Moral Skepticisms*, chapter 9.

For a rather different account of the possibility of moral knowledge—one which emphasizes the justificatory force of coherence among our moral beliefs—see Brink, *Moral Realism and the Foundations of Ethics*, chapter 5.

A careful discussion of the problem of the reliability of our moral beliefs can be found in Enoch, *Taking Morality Seriously*, chapter 7. The suggestion that reliability might be established by means of an appeal to evolution can be found there as well, at pp. 167–174.

Harman, *The Nature of Morality*, chapter 1, argues that moral truths or moral facts play no role in explaining moral beliefs and intuitions. The contrary view is implied by Temkin's defense of the causal efficacy of reasons in section 2 of "Has Parfit's Life Been Wasted?"

Some moral realists have argued that since there is a clear evolutionary advantage in our having a faculty of reason capable of reliably grasping at least some necessary truths (such as the truths of elementary arithmetic), once we agree that moral truths are also necessary there is no longer a puzzle as to why our moral intuitions should be thought reliable as well: we get insight into moral truths for free, as it were, as a result of having the evolutionarily advantageous faculty of reason. But this quick argument overlooks what in chapter 8 I call "the continuity problem." If all of morality lies beyond the home range of necessary truths for which it was advantageous to have true beliefs, why think that reason *remains* reliable when it generates intuitions about *moral* matters as well?

Evolution: For some quick sketches of possible evolutionary accounts of some central moral beliefs and behaviors, see Sinnott-Armstrong, *Moral Skepticisms*, pp. 40–43 (pp. 43-45 are also of interest). Further discussion, with particular emphasis on the evolutionary advantages of having a sense of moral obligation, can be found in Joyce, *The Myth of Morality*, pp. 135–148.

The most influential presentation of the claim that the possibility of such evolutionary accounts undermines (certain versions of) moral realism is Street, "A Darwinian Dilemma for Realist Theories of Value." The example of how evolution would never favor recognizing an obligation to kill one's children, supposing there were such an obligation, comes from Street, as does the suggestion that we can come to recognize the path dependence of our moral beliefs by thinking about the possibility of moral agents that evolved from social insects. There are, of course, other philosophers who have similarly argued that evolutionary accounts of our moral beliefs support the rejection of moral realism; see, for example, Joyce, *The Myth of Morality*, pp. 158–169.

I argued that one possible way for the moral realist to respond to evolutionary challenges is to suggest that there is a common ground for moral truth and moral beliefs. While differing in details, Enoch makes what I take to be the same basic suggestion in *Taking Morality Seriously*, pp. 167–174. Parfit may have something similar in mind in *On What Matters*, chapters 33 and 34 (though I find many of the details of Parfit's discussion difficult to follow).

Two examples of philosophers who think evolutionary theory poses no serious challenge to moral realism are Huemer, *Ethical Intuitionism*, pp. 214–219, and Fitzpatrick, "Debunking Evolutionary Debunking of Ethical Realism."

Explanation: The contemporary debate over whether moral facts would explain anything began with Harman, *The Nature of Morality*, chapter 1. Harman's initial treatment of the problem focused on the claim that moral facts don't explain moral observations and beliefs, but ensuing discussions quickly moved to the more general question of whether moral facts explain anything at all. See, for example, Sturgeon, "Moral Explanations." Sturgeon argues that it is a familiar thought that facts about someone's moral character can explain their behavior; the Hitler example comes from Sturgeon. A similar argument is made by Brink in *Moral Realism and the Foundations of Ethics*, pp. 182–197. Brink also makes the point that even if moral facts reduce to nonmoral ones, it may still be the former that are explanatorily primary, not the latter.

Useful discussions of the debate can be found in Miller, *An Introduction to Contemporary Metaethics*, chapter 8, and in Thomson, "Epistemological Arguments for Moral Skepticism," chapter 6 of *Moral Relativism and Moral Objectivity*. Thomson also raises the important question of whether we've really shown *moral* facts to be explanatory if we leave out their normative aspect. Sinnott-Armstrong argues that appeals to moral explanations inevitably beg the question against moral nihilism in *Moral Skepticisms*, pp. 153–167.

Temkin argues that even if normative facts are nonnatural ones, they can still explain our normative beliefs, and thus our behavior more generally; see section 2 of "Has Parfit's Life Been Wasted?" According to Railton's "Moral Realism," moral facts are *natural* facts that can affect our behavior "directly," as we might put it—that is, without doing so by means of our conscious beliefs.

The explanatory test for metaphysical legitimacy is rejected by Shafer-Landau in *Whatever Happened to Good and Evil?*, pp. 92–99, and in *Moral Realism*, pp. 98–115. It is rejected for somewhat similar reasons by Enoch in *Taking Morality Seriously*, chapter 3.

Motivation: A defense of motive externalism can be found in Brink, *Moral Realism and the Foundations of Ethics*, chapter 3, and in Shafer-Landau, *Moral Realism*, chapter 6. A defense of motive *internalism* can be found in Smith, *The Moral Problem*, chapter 3. The suggestion that an amoralist (for example, our hit man) making moral judgments may be like a blind person making claims about colors—that is, they are someone who doesn't fully grasp the relevant concept—comes from Smith. The suggestion that the amoralist may be speaking in "scare quotes" is made by Hare, *The Language of Morals*, pp. 124–126 and 163–165 (though Hare called this the "inverted-commas" use).

I noted parenthetically that it may be sufficient for the skeptic's purposes if we limit ourselves to a version of motive internalism according to which moral beliefs *can* suffice for providing motivation, rather than holding that they *always* do. Arguably, this more modest version of internalism is more plausible—after all, can't overwhelming depression or overwhelming anger, and so on, keep one from being moved even a little bit by one's sincerely held moral beliefs? At best, then, maybe all the internalist should insist upon is that moral beliefs *can* motivate, at least somewhat, and that they will do so in the *absence* of such "motivation blocking" psychological states. Combined with the Humean theory of motivation this still provides the materials for an argument to the conclusion that moral beliefs are not genuine beliefs after all. (How—the skeptic would ask—could genuine beliefs *ever* suffice for motivation, if desires are *always* required for motivation?) Nonetheless, for simplicity of exposition I discussed the argument in terms of the bolder ("always") version of internalism. Still, in thinking about whether amoralists like the hit man demonstrate the plausibility of motive externalism, it may be important to stipulate as well that the hit man is *not* suffering from depression, nor filled with rage, and so on.

The Humean theory of motivation was put forward by Hume in *A Treatise of Human Nature*, Book II, Part III, Section III. A contemporary explication and defense can be found in Smith, *The Moral Problem*, chapter 4, which also lays out the argument that considerations related to the direction of fit rule out the possibility of a single mental state being both a desire and a belief. The Humean theory, including appeals to the direction of fit, is criticized by Huemer in chapter 7 of *Ethical Intuitionism*, and by Shafer-Landau in chapter 5 of *Moral Realism*.

I noted, in passing, the possibility of a view according to which desires can motivate *only* when they are combined with, or consist in, relevant normative beliefs. I take Scanlon to be defending such a view in *What We Owe to Each Other*, chapter 1. The possibility of what I called the "less demanding" version of Humeanism, according to which although motivation requires desires, these desires can be generated along the way (rather than being among the initial mental states) is central to Nagel's argument in *The Possibility of Altruism*.

The particular motivation-focused argument we examined comes to a noncognitivist conclusion. But there is a variant of that argument (suggested by some comments made by Mackie in *Ethics: Inventing Right and Wrong*, chapter 1) that would support nihilism instead. It too assumes the truth of the Humean theory of motivation in its more demanding form. But unlike the original argument, it also assumes that moral beliefs are genuine beliefs, just as they appear to be; so it denies that moral beliefs per se are able to motivate. It does hold however that if there really were moral facts then *knowledge* of those facts should indeed be able to motivate. With these assumptions in place, the nihilist can argue that since no mere set of beliefs can suffice for motivation (given Humeanism)—not even when those beliefs are instances of knowledge—it turns out that knowledge of any supposed moral facts would be impossible. And since it is reasonable to hold that if there really were moral facts we could in principle come to know at least some of them, it follows that there actually are no moral facts at all and that all substantive moral beliefs are false. So we should embrace moral nihilism.

This new argument can be answered with replies similar to those offered in response to the original version. First, the realist might reject the internalist claim that lies at the heart of the argument and insist that even when our moral beliefs are based on knowledge of underlying moral facts they still cannot motivate on their own. Alternatively, second, the realist can reject the demanding version of Humeanism, holding instead that moral beliefs really can suffice for motivation even in the absence of an initial desire—or at the very least, that they can do so when those beliefs are instances of moral knowledge. Finally, third, the realist can reject the argument's implicit assumption that nothing can be both a belief and a desire, insisting rather that beliefs grounded in moral knowledge can be both; so even if motivation does require an initial desire, as the Humean account insists, moral knowledge can provide it on its own. Although realists will disagree among themselves as to which of these three replies is preferable, each suffices to block the nihilist's argument.

Reasons: The distinctions between explanatory, motivating, and normative or justifying reasons are laid out in Smith, *The Moral Problem*, pp. 92–98, and in Schroeder, *Slaves of the Passions*, pp. 10–14.

In the philosophical literature, the view I call "reasons internalism" is sometimes called "moral rationalism" instead. "Reasons internalism" is then used as the name for a different view, the one I later call "motive internalism about reasons."

Most moral realists, I suggested, accept reasons internalism. A prominent exception is Foot in "Morality as a System of Hypothetical Imperatives." Another is Brink, *Moral Realism and the Foundations of Ethics*, chapter 3. A defense of reasons internalism (there called "moral rationalism") can be found in Shafer-Landau, *Moral Realism*, chapter 8.

Skepticism about the very possibility of a categorical reason is expressed in Mackie, *Ethics: Inventing Right and Wrong*, chapter 1. This particular argument for moral skepticism is developed at greater length in Joyce, *The Myth of Morality*, chapters 2–5 (although, again, this may be rather difficult reading for those without a background in philosophy).

A classic defense of morality purely in terms of hypothetical reasons can be found in Hobbes, *Leviathan*. A contemporary argument along broadly the same lines is Gauthier, *Morals by Agreement*. Schroeder's *Slaves of the Passions* offers the fullest general account of the nature of hypothetical reasons, and it then argues that such reasons, once properly understood, provide a sufficient basis for morality. The classic defender of the view that morality should be understood as involving categorical reasons is Kant, *Groundwork of the Metaphysics of Morals*; indeed, he calls his fundamental moral principle "the categorical imperative." (Warning: Kant's book is especially difficult.)

Imagine a moral realist who accepts reasons internalism, who agrees there are no categorical reasons, but who also rejects views (like that of Hobbes or Gauthier) which attempt to show that everyone has hypothetical reasons to obey the very same set of moral requirements. Arguably, this precise combination of views would support a version of moral *relativism*, where which particular moral code you are required to obey depends on your particular desires. An argument for a view like this can be found in Harman, "Moral Relativism Defended."

Finally, let me say a quick word about the common view that if there is no god then everything is permissible (that is, there are no moral requirements and nothing is morally forbidden). The thinking behind this claim isn't altogether transparent, but perhaps people tempted by this idea believe that the following things are all true: (1) Genuine requirements must be backed by reasons (reasons internalism), but (2) the only genuine reasons are hypothetical ones. (3) If there *were* a god he could provide everyone with the requisite desire-based reasons to do as morality requires (perhaps by threatening to send us to hell if we don't obey him), but (4) if God doesn't exist then it just won't be true that everyone has a desire-based reason to do what morality supposedly demands. Hence (5) if there is no god there can be no genuine requirements and everything is permissible. If something like this is indeed the underlying argument then moral realists who deny the existence of God but who accept the existence of moral requirements can respond either by rejecting reasons internalism (denying (1)), by arguing for the existence of categorical reasons (denying (2)), or by offering accounts of morality based on hypothetical reasons that don't require a theological basis (denying (4)). Realists may of course disagree with one another as to which of these is the most plausible reply to give.

Reductionism: I've deliberately put aside a variety of puzzles about how best to understand the nature of reduction. Schroeder discusses a few of these issues with particular focus on reductionism for normativity in *Slaves of the Passions*, pp. 63–72.

The open question argument finds its classic statement in Moore, *Principia Ethica*, chapter 1. Moore took the argument to support simple realism. A careful recent presentation and analysis of the argument can be found in Miller, *An Introduction to Contemporary Metaethics*, pp. 12–24.

A largely sympathetic presentation of some contemporary reductionist views can be found in Miller, *An Introduction to Contemporary Metaethics*, chapter 9. A more critical discussion is Huemer, *Ethical Intuitionism*, chapter 4. The suggestion that we can simply see that nonnormative properties are of the wrong kind to provide a reduction base for normative ones is made by Huemer, pp. 94–95; my example involving planets and piano concertos is based on one of Huemer's. A similar objection to reductionism is raised by Parfit, *On What Matters*, Volume Two, pp. 324–327.

The suggestion that moral claims can be reduced to relevant claims about reasons can be developed in a variety of ways. The basic idea is laid out in Harman, *The Nature of Morality*, chapter 10. I describe one way of spelling out the suggestion in *The Limits of Morality*, pp. 64–80 (see also pp. 59–62). Scanlon's *What We Owe to Each Other* is an influential contemporary work that treats reasons as fundamental to morality and normativity more broadly. A similar claim is defended by Schroeder, *Slaves of the Passions*, pp. 79–83. Furthermore, since Schroeder—unlike Scanlon—goes on to offer a reductive account of reasons, his book as a whole is, in effect, a defense of reductionism. The thought that moral claims should be reduced to claims about appropriate *attitudes* is defended in Darwall, *The Second-Person Standpoint*, chapter 5, and in Gibbard, *Wise Choices, Apt Feelings*, chapter 1.

The idea of reducing facts about reasons to facts about an ideal reasoner or ideal deliberator is briefly outlined and defended in Harman, *The Nature of Morality*, chapter 11. Criticisms of approaches like this can be found in Dancy, *Ethics without Principles*. The objection that any attempt to characterize an "ideal deliberator" in strictly nonnormative terms must fall short—inevitably leaving open the possibility that anyone so characterized might fail to react appropriately to some reasons—is suggested by comments of Parfit's in *On What Matters*, chapter 3.

Simple Realism: Simple realists who argued for irreducible *moral* properties include Moore, *Principia Ethica*, and Ross, *The Right and the Good*. A classic statement of simple *normative* realism can be found in Sidgwick, *The Methods of Ethics*, Book I, Chapter III. Contemporary simple normative realists include Scanlon, *Being Realistic about Reasons*, and Parfit, *On What Matters*. Arguably, all of these philosophers believe the basic properties in question are nonnatural, although Scanlon and Parfit minimize the metaphysical significance of this claim.

Mackie complained in *Ethics: Inventing Right and Wrong*, chapter 1, that objective moral values would be "queer" and "utterly different" from other things. Criticism of this objection, including the reply that pretty much all broad classes of things are different from the other broad classes of things, is given in Huemer, *Ethical Intuitionism*, pp. 199– 201; several of the examples I use to illustrate this point are taken from Huemer.

Scanlon argues in *Being Realistic about Reasons* that there is nothing metaphysically troubling about the thought that facts about reasons are irreducible. A similar position is defended by Parfit in *On What Matters*, chapter 31.

Shafer-Landau discusses the difficulty of drawing a philosophically significant line between natural and nonnatural properties in *Moral Realism*, pp. 58–65. The examples I mention of noncausal but unobjectionable properties (being self-identical, being red or not, and being divisible by itself) come from Shafer-Landau, who takes them to show that being a natural property doesn't require causal efficacy (or, if it does, that being nonnatural isn't objectionable). Temkin argues for the causal efficacy of facts about reasons in section 2 of "Has Parfit's Life Been Wasted?"

Arguments to the effect that it must be false to claim that the only facts are those that can be established by science (because any such claim is self-defeating) are common among contemporary philosophers. See, for example, Shafer-Landau, *Whatever Happened to Good and Evil?*, pp. 100–101.

Moral Realism: Even though moral intuitions provide defeasible justification for belief in moral facts, that justification would indeed be defeated, as I noted, if we found ourselves unable to incorporate those intuitions into acceptable moral *theories*—systematic accounts of first-order moral facts and their ultimate basis. I provide an introduction to some of the most important proposals for such theories in *Normative Ethics*.

References

Ayer, A. J. *Language, Truth and Logic*. 1936.
Blackburn, Simon. *Essays in Quasi-Realism*. Oxford, 1993.
Brink, David. *Moral Realism and the Foundations of Ethics*. Cambridge, 1989.
Dancy, Jonathan. *Ethics without Principles*. Oxford, 2004.
Darwall, Stephen. *Philosophical Ethics*. Westview, 1998.
——. *The Second-Person Standpoint*. Harvard, 2006.
Dreier, James. "Meta-Ethics and the Problem of Creeping Minimalism." *Philosophical Perspectives* 18 (2004): 23–44.
Enoch, David. *Taking Morality Seriously*. Oxford, 2011.
——. "Why I Am an Objectivist about Ethics (And Why You Are, Too)" in Russ Shafer-Landau, editor, *The Ethical Life*. Oxford, 2015.
Fitzpatrick, William. "Debunking Evolutionary Debunking of Ethical Realism." *Philosophical Studies* 172 (2015): 883–904.
Foot, Philippa. "Morality as a System of Hypothetical Imperatives." Reprinted in *Virtues and Vices*. University of California, 1978. Originally published in *The Philosophical Review* 81 (1972): 305–316.
Gauthier, David. *Morals by Agreement*. Oxford, 1986.
Gibbard, Allan. *Wise Choices, Apt Feelings*. Harvard, 1990.
Hare, R. M. *The Language of Morals*. Oxford, 1952.
Harman, Gilbert. "Moral Relativism Defended." *The Philosophical Review* 84 (1975): 3–22.
——. *The Nature of Morality*. Oxford, 1977.
Hobbes, Thomas. *Leviathan*. 1651.
Huemer, Michael. *Ethical Intuitionism*. Palgrave Macmillan, 2005.
Hume, David. *A Treatise of Human Nature*. 1739.
Joyce, Richard. *The Myth of Morality*. Cambridge, 2001.
Kagan, Shelly. *The Limits of Morality*. Oxford, 1989.
——. *Normative Ethics*. Westview, 1998.
Kant, Immanuel. *Groundwork of the Metaphysics of Morals*. 1785.
Mackie, J. L. *Ethics: Inventing Right and Wrong*. Penguin, 1977.
Miller, Alexander. *An Introduction to Contemporary Metaethics*. Polity, 2003.
Moore, G. E. *Principia Ethica*. 1903.

Moser, Paul and Thomas Carson, editors. *Moral Relativism*. Oxford, 2001.

Nagel, Thomas. *The Possibility of Altruism*. Oxford, 1970.

Olson, Jonas. *Moral Error Theory*. Oxford, 2014.

Parfit, Derek. *On What Matters*. Oxford, 2011.

Rachels, James and Stuart Rachels. *The Elements of Moral Philosophy*, 5th edition. McGraw Hill, 2007.

Railton, Peter. "Moral Realism." *The Philosophical Review* 95 (1986): 163–207.

Ross, W. D. *The Right and the Good*. Oxford, 1930.

Scanlon, T. M. *Being Realistic about Reasons*. Oxford, 2014.

——. *What We Owe to Each Other*. Harvard, 1998.

Schroeder, Mark. *Noncognitivism in Ethics*. Routledge, 2010.

——. *Slaves of the Passions*. Oxford, 2007.

Shafer-Landau, Russ. *Moral Realism*. Oxford, 2003.

——. *Whatever Happened to Good and Evil?* Oxford, 2004.

Sidgwick, Henry. *The Methods of Ethics*. 1907.

Sinnott-Armstrong, Walter. *Moral Skepticisms*. Oxford, 2006.

Smith, Michael. *The Moral Problem*. Blackwell, 1994.

Stevenson, Charles. "The Emotive Meaning of Ethical Terms." Reprinted in *Facts and Values* (Yale, 1963). Originally published in *Mind* 46 (1937): 14–31.

Street, Sharon. "A Darwinian Dilemma for Realist Theories of Value." *Philosophical Studies* 127 (2006): 109–166.

Sturgeon, Nicholas. "Moral Explanations." Reprinted in Geoffrey Sayre-McCord, editor, *Essays on Moral Realism*. Cornell, 1988. Originally published in *Morality, Reason and Truth*, edited by David Copp and David Zimmerman. Rowman and Allanheld, 1985.

Temkin, Larry, "Has Parfit's Life Been Wasted?" in Peter Singer, editor, *Does Anything Really Matter?* Oxford, 2017.

Thomson, Judith Jarvis. "Epistemological Arguments for Moral Skepticism" in Gilbert Harman and Judith Jarvis Thomson, *Moral Relativism and Moral Objectivity*. Blackwell, 1996.

Index

absolutism *See* moral relativism
action guiding function of morality 16–18, 23–25, 155
amoralist *See* hit man
ant people 221, 222–23
argument from disagreement *See* disagreement
argument from evolution *See* evolution
argument from synonymy 95

basis of moral facts 31–34, 52–61, *see also* reductionism
bee people 221, 222–23
beliefs *See* moral beliefs
burden of proof 69–71, 186, 369–71

cognitivism
  basic idea 45, 374
  plausibility 67–68, 80–81, 87–88, 96–103
  See also noncognitivism
complex moral sentences 100–3, 376
constructivism
  basic idea 58, 373–74
  evolution and 208
  as moral skepticism 63, 132
  and intuition 180–82
  and moral relativism 132, 135–36, 140–41, 146–47, 150
  for reasons 241
  See also reductionism
content of morality 18–19, 155–56
continuity problem 215–20, 379

direction of fit 271–74
disagreement
  argument from 104–28
  explanations of moral 114–24, 148–51
  extent of moral 106–8, 121–22, 142–44, 175–76
  implications 108–14, 176–77
  between intuitions 173–77
  and noncognitivism 97–100
  nonconvergence 125–28

emotions *See* moral emotions
emotivism 81, *see also* noncognitivism
errors *See* moral errors
error theory 66–67
evolution
  argument from 191–92, 194–224
  common ground accounts 209–13, 228–29
  as connecting intuition and moral truth 184–85
  continuity problem 215–20, 379
  and observation 194–95, 198–201, 202–4, 215–19
  path dependence 220–24
  as shaping intuition and moral beliefs 191–94
  truth and advantage 199–213, 216–18, 228–29
explanation
  explanatory force and reality 225–28, 235, 242–44
  and moral facts 225–47
  and reduction 232–37
expressivism 81, *see also* noncognitivism
externalism *See* motive internalism; reasons internalism

facts *See* moral facts; normative facts
foundational theories in ethics 152–57
Frege-Geach problem *See* complex moral sentences

function of morality 16–18, 23–25, 155

general skepticism 3–4, 167–68, 169, 171, 172, 195, 198–99, 200–1, 212–13, 234, 246, 299, *see also* moral skepticism
God
  atheism 48, 50, 66
  conscience 185
  everything permissible without 383–84
  mind dependence of morality 32, 58, 182
  and moral relativism 135, 147, 150
  nonnatural properties 53, 54, 309, 355–56, 357
gravity 6–7

hit man 91–92, 94, 261–65, 287–88, 290, 293, 294–95, 302–3, 381
Humean theory of motivation
  basic idea 254–56
  and beliefs that are desires 269–75, 304–5, 306
  objections 265–69, 274, 303–4
  two versions 268–69
  See also motivation

ideal deliberator 241, 336–40, *see also* reasons
internalism *See* motive internalism; reasons internalism
intuitionism 185–88, *see also* intuitions
intuitions
  and belief 165–67, 175–76
  confirming 170–73
  connection to truth 178–85
  contingency 177–78
  disagreements between 173–77
  as fallible 161, 163–64, 165–67, 174, 177
  justificatory force 162–67, 168–88, 369–71
  nature of 162–66
  and noncognitivism 188–90
  and observations 159–68, 170–75, 176–77, 178–80, 182–83, 194–95
  path dependence 220–24
  reliability 178–85, 191–224

  as a source of knowledge 159–67
  skepticism about 167–85
  and systematic moral theory 224, 307
  See also evolution
irreducible normativity *See* simple normative realism

job description
  basic idea 11–16
  elements of morality's 16–39
  meeting morality's 39–41, 364–66

knowledge
  continuity problem 215–20
  intuitionism 185–88
  moral 23–26, 158–59, 214–15
  observation 159–67
  threat from evolution 191–92
  See also evolution; intuitions

metaethics 5–6, 111–12
mind dependence of morality 32–34, 57–58, 132, *see also* constructivism
moral beliefs
  and commands 93–95
  derivative 119–22, 124
  as also being desires 269–75
  motivated 122–24
  and motivation 90–93, 252–54
  See also moral opinions; motive internalism
moral emotions 191, 193–94
moral errors 21–23
moral facts
  basis 31–34
  causal powers 183, 204–5, 356–57
  disagreement 104–28
  existence 21, 47–48
  explanatory power 225–26, 244–47
  intuitions as evidence of 186
  mind dependence 57–58
  natural or nonnatural 53–55
  normative aspect 238–42
  reductionism and 55–57, 230–42, 308–13
  skepticism about 66, 67, 69, 79, 361–63
  See also moral properties; motive internalism; naturalism; normative facts

moral nihilism
    abolitionist 50, 62
    and the argument for noncognitivism 259, 260, 275–76
    arguing for 68–69, 382
    basic idea 49–50, 65–66, 375
    burden of proof 69–71
    coherence of 48–49
    disregarding arguments for 71–76
    and intuition 189–90
    as moral skepticism 62
    and the open question argument 321–22
    revisionist 50–52, 62, 88, 190
    See also normative nihilism
moral opinions 256–59, 276
moral properties
    causal powers 183, 204–5, 356–57
    mind dependence 57–58
    natural or nonnatural 53–55
    and properties of the wrong kind 325–29
    reducible to reasons 330–35, 361–63
    reduction of 55–57, 308–13
    See also moral facts; reduction
moral realism
    as moral skepticism 63–64
    basic idea 50, 373–74
    burden of proof 69–71
    disregarding arguments against 71–76
    and intuitionism 186–88
    threat of noncognitivism 82
    varieties 52–61
    vindicated 364–72
moral relativism
    arguments for 141–57
    basic idea 26–29, 129–41, 378
    constructivism 132, 135–36, 140–41, 146–47, 150
    in foundational theories 151–57
    implicit 136–40, 142, 149
    and noncognitivism 144–46
    realism or skepticism 129–32, 144, 154–55
    between species 221–22
    See also necessity of moral truths
moral requirements as reasons of the right sort 288, 301, 332–35

moral skepticism
    basic idea 61–64
    disregarding arguments for 71–76
    intuitionism 187–88
    See also general skepticism
motivated beliefs 122–24, 151
motivation
    and beliefs 90–93
    Humean theory 254–56, 265–69, 301–2, 303–6
    and moral relativism 147–48
    and reasons 300–6
    See also motive internalism
motive internalism
    about moral beliefs 37–39, 90–92, 248–54, 260–65, 278–79, 300–1, 381
    about reasons 300–3, 383
    See also reasons internalism

natural and nonnatural properties and facts
    basic idea 53–55
    causal powers 183, 204–5, 356–57
    constructivism and 58
    distinction between 355–58, 360–61
    in moral explanations 230–32
    objections to nonnatural properties 353–55, 359–61
    reductionism and 309–10
    simple realism 347, 353–61
necessity of moral truths 29–31, 130, 222
nihilism See moral nihilism; normative nihilism
noncognitivism
    arguments for 87–96, 256–59, 268–75
    as moral skepticism 62–63, 67, 79–80
    basic idea 45–47, 79–80, 374, 376–77
    complex moral sentences 100–3, 376
    disagreement 97–100
    expressing attitudes 81–85, 89–90, 91–92, 96–97
    giving commands 85–86, 93–95
    intuitions 188–90
    moral argument 98–100
    objections 96–103
    open question argument 321–22
    positive and negative theses 81, 85–86, 87–89, 91–92, 94

noncognitivism (*cont.*)
　plausibility 67–68, 80–81, 87–88, 96–103
　and revisionist moral nihilism 50–52
　and subjectivism 82–84
　uses of moral language 81–86, 100–3
　See also cognitivism
nonconvergence in ethics 125–28
normative ethics 5
normative facts and properties 240–42, *see also* moral facts; reasons
normative nihilism
　basic idea 77
　and evolution 205–7, 211
　implausibility 77–78, 289, 298–300, 343–44, 362–63
　and moral facts 240
　See also reasons

objectivity of morality 9–11, 20–21, 22–23, 27, 32–34, 39–41
observations *See* evolution; intuitions; knowledge
open question argument 317–25, *see also* reductionism

presupposition failure 48–50, 375
phenomenal conservatism 162–64, 168, 176–77, 197
projectivism 67
properties *See* moral properties

realism *See* moral realism
reasons
　categorical 279–80, 289–91, 296–307
　as explanatory 240–42
　hypothetical 291–300, 301–2, 305–6, 335–36
　ideal deliberator 241, 336–40
　kinds 280–84, 289–93
　and motivation 266–67, 300–6
　nature of 284–86, 296–300
　rational support 280–86, 296–300, 336–39, 345–47
　reduction of 241, 300, 311–13, 330–31, 335–41
　requirements as reasons of the right sort 288, 301, 332–35

　skepticism about moral 289–91, 293–307
　See also normative nihilism; reasons internalism; simple normative realism
reasons internalism 34–37, 39, 94–95, 238–40, 277–80, 283–84, 286–88, 300–1, 330–31, 383, *see also* motive internalism
reductionism
　appeal 308–13, 315
　basic idea 55–57, 313–17
　and explanation 230–37
　mind dependence 57–58
　open question argument 317–25
　and properties of the wrong kind 325–29
　for reasons 241, 300, 311–13, 330–31, 335–41
　See also simple realism; simple normative realism
relativism *See* moral relativism
representational content 271–74

simple normative realism
　basic idea 59–61, 345–47
　natural or nonnatural 347, 353–61
　objections 347–63
　plausibility 331, 341, 342–45
　See also simple realism
simple realism
　basic idea 58–61, 312–13, 331, 345–47
　natural or nonnatural 347, 353–61
　objections 347–61
　open question argument 321
　and the reliability of intuition 182–83
　See also simple normative realism
skepticism *See* general skepticism; moral skepticism
squirrels, life among the 243
subjectivism 82–84, 181, 259
systematic moral theory 307, 371–72
truth
　aptness 20–21, 43–44, 375
　aptness of moral sentences 44–47
　connection to intuitions 178–85
　of moral claims 19–21